lonely planet

Seattle

"All you've got to do is decide to go
and the hardest part is over.

So go!"

TONY WHEELER, COFOUNDER – LONELY PLANET

ROBERT BALKOVICH

Contents

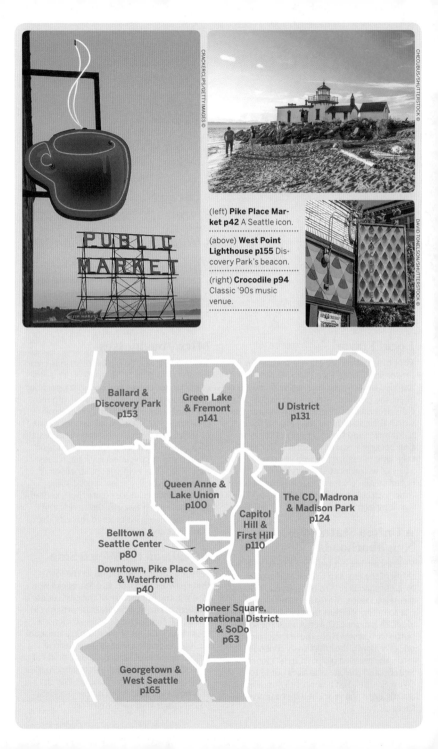

(left) **Pike Place Market p42** A Seattle icon.

(above) **West Point Lighthouse p155** Discovery Park's beacon.

(right) **Crocodile p94** Classic '90s music venue.

Welcome to Seattle

Blink and it's changed: Seattle is that ephemeral. Blending innovation and nature, it's a city always marching forward.

Local Flavor

First time in Seattle? Make a beeline for its proverbial pantry: Pike Place Market. It was founded in 1907, and its long-held mantra of 'meet the producer' still echoes enthusiastically around a city where every restaurateur worth their salt knows the name of their fishmonger and the biography of the cow that became yesterday's burgers. It doesn't take long to realize that you've arrived in a city of well-educated palates and wildly experimental chefs who are willing to fuse American cuisine with just about anything – as long as it's local.

A United States of Neighborhoods

Visitors setting out to explore Seattle should think of the city as a United States of Neighborhoods or – to put it in more human terms – a family consisting of affectionate but sometimes errant members. There's the aloof, elegant one (Queen Anne); the social butterfly (Capitol Hill); the artistic, bearded one (Fremont); the effortlessly cool one (Ballard); the grizzled old patriarch (Pioneer Square) and the one who lives out of town (West Seattle). You'll never fully understand Seattle until you've spent a bit of time with them all.

Micro-businesses

To outsiders, Seattle is an industrious creator of macro-brands. To insiders, it's a city of micro-businesses and boundary-pushing grassroots movements. For proof, dip into the third-wave coffee shops, the micro-breweries with their casual tasting rooms or the cozy informal bookstores that remain rock solid in a city that spawned Amazon. Then there are the latest national trends that Seattle has helped popularize: craft cider, weed dispensaries, specialist pie-makers, and vegan ice cream that's actually good, to name a few. Hit the streets and you'll see there's far more to this city than Starbucks and Boeing.

A Walk on the Weird Side

Seattle's current reputation as the town that spawned Amazon and Starbucks won't give you the full picture of the city's oddball cultural heritage. Crisscross its urban grid and you'll find all kinds of apparitions: a rocket sticking out of a building; a museum built to resemble a smashed-up electric guitar; a statue of Lenin; a mural made of used chewing gum; and fish-tossing market traders. Need help acclimating? The city's still-booming legal weed market will help you embrace your own weird side.

MATT MUNRO/LONELY PLANET ©

Why I Love Seattle

By Robert Balkovich, Writer

A friend once described Seattle to me as a 'great northern city,' and during a particularly cold February there I *really* learned what she meant. As much of a wonderland as it is in the summer, it's a city built for the rain and gloom. Everything is matched to it: the concrete buildings, handsome craftsman homes, restaurants serving hearty food, the mountains that hide themselves on cloudy days, and the way the downtown streetlights blinking on in the fog feels as warming as slipping into one of the city's ubiquitous cafes and lingering over a cup of coffee.

For more about our writers, see p256

Top: City skyline view from the Columbia Center (p48)

Seattle's
Top 10

Pike Place Market (p42)

1 Way more than just a market, 110-year-old Pike Place is a living community, a cabaret show, a way of life and an intrinsic piece of Seattle's soul. Strolling through its clamorous, sometimes chaotic thoroughfares, you simply couldn't be in any other city. There are fish that fly, shops that look like they've sprung from a Harry Potter movie, an art wall made out of chewing gum, and a multitude of lively old buskers jamming acoustic versions of Led Zeppelin songs outside the world's oldest Starbucks. Pure magic.

🔒 *Downtown, Pike Place & Waterfront*

Space Needle (p82)

2 The city icon that is as synonymous with Seattle as the letters S-E-A-T-T-L-E was built for the 1962 World's Fair by the architecture firm John Graham & Company, and in 2018 got a face-lift to bring it into a new era. Although it's no longer Seattle's tallest structure, one million annual visitors still squeeze into the Space Needle's slick, speedy elevators to enjoy views that are best described as awesome. Granted, tickets are expensive and you'll be elbow-to-elbow with tourists, but stop complaining and get in line: this is an essential Seattle pilgrimage.

◉ *Belltown & Seattle Center*

CORIN/SHUTTERSTOCK ©

LONNIE GORSLINE/SHUTTERSTOCK ©

Museum of Pop Culture *(p86)*

3 Paying homage to the left-handed, guitar-burning musical genius that was Jimi Hendrix, the Museum of Pop Culture is the brainchild of Microsoft co-founder Paul Allen (with fabulously bizarre architecture by Frank Gehry). It's an apt memorial to a region that has been a powerful musical innovator since the days of local boy Bing Crosby. Come and see the legends and how they were created, from Hendrix to Kurt Cobain, or experiment with your own riffs in the interactive Sound Lab. Marrying Captain Kirk with Nirvana Kurt is the on-site 'Infinite Worlds of Science Fiction' exhibit, where *Star Trek* meets *Doctor Who*.

◉ *Belltown &*
Seattle Center

Puget Sound Ferries *(p177)*

4 Tap the average Seat-tleite about their most cherished weekend excursion and they could surprise you with a dark horse – a cheap and simple ride on the commuter ferry across Puget Sound to Bainbridge Island. There's nothing quite like being surrounded by water and seeing Seattle's famous skyline disappearing in the ferry's foamy wake, the only commentary the cry of the seagulls and the only entertainment the comedic antics of escaping families bound for a day out on the nearby Olympic Peninsula.

◉ *Downtown, Pike*
Place & Waterfront

Public Art *(p87)*

5 Seattle likes to dis-play its art out in the open with no holds barred. Sculptures and statues decorate parks, streets and squares, from the weird (a stone troll underneath a bridge), to the iconic (Hendrix in classic rock-and-roll pose), to the existential (a group of people waiting for a bus that never comes). The city even has its own sculpture park, an outpost of the Seattle Art Museum that spreads its works across a beautifully landscaped outdoor space overlooking glassy Elliott Bay. ABOVE: THE FREMONT TROLL BY SCULPTORS STEVE BADANES, WILL MARTIN, DONNA WALTER AND ROSS WHITEHEAD.

◉ *Belltown &*
Seattle Center

Coffee Culture (p117)

6 Every rainy day in this city is just another opportunity to warm up with a cup of joe. Seattle practically invented modern North American coffee culture, thanks to a small store in Pike Place Market that went global: Starbucks. But, while the rest of the world has been quick to lap up the green mermaid logo, Seattle has moved on. Starbucks is merely the froth on the cappuccino in a city where hundreds of small-scale micro-roasteries, cafes, baristas and knowledgeable caffeine connoisseurs continue to experiment and innovate. BELOW: STARBUCKS RESERVE ROASTERY & TASTING ROOM (P118)

🍷 *Capitol Hill & First Hill*

Capitol Hill (p110)

7 While other neighborhoods have their tourist shrines, Capitol Hill has its people and its culture – both thoroughly eclectic. Although the neighborhood has faced gentrification issues in recent years, its wonderfully offbeat soul is ever present. There are dive bars in old autoshops, cabaret venues where folks across the spectrum of gender and sexual identity perform to enthralled crowds, body-positive sex shops and enough vinyl and books to make you think that Amazon.com never happened. Welcome to Seattle's most colorful 'hood. Visiting isn't an option – it's a duty.

◉ *Capitol Hill & First Hill*

8

Beer Culture in Ballard *(p163)*

8 A one-time fishing village founded by Nordic immigrants, the Ballard neighborhood has been reincarnated as Seattle's beer capital with enough bars in its own right to satisfy a city. Boldly experimental, Ballard's small breweries concoct big flavors that are served in a cornucopia of drinking establishments. There are nano-breweries, brewpubs, old-school biker hangouts, tasting rooms, whiskey bars, sports bars, dives peddling rock, and bars with book corners. Bonus: once you're done with the booze, you can immerse yourself in Ballard's unique Nordic Museum and a necklace of waterside parks.

🍷 *Ballard &*
Discovery Park

Discovery Park (p155)

9 Seattle justifies its 'Emerald City' moniker in the rugged confines of 534-acre Discovery Park, a one-time military installation reborn as a textbook example of urban sustainability. Speckled with Douglas fir trees, hunting eagles, log-littered beaches and wild meadows, it resembles a lonely tract of Pacific Northwestern wilderness picked up and dropped into the middle of a crowded metropolitan area. Come here for breathing space, coexistence with nature, and a chance to slow down and reflect on the magic that lured people to Seattle in the first place. RIGHT: WEST POINT LIGHTHOUSE

🏃 *Ballard & Discovery Park*

Belltown Dining (p89)

10 Belltown, the high-spirited neighborhood where flannel-shirted grunge groupies once practiced their stage-dives, is now better known for its restaurants – cramming over 100 of them into a strip abutting downtown. Considered a microcosm of Seattle's gastronomic scene, this UN of food places a strong emphasis on 'locavore' cuisine, showcasing ingredients from Seattle's adjacent waters and farms. Look out for artisanal bakeries, sushi, creative pizzas, Basque-style tapas, Greek fusion, make-your-own poke bowls, seafood from Pike Place Market and homemade pasta, served around communal tables.

✗ *Belltown & Seattle Center*

What's New

Farewell Alaskan Way Viaduct

After many years of planning, the Alaskan Way Viaduct, an elevated stretch of highway that many saw as an eyesore on the city's otherwise stunning waterfront, has finally been demolished.

Space Needle remodel

Even if you've been to the top of the city's most iconic building (p82), it's now worth a second trip thanks to an extensive renovation to the observation decks of the Space Needle.

Nordic Museum reborn

The Nordic Museum (p156; formerly Nordic Heritage Museum) reopened in 2018 in a brand-new water-adjacent building, a huge upgrade from its former home in a charming, but small, historic schoolhouse.

Museums under renovation

Both the Burke Museum (p133), specializing in earth sciences and Native American history, and the Seattle Asian Art Museum (p112) were undergoing extensive remodels at the time of writing, with plans to reopen in late 2019.

The Spheres

In 2018 Amazon opened its second new building in the Denny Triangle. Contrasting the rather streamlined Amazon Tower I (p88), the Spheres (p87) is a complex made up of three orbs constructed from latticed white metal and glass. Inside plants intermingle with the architecture, giving you the feeling of being in a futuristic artificial forest.

The Key Arena is dead

Long live the Seattle Center Arena (p97)!

The Nest

Seattle has a new breathtaking view courtesy of high-up hotel bar the Nest (p54). It's crowded and expensive, but worth it on a clear day for a peek at Mt Rainier in the distance.

Ballard rising

Once its own city, then viewed as not *really* part of Seattle, a recent influx of quality restaurants, bars and shops into Ballard (p153) has transformed the neighborhood into one of the city's cultural hot spots.

Art in the Central District

Event programming at the historic Langston Hughes Performing Arts Center (p126) is now being handled by the newly formed LANGSTON non-profit arts organization (p130). Be sure to check the event schedule when you're in town.

Cocktails are the new craft beer

Don't get us wrong: Seattle is still a beer city, but earthy, unpretentious craft cocktails have taken up the mantle of the alcoholic libation of the moment. You'll find many new lounges and restaurants – such as Heartwood Provisions (p51), which opened in 2018 – that specialize in mixed drinks, as well as older establishments that have updated their menus to reflect the culture shift.

For more recommendations and reviews, see **lonelyplanet. com/seattle**

Need to Know

For more information, see Survival Guide (p211)

Currency
US dollar ($)

Language
English

Visas
Visa requirements vary widely for entry to the US and are liable to change. For up-to-date information, check www.travel.state.gov.

Money
ATMs are widely available. Credit and debit cards are accepted at most hotels, restaurants and shops, even for small transactions.

Cell Phones
The US uses CDMA-800 and GSM-1900 bands. SIM cards are relatively easy to obtain.

Time
Pacific Standard Time (GMT/UTC minus eight hours)

Tourist Information
Visit Seattle (Map p232; ☑20 6-461-5800; www.visitseattle. org; 705 Pike St; ⊙9am-5pm daily Jun-Sep, Mon-Fri Oct-May; ☒Westlake) The main tourist information center is in the Washington State Convention Center in downtown.

Daily Costs

Budget:
Less than $150
➡ Dorm bed in a hostel: $35

➡ Pike Place Market take-out snacks: $3–6

➡ Certain days at museums: free

➡ Public transportation average fare: $2.75

Midrange:
$150–300
➡ Online deal at a no-frills hotel: $130–180

➡ Pub, bakery or sandwich-bar meal: around $10

➡ Cheap tickets for sports games: from $12

➡ Short taxi trip: $12–15

Top end:
More than $300
➡ Downtown hotel room: more than $250

➡ Meal at trendy Capitol Hill restaurant: from $50

➡ Tickets to the theater or a concert: from $40

Advance Planning

One month before Start looking at options for car rental, accommodations, tours and train tickets.

Two weeks before If you're hoping to see a particular performance or game, whether it's the Mariners or the opera, it's wise to buy tickets in advance.

One to two days before Book popular restaurants in advance. Search the *Stranger* and the *Seattle Times* for upcoming art and entertainment listings.

Useful Websites

The Stranger (www.the stranger.com) Seattle's best newspaper for entertainment listings – and it's free.

Seattle Weekly (www.seattle weekly.com) The city's other free newspaper can be picked up in coffee bars or from metal street-side dispensers.

Seattle Post-Intelligencer (www.seattlepi.com) Online-only newspaper.

Real Change (www.realchange news.org) Weekly newspaper sold on the streets for and by unhoused people.

Eater (https://seattle.eater. com) The place to turn for food news and restaurant recommendations.

WHEN TO GO

Winter is dreary. Spring brings a few gorgeous days. July to September is dry and sunny. Early fall has more change-able weather.

Seattle

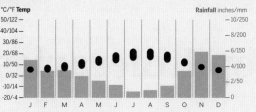

Arriving in Seattle

Sea-Tac International Airport (SEA) Link light rail connects to downtown Seattle in 30 minutes; shuttle buses stop on the 3rd floor of the airport garage and cost from $24.45 one way; taxi fares start around $55 to downtown (25 minutes).

King Street Station Situated in Pioneer Square and on the cusp of downtown with good, fast links to practically everywhere in the city. Use light rail to Westlake in the heart of downtown or take the streetcar to First Hill (both fares $2.25).

The Piers Metro buses 24 and 19 connect Pier 91 in Magnolia with downtown via the Seattle Center. Fares are a flat $2.75. Shuttle Express (p212) links piers 66 and 91 with Sea-Tac airport ($34) or downtown ($22). Washington State Ferries dock at Pier 52 in downtown Seattle.

For much more on **arrival** see p212

Getting Around

There is a large and growing network of public transportation in Seattle.

Bus A wide number of routes. Pay as you enter the bus; there's a flat fee of $2.75/1.50 per adult/child; you'll receive a slip that entitles you to a transfer until the time noted.

Light rail Regular all-day service on one line between Sea-Tac Airport and the University of Washington via downtown.

Streetcar Two lines: the South Lake Union line runs from Westlake Center to South Lake Union every 15 minutes, and the First Hill line runs from Pioneer Square to Capitol Hill. Fares are $2.25/1.50 per adult/child.

Water taxi Runs between Pier 50 on the waterfront to West Seattle; daily in summer, weekdays only in winter. The fare is $5.75 for the 10-minute crossing.

Taxi Initial charge $2.60, then $2.50 per mile.

For much more on **getting around** see p214

Sleeping

In common with many US cities, Seattle's sleeping options are plentiful and varied. Want to drive up to a motel and park your car where you can see it through the window? You can do that. Rather toss your keys to the valet while a bellhop whisks your bags to your suite? You can do that too, as well as everything in between.

Useful Websites

Lonely Planet (lonelyplanet.com/usa/seattle/hotels) Recommendations and bookings.

Visit Seattle (www.visitseattle.org) Deals available through the 'Lodging' page of the official Seattle/King County website.

Seattle Bed & Breakfast Association (www.lodginginseattle.com) Portal of the city's 20 best B&Bs; navigate to the 'Specials' page for info on packages and deals.

For much more on **sleeping** see p186

Top Itineraries

Day One

Pike Place (p40)

Early birds catch more than worms at **Pike Place Market**. Arrive promptly at 9am for some real-life street theater at market roll call before wandering over to the Main Arcade to see the fish throwers warming up. Spend the morning getting lost, browsing, tasting, buying and bantering with the producers, but don't miss the **gum wall** or **Rachel the Market Pig**. Afterward, be sure to wander down to the market extension overlooking the waterfront.

> **Lunch** Grab some mac 'n' cheese at Beecher's Handmade Cheese (p51).

Downtown & Waterfront (p40)

Scamper across Alaskan Way and marvel at the vistas created by the demolition of the viaduct that used to blight this area. Be a tourist and head for the **Aquarium** on Pier 59, or become a local and jump on a **Puget Sound ferry** just for the ride. Allow a good hour to browse the latest exhibits at **Seattle Art Museum** (SAM) on the western edge of downtown.

> **Dinner** Enjoy a seafood feast on the water at Elliott's Oyster House (p53).

Pioneer Square (p63)

Head to Pioneer Square for a drink in the amiable sports bar **Fuel** before hitting the **Comedy Underground**, where even poker-faced *misérables* have been known to break.

Day Two

Seattle Center (p80)

Give in to your most touristy instincts and head to the Seattle Center. After a cursory orientation of the complex, opt first for the crystallized magnificence of **Chihuly Garden & Glass**. If you buy a joint-admission ticket you can zip up the adjacent **Space Needle** afterwards for equally dazzling views.

> **Lunch** Pop into Belltown for lunch at lauded Tilikum Place Cafe (p90).

Seattle Center (p80)

After lunch, enjoy glittering Elliott Bay views and giant, imaginative art at the **Olympic Sculpture Park** before returning to the Seattle Center for an afternoon of rock-n-roll nostalgia at the **Museum of Pop Culture**. Stroll along 6th Ave afterward and pop into the **Assembly Hall** for a cup of coffee and a free game of pool.

> **Dinner** Decamp for a plate of home-made pasta to Tavolàta (p91).

Belltown (p80)

Start off with a game of pinball in **Shorty's**. If you like your bars divey, stay put. For a taste of modern Belltown, hit the **Whisky Bar** and order a Westland single malt, or agonize over the selection of truly novel cocktails at **No Anchor**. End the night by seeing who's playing at the **Crocodile**.

Day Three

Pioneer Square (p63)

Start the morning like a true Seat-tleite with a latte in **Zeitgeist**, possibly the city's best indie coffee shop. Cross the road, admiring 1890s redbrick architecture, and visit the entertaining, educational and free **Klondike Gold Rush National Historical Park**. If there's time, take a gilded-age elevator up the **Smith Tower** before lunch.

> **Lunch** Hit the International District for dim sum in Jade Garden (p71).

International District (p63)

In the ID, call in on its most famous sight, the **Wing Luke Museum**, and its most esoteric, the **Pinball Museum** (for a quick game), before imbibing tea and Japanese American history in the **Panama Hotel Tea & Coffee House**. From here, climb up through genteel First Hill to Capitol Hill.

> **Dinner** Indulge in Seattle's locavore culture at Sitka & Spruce (p116).

Capitol Hill (p110)

Spontaneous evenings in Capitol Hill start early and go on till late. Warm up on the Pike–Pine corridor with a cocktail on the patio at **Pony** before heading over to **Optimism Brewing Co** for a straight-from-the-beer-vat microbrew. Those with high alcohol thresholds can keep mixing at **Capitol Cider**. Those with a penchant for cool indie music delivered live should check out **Neumo's**.

Day Four

Lake Union (p100)

It's time for a journey through Seattle's outer neighborhoods. Start the morning in South Lake Union, where a lakeside park hosts the **Museum of History & Industry**, a roller-coaster journey through Seattle's past. If there's time afterward, pop into the **Center for Wooden Boats** to plan future sailing sorties.

> **Lunch** Dine at Serious Biscuit (p105), owned by celebrity chef Tom Douglas.

Fremont (p141)

Stroll through Westlake along the **Cheshiahud Loop**, or flag a bus to take you to Fremont. Soon after crossing the Fremont Bridge, you'll spy *Waiting for the Interurban* and plenty of other whimsical sculptures. It would be foolish to leave Fremont without a visit to **Theo Chocolate Factory**. Share coffee with the locals afterward at **Milstead & Co** before hitting the **Burke-Gilman Trail** (or getting a bus) to Ballard.

> **Dinner** Go Mexican at La Carta de Oaxaca (p158) on Ballard Ave NW.

Ballard (p153)

If weather permits, stroll out to **Hiram M Chittenden Locks** for sunset, before returning to Ballard Ave to experience the neighborhood's self-contained nightlife. There's no friendlier beer nook than **Populuxe Brewing**, a pioneering nano-brewery. More rambunctious is **King's Hardware**. Louder still is the **Tractor Tavern**, a legendary hive of indie rock and alt-country music.

If You Like...

Views

Columbia Center The highest human-made view in Seattle can be seen for $20. (p48)

Space Needle The (expensive) rite of passage for every tourist since 1962. (p82)

Kerry Park Climb to this park in Seattle's salubrious Queen Anne quarter and watch the sun set. (p103)

Rainier Vista The University of Washington's campus is designed to lead your eyes right to its stunning mountain views. (p134)

Pier 66 Close enough to the skyline to enjoy its visceral urban charms. (p87)

Bhy Kracke Park A lesser known Queen Anne viewpoint that delivers the goods. (p103)

Museums

Seattle Art Museum A leading player in modern art from around the globe, with an enviable Native American collection. (p46)

Nordic Museum Newly reopened in a breathtaking space and boasting a stunning collection of exhibits on Nordic culture and history. (p156)

Museum of History & Industry Seattle's boom-bust history is laid out in an erstwhile armory building on the shores of Lake Union. (p102)

Chihuly Garden & Glass Tacoma-born Dale Chihuly honored in a dazzling glass-art display beneath the Space Needle. (p84)

ROMAN KHOMLYAK/SHUTTERSTOCK ©

Bird in Discovery Park (p155)

Museum of Pop Culture Super-modern rock-and-roll museum that lets you play on some of the exhibits. (p86)

Northwest African American Museum Small but powerful homage to the history and cultural contributions made by the Pacific Northwest's African American communities. (p126)

Klondike Gold Rush National Historical Park Interactive museum that details Seattle's role in the 1897 gold fever that gripped the Yukon. (p66)

Offbeat Stuff

Gum wall Get rid of your chewing gum and contribute to Seattle's biggest (and most unhygienic) art wall. (p49)

Fish throwers Watch huge salmon flying through the air at Pike Place Market. (p42)

Statue of Lenin Come and pay your respects, or hurl a few insults, at Vladimir Ilyich Ulyanov, aka Lenin. (p143)

Solstice cyclists Fremont's Solstice Fair includes an artsy parade, where nude cyclists pedal through the neighborhood. (p142)

Hat 'n' Boots This giant cowboy hat and boots once embellished a Washington gas station. (p168)

Café Racer Both an eclectic neighborhood dive and home to the OBAMA Room (Official Bad Art Museum of Art). (p137)

Green Spaces

Green Lake Park Amateur athletics track? Body-beautiful competition? Giant alfresco community center? Green Lake Park is where it all happens. (p145)

Volunteer Park Follow Millionaires Row to this elegant park on Capitol Hill, where a water tower offers panoramic views. (p112)

Discovery Park A former military installation that became a park in the 1970s, it retains an element of wilderness lacking elsewhere. (p155)

Washington Park Arboretum Pleasant green corridor that bisects Seattle's eastern neighborhoods with multiple paths and a Japanese garden. (p126)

Madison Park Beach Popular in-town lounging and swimming spot. (p127)

Lincoln Park Forested trails lead to large stretches of undeveloped beachfront far from busy downtown. (p168)

Architecture

Pioneer Square The homogeneous historic quarter where Seattle was born guards the city's most valuable architectural legacy. (p65)

Queen Anne Hilly, well-to-do neighborhood with fine residential houses designed in the elegant Queen Anne Revivalist style. (p39)

Seattle Central Library A 21st-century architectural marvel that looks like a giant diamond dropped from outer space. (p48)

Museum of Pop Culture Frank Gehry allegedly designed this avant-garde building to resemble one of Hendrix' smashed guitars. (p86)

University of Washington A campus full of grandiose structures. (p133)

Spheres Amazon's newest building, a futuristic marriage of architecture and nature. (p87)

Free Stuff

Boat rides on Lake Union Free sailing trips at 10am Sunday at the Center for Wooden Boats; first come, first served. (p104)

Music in Pike Place Everyone from concert violinists to punk poets busks for free at Pike Place Market. (p42)

Occidental Park This refurbished Pioneer Square park offers free outdoor games, including chess and table tennis. (p66)

Borrow a bike Numerous hotels offer free bikes, so grab some wheels and hit the beautiful Burke-Gilman Trail. (p139)

Public art Viewing all of Seattle's alfresco art, including at the Olympic Sculpture Park, costs precisely zero dollars. (p87)

Green Lake Park A favorite for runners, personal trainers and artistically tattooed sunbathers. (p145)

Fremont public sculpture Fremont's sculptures are an eclectic amalgamation of the scary, the politically incorrect and the, well, weird. (p143)

Bill & Melinda Gates Foundation Discovery Center See what one of the world's richest families does with their money. (p88)

For more top Seattle spots, see the following:

➡ Eating (p24)

➡ Drinking & Nightlife (p27)

➡ Entertainment (p29)

➡ Sports & Activities (p31)

➡ Shopping (p34)

Month By Month

January

The year starts with a hangover and occasional flurries of snow. Plan indoor activities or bring your skis and head to the nearby mountains.

✨ Chinese New Year

Beginning toward the end of January or at the start of February and lasting for two weeks, the year's first notable festival (www.cidbia.org) takes place in the International District with parades, firecrackers, fireworks and plenty of food.

February

Dark, dreary days and occasional bouts of genuine cold keep most in figurative hibernation. Scour the internet for hotel deals and book a night at the theater.

March

The odd warm day can see restaurants opening up their patios, but more often than not rain persists. St Patrick's Day provides a good excuse to shrug off the long, hard winter.

✨ Moisture Festival

This increasingly prominent comedy/varieté festival (moisturefestival. org) takes place over four weeks from mid-March to mid-April.

April

This is usually the month where you'll find the center of the 'nice weather' and 'cheaper hotel rates' Venn diagram. It's not always sunny, but there are plenty of stunner days.

May

People start hitting the waterside attractions. Visit before Memorial Day (last Monday in May): this could be your last chance for a hotel deal for a while.

✨ Northwest Folklife Festival

This humongous festival (www.nwfolklife.org) takes over Seattle Center during Memorial Day weekend. More than 5000 performers and artists from over 100 countries present music, dance, crafts and food in celebration of the rich cultural heritage of the Pacific Northwest.

☆ Seattle International Film Festival

Held over three weeks from mid-May to early June, this prestigious film festival (p29) uses a half-dozen cinemas to screen over 400 movies. Major venues include the SIFF Cinema Uptown in Lower Queen Anne and the festival's own dedicated SIFF Film Center in the Seattle Center.

June

Showers can linger in the early part of June, but summer's in the post. When the temperatures rise you can feel the

city loosen up and sigh
contentedly.

🎺 Fremont Solstice Fair

Off-kilter Fremont offers a
June fair (p142) with live
music, food and crafts, and
the overtly artsy Solstice
Parade, where human-
powered floats and –
ahem – nude cyclists trickle
through the neighborhood.

🎺 Seattle Pride Festival

Seattle Pride (p218), the
city's pioneering LGBTIQ+
event (held every year
since 1974) usually falls on
the last Sunday in June. It
includes a huge downtown
parade followed by a festival in Capitol Hill's Volunteer Park.

July

**Peak temperatures
(75°F/24°C) and peak
prices mark Seattle's
peak season, when you'd
be wise to book ahead for
pretty much everything.**

🎺 Seafair

Huge crowds attend the
Seafair (www.seafair.com)
festival held on the water
from mid-June to mid-
August, with a pirate's landing, a torchlight parade, an
air show, a music marathon
and even a Milk Carton
Derby (look it up!).

August

**Salmon bakes,
neighborhood street fairs
and lazy beach afternoons
give August a laid-back
feel. But school's out, so
expect ubiquitous cries of
excited kids.**

🎺 Nordic Sól

Citizens of Ballard redis-
cover their inner Viking
and celebrate Seattle's
Scandinavian heritage in
the grounds of the Nordic
Museum (p156)at the
Nordic Sól celebration (formerly called Viking Days).

🎺 Hempfest

Seattle's Hempfest (www.
hempfest.org) is a large
annual festival celebrating
weed culture. Needless to
say it has been even more
of a blast since recreational
marijuana became legal
in 2012.

September

**The best month to
visit? Possibly. Once
Bumbershoot's over,
the tourists go home
and hotel prices deflate,
but the weather usually
remains sunny and
relatively warm until early
October.**

🎺 Bumbershoot

One of the biggest events
(bumbershoot.com) of the
year in the Pacific Northwest for those who want to
be seen. Some come for the
Instagram moments, oth-
ers for the incredible live
music, comedy, theater and
dance, and everyone has a
good time.

October

**There's the possibility of
an Indian summer in the
first half of the month
when the start of the
shoulder season brings
cheaper prices. As the
clouds roll in, people
get out to celebrate
Halloween.**

☆ TWIST: Seattle Queer Film Festival

This popular film festival
(p218) shows new queer-
themed movies from direc-
tors worldwide. It's curated
by the Three Dollar Bill
Cinema and held at various
venues.

November

**November can be a dismal
month for weather, but
most sights stay open
and, with low season
kicking in, some hotels
slash their prices to half
summer rates.**

🔒 Best of the Northwest

The Best of the Northwest
(nwartalliance.org) art
and fine craft show is held
in Magnuson Park in the
Sand Point neighborhood
just north of the U District.
It showcases artists and
designers of all genres from
jewelry to glass.

December

**Seattle's surrounding ski
resorts open up, making
the city a good urban
base for snow-related
activities. Hotel prices
continue to drop along
with the temperatures.**

🎺 Winterfest

Seattle Center holds a
month-long celebration
of holiday traditions from
around the globe, starting
with Winter Worldfest, a
massive concert and dance
performance, and continu-
ing with exhibits, dances,
concerts and ice skating
(www.seattlecenter.com/
winterfest).

With Kids

Take it easy, overworked parent. Seattle will entertain, pacify and often educate your energetic kid(s) without their even realizing it. Some of the attractions are obvious – a children's theater and a zoo. Others are more serendipitous: don't miss the pinball museum or the exciting urban theater of Pike Place Market.

Seattle Pinball Museum (p68)

Where to Eat

Most restaurants in Seattle are kid-friendly. The only places you're likely to see 'No Minors' signs are pubs, gastropubs and dive bars (notwithstanding that, many pubs will serve families as long as you don't sit at the bar). Some places introduce a no-kids policy after 10pm.

Pike Place Market has the widest selection of cheap, immediately available food and is a fun place to hang out and eat. You'll struggle to find anyone (kid or adult) who doesn't fall instantly in love with the mac 'n' cheese cartons sold at Beecher's Handmade Cheese (p51) or the flaky pastries rolled before your eyes at Piroshky Piroshky (p51). Elsewhere, Pie (p147) in Fremont cooks up some excellent crusty fare, and Belltown's La Vita é Bella (p90) is a traditional family-friendly Italian trattoria. Every youthful visitor to Seattle should be allowed at least one 'treat' from Top Pot Hand-Forged Doughnuts (p89) – preferably for breakfast. Ivar's Acres of Clams (p53) makes a good post-aquarium fish-and-chips lunch. Watch out for the hungry seagulls!

Outdoor Activities

Discovery Park

There are sometimes organized nature walks in the park (p155); check schedules at the Environmental Learning Center (p155). Otherwise this giant green space has a kids' play area, wonderful beach-combing opportunities and several miles of safe trails.

Hiram M Chittenden Locks

Watch the boats traverse the locks (p156) and see the fish ladder. The adjacent park is good for a picnic, weather permitting.

Center for Wooden Boats

You can sail model boats on the pond in Lake Union Park at weekends from 11am to 2pm. The center (p104) also offers free sailboat rides (first come, first served) on Lake Union on Sunday (sign-up from 10am).

DAVID TONELSON/SHUTTERSTOCK ©

Cycling the Burke-Gilman Trail

Recycled Cycles (p140) in the U District rents trail-a-bikes or trailers (chariots) so you can cycle safely with your kids.

Alki Beach Park

The main part of West Seattle's beach (p168) is sandy – ideal for sandcastle building and all of those other age-old seaside pleasures. There are good tide pools further west around the lighthouse.

Shops for Kids

Market Magic

Pike Place Market's resident joke and magic shop (p59).

Card Kingdom

Ballard games emporium (p164) with on-site board games to buy or just play.

Pink Gorilla Games

New and retro video games and related toys can be found at Pink Gorilla (p77).

Golden Age Collectables

A haven (p60) for kids who prefer to keep their toys in the packaging to preserve their value.

Seattle Center

The Seattle Center has the most concentrated stash of kid-friendly activities, including the professional Seattle Children's Theater (p96; performances Thursday to Sunday) and the Children's Museum (p89; better for the under 10s). In the summer, balloon-twisters, singers and dancers entertain the crowds alfresco. Aside from the interesting and educational permanent displays, the Pacific Science Center (p89) has some excellent touring exhibits. Past shows have included Harry Potter movie memorabilia and King Tutankhamun's jewels. In the Museum of Pop Culture (p86) you could fill an afternoon in the Sound Lab, where adults and kids can requisition drum kits, guitars and keyboards, and even form their own

band for the special 'On Stage' feature. The elevator ride in the Space Needle (p82) is an adventure and there are plenty of things to press at the top.

Rainy Day Activities

Seattle Pinball Museum

Pay $12 to $15 for unlimited use of several dozen pinball machines (stools are available for the vertically challenged and snacks are sold) at this museum (p68). The catch: getting your kid out afterward!

Museum of Flight

Huge museum (p167) with plenty of interactive exhibits, including a flight simulator.

Museum of History & Industry

Learn about Seattle's past through film, music, quizzes and questions at the Museum of History & Industry (p102).

Animal Viewing

Woodland Park Zoo

Woodland Park (p145) is considered one of the best zoos in the US, with 300 species including snow leopards, lions and tigers.

Seattle Aquarium

Designed with kids in mind, the aquarium (p50) has a fish 'touching tank' and daily feeding shows.

NEED TO KNOW

Activities ParentMap (www.parent map.com) has child- and family-friendly activity listings around the city.

Geography Watch out for Seattle's ultra-steep hills if you're pushing a stroller or have kids on scooters.

Diapers Bathrooms in larger stores and venues will usually have changing tables.

Transport Kids often qualify for discounted metro bus and ferry fares.

Pike Place Market (p42) fish stall

Eating

Seattle's food scene was always noteworthy, but in recent years it has exploded, thanks to the popularity of farm-to-table practices and new American cuisine, with all of its simple preparations and locally sourced ingredients. As with other major cities you'll also find that immigrant communities have made their mark, as have contemporary dining trends.

What is Northwest Cuisine?

A lot of Seattle's gourmet restaurants describe their food as 'Northwest cuisine.' Its cornerstone is high-quality regional ingredients that grow abundantly in Washington State: seafood so fresh it squirms, fat berries freshly plucked, mushrooms dug out of the rich soil and a cornucopia of fruit and vegetables. Another distinguishing feature is pan-Asian cooking, often referred to as Pacific Rim cuisine or fusion food. The blending of American or European standards with ingredients from Asia, it results in some unusual combinations – don't be surprised if you get wasabi on your French fries.

Things Seattle Does Well

Surrounded by water, Seattle is an obvious powerhouse of fresh seafood. Local favorites include Dungeness crab, salmon, halibut, oysters, spot prawns and clams.

Although it's not one of the most cosmopolitan cities in the US, Seattle has a sizable Chinese population and a strong selection of dim sum restaurants in the International District (ID). The ID also harbors a good cluster of Vietnamese restaurants in its 'Little Saigon' quarter.

Seattle's Italian restaurants are often highly progressive, many of them specializing in regional food such as Roman or Piedmontese.

Chef Ethan Stowell has successfully married Italian cuisine with Northwest traditions and popularized the use of homemade pasta.

Other genres in which Seattle excels are bakeries (a by-product of its cafe culture), Japanese food (the sushi is unwaveringly good) and – perhaps surprisingly – spicy Ethiopian food; the bulk of the East African restaurants are in the Central District (CD). The city used to be noted for its dearth of Mexican restaurants, but in the past decade or so many shockingly good ones have opened. While the Indian fare can't compete with that found in Vancouver, the appearance of Nirmal's (p70) in Pioneer Square has upped the ante somewhat.

Seattle also loves a good steak – especially one that's led a happy, grass-fed life on a farm just outside of town. Recent booming food trends are southern-style biscuits, *pho*, Cuban sandwiches and New York–style pizza.

Mold-Breaking Chefs

Tom Douglas The biggest name on the Seattle food scene, Douglas helped define what people mean when they talk about Northwest cuisine. He opened his first restaurant, Dahlia, in 1989 and has since followed it with 16 more. Douglas won the prestigious James Beard Award for Best Restaurateur in 2012 and once battled Masaharu Morimoto in an episode of *Iron Chef America* – and won.

Ethan Stowell With 13 Seattle restaurants, Stowell is now considered an established star. His specialty is marrying creative Italian cuisine with classic Northwest ingredients, especially seafood.

Matt Dillon Seattle's most devotedly sustainable chef owns a farm on Vashon Island and is a strong proponent of food foraging. In 2012 he shared James Beard honors with Tom Douglas when he won the Best Northwest Chef award. His don't-miss restaurant is Sitka & Spruce (p116), one of the best in the city overall, where pretty much all the ingredients are local.

Eating by Neighborhood

Downtown, Pike Place & Waterfront (p50) Enjoy fine dining in downtown; grab cheap, on-the-go, artisanal food at Pike Place Market; seafood is order of the day at the Waterfront.

Pioneer Square, International District & SoDo (p69) New veg-friendly bistros and old steakhouses dot Pioneer Square; Vietnamese food and dim sum characterize the ID.

NEED TO KNOW

Price Ranges
The following price ranges refer to the average cost of a main dish:

$ less than $15

$$ $15–25

$$$ more than $25

Opening Hours
Breakfast is typically served from 7am to 11am, brunch from 9am to 3pm, lunch from 11:30am to 2:30pm and dinner from 5:30pm to 10pm. It's not unusual for restaurants to close between lunch and dinner.

Tipping
Tips are not figured into the check at a restaurant. In general, 15% is the baseline tip, but 20% is usually more appropriate, and 25% if you enjoyed the service. Some restaurants have begun an automatic 18% gratuity on all tickets.

Reservations
Most Seattle restaurants don't require bookings, but the hot new places fill up quickly, so it's best to call ahead or book online to avoid disappointment.

Belltown & Seattle Center (p89) Belltown vies with Capitol Hill for Seattle's best selection of restaurants covering every genre and budget.

Queen Anne & Lake Union (p104) Hilltop bistros and corporate lunch spots dominate.

Capitol Hill & First Hill (p114) Cuisine from over the map, with Seattle's hottest chefs competing alongside the next big thing.

The CD, Madrona & Madison Park (p127) A plateful of surprises that'll satisfy everyone from French-haute-cuisine snobs to soul-food purists.

U District (p134) Cheap, no-frills, food that caters to the college crowd and is kind to vegetarians.

Green Lake & Fremont (p146) Fremont specializes in unusual noncorporate fast food; Green Lake exhibits warm, family-friendly restaurants.

Ballard & Discovery Park (p157) Seafood, with some cool Mexican places making an interesting cameo.

Georgetown & West Seattle (p169) A wide array of mostly undiscovered spots, often very family friendly.

Lonely Planet's Top Choices

Sitka & Spruce (p116) If you had to sum up Seattle cuisine in three words, this is it.

La Carta de Oaxaca (p158) Unmissable regional Mexican cuisine and the best brunch in town.

Staple & Fancy (p159) It's worth blowing your budget on the tasting menu at this rustic Italian spot.

Heartwood Provisions (p51) Makes its mark with brilliantly executed Northwest cuisine with some Southeast Asian flair.

Maneki (p72) This traditional Japanese restaurant is one of the most distinctive dining opportunities in town.

Taco Chukis (p127) They only do tacos, but when they are this good, what else could you need?

Best by Budget

$

Taco Chukis (p127) The best bite of food for under $3 you're likely to find.

Crumpet Shop (p52) Pike Place phenomenon where thick toppings are lashed on homemade crumpets.

Piroshky Piroshky (p51) Russian buns are rolled in the window of this Pike Place Market hole-in-the-wall.

Bakery Nouveau (p169) Best bakery this side of...Paris.

$$

Café Campagne (p53) French cuisine that stands an Eiffel Tower above all its competitors.

Bitterroot (p158) Perfectly smoked meat plus a huge whiskey list is always a winning equation.

Portage Bay Cafe (p136) Astoundingly good brunch.

Ma'Ono (p170) Fried chicken sandwiches Hawaiian-style.

Wild Ginger (p51) Asian fusion with plenty of flair.

$$$

Nirmal's (p70) Elegant Indian fine dining that doesn't skimp on the flavors.

Cascina Spinasse (p116) Italian nosh that's worth the extra investment.

Canlis (p106) Queen Anne's oasis of 'posh' with food to boot.

The Whale Wins (p148) A new vegetable-friendly haven of good taste.

Best Recently Opened Restaurants

Heartwood Provisions (p51) New fine dining that actually makes a splash on the scene.

San Fermo (p159) A welcome recent addition to Ballard in one of the neighborhood's oldest buildings.

Kamonegi (p147) The traditional soba noodles and tempura here have shaken up the Fremont dining scene.

Arthur's (p170) Aussie-inspired breakfast and lunch bites sure to keep the bad-weather blues away.

Best by Cuisine

Asian

Maneki (p72) Come for fish so fresh it's legendary.

7 Star Pepper (p72) Hand-shaved noodles that are worth the trek to this out-of-the-way restaurant.

Nuna Ramen (p147) Rich broth, chewy noodles and plenty of mix-ins put this ramen joint a cut above.

Pho Bac (p71) Newly renovated International District institution well loved for its *pho*.

Jade Garden (p71) Regarded as the best dim sum around.

Seafood

Walrus & the Carpenter (p159) Ballard oyster bar where they serve 'em raw with white wine.

Steelhead Diner (p53) Located in Pike Place Market, with fresh fish bought yards from your plate.

Sunfish (p170) Head to Alki Beach for some of the best fish-and-chips in the city.

Pike Place Chowder (p52) Pike Place institution where there's always 40 people queuing for four tables.

Best With a View

Canlis (p106) Up on Queen Anne Hill, Canlis overlooks the watery action of Lake Union.

Ray's Boathouse (p160) Fine dining on Puget Sound where shimmering water views add a sparkle on sunny days.

Salty's on Alki (p170) Top-notch food overlooking Elliott Bay with the Seattle skyline as a backdrop.

Cutter's Crabhouse (p53) Ferries, gulls and snowcapped mountains enhance the food experience at this waterfront crab restaurant.

Drinking & Nightlife

It's hard to complain too much about Seattle's crappy weather when the two best forms of rainy-day solace – coffee and alcohol – are available in such abundance. There's no doubt about it: Seattle's an inviting place to enjoy a drink, whatever your poison.

Coffee Culture

When the first Starbucks opened in Pike Place Market in 1971, Seattle was suddenly the center of the coffee universe. It still is, although these days Starbucks is loved and loathed in equal measure.

After Starbucks came the 'third wave': coffee shops that buy fair-trade coffee with traceable origins and concoct it through a micro-managed, in-house roasting process that pays attention to everything from the coffee's bean quality to its 'taste notes'. These shops are now as ubiquitous as Starbucks, though they remain independent and adhere strictly to their original manifesto: quality not quantity.

Macro Amounts of Microbrews

The microbrew explosion rocked the Northwest around the same time as the gourmet-coffee craze, but not coincidentally: Seattle's Redhook Brewery was co-founded in 1981 by Gordon Bowker, one of the guys who founded Starbucks.

Most local microbreweries started out as tiny craft breweries that produced European-style ales. Many of these small producers initially lacked the capital to offer their brews for sale anywhere but in the brewery building itself, hence the term 'brewpub' – an informal pub with its own on-site brewery.

Though you can find microbrews at practically every bar in town, brewpubs often feature signature brews and ales not available anywhere else. It's worth asking about specialty brews or seasonal beers on tap. Most of the brewpubs offer a taster's selection of the house brews. Pints range in price from $5 to $7, and you can usually get a small sample to try before committing.

Drinking & Nightlife by Neighborhood

Downtown, Pike Place & Waterfront (p54) Hotel bars and pleasant old-school drinking nooks tucked away in Pike Place.

Pioneer Square, International District & SoDo (p72) Gritty saloons in Pioneer Square; bubble tea and restaurant lounges in the ID.

Belltown & Seattle Center (p92) Belltown's bar-hopping, late-night drinking scene is not as grungy as it once was.

Queen Anne & Lake Union (p106) Lower Queen Anne has a lively bar scene and is a coffee-culture epicenter.

Capitol Hill & First Hill (p117) *The* place for a night out, with gay bars, dive bars, cocktail lounges and third-wave coffee shops.

The CD, Madrona & Madison Park (p129) Mostly quiet with a few local taverns.

U District (p137) No-frills dives and a plethora of coffee shops designed for the laptop crowd.

Green Lake & Fremont (p148) Mix of new-ish brewpubs and old-school neighborhood pubs.

Ballard & Discovery Park (p160) Beer heaven, with old-fashioned pubs sitting alongside boisterous brewpubs and cozy nano-breweries.

Georgetown & West Seattle (p171) Blue-collar pubs reborn as bohemian Georgetown bars.

NEED TO KNOW

Opening Hours

This is caffeine-addicted Seattle, so some coffee bars open as early as 5am and close at around 11pm, but 7am until 6pm is more standard. Bars usually serve from lunchtime until 2am (when state liquor laws demand they stop selling booze), although some don't open until 5pm and others start as early as 7am.

Ha-Ha-Happy Hours

The term happy 'hour' is a misnomer: most Seattle bars run their happy hours from around 3pm until 6pm. Some bars also offer happy-hour deals on bar snacks, appetizers or even full-blown meals. Late night happy hours, usually 10pm until 1am, are becoming more common.

Lonely Planet's Top Choices

Zeitgeist Coffee (p74) Best coffee in Seattle? Go and find out!

Fremont Brewing Company (p148) The secret's in the hops.

Bookstore Bar (p54) Buy a whiskey; snuggle down with a great novel.

Pony (p117) Gay bar that welcomes all to its legendarily fun patio.

Owl & Thistle (p56) No one does pubs like the Irish.

Unicorn (p117) Whimsical bar in which to enjoy the sweeter things in life.

Best Brewpubs & Tasting Rooms

Fremont Brewing Company (p148) New old-school brewery where you can taste beer at wooden tables on the factory floor.

Populuxe Brewing (p160) Beloved Ballard micro-brewery made for lazy summer afternoons.

Pike Pub & Brewery (p57) One of the oldest and most cherished brewpubs in Seattle.

Optimism Brewing Co (p118) At long last, a new industrial-style brewery and tasting room on Capitol Hill.

Machine House Brewery (p171) Small friendly peddler of British-style ales in an old Georgetown beer factory.

Best Dive Bars

Blue Moon (p137) Romanticism with a rough edge in a poets' haven in the U District.

Shorty's (p94) Pinball, hot dogs, punk rock and beer – a devastating combination in Belltown.

5 Point Café (p94) That stale-beer smell has been here since 1929.

Monkey Pub (p138) A dive by nature not design in the U District.

Café Racer (p137) Improv jazz, eccentric decor and a bad art museum are just three of the flavors in this U District dive.

Best LGBTIQ+ Bars

Pony (p117) Capitol Hill's own agora, located in a renovated auto shop.

Wildrose (p118) Lesbian pub in Capitol Hill.

R Place (p118) The place to watch go-go boys gyrate before trying some moves of your own.

Re-Bar (p94) What? A gay club that's not in Capitol Hill?

Outwest Bar (p171) A mellow LGBTIQ+ outpost in West Seattle.

Best Whiskey Bars

Westland Distillery (p77) Micro-distillery with tasting room and the yardstick against which other Seattle whiskeys are measured.

Bookstore Bar (p54) Try a couple of their more than 100 varieties of Scotch and bourbon.

Radiator Whiskey (p56) Pike Place bar with a penchant for delicious Manhattans.

Whisky Bar (p94) A new location hasn't dampened the throat-warming effects of the numerous whiskeys.

MacLeods (p162) Genuine Scottish pub in the bar bonanza of Ballard.

Best Coffee Bars

Zeitgeist Coffee (p74) At Zeitgeist it's all about the coffee – and the gorgeous almond croissants.

Storyville Coffee (p56) New kid on the block, but already making a name for itself.

Espresso Vivace at Brix (p117) Drink coffee, listen to the Ramones and check out the latest street style.

Milstead & Co (p148) Multi-roaster in Fremont choosing the best coffee on the market; the menu changes daily.

Victrola Coffee Roasters (p117) When hipsters go to heaven they probably get teleported to Victrola in Capitol Hill.

⭐ Entertainment

Quietly aggrieved that it was being bypassed by big-name touring acts in the 1980s, Seattle shut itself away and created its own live-music scene. This explosive grassroots movement is backed up by plenty of other artistic strands, including independent cinema, burlesque theater, bookstore poetry readings and some high-profile opera, classical music and drama.

Live Music

For simplicity's sake, Seattle's music venues can be stacked in a kind of triangular tower. At the summit sits the 17,000-capacity Seattle Center Arena (p97). Below this is a trio of medium-sized historic theaters: the 2807-capacity Paramount (p58), the 1800-capacity Moore (p96), dating from 1907, and the 1137-capacity Showbox (p58), dating from 1939. Next is a handful of more clamorous venues, small enough to foster the close band-audience interaction that was so crucial in the development of Seattle's 1990s music revolution. Some of these '90s bastions still exist, though in a more sanitized form. Still pulling less-mainstream big-name acts are the 560-capacity Crocodile (p95) in Belltown and 650-capacity Neumo's (p120) in Capitol Hill.

Hosting lesser-known local talent are various neighborhood venues such as Ballard's 360-capacity Tractor Tavern (p163) and Fremont's High Dive (p151). Right at the bottom of the triangle are the ubiquitous pubs, clubs and coffee bars that showcase small-time local talent from Irish fiddlers to Björk-like singers. Seattle has two jazz venues: Tula's (p96) and Dimitriou's Jazz Alley (p95). For a swankier dinner-show scene, hit downtown's Triple Door (p58).

The Arts

Seattle is a book-loving town and there's a literary event practically every night. The film industry also has national stature. The **Seattle International Film Festival** (SIFF; ☑20 6-464-5830; www.siff.net; ☺May-Jun) is among the most influential festivals in the country, and a thriving independent scene has sprung up in a handful of underground venues. Theater runs the gamut from big productions, such as Ibsen at the Intiman (p96), to staged readings of obscure texts in cobbled-together venues or coffee shops. The Seattle Symphony (p58) has become nationally known and widely respected, primarily through its excellent recordings. Meanwhile the Central District has revitalized two of its historic arts venues: the Langston Hughes Performing Arts Center (p126) and Washington Hall (p126).

Entertainment by Neighborhood

Downtown, Pike Place & Waterfront (p57) Classical music and historic Showbox theater in downtown.

Pioneer Square, International District & SoDo (p75) Comedy shows and a few tough pubs peddling punk and metal.

Belltown & Seattle Center (p94) Alt-rock and jazz venues in Belltown; opera, ballet and theater in Seattle Center.

Queen Anne & Lake Union (p107) Fringe theater and hallowed rock venues such as El Corazon.

Capitol Hill & First Hill (p120) Everything outside the mainstream, including alt-rock and electronica.

The CD, Madrona & Madison Park (p130) Jimi Hendrix played his first gig here; the LANGSTON arts center is keeping the area entertained today.

U District (p138) Small pub strummers and stand-up comedy plus name acts at the revived Neptune Theater.

NEED TO KNOW

Opening Hours

Typically, live music starts between 9pm and 10pm and goes until 1am or 2am.

Tickets & Reservations

Tickets for big events are available through Ticket-Master (www.ticketmaster.com). **Brown Paper Tickets** (☑800-838-3006; www.brownpapertickets.com) handles sales for a number of smaller and quirkier venues, from theater to live music. Alternatively, you can often book via the venue website.

Cover Charge

For most venues you can pay admission at the door; for a small- to medium-size venue, the cover charge can be anywhere from $5 to $20.

Green Lake & Fremont (p151) Intimate High Dive and Nectar Lounge in Fremont book small-name live acts.

Ballard & Discovery Park (p163) Pubs and clubs plus the Sunset and Tractor taverns cement a good live-music scene.

Lonely Planet's Top Choices

Crocodile (p94) Even 25 years on, it hasn't lost its ability to rock and roll.

Dimitriou's Jazz Alley (p95) Be-bopping the crowds in Belltown since 1985.

Seattle International Film Festival (p29) One of the best and most multifarious film festivals in the US.

Benaroya Concert Hall (p58) The spectacular HQ for Seattle's prestigious symphony orchestra.

Langston Hughes Performing Arts Center (p126) Historic venue whose programming is dedicated to 'cultivating black brilliance.'

Best Live-Music Venues

Crocodile (p94) Nationally renowned midsize live venue that helped promote grunge.

Neumo's (p120) The other pillar of Seattle's dynamic scene has updated and remains relevant.

McCaw Hall (p95) Go and hear the Seattle Opera raise the roof.

Chop Suey (p120) Diverse selection of live acts, with indie alternating with hip-hop.

Tractor Tavern (p163) The anchor of Ballard's live scene specializes in alt country.

Best Theaters

A Contemporary Theatre (p58) With its central stage and gilded decor, this is Seattle's best all-round theater.

On the Boards (p108) Cutting-edge contemporary drama in Queen Anne.

Jewel Box Theater (p96) Small gem specializing in burlesque hidden in a Belltown cocktail bar.

Paramount Theater (p58) Touring Broadway shows.

Best Small Live Venues

Espresso Vivace at Brix (p117) Hip coffee bar where local bands play regular laid-back sets.

High Dive (p151) Small Fremont dive for up-and-coming bands.

Nectar Lounge (p151) Early promoter of Seattle's now-famous hip-hop scene.

Owl & Thistle (p56) Downtown Irish pub with fine fiddlers and folk music.

Best Cinemas

Grand Illusion Cinema (p138) Tiny U District nook run by passionate film buffs.

Cinerama (p96) This unique curved screen is the best place to see the latest blockbuster.

Northwest Film Forum (p120) Arts-club feel lends expertise to this film geek's heaven.

Central Cinema (p130) Best cinema in Seattle to bring in food and drink as you watch the movie.

Kayaking on Lake Union (p103)

Sports & Activities

Never mind the rain – that's why Gore-Tex was invented. When you live this close to the mountains, not to mention all that water and impressive parks, it's just criminal not to get outdoors. One of Seattle's greatest assets is that it's a large city that doesn't require you to leave to find outdoor recreation.

Spectator Sports

With state-of-the-art stadiums and teams that have recently won with a lot of glory, Seattle is a great town in which to watch the pros play. College games too, are hugely popular with locals and a fun way to spend an afternoon.

Formed in 1977 and former tenants of the erstwhile Kingdome, the beloved Seattle Mariners (p75) **baseball** team play at T-Mobile Park. They are yet to win a World Series title.

The Northwest's only **National Football League** (NFL) franchise, the Seattle Seahawks (p75) play in 72,000-seat CenturyLink Field. The team won Super Bowl XLVIII in February 2014.

Women's basketball team the Seattle Storm (p140) is the city's most successful franchise, winning the **Women's National Basketball Association** (WNBA) title three times, most recently in 2018. They are playing mostly at the Hec Edmundson Pavilion at the University of Washington until 2021, while the Seattle Center Arena is renovated to accommodate a new **National Hockey League** (NHL) franchise.

The University of Washington Huskies (p138) **football and basketball** teams are another Seattle obsession. The Huskies football team plays at 70,000-capacity Husky Stadium and you'll find the men's and women's basketball teams at the 'Hec Ed'.

Reincarnated in 2008, **soccer** team the Seattle Sounders (p75) has fanatical supporters and lots of 'em: 67,000 once attended a

NEED TO KNOW

Costs

The following is a price guide for tickets to see Seattle's main pro sports teams: the Mariners (baseball), the Sounders (soccer), the Seahawks (American football) and the Storm (basketball).

➡ Mariners $15–150

➡ Sounders $30–100

➡ Seahawks $110–550

➡ Storm $15–80

Buying Tickets

You can buy tickets either in person at the box offices (at CenturyLink Field for soccer and football, at T-Mobile Park for baseball), or online through TicketMaster (www.ticketmaster.com).

Planning Ahead

Seattle's pro sports teams enjoy fanatical support and games regularly sell out. It is wise to book weeks, if not months, ahead. For match schedules, check the club websites.

➡ Seattle Mariners (p75)

➡ Seattle Sounders (p75)

➡ Seattle Seahawks (p75)

➡ Seattle Storm (p140)

friendly against Manchester United. Highly successful, they share digs at CenturyLink Field with the Seahawks.

Hiking

In Seattle, it's possible to hike (or run) wilderness trails without ever leaving the city. **Seward Park**, east of Georgetown, offers several miles of trails in a remnant of the area's old-growth forest, and an even more extensive network of trails is available in 534-acre Discovery Park (p155), northwest of downtown. At the northern edge of Washington Park Arboretum (p126), Foster Island has a 20-minute wetlands trail winding through marshlands created upon the opening of the Lake Washington Ship Canal. This is also a great place for bird-watching, fishing and swimming.

Running

With its many parks, Seattle provides a number of good trails for runners. If you're in the downtown area, the trails along Myrtle Edwards Park (p87) – just north of the waterfront along Elliott Bay – make for a nice run, affording views over the Sound and of the downtown skyline. Green Lake (p145) includes two paths: the 2.75-mile paved path immediately surrounding the lake and a less-crowded, unpaved path going around the perimeter of the park. The Washington Park Arboretum (p126) is another good choice for running, as the trails lead through some beautiful trees and flower gardens. The trails in the arboretum connect to the Lake Washington Blvd trail system, which extends all the way south to Seward Park, just in case you happen to be training for a marathon.

Cycling

Despite frequent rain and hilly terrain, cycling is still a major form of both transportation and recreation in the Seattle area. In 2014 the city finally inaugurated a public bike-sharing scheme, which closed in March 2017 due to lack of ridership. In 2018 several private companies, including Lyft and Lime, began the practice again.

In the city, commuter bike lanes are painted green on many streets, city trails are well maintained, and the friendly and enthusiastic cycling community is happy to share the road. The wildly popular 20-mile Burke-Gilman Trail (p139) winds from Ballard to Log Boom Park in Kenmore on Seattle's Eastside. There, it connects with the 11-mile long **Sammamish River Trail**, which winds past the Chateau Ste Michelle winery in Woodinville before terminating at Redmond's Marymoor Park.

Other good places to cycle are around Green Lake (p145) (congested but pretty), at Alki Beach (p168)(sublime) or, closer to downtown, through scenic Myrtle Edwards Park (p87). The latter trail continues through Interbay to Ballard, where it links with the Burke-Gilman.

Anyone planning on cycling in Seattle should pick up a copy of the *Seattle Bicycling Guide Map,* published by the City of Seattle's Transportation Bicycle & Pedestrian Program and available online (www.cityofseattle.net/transportation/bikemaps.htm) and at bike shops.

On the Water

Seeing Seattle from the water is a surefire way to fall in love with the city. A number of places rent **kayaks and canoes**, or you can arrange a guided tour through the Northwest Outdoor Center (p109), the Agua Verde Paddle Club (p140) or the Moss Bay Rowing & Kayak Center (p109). The Center for Wooden Boats (p104) on Lake Union offers **sailing** lessons, sailboat rentals and free 45-minute sailboat rides every Sunday morning (first come, first served).

The calmest, safest places to launch are Green Lake (p145), Lake Union (p103) or near the water-taxi dock in Seacrest Park in West Seattle. If you're not confident, take a lesson. Several of the rental companies in Green Lake, Westlake (Lake Union) and the U District offer instruction from around $70 per hour.

Seattle's chilly waters are good for **diving**, with regular sightings of octopus, huge ling cod, cabezon, cathedral-like white anemones and giant sea stars. Most of the area's best dive sites are outside of Seattle, in sheltered coves and bays up and down the coast. Popular spots include Alki Cove, on the eastern side of Alki Point; Saltwater State Park, south of Seattle in Des Moines; and Edmonds Underwater Park near the Edmonds Ferry Dock, north of Seattle.

Activities by Neighborhood

Downtown, Pike Place & Waterfront (p62) Bike-tour companies and hotel gyms.

Pioneer Square, International District & SoDo (p77) Home of Seattle's two pro sports stadiums.

Belltown & Seattle Center (p97) Free yoga classes in the Olympic Sculpture Park during summer months.

Queen Anne & Lake Union (p109) Multiple water activities available on Lake Union and a multipurpose path that circumnavigates the lake.

Capitol Hill & First Hill (p121) Tennis courts and baseball diamonds in Cal Anderson Park; paths for jogging in Volunteer Park.

The CD, Madrona & Madison Park (p130) Parks, beaches and waterside attractions on Lake Washington.

U District (p140) Cycling on the Burke-Gilman Trail; boating access on Lake Union; Husky Stadium for college football.

Green Lake & Fremont (p152) Running, cycling and boating bonanza around Green Lake.

Ballard & Discovery Park (p164) Two wild waterside parks and a climbing center.

Georgetown & West Seattle (p173) Cycling, kayaking, swimming and skating along Alki Beach.

Lonely Planet's Top Choices

Discovery Park (p155) Get a taste of the Pacific Northwest's great outdoors in the city.

Burke-Gilman Trail (p139) Much-loved non-motor-traffic trail through some of Seattle's best neighborhoods.

Green Lake Park (p145) Where to watch other people puff, pant and pose in their REI gear.

REI (p108) Tackle the climbing wall in the Northwest's outdoor megastore.

Seattle Sounders (p76) Think soccer's not big in the US? Go and hear Sounders' fans sing at CenturyLink Field.

Best Places to Go Running

Myrtle Edwards Park (p87) A quick exit out of downtown for gulps of sea air on traffic-free paths.

Green Lake Park (p145) See how many people you can overtake – or get overtaken by – on the 2.5-mile loop.

Burke-Gilman Trail (p139) The most pleasurable way to get from A to B in Seattle's northern neighborhoods.

Washington Park Arboretum (p126) Lose yourself in a veritable tree museum.

Best Bike Trails

Burke-Gilman Trail (p139) Join the masses – commuting, flirting, having on-the-go business meetings, or just having fun.

Alki Beach Park (p168) Hire a bike to breeze you along this seaside promenade.

Green Lake Park (p145) Play 'dodge the jogging lovers' on a bike in this always-busy park.

Best Water Activities

Center for Wooden Boats (p104) Go sailing on Lake Union – it's free on Sundays!

Agua Verde Paddle Club (p140) Head out solo, take a lesson or sign up for a moonlit kayak tour.

Green Lake Boat Rental (p152) Take it easy and have fun in a paddleboat on the waters of this calm sheltered lake.

Alki Beach Park (p168) Swim, splash, windsurf, kayak, paddleboard and generally get wet.

Shopping

Seattle, like any big US city, has a whole range of big-name stores. You won't have to look hard – they'll find you. More precious and of more interest are the one-of-a-kind shops you'll find hidden down alleys and crammed between coffee shops. The city's tour de force is its bookstores and record stores, surely some of the best in the nation.

Independent Bookstores

Ironically, the city that spawned Amazon guards one of the best collections of indie bookstores in the US. Established local operators include University Book Store (p139), a veritable book emporium founded in 1900 that offers the kind of well-informed personal touches that online shopping can never replicate. Equally revered is Elliott Bay Book Company (p120), where a tranquil cafe, a team of well-read staff and regular author signings provide multiple excuses to linger. Ada's Technical Books & Cafe (p120) is a new-ish book specialist in Capitol Hill with beautiful decor and fine cafe. There are also more specialist booksellers such as Metsker Maps (p59), for travel-related books; Left Bank Books (p59), just in case you lost your copy of *Das Kapital*; and Fantagraphics (p173), for graphic novels and comic strips. In 2015, Seattle prepared itself for the ultimate oxymoron when Amazon opened its first bricks-and-mortar bookstore in the U District (you can give it a miss). With print book sales on the rise for the first time in over a decade, it's proof that bookstores can and will survive.

Marijuana

Adults aged 21 and over may buy up to 1oz of pure weed (or 16oz of solid edibles, or 72oz of liquid product) for private consumption in Seattle from a licensed seller. There are now weed dispensaries in just about every neighborhood in the city and inside them you'll find a truly jaw-dropping amount of product including flower (think what you'd load a bong or bowl with), pre-rolls (joints), edibles, vape cartridges and a plethora of more advanced options. Also inside? Some of the friendliest customer service you're likely to experience anywhere in the city. The 'bud tenders' who work behind the counter are knowledgeable, chatty and always ready with recommendations and advice. You do not need to know anything about weed before you go in and you shouldn't feel intimidated to do so. If you're a total novice just let the staff know. Dispensaries tend to be total judgment-free zones and you're just as likely to be in line behind someone's sweet old grandma as you are a tattooed college senior.

Shopping by Neighborhood

Downtown, Pike Place & Waterfront (p59) Big-name brands in downtown; small-time no-brands in Pike Place; tourist kitsch on the waterfront.

Pioneer Square, International District & SoDo (p76) Expensive antiques and carpets in Pioneer Square; cheap Asian supermarkets in the ID.

Capitol Hill & First Hill (p120) Huge selection of indie boutiques, esoterica, sex toys, and one of the nation's best bookstores.

U District (p139) Cheap vintage clothing for tight student budgets and abundant bookstores for fact-hungry undergraduates.

Green Lake & Fremont (p151) Junk stores and vintage-clothing shops being gradually pushed out by fancier boutiques.

Ballard & Discovery Park (p163) Card-game emporium, weird T-shirt prints, rare vinyl and artsy Sunday market stalls.

Georgetown & West Seattle (p172) Upscale vintage, low-end vintage and plenty of one-off boutiques.

Lonely Planet's Top Choices

Elliott Bay Book Company (p120) Great books, top readings and snug on-site cafe.

Ballyhoo (p163) Weird and wonderful oddities store with tons of affordable esoterica.

Bop Street Records (p164) Every musical genre, overseen by passionate staff.

Lucca Great Finds (p164) A bounty of effortlessly tasteful gifts, homewares and all manner of stationery.

Susan Wheeler Home (p172) Thoughtfully selected antique homewares, art and furniture.

Market Magic (p59) Classic Pike Place Market throwback.

Best Record Stores

Bop Street Records (p164) Astounding array of every musical genre known to Homo sapiens.

Easy Street Records & Café (p172) Drink coffee, imbibe beer, eat snacks and...oh...browse excellent records.

Georgetown Records (p173) Rare picture-cover 45s and vintage LPs next door to Fantagraphics comic shop.

Singles Going Steady (p97) If this name means anything to you, this punkish record shop is your nirvana.

Best Vintage Clothes

Fremont Vintage Mall (p151) There's a bit of vintage everything here, including clothes.

Revival (p121) Vintage jewels hand-picked by the owner.

Throwbacks NW (p121) Novel vintage-sportswear shop.

Crossroads Trading Co (p121) Used-clothing store with lower hipster quotient.

Best Shopping Strips

Ballard (p163) In terms of overall variety, quantity and quality of stores nowhere in the city bests it.

Pike Place Market (p42) Support your local farmer/craftsperson/third-generation store owner in Seattle's bustling heart.

Downtown (p59) Big-name stores deliver the goods in the city's retail core.

Broadway (p120) Check your hipster rating by going shopping on Capitol Hill's main strip.

'The Ave' (p137) A dearth of designer labels but an abundance of welcome bargains beckon in the U District.

Dispensaries

Herban Legends (p97) Professional, but, as the name suggests, doesn't take itself too seriously.

Hashtag Cannabis (p152) Huge variety of products, especially for those looking for specialty goods.

Origins Cannabis (p173) Things are a little bit friendlier in West Seattle, including their dispensaries.

Ganja Goddess (p77) At the time of writing one of the few dispensaries accepting payment by card.

Have a Heart (p97) Popular, high-tech and right near downtown.

Markets

Pike Place Market (p42) No intro required – lose yourself for a day, at least!

U District Farmers Market (p136) Produce-only market that's been running since 1993.

Ballard Farmers Market (p164) With food and some crafts, this is *the* place to go on a Sunday.

Melrose Market (p116) Attractive sustainable market plying high-end food products in the Pike–Pine corridor.

Uwajimaya (p76) Get lost in this mall of Japanese goods.

Best Esoterica

Ballyhoo (p163) Sells everything from antique nudie postcards to a taxidermied two-headed calf.

Market Magic (p59) All the tricks a young aspiring magician could dream of.

Tenzing Momo (p60) Atmospheric apothecary where you might expect to see a wizard.

Card Kingdom (p164) Interactive games emporium in Ballard that could delay you for...oh... hours.

Pink Gorilla Games (p77) Small retailer of nostalgia trip–inducing, vintage video games.

PLAN YOUR TRIP SHOPPING

NEED TO KNOW

Opening Hours

Shops are usually open from 9am or 10am to 5pm or 6pm (9pm in shopping malls) Monday to Friday, as well as noon to 5pm or so (later in malls) on weekends. Some places, like record stores and bookstores, may keep later hours, such as from noon to 8pm or 9pm.

Taxes & Refunds

A 10.1% sales tax is added to all purchases except food to be prepared for consumption (ie groceries). Unlike the European VAT or Canadian GST, the sales tax is not refundable to tourists.

Explore Seattle

◉ SEATTLE'S
TOP SIGHTS

Neighborhoods at a Glance

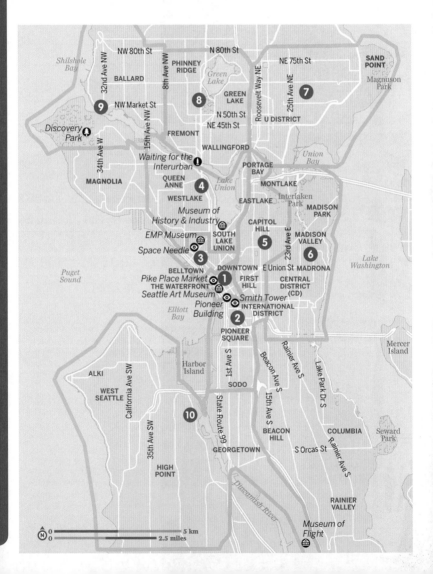

❶ Downtown, Pike Place & Waterfront p40

Downtown Seattle is a standard (though hilly) American amalgam of boxy skyscrapers and brand-name shopping opportunities that's given welcome oomph by Pike Place Market, the city's number-one must-see sight. The waterfront is home to kitschy tourist attractions and Puget Sound views.

❷ Pioneer Square, International District & SoDo p63

Seattle's birthplace retains the grit of its 'Skid Row' roots with red-brick architecture and a rambunctious street life tempered by art galleries and locavore restaurants. The International District's legacy as home to many of the city's southeast Asian immigrant communities makes for exquisite dining, while SoDo (south of downtown) is an austere warehouse district that's attracting new distilleries and dispensaries.

❸ Belltown & Seattle Center p80

Where industry once roared, condos now rise in Belltown. The neighborhood gained a reputation for its grungy nightlife in the 1990s, but these days it's more renowned for its 100-plus restaurants. It's also near the Seattle Center, where the green lawns and fountains attract, in equal measure, gawking tourists and families looking for a retreat from the bustle of downtown.

❹ Queen Anne & Lake Union p100

Queen Anne is a neighborhood double bill: the top of the hill hoards old money in beautiful early-20th-century mansions, while the bottom is more egalitarian and features a bevy of solid restaurants and cafes. Nearby Lake Union's southern shores are changing more quickly than the fresh-faced influx of techies can tweet about them.

❺ Capitol Hill & First Hill p110

Capitol Hill is Seattle's most unashamedly hip neighborhood, where the rich mix with the eccentric. While gentrification has let some of the air out of its tires, this is still Seattle's best crash pad for dive-bar rock and roll, LGBTIQ+ mirth and on-trend dining. More straitlaced First Hill is home to an art museum and multiple hospitals.

❻ The CD, Madrona & Madison Park p124

The Central District (CD) has long been the center of Seattle's African American community, an oasis of incredible Ethopian food, birthplace of the city's rap/hip-hop movement and, more recently, a gentrification battleground. Madison Park and Madrona have popular beaches and attractive parks, while Madison Valley features a cluster of eclectic restaurants.

❼ U District p131

This neighborhood of young, studious out-of-towners places the beautiful, leafy University of Washington campus next to the shabbier 'Ave,' an eclectic strip of cheap boutiques, dive bars and take-out spots.

❽ Green Lake & Fremont p141

Fremont pitches young hipsters among old hippies in an unlikely urban alliance, with junk shops, urban sculpture and a healthy sense of its own ludicrousness. To the north, family-friendly Green Lake is a more affluent suburb centered on a park favored by fitness devotees.

❾ Ballard & Discovery Park p153

A former seafaring community with Nordic heritage, Ballard still feels like a small town engulfed by a bigger city. The neighborhood has come into its own as one of the city's best locals for exciting restaurants, lively bars and killer shopping. Just across Salmon Bay is Discovery Park, one of the largest in the city and a must for those who love easy-to-tackle hikes ending in stunning views.

❿ Georgetown & West Seattle p165

South of Seattle's city center things are decidedly more mellow, but the neighborhoods are full of unique attractions for curious visitors. West Seattle is teeming with cute commercial strips and some of the best parks and beaches in the city. To the east is Georgetown, an arty enclave hammered out of a former industrial district.

Downtown, Pike Place & Waterfront

Neighborhood Top Five

❶ Pike Place Market (p42) Seeing, smelling and tasting the unique energy of this Seattle icon, from the charismatic fish throwers to the creative – but disgusting – gum wall.

❷ Seattle Art Museum (p46) Experiencing the latest surprise lighting up

this constantly evolving museum.

❸ Bainbridge Island ferry (p214) Riding on the Bainbridge Island ferry just for the hell of it and watching Seattle's famous skyline disappear in its foamy wake.

❹ Seattle Great Wheel (p50) Viewing Seattle's on-

going waterfront regeneration from inside an enclosed pod on this giant wheel.

❺ Beecher's Handmade Cheese (p51) Joining the line for take-out tubs of gooey and hot mac 'n' cheese at Pike Place Market's artisanal cheese phenomenon.

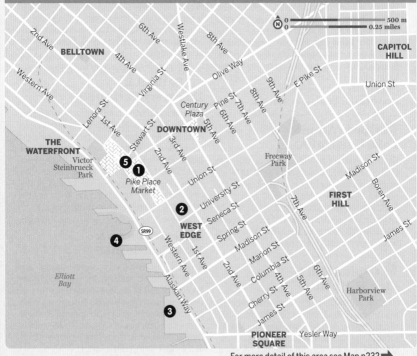

For more detail of this area see Map p232 ➡

Explore Downtown, Pike Place & Waterfront

You don't have to search long to find Seattle's soul: head directly to Pike Place Market (p42) and throw away any map you might have acquired – your nose, eyes and ears are the only compasses you'll need here.

It's particularly important to get to the market early if you want to avoid that cattle-truck feeling (40,000 visitors per day!). Weekdays and before 10am on weekends are best. That said, many enjoy the organized chaos of the arcades at Saturday lunchtime. The waterfront is more weather dependent; a sunny weekend afternoon finds it swarming, while on a misty weekday morning you'll have the place pretty much to yourself.

Downtown Seattle, though impressive from a distance, is a bit of an anomaly. Instead of being the beating heart of the city, it's a fairly quiet, functional business district adjacent to Seattle's twin lures: Pike Place Market and Pioneer Sq (p65). It's best to visit on a weekday, when throngs of people are working and shopping in the area. At night and on weekends it can feel rather desolate.

Seattle's retail heaven extends from the corner of 5th Ave and Pike St for a few blocks in all directions. A block north, on 5th Ave at Pine St, is the flagship store of Nordstrom (p60), the national clothing retailer that got its start in Seattle. Just to the west is Westlake Center.

Local Life

Early-morning market Get to Pike Place (p42) early and listen to the vendors chitchat as they set up their stalls. Be sure to witness the 'market roll call' in the North Arcade, when day-stall vendors are allocated spaces.

Ferry across the Sound Pretend you're a Puget Sound commuter and stow away on a Bainbridge Island ferry just for the scenic ride.

Getting There & Away

Light rail Sound Transit's Central Link light rail from Sea-Tac Airport has two downtown stations: Westlake, and University St and 3rd Ave.

Streetcar Services run to South Lake Union from Westlake.

Bus You can get downtown easily from any part of Seattle by bus.

Lonely Planet's Top Tip

Look down! Seattle's public art extends to its hatch covers (manholes). Nineteen of them have been emblazoned with an imprint of a downtown map with your location marked. It's impossible to get lost.

✖ Best Places to Eat

➡ Heartwood Provisions (p51)

➡ Café Campagne (p53)

➡ Wild Ginger (p51)

➡ Beecher's Handmade Cheese (p51)

➡ Piroshky Piroshky (p51)

For reviews, see p50.➡

☕ Best Places to Drink

➡ Bookstore Bar (p54)

➡ Storyville Coffee (p56)

➡ Radiator Whiskey (p56)

➡ Ancient Grounds (p54)

➡ Owl & Thistle (p56)

For reviews, see p54.➡

🔒 Best Places to Shop

➡ Old Seattle Paperworks (p59)

➡ Pure Food Fish (p59)

➡ Metsker Maps (p59)

➡ Market Magic (p59)

For reviews, see p59.➡

DOWNTOWN, PIKE PLACE & WATERFRONT

TOP SIGHT
PIKE PLACE MARKET

A cavalcade of noise, smells, personalities, banter and urban theater sprinkled liberally around a spatially challenged waterside strip, Pike Place Market is Seattle in a bottle. In operation since 1907 and still as soulful today as it was on day one, this wonderfully local experience highlights the city for what it really is: all-embracing, eclectic and proudly unique.

Some History

Pike Place Market is the oldest continuously operating market in the nation. It was established in 1907 to give local farmers a place to sell their fruit and vegetables and bypass the middleman. Soon, the greengrocers made room for fishmongers, bakers, butchers, cheese sellers, grocers selling imported wares, and purveyors of the rest of the Northwest's agricultural bounty. The market wasn't exactly architecturally robust – it's always been a thrown-together warren of sheds and stalls, haphazardly designed for utility – and was by no means an intentional tourist attraction. That came later.

An enthusiastic agricultural community spawned the market's heyday in the 1930s. Many of the first farmers were immigrants, a fact the market celebrates with annual themes acknowledging the contributions of various ethnic groups; past years have featured Japanese Americans, Italian Americans and Sephardic Jewish Americans.

By the 1960s, sales at the market were suffering from suburbanization, the growth of supermarkets and the move away from local, small-scale market gardening. Vast tracts of agricultural land were disappearing, replaced by such ventures as the Northgate Mall and Sea-Tac airport. The internment of Japanese American farmers during WWII had also

DON'T MISS
➡ Fish throwers
➡ Gum wall
➡ Market roll call
➡ World's oldest Starbucks

PRACTICALITIES
➡ Map p232, C4
➡ 206-682-7453
➡ www.pikeplacemarket.org
➡ 85 Pike St, Pike Place
➡ 9am-6pm Mon-Sat, to 5pm Sun
➡ Westlake

taken its toll. The entire area became a bowery for the destitute and was known as a center of ill repute.

In the wake of the 1962 World's Fair, plans were drawn up to bulldoze the market and build high-rise office and apartment buildings on this piece of prime downtown real estate. Fortunately, public outcry prompted a voter's initiative to save the market. Subsequently, the space was cleaned up and restructured, and it has become once again the undeniable pulse of downtown; some 10 million people mill through the market each year. Thanks to the unique management of the market, social-services programs and low-income housing mix with commerce, and the market has maintained its gritty edge. These initiatives have prevented the area from ever sliding too far upscale. A market law prohibits chain stores or franchises from setting up shop and ensures all businesses are locally owned. The one exception is, of course, Starbucks, which gets away with its market location because it is the coffee giant's oldest outlet, moving here from its original location in 1976.

Orientation

If you're coming from downtown, simply walk down Pike St toward the waterfront; you can't miss the huge **Public Market sign** etched against the horizon. Incidentally, the sign and clock, installed in 1927, constituted one of the first pieces of outdoor neon on the West Coast. From the top of Pike St and 1st Ave, stop and survey the bustle and vitality. Walk down the cobblestone street, past perpetually gridlocked cars (don't even think of driving down to Pike Pl) and, before walking into the market, stop and shake the bronze snout of **Rachel the Market Pig**, the de-facto mascot and presiding spirit of the market. This life-size piggy bank, carved by Whidbey Island artist Georgia Gerber and named after a real pig, collects about $10,000 each year. The funds are pumped back into market social services. Nearby is the **information booth** (Map p232; ☑206-682-7453; cnr Pike St & 1st Ave; ☺9am-6pm Mon-Sat, 9am-5pm Sun), which has maps of the market and information about Seattle in general. It also serves as a ticket booth, selling discounted tickets to various shows throughout the city.

Main & North Arcades

Rachel the Market Pig marks the main entrance to the **Main & North Arcades** (Map p232; Western Ave), thin shed-like structures that run along the edge of the hill; these are the busiest of the market buildings. With banks of fresh produce carefully arranged in artful displays, and fresh fish, crab and

BUSKERS

Anyone can busk in the market as long as they register with the market office, pay a $30 annual fee and perform in one of 13 designated spots. With a guaranteed annual audience of 10 million people passing through, pitches are understandably popular. Well-known market performers include Johnny Hahn, who has been tickling the keys of an upright piano for nearly 30 years, and Emery Carl, who plays guitar while spinning a Hula-Hoop.

In a city as fast-moving as Seattle, not even a historical heirloom like Pike Place Market escapes a makeover. In 2015 ground was broken on the 'Pike Up' project, a 30,000-sq-ft extension of Pike Place. Made possible by the demolition of the Alaskan Way Viaduct, the MarketFront complex opened in 2017 with new shops, restaurants and stalls, and links the market to the waterfront via terraces, staircases and green space.

other shellfish piled high on ice, this is the real heart of the market. Here you'll see fishmongers tossing salmon back and forth like basketballs (many of these vendors will pack fish for overnight delivery). You'll also find cheese shops, butchers, stands selling magazines and candy from around the world, tiny grocery stalls and almost everything else you need to put together a meal. The end of the North Arcade is dedicated to local artisans and craftspeople – products must be handmade to be sold here. It's also abloom with flower sellers, most of them of Vietnamese Hmong origin. The Main Arcade was built in 1907, the first of Frank Goodwin's market buildings.

Down Under

As if the levels of the market that are above ground aren't labyrinthine enough, below the Main Arcade are three lower levels called the Down Under. Here you'll find a fabulously eclectic mix of pocket-size shops, from Indian spice stalls to magician supply shops and vintage magazine and map purveyors.

Economy Market Building

Once a stable for merchants' horses, the Economy Market Building on the south side of the market entrance has a wonderful Italian grocery store, DeLaurenti's (p60) – a great place for any aficionado of Italian foods to browse and sample. There's also Tenzing Momo (p60), one of the oldest apothecaries on the West Coast, where you can pick up herbal remedies, incense, oils and books. Tarot readings are available here on occasion. Look down at the Economy Market floor and you'll see some of its 46,000 tiles, sold to the public in the 1980s for $35 apiece. If you bought a tile, you'd get your name on it and be proud that you helped save the market floor. Famous tile owners include *Cat in the Hat* creator Dr Seuss and former US president Ronald Reagan.

South Arcade

If you continue past DeLaurenti's, you'll come into the South Arcade, the market's newest wing, home to upscale shops and the lively Pike Pub & Brewery (p57). It's not technically part of the historic market, but is with it in spirit and rambunctious energy.

Corner & Sanitary Market Buildings

Across Pike Pl from the Main Arcade are the 1912 **Corner & Sanitary Market Buildings** (Map p232; 1st Ave, btwn Pike & Pike Sts), so named because they were the first of the market buildings in which live animals were prohibited. It's now a maze of ethnic groceries and great little eateries, including Three Girls Bakery (p52), which is as old as the building itself; Storyville Coffee (p56), one of the market's newest businesses; and the insanely popular Crumpet Shop (p52). When you've finished digesting your baked goods, you can digest a bit of radical literature in bolshie bookstore, Left Bank Books (p59).

Post Alley

Between the Corner Market and the Triangle Building, narrow Post Alley (named for its hitching posts) is lined with shops and restaurants. Extending north across Stewart St, it offers two of the area's best places for a drink: the Pink Door Ristorante (p53), an Italian hideaway with a cool patio, and Kells (p57), an Irish pub. In Lower Post Alley, beside the market sign, is the **LaSalle Hotel**, which was the first bordello north of Yesler Way. Originally the Outlook Hotel, it was taken over in 1942 by the notorious Nellie Curtis, a woman with 13 aliases and a knack for running suspiciously profitable hotels with thousands of

Part of the gum wall (p49)

➡ If you dislike crowds, visit the market early (before 10am).

➡ Wander over to adjacent Victor Steinbrueck Park for beautiful clear-weather views of Mt Rainier.

➡ Join a Seattle walking tour; plenty of them start in or around the market and all skillfully explain its history.

Watching Pike Place's daily market roll call, rung in by an old-fashioned hand bell promptly at 9am (9:30am on Sunday from January to April), is like watching a boisterous cattle auction. The purpose of roll call is allocating space to the market's temporary craft-sellers. As Pike Place has over 200 registered vendors but only 130 available trading spots, each day is nail-biting. Roll call is held at the north end of the North Arcade.

lonely sailors lined up nightly outside the door. The building, rehabbed in 1977, now houses commercial and residential space.

Post Alley continues on the southern side of Pike St where you'll find the beautifully disgusting gum wall (p49) and one of the market's best hideaway spots, the bar and pizza restaurant Alibi Room (p56).

Triangle Building

All in a row in the diminutive Triangle Building, sandwiched between Pike Pl, Pine St and Post Alley, is a huddle of cheap food take-outs including Mee Sum Pastry (p52; try the steamed pork bun), a juice bar and Cinnamon Works (p52) – all great choices for a stand-up snack.

First Avenue Buildings

These downtown-facing buildings, added mainly in the 1980s, blend seamlessly into the older hive. Here you'll find Pike Place's only two accommodations – Pensione Nichols (p189) and Inn at the Market (p190).

North End

The market's North End stretches along Pike Pl from Pine St to Victor Steinbruck Park (p49). The 1918 **Soames-Dunn building**, once occupied by a seed company and a paper company, is now home to the world's oldest Starbucks.

 TOP SIGHT
SEATTLE ART MUSEUM

While it doesn't have the size or star power of its contemporaries in New York and Chicago, the Seattle Art Museum (SAM) has a collection that feels uncommon, intimate and extraordinary. Its sterling selection of contemporary and antique art of the indigenous peoples of the Pacific Northwest alone makes this a required stop on any visit to the Emerald City.

Entrance Lobby

SAM is a three-site museum incorporating the Olympic Sculpture Park (p87), the Seattle Asian Art Museum (p112) and this splendid 150,000-sq-ft downtown facility. The main building is guarded by a 48ft-high sculpture known as Hammering Man (p48) and contains a cascading stairway inside guarded by Chinese statues called the 'Art Ladder.' Look up to take in 'Middle Fork' by John Grade, a giant plaster cast of an actual tree that hangs over the ticket desk. You'll get a good view of it from above as you take the escalator.

Modern & Contemporary Art

SAM has an enviable collection of modern art. Level 3 is home to Andy Warhol's *Double Elvis*, a silk-screen image of a young Presley firing a pistol right at the viewer, and Jackson Pollock's drippy (and trippy) *Sea Change*. The broad hallway at the top of the escalators has a small collection of exhibits from the Pilchuck Glass School (p85), an excellent appetite whetter if you're heading over to Chihuly Garden & Glass (p84) later.

DON'T MISS

→ Native American art
→ *Walkabout: the Art of Dorothy Napangardi*
→ *Double Elvis* by Andy Warhol
→ Van Dyck's *Pomponne II de Bellièvre*
→ Art ladder

PRACTICALITIES

→ Map p232, D5
→ ☎206-654-3210
→ www.seattleart museum.org
→ 1300 1st Ave, Downtown
→ adult/student $24.95/14.95
→ ☉10am-5pm Wed & Fri-Mon, to 9pm Thu
→ ☒University St

Native American Art

The Hauberg Gallery on level 3 is dedicated to the museum's impressive collections of art from the indigenous peoples of the Pacific Northwest coastal regions, including the Tlingit, Haida and Kwakwaka'wakw. Large wooden masks and colorful textiles are displayed thoughtfully here and the exhibits are accompanied by a video installation on contemporary Native American culture. There are also pieces from elsewhere in the Americas before European colonization, including a small room of artifacts from pre-Columbian Mesoamerica.

Top Floor

Level 4 has a rather scattered collection of world art from Greek pottery and ancient Egyptian statues to pieces from the Italian renaissance. Standout works include *Pomponne II de Bellièvre* by Van Dyck and *Saint Augustine in Ecstasy* by the Spanish baroque painter Esteban Murillo. The 19th century is represented with works by Monet, Matisse and Vuillard.

The adjacent Simonyi Galleries are generally reserved for temporary exhibitions. Recent shows have included contemporary Native American art and a large psychedelic mixed-media installation depicting spiritual energy (in the form of a prismatic rainbow of colors) flowing between three seated figures.

Walkabout: the Art of Dorothy Napangardi

If you visit the museum before March 7, 2021 do not miss this exhibit of art by the late Australian Aboriginal painter Dorothy Napangardi (1956–2013) on display in the museum's dedicated Australian Art gallery. The paintings here are arresting: huge canvases filled with dots, some in lines quite straight and linear, others flowing and whirling like dry riverbeds or starry skies. At first glance they may appear as abstract to those of us uninformed about Aboriginal culture, but each work represents very literal landscapes and the journeys that Napangardi and her ancestors undertook on foot across their homeland, the Tanami Desert in Central Australia. Although Napangardi herself rarely extrapolated on her paintings, each is accompanied by words from her friends and admirers which illuminate the intimate stories of her work.

FROM ONE TO THREE

From its inception in 1933 until the early 1990s, the Seattle Art Museum was a single-site museum tucked away in Volunteer Park, in the building now occupied by the Seattle Asian Art Museum. The main collection shifted to its present downtown location in 1991, the Volunteer Park facility re-opened with an Asian-themed moniker in 1994, and the Olympic Sculpture Park was added in 2007.

One notable artist with multiple works on display in the Seattle Art Museum is Mark Tobey (1890–1976), an abstract impressionist with a penchant for Asian calligraphy who some view as an avant-garde precursor to Jackson Pollock. Works of Tobey to look out for include the dense, colorful *Festival* and the mask-etched *Esquimaux Idiom*, with its strong Native American undertones.

◉ SIGHTS

Many of the city's most iconic buildings, areas, landmarks and businesses are found in these neighborhoods. Every time you turn a corner it'll feel like you're bumping into one, such as the Pike Place Market's neon sign and the Seattle Art Museum's Hammering Man sculpture. The structures on the waterfront are perhaps less iconic, but the views of the Puget Sound and surrounding mountains from the piers more than make up for it.

◉ Downtown

SEATTLE ART MUSEUM   MUSEUM
See p46.

HAMMERING MAN   MONUMENT
Map p232 (1300 1st Ave; ꔹUniversity St) Although not unique to Seattle, *Hammering Man,* the 48ft-high metal sculpture that guards the entrance to the Seattle Art Museum (p46) on the corner of 1st Ave and University St, has become something of a city icon since it was raised in 1992.

The sculpture, whose moving motor-powered arm silently hammers four times per minute, 364 days a year (he has Labor Day in September off), is supposed to represent the worker in all of us. It was conceived by Jonathan Borofsky, an American artist from Boston, who has designed similar hammering men for various other cities. There are taller and heavier models in Frankfurt, Germany, and Seoul, South Korea.

SEATTLE CENTRAL LIBRARY   LIBRARY
Map p232 (🖉206-386-4636; www.spl.org; 1000 4th Ave; ⊙10am-8pm Mon-Thu, to 6pm Fri & Sat, noon-6pm Sun; 🅿; ꔹPioneer Sq) Rivaling the Space Needle and the Museum of Pop Culture for architectural ingenuity, Seattle Central Library looks like a giant diamond that's dropped in from outer space. Conceived by Rem Koolhaas and LMN Architects in 2004, the $165.5 million sculpture of glass and steel was designed to serve as a community gathering space, a tech center, a reading room and, of course, a massive storage facility for its one-million-plus books. Come here to enjoy art, architecture, coffee and literary comfort.

The overall style of the library is phenomenal both outside and in. Lemon-yellow escalators, hot-pink chairs and zippy wi-fi connections make for a modern, tech-friendly experience. There are also 132 research computers available in the **Mixing Chamber**, where librarians in teams help with in-depth research. The **Book Spiral**, spanning several floors, holds most of the library's nonfiction books. Guests can take self-guided tours using their cell phones (signs display which stop number you need to enter).

The library is spread over 11 levels with parking provided underground. Public art is spread liberally around the facility, but the design pinnacle is undoubtedly the 12,000-sq-ft **reading room** on level 10 with 40ft glass ceilings. It has amazing light, great views of downtown and seating for up to 400 people.

COLUMBIA CENTER   VIEWPOINT
Map p232 (🖉206-386-5564; www.skyview observatory.com; 701 5th Ave; adult/child $20/14; ⊙10am-10pm late May-early Sep, to 8pm rest of year; ꔹPioneer Sq) Everyone rushes for the iconic Space Needle, but it's not the tallest Seattle viewpoint. That honor goes to the sleek, tinted-windowed Columbia Center at 932ft high with 76 floors. An elevator in the lobby takes you up to the free-access 40th floor, where there's a Starbucks. From here you must take another elevator to the plush Sky View Observatory on the 73rd floor, from where you can look down on ferries, cars, islands, roofs and – ha, ha – the Space Needle!

Built between 1982 and 1985, it's the loftiest building in the Pacific Northwest.

ARCTIC BUILDING   LANDMARK
Map p232 (700 3rd Ave; ꔹPioneer Sq) Like the psychedelic Beatles' song, the unique Arctic Building, completed in 1917, is celebrated for its walruses. Their heads (25 of them), surrounded by intricate terracotta ornamentation, peek out from the building's exterior.

Though the walruses' tusks were originally authentic ivory, an earthquake in the 1940s managed to shake a few of them loose to the ground. To protect passersby from the unusual urban hazard of being skewered by falling tusks, the ivory was replaced with epoxy.

COBB BUILDING   LANDMARK

Map p232 (1301 4th Ave; ⓡUniversity St) Look up at the beaux-arts style Cobb Building (1910) and see remnants of an older Seattle. Peering out from the 11-story edifice you'll see several stern-looking terracotta heads of the same Native American chief.

1201 THIRD AVENUE   LANDMARK

Map p232 (1201 3rd Ave; ⓡUniversity St) The beauty of the Seattle skyline is reflected in the 55-story 1201 Third Avenue building at 3rd and Seneca, which changes colors with the clouds and sunsets. This is the second-tallest building in Seattle and dates from 1988. Seattleites have nicknamed it 'the Spark Plug.' Enter off 3rd Ave to explore the building's interior, which got a makeover in 2016.

RAINIER TOWER   LANDMARK

Map p232 (1333 5th Ave; ⓡUniversity St) With its inverted base that looks like a tree that's been nibbled by a beaver, this urban behemoth was finished in 1977, after which it quickly acquired the nickname 'the Beaver Building.' Taking up an entire block between 4th and 5th Aves and University and Union Sts is Rainier Sq, a shopping center connected to the top-heavy tower.

SEATTLE TOWER   LANDMARK

Map p232 (1218 3rd Ave; ⓡUniversity St) Formerly the Northern Life Tower, this 26-story art deco skyscraper, built in 1928, was designed to reflect the mountains of the Pacific Northwest. The brickwork on the exterior blends from dark at the bottom to light on top, the same way mountains appear to do. Check out the 18-karat-gold relief map in the lobby.

WASHINGTON STATE
CONVENTION CENTER   NOTABLE BUILDING

Map p232 (☏206-447-5000; 705 Pike St; ⓡWestlake) It's hard to miss this gigantic complex decked out with ballrooms, meeting rooms, space for exhibitions and the Seattle Convention and Visitors Bureau (p220). An arched-glass bridge spans Pike St between 7th and 8th Aves, with what looks like a giant eye in the middle of it.

The main entrance is on the corner of 7th Ave and Pike St. **Freeway Park** nearby provides a leafy, fountain-laden downtown oasis.

SAFECO PLAZA   LANDMARK

Map p232 (1001 4th Ave; ⓡUniversity St) Built in 1969 and originally known as 1001 Fourth Avenue Plaza, this was one of the city's first real skyscrapers. At the time, it was a darling of the architectural world, though nowadays the 50-story bronze block looks dated. Locals nicknamed it 'the box that the Space Needle came in.'

In the plaza outside is the **Three Piece Sculpture: Vertebrae** by Henry Moore – a result of Seattle's '1% for art' clause, under which 1% of the construction cost of the building is invested in public art.

⊙ Pike Place

PIKE PLACE MARKET   MARKET
See p42.

GUM WALL   PUBLIC ART

Map p232 (Post Alley; ⓡUniversity St) Seattle's famous gum wall is one of those cultural monuments you can smell before you even see it. The sweet aroma of chewed gum wafts from this strip of Post Alley, which is completely covered in the stuff. It's a popular selfie spot, and is worth a peek for the sheer magnitude of it alone. It cannot be emphasized enough just how much gum there is!

VICTOR STEINBRUECK PARK   PARK

Map p232 (☏206-684-4075; 2001 Western Ave; ◷6am-10pm; ⓡWestlake) When you've had enough of Pike Place Market and its crowds, wander out the end of the North Arcade and cross Western Ave to Victor Steinbrueck Park, a small grassy area designed in 1982 by Steinbrueck and Richard Haag.

A historic armory building once stood on the site, but it was knocked down in 1968, much to the disgust of Steinbrueck, a major preservationist who worked hard to save both Pike Place and Pioneer Sq from the wrecking ball. As consolation, this small breathing space between the waterfront and downtown was created. Perched over Elliott Bay, it has benches, a couple of totem poles carved by Quinault tribe members James Bender and Marvin Oliver, and great views over the waterfront and bay. Rallies and political demonstrations are often held here.

STARBUCKS – IT STARTED HERE (ALMOST)

It's practically impossible to walk through the door of Starbucks (p57) in Pike Place Market without appearing in someone's Facebook photo, so dense is the tourist traffic. But, while this hallowed business might be the world's oldest surviving Starbucks store, it is not – as many assume – the world's first Starbucks location, nor is it Seattle's oldest espresso bar. The original Starbucks opened in 1971 at 2000 Western Ave (at Western Ave's north end). It moved to its current location, a block away, in 1976. The honor of Seattle's oldest continuously running coffee bar goes to Café Allegro in the U District, which opened in 1975. Until the early 1980s Starbucks operated purely as a retail store that sold coffee beans and equipment (plus the odd taster cup). The company didn't open up its first espresso bar until 1984, after CEO Howard Shultz returned from an epiphanic trip to Italy. The Pike Place cafe is unique in that, in keeping with the traditional unbranded ethos of the market, it doesn't sell food or baked goods – just coffee.

Other interesting Starbucks facilities in Seattle include the cafe on the 40th floor of the Columbia Center (p48), Seattle's tallest building; the company's first LEED-certified cafe that opened downtown on the corner of Pike St and 1st Ave in 2009 and sports the original brown logo; and the Starbucks Reserve Roastery (p118) in Capitol Hill. The latter is a veritable coffee emporium that opened in 2014 and, ostensibly at least, appears to be the antithesis of everything you normally find in a Starbucks cafe.

⊙ Waterfront

SEATTLE AQUARIUM   AQUARIUM

Map p232 (⌖206-386-4300; www.seattle aquarium.org; 1483 Alaskan Way; adult/child $34.95/24.95; ⊙9:30am-5pm; ⋒; ⋒University St) Though not on a par with Seattle's nationally lauded Woodland Park Zoo, the aquarium – situated on Pier 59 in an attractive wooden building – is probably the most interesting sight on the waterfront, and it's a handy distraction for families with itchy-footed kids.

The entry lobby instantly impresses with a giant fish-filled tank called 'Window on Washington Waters'; background music is sometimes provided by live string quartets. The aquarium houses harbor seals and resident sea and river otters, who float comically on their backs. An underwater dome on the lower level gives a pretty realistic glimpse of the kind of fish that inhabit the waters of Puget Sound, and the daily diver show here is probably the best of the aquarium's live events. For kids there are plenty of hands-on exhibits, including a pool where they can stroke starfish and caress sea urchins.

SEATTLE GREAT WHEEL   FERRIS WHEEL

Map p232 (www.seattlegreatwheel.com; 1301 Alaskan Way; adult/child $14/9; ⊙10am-11pm Sun-Thu, to midnight Fri & Sat late Jun-early Sep, 11am-10pm Mon-Thu, to midnight Fri, 10am-midnight Sat, to 10pm Sun rest of year; ⋒University St) This 175ft Ferris wheel was installed in June 2012 with 42 gondolas, each capable of carrying eight people on a 12-minute ($14!) ride. The wheel sticks out over the water on Pier 57 and has quickly become synonymous with Seattle's ever-improving waterfront. It's the tallest of its type on the West Coast, though it pales in comparison with other behemoths such as the London Eye.

✖ EATING

Downtown is home to both ultra-posh restaurants and casual grab-and-go eateries. You'll have to pick through the overpriced and underwhelming options, but there are plenty of diamonds in that rough.

Pike Place is where you go for cheap on-the-go grub, invariably sold to you by the person who picked/made/reared it. Explore the market on an empty stomach and you'll be full by the time you leave, and it won't have cost you much.

The waterfront is where to descend for oysters, clams and fish-and-chips. It's much more touristy so be prepared for menu price shock and long waits.

✖️ Downtown

TASTE RESTAURANT NORTHWESTERN US $
Map p232 (☑206-903-5291; www.tastesam.
com; 1300 1st Ave; mains $8-14; ⊘11am-5pm
Wed, Fri, Sat & Sun, to 9pm Thu; ☒University
St) Inside the Seattle Art Museum (p46),
Taste has been known to change its menu
to honor the gallery's various temporary
exhibitions.

★HEARTWOOD PROVISIONS FUSION $$$
Map p232 (☑206-582-3505; www.heartwood
sea.com; 1103 1st Ave; mains $24-37; ⊘4:30-
10pm Sun-Thu, to 11pm Fri & Sat, also 9:30am-
2pm Sat & Sun; ☒University St) Cocktails are
having a moment as the alcoholic libation
du jour in Seattle and nowhere is that more
clear than at Heartwood, a handsome
restaurant and bar with a menu of mixed
drinks that is unmatched. Come for dinner,
where each dish is infused with Southeast
Asian flavors and has its own cocktail pair-
ing (optional for an additional $7).

You can also hang out at the bar section
(3pm to 11pm Sunday to Thursday, to midnight Friday and Saturday) where a menu
of small plates and simple meals ($4 to
$20) is served. For those looking to splash
out, the chef's tasting menu for $75 a head
is highly recommended.

★WILD GINGER ASIAN $$$
Map p232 (☑206-623-4450; www.wildginger.
net; 1401 3rd Ave; mains $19-34; ⊘11:30am-
10pm Mon-Thu, to 11pm Fri & Sat, 4-9pm Sun;
☒University St) A tour of the Pacific Rim –
via China, Indonesia, Malaysia, Vietnam
and Seattle, of course – is the wide-ranging
theme at this highly popular downtown
fusion restaurant. The signature fragrant
duck goes down nicely with a glass of Ries-
ling. The restaurant also provides food for
the swanky Triple Door (p58) dinner club
downstairs.

GEORGIAN BRITISH $$$
Map p232 (☑206-621-7889; www.fairmont.
com/seattle; 411 University St; afternoon tea
$49; ⊘6:30am-2:30pm Mon-Fri, from 7am Sat
& Sun; ☒University St) Once *the* place for
Seattle fine dining, the Georgian at the
Fairmont Olympic Hotel (p189) discontin-
ued its dinner service in 2016. Its elegantly
attired restaurant still serves lunch, but
it's probably best reserved for afternoon

tea – technically 'high tea' – with its proper
British platter of scones, sandwiches and
tea in china tea cups. For $16 extra you can
add champagne.

PURPLE CAFE
& WINE BAR INTERNATIONAL $$$
Map p232 (☑206-829-2280; www.thepurple
cafe.com; 1225 4th Ave; mains $16-39; ⊘11am-
11pm Mon-Thu, to midnight Fri, noon-midnight
Sat, to 11pm Sun; ☒University St) Instantly
impressive with its high ceiling, lofty mezzanine floor and spectacular tower of wine
bottles, the Purple Cafe almost always
seems to fill its ostentatious interior, providing an atmosphere not unlike King
Street Station five minutes after the Chicago train has pulled in. The multifarious
menu reads like *War and Peace*.

To save time, opt for the lobster mac 'n'
cheese and a bottle of wine pulled from the
collection of 5000 stashed in the tower.

✖️ Pike Place

★BEECHER'S
HANDMADE CHEESE DELI $
Map p232 (☑206-956-1964; www.beechershand
madecheese.com; 1600 Pike Pl; snacks $5-12;
⊘9am-6pm; ☒Westlake) ✦ Artisanal beer,
artisanal coffee...next up, Seattle brings
you artisanal cheese and it's made as you
watch in this always-crowded Pike Place
nook, where you can buy all kinds of
cheese-related paraphernalia. As for that
long, snaking, almost permanent queue
– that's people lining up for the wonderful homemade mac 'n' cheese that comes
in two different-sized tubs and is simply
divine.

★PIROSHKY PIROSHKY BAKERY $
Map p232 (☑206-441-6068; www.piroshky
bakery.com; 1908 Pike Pl; snacks $3-6; ⊘8am-
7pm Mon-Fri, to 7:30pm Sat & Sun; ☒Westlake)
Piroshky knocks out its delectable sweet
and savory Russian pies and pastries in a
space about the size of a walk-in closet. Get
the savory smoked-salmon pâté or the sau-
erkraut with cabbage and onion, and follow it with the chocolate-cream hazelnut
roll or a fresh rhubarb piroshki.

LOPRIORE BROS. PASTA BAR ITALIAN $
Map p232 (☑206-621-7545; 1530 Post Alley;
mains $10-11; ⊘10am-5pm; ☒Westlake) Often

hidden behind a queue for the riotously popular Pike Place Chowder, this theatrical sales counter is staffed by wise-cracking servers who wouldn't look out of place in an early-career Scorsese movie. Oscar-worthy service is backed up by the *cibo*, in particular the open meatball sandwich doused in tomato sauce and Parmesan and spread over a crispy baguette.

CRUMPET SHOP
BAKERY $

Map p232 (206-682-1598; www.thecrumpet shop.com; 1503 1st Ave; crumpets $3-6; ⏰7am-3pm Mon, Wed & Thu, to 4pm Fri-Sun; ⓡWestlake) The treasured British crumpet has been given a distinct American twist with lavish toppings such as pesto, wild salmon or lemon curd at this casual Pike Place Market eatery, family owned and operated for 40 years. Organic ingredients make it very Pacific Northwest, though there's Marmite for homesick Brits and curious Americans.

PIKE PLACE CHOWDER
SEAFOOD $

Map p232 (206-267-2537; www.pikeplace chowder.com; 1530 Post Alley; medium chowder $8.75; ⏰11am-5pm; ⓡWestlake) Proof that some of the best culinary ideas are almost ridiculously simple, this Pike Place Market hole-in-the-wall takes that New England favorite (clam chowder) and gives it a dynamic West Coast makeover. You can choose from four traditional chowders in four different sizes accompanied by four different salads. Then you can fight to eat it at one of four tables.

The chowder has been voted the nation's best more than once – in competitions held in New England!

CAFFÈ LIETO
BREAKFAST $

Map p232 (Biscuit Bitch; 206-441-7999; www. biscuitbitch.com; 1909 1st Ave; biscuits $6.40-9.50; ⏰7am-2pm Mon-Fri, 8am-3pm Sat & Sun; ⓡWestlake) This tiny Pike Place Market storefront houses two casual dining juggernauts: Cafe Lieto and Biscuit Bitch. The former specializes in strong coffee, while the latter does giant, flaky biscuits totally smothered in toppings. Go with a classic biscuits and gravy, or the 'hot mess bitch' with eggs, grits, cheese and jalapeños.

Expect long lines and very friendly customer service. There are several other independently run Biscuit Bitch locations, including a larger shop in Pioneer Square (p69).

CINNAMON WORKS
BAKERY $

Map p232 (206-583-0085; 1536 Pike Pl; baked goods from $2.25; ⏰7:30am-5pm Mon-Fri, from 8am Sat & Sun; ⓡWestlake) It's hard to walk past this bakery in Pike Place – part of the market's furniture since the early 1980s – and not stop. Not surprisingly, the cinnamon buns are warm and delicious (and not too sweet), and there are tons of gluten-free and vegan options.

MEE SUM PASTRY
ASIAN $

Map p232 (206-682-6780; 1526 Pike Pl; bao from $3.18; ⏰9am-7pm; ⓡWestlake) This little storefront window is famed for its giant *hum bao* – eminently portable meat- or vegetable-filled steamed buns that make a great snack or small meal. The steamed pork *bao* is tops. Next door is a smoothie stand, where you can round out your tidy little meat bomb with some fresh fruits and vegetables.

THREE GIRLS BAKERY
BAKERY $

Map p232 (206-244-1045; www.threegirls bakery.com; 1514 Pike Pl; sandwiches $8-9.50; ⏰6am-6pm; ⓡWestlake) The 'three girls' in this pioneering business in Pike Place Market first set up shop in 1912, eight years before women in the USA got the vote. Times have obviously changed, but the quality of the baking laid down by that trio of ladies hasn't.

LE PICHET
FRENCH $$

Map p232 (206-256-1499; www.lepichet seattle.com; 1933 1st Ave; dinner mains $22-25; ⏰8am-midnight; ⓡWestlake) Say *bonjour* to Le Pichet, just up from Pike Place Market, a cute and very French bistro with pâtés, cheeses, wine, *chocolat* and a refined Parisian feel. Dinner features delicacies such as Niçoise chickpea crepes and Basque seafood stew. The specialty is a roast chicken (for two $45) – just know that there's an hour's wait when you order one.

MATT'S IN
THE MARKET
NORTHWESTERN US $$$

Map p232 (206-467-7909; www.mattsinthe market.com; 94 Pike St; mains lunch $15-21, dinner $38-48; ⏰11:30am-2:30pm & 5:30-10pm Mon-Sat; ⓡWestlake) Matt's, now run by a former Pike Place Market fish-thrower, is perched above the bustle of the market with views out over the famous clock. Most of the ingredients on the menu come from down below. Expect plenty of fish, fresh veg and organic meats.

For economy, come for the lunchtime sandwiches (the catfish is good). For fruity fish glazes and atmosphere, come for dinner.

STEELHEAD DINER
SEAFOOD $$$

Map p232 (📞206-625-0129; www.steelhead diner.com; 95 Pine St; mains $18-38; ☺11am-10pm; 🚇Westlake) It's all about the fish at the Steelhead, one of Pike Place Market's posher posts. The fish-and-chips are a given, but you're better off trying the more typically Northwestern smoked salmon cakes, sautéed sole or the multifarious *cioppino* (fish stew) here. The place has a good reputation so it's wise to book ahead.

★CAFÉ CAMPAGNE
FRENCH $$$

Map p232 (📞206-728-2233; www.cafecamp agne.com; 1600 Post Alley; mains $18-28; ☺10am-10pm Mon-Fri, from 8am Sat & Sun; 🚇Westlake) Short of teleporting over to Paris, this is about as Gallic as a Seattleite can get. Inside Café Campagne's effortlessly elegant interior you can live vicariously as a French poseur over steamed mussels, hanger steaks, generous portions of *frites* and crispy vegetables. Save room for the crème brûlée dessert. Should you be sufficiently satisfied, consider coming back for weekend brunch.

PINK DOOR RISTORANTE
ITALIAN $$$

Map p232 (📞206-443-3241; www.thepinkdoor. net; 1919 Post Alley; mains $19-30; ☺11:30am-10pm Mon-Thu, to 11pm Fri & Sat, 4-10pm Sun; 🚇Westlake) A restaurant like no other, the Pink Door is probably the only place in the US (the world?) where you can enjoy fabulous *linguine alle vongole* (pasta with clams and pancetta) and other Italian favorites while watching live jazz, burlesque cabaret, or – we kid you not – a trapeze artist swinging from the 20ft ceiling.

ETTA'S SEAFOOD
SEAFOOD $$$

Map p232 (📞206-443-6000; www.ettasrest aurant.com; 2020 Western Ave; mains $17-29; ☺11:30am-9pm Mon-Thu, to 10pm Fri, 9am-10pm Sat, to 9pm Sun; 🚇Westlake) Famous for its gourmet seafood brunch, which includes mouthwatering poached eggs with Dungeness crab and crab-butter hollandaise, Etta's is a reliable and classy place with a fish-focused dinner menu. Look out for

'crabby hour' (weekdays from 3:30pm to 5:30pm and weekends 3pm to 5pm) when the crustaceans come in all shapes and sizes (and sauces).

CUTTER'S CRABHOUSE
SEAFOOD $$$

Map p232 (📞206-448-4884; www.cutterscrab house.com; 2001 Western Ave; mains $19-45; ☺11am-9pm Mon-Thu, to 9:30pm Fri, 10:30am-9pm Sat, to 8pm Sun; 🚇Westlake) When you're located 70 sailing miles from Dungeness Spit there's no avoiding the crabs. Waterfront-facing Cutter's ain't cheap, but it will deliver the freshest crab catch in Seattle in cakes, gnocchi or just steamed whole.

🍴 Waterfront

ELLIOTT'S OYSTER HOUSE
SEAFOOD $$

Map p232 (📞206-623-4340; www.elliottsoyster house.com; 1201 Alaskan Way, Pier 56; ½ dozen oysters $16.50-22.50; ☺11am-10pm; 🚇University St) One of the best oyster houses in Seattle overhangs the water on Pier 56. The oyster menu lists over 30 different varieties plucked from practically every inlet and bay in Puget Sound and they're nicely paired with Washington white wines. Reservations are recommended, especially for outside seating.

The restaurant is most popular for its progressive oyster happy hour: starting at 3pm chef's choice oysters are $1.50 a piece and the price raises by 50c an hour until 6pm.

IVAR'S ACRES OF CLAMS
SEAFOOD $$

Map p232 (📞206-624-6852; www.ivars.com; 1001 Alaskan Way, Pier 54; mains $16-27; ☺11am-9pm Sun-Thu, to 10pm Fri & Sat; 🚼; 🚇University St) Ivar Haglund was a beloved local character famous for silly promotional slogans ('Keep clam!'), but he sure knew how to fry up fish-and-chips. Ivar's is a Seattle institution that started in 1938, and its founder still stands sentinel at the door (albeit as a statue).

Forgo the dining room for the outdoor lunch counter; the chaotic ordering system involves a lot of yelling, but it seems to work, and then you can enjoy your clam strips or fish-and-chips outdoors on the pier. The tradition at Ivar's is to feed chips to the seagulls, who'll swoop down and take them out of your hand.

🍷 DRINKING & NIGHTLIFE

Hotel bars are your best bet for drinking here, as there aren't too many watering holes in the downtown commercial core. Some of the finer hotel lounges serve as nice little oases. Coffee shops abound, but those with character are scarce.

There are some extremely romantic and very cozy drinking spots tucked away among the warrenlike market buildings in Pike Pl, and many of them have incredible views across the water. Post Alley has a couple of atmospheric Irish pubs and a wine-tasting room.

Head to the waterfront with a booking for rosé and oysters on the water.

🍷 Downtown

★ANCIENT GROUNDS
CAFE

Map p232 (☑206-7749-0747; 1220 1st Ave; ⊙7:30am-4:30pm Mon-Fri, noon-6pm Sat; ☒University St) If it's not enough that this cozy coffee nook serves some of the best espresso shots in the city, Ancient Grounds also doubles as a showroom for a well-curated selection of antiques. While waiting for your latte you can pick through a rack of vintage kimonos or peruse a display of wooden masks from indigenous communities of the Pacific Northwest.

★BOOKSTORE BAR
BAR

Map p232 (☑206-624-4844; www.alexishotel. com; 1007 1st Ave; ⊙7am-11pm Mon-Fri, from 8am Sat, 8am-10pm Sun; ☒Pioneer Sq) Cementing downtown's reputation as a fount of good hotel bars is the Bookstore, encased in the front window of the Alexis Hotel (p190), which mixes books stacked on handsome wooden shelves with whiskey – an excellent combination (ask Dylan Thomas). There are over 100 varieties of Scotch and bourbon available, plus a full gamut of weighty literary tomes from Melville to Twain.

NEST
ROOFTOP BAR

Map p232 (☑206-512-1096; 110 Stewart St; ⊙5pm-midnight Sun-Thu, from 3pm Fri & Sat) Like other modern rooftop bars in major American cities, the Nest is overpriced and usually crowded with cliques of lawyers and PR executives. But the views of the downtown skyline rolling out along

🏃 Neighborhood Walk
Downtown Architecture

....

START ARCTIC BUILDING
END WESTLAKE CENTER
LENGTH 2 MILES; ONE HOUR

....

Downtown isn't Seattle's most buzzing or creative neighborhood, but its modern edifices contain some interesting architectural details rarely spared a glance by the suited office workers who hurry from building to building at street level.

Start this walk at the south end of downtown at the ❶ **Arctic Building** (p48), built in 1917 as a club for Klondike gold-rush veterans. Crane your neck to get a look at the 25 walrus heads that embellish the building's exterior a couple of floors up. Then walk up Cherry St and take a left onto 4th Ave.

The ❷ **Columbia Center** (p48), formerly the Bank of America Tower and the Columbia Seafirst Center, takes up the block between 4th and 5th Aves and Columbia and Cherry Sts. This is the tallest building on the West Coast. If you have time (and $20), check out the observation deck on the 73rd floor.

Follow 4th Ave to Madison St and the ❸ **Safeco Plaza** (p49). Built in 1969, this was one of the city's first real skyscrapers, and it ended the Space Needle's short seven-year reign at the top. The building ushered in an era of massive downtown growth – most of it in a vertical direction. It is now Seattle's fifth-tallest skyscraper.

Just across 4th Ave, you certainly won't miss the dramatically post-modern ❹ **Seattle Central Library** (p48), spectacular from the outside with its rough-cut diamond shape. It's worth going inside for a quick ride up the bright-yellow escalators to see how good architecture can combine practicality and beauty. There are wide-ranging views from the top levels.

Continue on 4th Ave to University St and take a left, walk half a block and look up on your left. Formerly the Northern Life Tower, the ❺ **Seattle Tower** (p49), an art-deco skyscraper built in 1928, was designed to reflect the mountains of the Pacific Northwest.

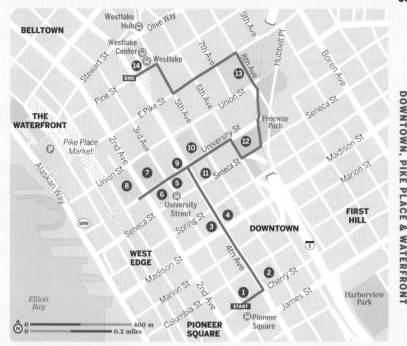

Continue down University St to the ❻**1201 Third Avenue** (p49) building, which acts like a mirror to the surrounding mountains. Nicknamed 'the Spark Plug,' it is particularly charming at sunset. Enter off 3rd Ave and examine the plush lobby of Seattle's second-tallest building.

Cross University St to ❼**Benaroya Concert Hall** (p58). Walk into the glass-enclosed lobby, where you can take in excellent views of Elliott Bay. Look up at the two giant 20ft-long chandeliers sculpted by Tacoma-born glass artist Dale Chihuly.

Continue along University to get an eyeful of the ❽**Seattle Art Museum** (p46). It may not be one of the seven wonders of the architecture world, especially from the outside, but it is a clever solution to the problem of finding more and better gallery space in the crowded downtown core.

Walk back up University St, across 3rd Ave to the corner of 4th Ave. Look up at the ❾**Cobb Building** (p49), one of downtown Seattle's more ornate edifices. On a decorative band, several sculpted heads of an erstwhile Native American chief survey the modern car chaos below.

Continue on University St across 4th Ave to ❿**Rainier Tower** (p49), which, with its precarious-looking inverted base, has been nicknamed the 'Beaver Building.' A clever piece of modern engineering, the building takes up an entire block between 4th and 5th Aves and University and Union Sts as Rainier Sq.

Cross University St and enter the domain of the Jazz Age ⓫**Fairmont Olympic Hotel** (p189), built in 1924 and undoubtedly one of the classiest remnants of Seattle's early-20th-century heyday. The block-square building looks sober and unrevealing on the outside, but journey through the revolving doors to discover a plush lobby dominated by chandeliers, marble walls and exotic carpets.

Continue northeast on University St past 6th Ave; duck around into ⓬**Freeway Park**. Meander through it, then follow the signs to the ⓭**Washington State Convention Center** (p49) and the visitor center inside. Leave the convention center through its front doors on Pike St. Follow Pike (if you squint you might see Pike Place Market at the end of the street) to 5th Ave.

Take a right on 5th Ave to Pine St; turn left, toward the utilitarian ⓮**Westlake Center** (p61). Stop for a latte and park yourself in the at one of the tables in the park opposite where you'll also find games and food trucks.

the Puget Sound with Mt Rainier visible in the distance on clear evenings make it well worth at least one drink.

It's at the top of the Thompson Seattle (p190). Enter through the lobby and you'll be directed to the line for the elevator up to the bar.

★ OWL & THISTLE   IRISH PUB

Map p232 (☑206-621-7777; www.owlnthistle. com; 808 Post Ave; ☺11am-2am; ☒Pioneer Sq) One of the best Irish pubs in the city, the dark, multiroomed Owl & Thistle is located slap-bang downtown but misses most of the tourist traffic because it's hidden in Post Ave.

Aside from hosting Celtic folk bands or acoustic singer-songwriters, it serves excellent beer and possibly the cheapest fish-and-chips in the city ($5.25 during happy hour 3pm to 7pm daily). Most importantly, it's run by an Irish couple.

SEATTLE COFFEE WORKS   CAFE

Map p232 (☑206-340-8867; www.seattlecoffee works.com; 107 Pike St; ☺6:30am-7pm Mon-Fri, 7am-7pm Sat, 7:30am-6pm Sun; ☎; ☒Westlake) 🍴 Amid the frenetic action of downtown is a cafe that truly treats its coffee like wine. Seattle Coffee Works' woody interior is split in two, with a normal walk-up counter and a 'slow bar' where staff will brew your coffee to order and discuss its taste notes like enthusiastic oenologists.

SHUCKERS   BAR

Map p232 (☑206-621-1984; www.shuckers seattle.com; 411 University St; ☺11:30am-9pm Mon-Thu, to 10pm Fri & Sat, 5-9pm Sun; ☒University St) Even if you're not a guest at the adjoining Fairmont Olympic Hotel (p189), stop in at this classy oyster bar for a menu of ultra-fresh bivalves that changes daily ($3.50 per oyster) and a glass of wine from its exhaustive collection.

📍 Pike Place

STORYVILLE COFFEE   CAFE

Map p232 (☑206-780-5777; www.storyville. com; 94 Pike St; ☺6:59am-6pm; ☎; ☒Westlake) There are so many coffee bars in Seattle that it's sometimes hard to see the forest from the trees, unless it's the kind of wood that adorns the curved bar of Storyville. Welcome to one of Seattle's newer luxury coffee chains, whose two downtown

locations (another at 1st and Madison) attract a mixture of tourists and locals looking for excellent coffee.

RADIATOR WHISKEY   WHISKEY BAR

Map p232 (☑206-467-4268; www.radiator whiskey.com; 94 Pike St; ☺4pm-midnight Mon-Sat; ☒University St) A fruitful marriage of style and substance, Radiator Whiskey, on the top floor of the Pike Place Market (p42), has exactly the amount of rustic design you'd want from a whiskey bar that has dozens of bourbons, ryes and single malts on offer. There are other spirits too, as well as a drink list that includes four takes on the classic Manhattan.

ZIG ZAG CAFÉ   COCKTAIL BAR

Map p232 (☑206-625-1146; www.zigzagseattle. com; 1501 Western Ave; ☺5pm-2am; ☒University St) If you're writing a research project on Seattle's culinary history, you'll need to reserve a chapter for the Zig Zag Café. This is the bar that repopularized gin-based Jazz Age cocktail 'The Last Word' in the early 2000s. The drink went viral and the Zig Zag's nattily attired mixers were rightly hailed as the city's finest alchemists.

Times have moved on and the Zig Zag does some mean food these days, but the cocktails are still good, and remarkably cheap during happy hour.

The bar is tucked away on the Pike St Hill Climb.

ALIBI ROOM   BAR

Map p232 (☑206-623-3180; www.seattlealibi. com; 85 Pike Pl; ☺11:30am-2am, food until 1am; ☒University St) Hidden down Post Alley opposite the beautifully disgusting 'gum wall,' the Alibi feels like an old speakeasy or perhaps the perfect place to hide from the perfect crime (or all the Pike Place crowds). Dark and cavernous, it provides surprisingly good entertainment with regular DJ nights, art installations, stand-up performances and experimental-film screenings.

If you're peckish it has a menu of pretty damn good pizza ($19 to $23) and other snacky bar foods.

TASTING ROOM   WINE BAR

Map p232 (☑206-770-9463; www.winesof washington.com; 1924 Post Alley; ☺noon-8pm Sun-Thu, to 10pm Fri & Sat; ☒Westlake) Pike Place Market is a good spot to sample the wares of some of Washington's best wine producers, and there are few better places

LOCAL KNOWLEDGE

WINE TASTING

Although it's a long way behind California in terms of annual grape yield, Washington State is the second-largest wine-producing region in the US – and it's growing. Ninety-nine percent of the state's grapes are grown on the eastern side of the Cascade Mountains in 10 different AVAs (American Viticultural Areas) that support over 800 private wineries, many of which are small and family-run. Unlike other wine regions that have become famous for one particular type of grape, Washington is known as a good all-rounder whose youthful wines – in particular the reds – are trumpeted for fruitiness and fresh acidity. Not surprisingly, Pike Place Market is a good place to sample the wares of some of Washington's best small producers, especially the Tasting Room (p56), which offers daily tastings from $12 for four 1oz pours.

than the Tasting Room, which offers four-glass tastings for $12. Friendly experts will talk you through the taste notes and tannins of prized vintages from Walla Walla, the Yakima Valley and the Columbia River region.

ATHENIAN INN
BAR

Map p232 (⎘206-624-7166; www.athenianinn. com; 1517 Pike Pl; ⊗8am-9pm Mon-Sat, 9am-4pm Sun Mar-Oct, to 8pm Mon-Thu Nov-Feb; ⍟Westlake) There's nothing fancy about Pike Place Market's Athenian, but it's a landmark and a bastion of unpretentious, frontier-era Seattle. Consider, as you sink that hoppy beer, that this joint has been here since 1909, opening two years after the market itself.

PIKE PUB & BREWERY
BREWERY

Map p232 (⎘206-622-6044; www.pikebrewing. com; 1415 1st Ave; ⊗11am-midnight Sun-Thu, to 1am Fri & Sat; ⍟University St) 🌿 Leading the way in the US microbrewery revolution, this brewpub was an early starter, opening in 1989 underneath Pike Place Market. Today it continues to serve good pub food (mains $15 to $26) and hop-heavy, made-on-site beers in a busily decorated but fun multilevel space. Free tours of the brewery are available.

Friendly bar staff will help you pair beer with your food.

KELLS
IRISH PUB

Map p232 (⎘206-728-1916; www.kellsirish. com/seattle; 1916 Post Alley; ⊗11:30am-2am; ⍟Westlake) One of three West Coast Kells, this Pike Place Market Irish pub is the most atmospheric and authentic, with its exposed-brick walls, multiple nooks and crannies, and a rosy-cheeked crowd. The perfectly poured Imperial pints of

Guinness are divine and there's regular live Irish-inspired music to enjoy while you give yourself a foam mustache.

VIRGINIA INN
PUB

Map p232 (⎘206-728-1937; www.virginiainn seattle.com; 1937 1st Ave; ⊗11:30am-midnight Sun-Thu, to 2am Fri & Sat; ⍟Westlake) Near Pike Place Market (which it predates by four years) is one of Seattle's most likable bars. Lots of draft beers, a bright brick interior and modern menu consisting of 'small plates' like pork belly with Washington-grown apples make this a good rendezvous point for forays elsewhere.

STARBUCKS
CAFE

Map p232 (⎘206-448-8762; www.1912pike. com; 1912 Pike Pl; ⊗6am-9pm; ⍟Westlake) The world's oldest surviving Starbucks store, but not – as many assume – the first. The original Starbucks opened in 1971 at 2000 Western Ave (roughly a block away). Historical value aside, the shop is small, perennially crowded, and doesn't sell snacks – just coffee. Another curiosity is that it, unusually, displays the original brown Starbucks logo of a topless mermaid.

☆ ENTERTAINMENT

Not surprisingly, downtown is where to see big-ticket items such as touring Broadway shows and the Seattle Symphony orchestra. There's also at least one good live-music venue and a well-regarded dinner theater that books diverse musical acts.

For more traditionally Seattle entertainment, check out the live-music scenes in nearby Belltown and Capitol Hill.

★A CONTEMPORARY
THEATRE   THEATER

Map p232 (ACT; ☎206-292-7676; www.act theatre.org; 700 Union St, Downtown; ☒University St) One of the three big theater companies in the city, the ACT fills its $30 million home at Kreielsheimer Pl with performances by Seattle's best thespians and occasional big-name actors. Terraced seating surrounds a central stage and the interior has gorgeous architectural embellishments.

★BENAROYA
CONCERT HALL   CONCERT HALL

Map p232 (☎206-215-4747; www.seattlesym phony.org/benaroyahall; 200 University St, Downtown; ☒University St) With a bill of almost $120 million in construction costs, it's no wonder the Benaroya Concert Hall, the primary venue of the Seattle Symphony, oozes luxury. The minute you step into the glass-enclosed lobby of the performance hall you're overwhelmed by views of Elliott Bay; on clear days you might even see the snowy peaks of the Olympic Range in the distance.

Even if you're not attending the symphony, you can walk through the foyer and marvel at the 20ft-long chandeliers, specially created by Tacoma glassmaker Dale Chihuly.

TRIPLE DOOR   LIVE PERFORMANCE

Map p232 (☎206-838-4333; www.thetriple door.net; 216 Union St, Downtown; ☒University St) This club downstairs from the Wild Ginger (p51) restaurant is a Seattle mainstay with a liberal booking policy that includes country and rock as well as jazz, gospel, R&B, world music and burlesque performances. There's a full menu and a smaller lounge upstairs called the **Musicquarium** with an aquarium and free live music.

SEATTLE SYMPHONY   CLASSICAL MUSIC

Map p232 (☎206-215-4747; www.seattlesym phony.org; 200 University St, Downtown; ☒University St) A major regional ensemble, the Seattle Symphony orchestra plays at the Benaroya Concert Hall, which you'll find downtown at 2nd Ave and University St.

PARAMOUNT THEATER   THEATER

Map p232 (☎206-682-1414; www.stgpresents. org; 911 Pine St, Downtown; ☒10) Saved from demolition and listed as a historic monument in the mid-1970s, the Paramount Theater dates back to 1928 and was restored to its Jazz Age finery in 1995. It has operated ever since as an esteemed multi-performance venue (rock, comedy, theater), though its forte is touring Broadway shows.

The theater was originally conceived as a movie house with back-up from the popular vaudeville acts of the day. It continued as a cinema until 1971 (Bruce Lee was briefly an usher), whereupon it became a rock venue, lost money and degenerated into a tatty shadow of its former self.

5TH AVENUE THEATER   THEATER

Map p232 (☎206-625-1900; www.5thavenue. org; 1308 5th Ave, Downtown; ☺box office 9am-5:30pm Mon-Fri; ☒University St) Built in 1926 with an opulent Asian motif, the 5th Avenue opened as a vaudeville house; it was later turned into a movie theater and then closed in 1979. An influx of funding and a heritage award saved it in 1980, and now it's Seattle's premier theater for Broadway musical revivals. It's worth going just for a look at the architecture.

Tickets are available by phone or at the theater box office.

SHOWBOX   LIVE MUSIC

Map p232 (☎206-628-3151; www.showbox presents.com; 1426 1st Ave, Pike Place; ☒University St) This cavernous 1137-capacity showroom – which hosts mostly national touring acts, ranging from indie rock to hip-hop – reinvents itself every few years and successfully rode the grunge bandwagon while it lasted. It first opened in 1939 and its dressing-room walls could probably tell some stories – everyone from Duke Ellington to Ice Cube has played here.

MARKET THEATER   THEATER

Map p232 (☎206-587-2414; www.unexpected productions.org; 1428 Post Alley, Pike Place; ☒Westlake) The Market Theater is Seattle's bona fide improv comedy theater with shows staged by Unexpected Productions. It was patrons queuing for this theater who started off the famed gum wall (p49) in the 1990s. With the advent of online booking, the queues are more for photos these days. See website for schedule and tickets.

SHOPPING

The main shopping area in Seattle is downtown between 3rd and 6th Aves and between University and Stewart Sts. If you're anywhere nearby, you can't miss it. For the compulsive browser, amateur chef, hungry traveler on a budget, or anyone else with their five senses fully intact, Seattle has no greater attraction than Pike Place Market. This is shopping central in Seattle: dozens of market food stalls hawk everything from geoduck clams to fennel root and harissa. Locals shop here just as much as tourists.

For the full gamut of souvenirs, simply stroll the boardwalk along the waterfront.

★ OLD SEATTLE PAPERWORKS
POSTERS, MAGAZINES

Map p232 (☏206-623-2870; 1501 Pike Place Market, Pike Place; ⏰10am-5pm; ☒Westlake) If you like decorating your home with old magazine covers from *Life, Time* and *Rolling Stone,* or have a penchant for art deco tourist posters from the 1930s, or are looking for that rare Hendrix concert flyer from 1969, this is your nirvana. It's in Pike Place Market's Down Under section.

★ MARKET MAGIC
MAGIC

Map p232 (☏206-624-4271; www.marketmagicshop.com; 1501 Pike Pl, Pike Place; ⏰10am-5pm Mon-Sat, from 10:30am Sun; ☒Westlake) Selling fake dog poop, stink bombs, water-squirting rings and magic tricks, this Pike Place Market magic shop is heaven for aspiring magicians, pranksters, school kids, and grown-ups who wish they were still school kids.

METSKER MAPS
MAPS

Map p232 (☏206-623-8747; www.metskers.com; 1511 1st Ave, Pike Place; ⏰9am-8pm Mon-Fri, from 10am Sat, 10am-6pm Sun; ☒Westlake) In its high-profile location on 1st Ave, this 65-year-old map shop sells all kinds of useful things for the traveler, from maps and guidebooks to various accessories. It also has a good selection of armchair-travel lit and pretty spinning globes for the dreamers.

LEFT BANK BOOKS
BOOKS

Map p232 (☏206-662-0195; www.leftbankbooks.com; 92 Pike St, Pike Place; ⏰10am-7pm Mon-Sat,

11am-6pm Sun; ☒Westlake) This collective of more than 40 years displays zines in *español,* revolutionary pamphlets, essays by Chomsky and an inherent suspicion of authority. You're in Seattle, just in case you forgot.

WATSON KENNEDY FINE HOME
HOMEWARES

Map p232 (☏206-652-8350; www.watsonkennedy.com; 1022 1st Ave, Downtown; ⏰10am-6pm Mon-Sat, noon-5pm Sun; ☒University St) Watson Kennedy is one of those delightful homewares stores where you feel that you could spend hours smelling soaps and picking out frivolous, but fun, kitchen gadgets. The merchandise is all a cut above and the store is organized by theme (roses, nautical etc), which adds an extra layer of effortless whimsy.

TRUFFLE QUEEN
FOOD

Map p232 (☏206-292-5555; https://trufflequeen.com; 1524 Pike Pl, Pike Place; ⏰10am-6pm; ☒Westlake) If you're struggling to work out which fine Pike Place Market artisanal product to take home with you, here's some friendly advice: proceed directly to Truffle Queen (formerly La Buona Tavola) and buy its truffle oil. Made from high-quality Italian truffles, this is the real deal and well worth the investment.

Bonus: there are daily wine tastings until 5:30pm ($10), as well as a happy hour from 5pm to 6pm where $5 gets you a glass of wine from whatever bottle happens to be open at the time.

FIRST & PIKE NEWS
BOOKS

Map p232 (☏206-624-0140; 93 Pike St, Pike Place; ⏰8am-6:30pm; ☒University St) Who said magazines are dead? You can read all about it at this Pike Place Market newsstand peddling *Jazz Times, Surfer Journal, Cigar Aficionado,* Spanish tattoo mags, Italian gossip tabloids, Russian comics and the good old *Buddhist Times.*

PURE FOOD FISH
FOOD

Map p232 (☏206-622-5765; www.freshseafood.com; 1511 Pike Pl, Pike Place; ⏰7am-6pm; ☒Westlake) Perhaps the gift that says 'I *heart* Seattle' the most is a whole salmon or other fresh seafood from the fish markets. All the markets will prepare fish for transportation on the plane ride home, but Pure Food Fish has been around for four generations and has the best reputation for quality and value.

NORDSTROM RACK   CLOTHING
Map p232 (☑206-448-8522; https://stores. nordstromrack.com; 400 Pine St, Downtown; ☺9:30am-9pm Mon-Fri, 10am-8pm Sat, to 7pm Sun; 🚇Westlake) Nordstrom Rack offers closeouts and returns from its parent store across the street. It's a favorite among those with chichi taste and a limited budget.

DELAURENTI'S   FOOD
Map p232 (☑206-622-0141; www.delaurenti. com; 1435 1st Ave, Pike Place; snacks $5-12; ☺9am-6pm Mon-Sat, 10am-5pm Sun; 🚇University St) A Pike Place Market veteran, this Italian grocery stºre/deli has been run by the same family since 1946. Not needing to roll with the times, it offers a beautifully old-fashioned selection of wine, cheese, sausages, hams and pasta, along with a large range of capers, olive oils and anchovies. The sandwich counter is a great place to order panini, salads and pizza.

MADE IN WASHINGTON   GIFTS & SOUVENIRS
Map p232 (☑206-467-0788; www.madein washington.com; 1530 Post Alley, Pike Place; ☺10am-6pm; 🚇Westlake) If you're looking for something authentically Northwest, head to Made in Washington. One of several locations around the city, this one in Pike Place Market stocks arts and crafts, T-shirts, coffee and chocolate, smoked salmon, regional wines, books and other creative ephemera made in the Evergreen state. There's **another branch** (Map p232; ☑206-623-1063; 400 Pine St, Downtown; ☺10am-8pm Mon-Sat, 11am-6pm Sun; 🚇Westlake) in the Westlake Center.

TENZING MOMO   GIFTS & SOUVENIRS
Map p232 (☑206-338-0193; www.tenzingmomo. com; 93 Pike St, Pike Place; ☺10am-6pm Mon-Sat, to 5pm Sun; 🚇University St) Doing a good impersonation of one of the magic shops in Diagon Alley from the *Harry Potter* books, Tenzing Momo is an old-school natural apothecary with shelves of mysterious glass bottles filled with herbs and tinctures to treat any ailment. It's in the Economy Market Building.

NORDSTROM   DEPARTMENT STORE
Map p232 (☑206-628-2111; www.nordstrom. com; 500 Pine St, Downtown; ☺9:30am-9pm Mon-Sat, 10am-7pm Sun; 🚇Westlake) Born and fostered in Seattle by a Klondike gold-rush profiteer, this upscale department store occupies a giant space in the former Frederick and Nelson Building.

SUR LA TABLE   HOMEWARES
Map p232 (☑206-448-2244; www.surlatable. com; 84 Pine St, Pike Place; ☺9am-6:30pm; 🚇Westlake) It's hard to miss this gigantic cookware store. It's a chain, but a good one, and it started here in Seattle. The rich supply of cookware, books, gear and gadgets is bound to entice any food critic, gourmand or gourmet.

GOLDEN AGE COLLECTABLES   TOYS
Map p232 (☑206-622-9799; www.goldenage collectables.com; 1501 Pike Pl, Pike Place; ☺9:30am-6pm Mon-Thu, to 6:30pm Fri, 9am-6:30pm Sat, from 9:30am Sun; 🚇Westlake) A haven for geeks, kids and, especially, geeky kids, this shop has comics and comic-book–inspired toys, novelty items (hopping nuns etc), costumes and loads of goth-friendly knickknacks.

BARNES & NOBLE   BOOKS
Map p232 (☑206-264-0156; www.barnesand noble.com; 600 Pine St, Downtown; ☺9am-9pm Mon-Thu, to 10pm Fri & Sat, 10am-9pm Sun; 🚇Westlake) Since the demise of Borders in 2011 and the relocation of Elliott Bay Book Company (p120) to Capitol Hill, Barnes & Noble remains downtown's main book emporium, with generous opening hours and helpful, well-read staff.

PACIFIC PLACE   MALL
Map p232 (www.pacificplaceseattle.com; 600 Pine St, Downtown; ☺10am-8pm Mon-Sat, 11am-7pm Sun; 🚇Westlake) Seattle's best-quality boutique mall feels a bit like the lobby of an upscale hotel – it's cylindrical, and the total lack of that hectic shopping-mall vibe makes it very pleasant to walk around. Stores include **J Crew** (Map p232; ☑206-652-9788; www.jcrew.com; ☺10am-8pm Mon-Sat, 11am-7pm Sun), **Club Monaco** (Map p232; ☑206-264-8001; www.clubmonaco.com; ☺10am-8pm Mon-Sat, 11am-7pm Sun) and Barnes & Noble.

Take a moment to gape in the window at **Tiffany & Co** (Map p232; ☑206-264-1400; www.tiffany.com; ☺10am-8pm Mon-Sat, 11am-6pm Sun) or saunter inside for a special gift. The mall's top level features a movie theater, a pub and a couple of restaurants. This is also where you'll find the nicest public restrooms in downtown Seattle.

YE OLDE
CURIOSITY SHOP
GIFTS & SOUVENIRS

Map p232 (☑206-682-5844; https://yeolde curiosityshop.com; 1001 Alaskan Way, Pier 54, Waterfront; ⊙10am-6pm Mon-Thu, 9am-9pm Fri & Sat, 10am-7pm Sun; ⍰University St) This landmark shop on Pier 54 has been around since 1899 – ancient history by Seattle standards. It has changed quite a bit since then and now mostly hawks replica oddities and Seattle souvenirs. Half the stuff it displays, such as Chief Seattle's hat, a variety of stalagmites and 'tites, and some pretty cool fortune-telling machines, isn't for sale.

WESTLAKE CENTER
MALL

Map p232 (☑206-467-3044; www.westlake center.com; 400 Pine St, Downtown; ⊙10am-8pm Mon-Sat, 11am-6pm Sun; ⍰Westlake) This 'boutique mall' – also the starting point for the monorail – has an assortment of stores. There are some well-established chains like Nordstrom Rack, as well as those with a more local bent like Made in Washington and an outlet of **Fireworks** (Map p232; ☑206-682-6462; www.fireworksgallery. net; ⊙10am-8pm Mon-Sat, 11am-6pm Sun), which offers inexpensive arty products by regional craftspeople – they make great gifts.

MACY'S
DEPARTMENT STORE

Map p232 (☑206-344-2121; www.macys.com; 1601 3rd Ave, Downtown; ⊙10am-8pm Mon-Wed, to 9pm Thu-Sat, 11am-7pm Sun; ⍰Westlake)

WALKING TOURS

Downtown Seattle, and in particular Pike Place Market, is awash with good, independent walking tours of many types, but with a strong bias toward food and drink. As a rule, the tours are organized by small private individuals or companies who offer a professional but highly personal service. All of them will give you a candid view of Seattle, its market and its people. With wet weather rarely off the menu, tours usually go ahead rain or shine.

Seattle Free Walking Tours (Map p232; www.seattlefreewalkingtours.org; 2001 Western Ave, Pike Place) FREE A non-profit set up by a couple of world travelers and Seattle residents in 2012, who were impressed with the free walking tours offered in various European cities, these tours meet daily at 11am on the corner of Western Ave and Virginia St. The intimate two-hour walk takes in Pike Pl, the waterfront and Pioneer Sq. If you have a rip-roaring time (highly likely), there's a suggested $20 donation. Reserve online.

Seattle by Foot (☑206-508-7017; www.seattlebyfoot.com; per person from $39) This company runs a handful of tours including the practically essential (this being Seattle) Coffee Crawl, which will ply you liberally with caffeine while explaining the nuances of latte art and dishing the inside story on the rise (and rise) of Starbucks. It costs $39 including samples. Registration starts at 9:50am Thursday to Sunday at the Hammering Man (p48) outside Seattle Art Museum. The same company also offers a unique Seattle Kids Tour: two hours of educational fun involving art, music and chocolate. Prices are from $125 per family. Reserve ahead.

Savor Seattle (☑206-209-5485; www.savorseattletours.com; tours from $44) These guys lead a handful of gastronomic tours, the standout being the two-hour Booze-n-Bites that runs several times daily and costs $69. Prepare yourself for some sublime cocktails, wine and food.

Seattle Bites (☑425-888-8837; www.seattlebitesfoodtours.com; tours from $44) Try Lummi Island salmon, Nutella crepes, clam chowder, Washington wine and German sausage all in one market tour. This 2½-hour stroll costs $44 and leaves at 10:30am year-round (and 2:30pm May through September), so go easy on breakfast. Participants are given listening devices, enabling them to wander off and still hear the guide's words of wisdom.

Seattle's oldest and largest department store, this hard-to-miss classic – formerly Bon-Marché, but renamed Bon-Macy's in August 2003 when it was bought by Macy's, then shortened for convenience – is a mainstay of clothing and homewares shopping.

SOUK
FOOD

Map p232 (☑206-441-1666; 1916 Pike Pl, Pike Place; ☺10am-6pm Mon-Sat, 11am-5pm Sun; ⓡWestlake) Supplies here include Middle Eastern and North African spices and foods. Named after the Arabic word for marketplace, the shop sells everything you'll need to get from cookbook to curry – including cookbooks and curries.

🏃 SPORTS & ACTIVITIES

ROAD DOGS SEATTLE BREWERY TOUR
TOURS

Map p232 (☑206-249-9858; www.seattlebrewerytour.com; 1427 Western Ave, Pike Place; tours $79; ☺10:30am, 2:30pm & 6pm Sun-Fri, 10:30am, 2:30pm & 6:30pm Fri & Sat) Road Dogs' popular three-hour Seattle Brewery tour takes in three breweries from a list of 25, from long-established microbreweries to nascent nano-businesses. To allow you to safely sup samples en route, you'll be picked up and whisked around in a minibus driven by a beer expert/driver.

The company also runs local coffee and distillery tours. Book online.

KUSH TOURISM
TOURS

Map p232 (☑206-633-2489; www.kushtourism.com; 1620 4th Ave, Ste 1, Downtown; tours $99; ☺10am Mon-Sat; ⓡWestlake) Seattle's first specialist marijuana tour company can also help you clear up some of the red tape surrounding the state drug laws. Its 3½-hour tour visits marijuana grows, pot shops and glass blowers. Check out the website for up-to-date information on stores, pot-friendly accommodations and legal matters.

COPPERWORKS DISTILLING
DISTILLERY

Map p232 (☑206-504-7604; www.copperworksdistilling.com; 1250 Alaskan Way, Waterfront; tours $15; ☺noon-6pm Mon-Thu, to 7pm Fri & Sat, to 5pm Sun; ⓡUniversity St) Smack in the middle of downtown, this craft distiller is so new its first batch of whiskey hasn't even finished aging yet. Notwithstanding, Copperworks has already made a name for itself with its vodka and – more emphatically – its gin made with Washington State barley in Scottish stills before being aged in Kentucky barrels.

Tours occur on Friday (5pm) and Saturday (3pm and 5pm) and cost $15. You can come in anytime during business hours for a tasting ($10) of a flight of four spirits.

SEATTLE CYCLING TOURS
CYCLING

Map p232 (☑206-356-5803; www.seattle-cycling-tours.com; 714 Pike St, Downtown; tours from $59; ⓠ10) Perhaps one of the best ways for new visitors to get oriented with Seattle's streets is with a bike tour. Seattle Cycling Tours organizes some of the best in town. The tour that goes all the way to Ballard Locks avoiding Seattle's famous hills is highly recommended. Another popular option is the longer weekend ride to Bainbridge Island.

ARGOSY CRUISES SEATTLE HARBOR TOUR
CRUISE

Map p232 (☑206-623-1445; www.argosycruises.com; 1101 Alaskan Way, Pier 55, Waterfront; 1hr tour adult/child $31/17; ⓡUniversity St) Argosy's popular Seattle Harbor Tour is a one-hour narrated excursion around Elliott Bay, the waterfront and the Port of Seattle. It departs from Pier 55.

DOWNTOWN SEATTLE YMCA
GYM

Map p232 (☑206-382-5010; www.seattleymca.org; 909 4th Ave, Downtown; day pass $10-15; ☺5am-9pm Mon-Fri, 7am-5pm Sat; ⓡPioneer Sq) The Y is notably traveler-friendly and this location has clean, classy, updated equipment including a pool, free weights, cardio equipment and child care.

Pioneer Square, International District & SoDo

Neighborhood Top Five

❶ **Klondike Gold Rush National Historical Park** (p66) Reliving the spirit of the gold rush at this inspiring museum, set in one of the many red-brick Richardsonian Romanesque buildings that sprang up after the 1889 Great Fire.

❷ **Zeitgeist Coffee** (p74) Diving mouth first into

Seattle's famous coffee scene with a damn fine cup of coffee.

❸ **Jade Garden** (p71) Satisfying lunchtime Asian food cravings at this boisterous dim-sum restaurant in the International District.

❹ **CenturyLink Field** (p75) Warming up in the bars of Pioneer Square before at-

tending a football or soccer game.

❺ **Westland Distillery** (p77) Getting a taste of the up-and-coming SoDo neighborhood with a throat-warming glass of single malt whiskey.

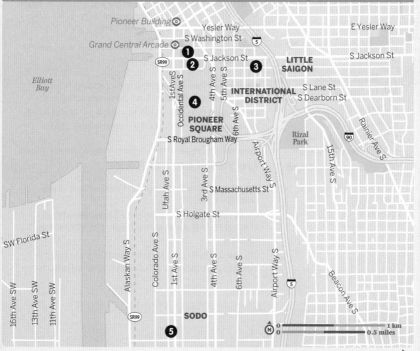

For more detail of this area see Map p234 ➡

Lonely Planet's Top Tip

Pioneer Square social life is heavily affected by the sports events that go on at the two adjacent stadiums. If you like your pubs and restaurants loud and boisterous, come on a game day. If you don't, go elsewhere.

✕ Best Places to Eat

➡ Maneki (p72)

➡ Nirmal's (p70)

➡ London Plane (p70)

➡ Il Corvo Pasta (p69)

For reviews, see p69. ➡

☕ Best Places to Drink

➡ Zeitgeist Coffee (p74)

➡ Saké Nomi (p72)

➡ Panama Hotel Tea & Coffee House (p74)

➡ Pyramid Ale House (p74)

For reviews, see p72. ➡

🛍 Best Places to Shop

➡ Filson (p76)

➡ Uwajimaya (p76)

➡ Glasshouse Studio (p77)

➡ Ganja Goddess (p77)

For reviews, see p76. ➡

Explore Pioneer Square, International District & SoDo

Browsing the Pioneer Square Historical District is rather like visiting a movie set of early-20th-century Seattle, except that the food and the shopping are better. This is the birthplace of Seattle, and the redbrick district of historical buildings is still a real crossroads of the modern city.

Some visitors arrive by long-distance bus or train at King Street Station (p68), a good place to get oriented due to its proximity to a trio of local squares. A few blocks west of the station is Pioneer Square Park (p67), an architectural showpiece, and neighboring Occidental Park (p66) was recently given a beautiful face-lift.

To the east of King Street Station is the International District (ID). The 'international' moniker has some merit: while predominantly Chinese, there is a strong Vietnamese presence and a few reminders of the city's Japantown, which never recaptured its pre-WWII vibrancy after its citizens were detained in internment camps during the war.

The ID is perfect hunting ground for cheap food: dim sum and Vietnamese *pho* predominate. You'll also find the Wing Luke Asian Museum (p68) and the delectable Panama Hotel Tea & Coffee House (p74).

Access spread-out SoDo by strolling south on 1st Ave S. Beyond its two sports stadiums you'll stumble upon weed dispensaries, a whiskey distillery (p77) and a little-known computer museum (p69).

Local Life

Uwajimaya Shop for exotic fruit and vegetables or Korean beauty products at this giant Asian community market (p76).

Occidental Park You can play table tennis or talk recipes with a food-cart vendor in this recently cleaned-up park (p66).

Getting There & Away

Bus Pioneer Square is a few blocks from downtown and its plentiful bus options.

Light rail Central Link light rail from Sea-Tac Airport stops at Pioneer Square station or International District/Chinatown station.

Streetcar The First Hill Streetcar runs from S Jackson St in Pioneer Square through the ID, CD and First Hill to Capitol Hill.

TOP SIGHT
PIONEER SQUARE ARCHITECTURE

Many important architectural heirlooms are concentrated in Pioneer Square, the district that sprang up in the wake of the 1889 Great Fire. Instantly recognizable by its handsome red-brick buildings, the neighborhood showcases the Richardsonian Romanesque architectural style, strongly influenced by America's Chicago School.

Grand Central Arcade

The lovely Grand Central Arcade (p67) was originally Squire's Opera House, erected in 1879. When the Opera House was destroyed in the Great Fire it was rebuilt as the Squire-Latimer Building in 1890 and later became the Grand Central Hotel. The hotel underwent a major restoration in the 1970s and now contains two floors of shops.

Smith Tower

A mere dwarf amid Seattle's impressive skyline, the 42-story neoclassical Smith Tower (p68) was, for half a century after its construction in 1914, the tallest building west of Chicago. The beaux arts–inspired lobby is paneled in onyx and marble, and the elevator is still manually operated by a uniformed attendant. You can visit the observation deck in the 35th-floor Observatory, which has an ornate wooden ceiling.

Pioneer Building

Built in 1891, the magnificent Pioneer Building (p67) facing Pioneer Square Park is one of the finest Victorian buildings in Seattle and features many of the classic components of Richardsonian Romanesque; look for the Roman arches, a recessed main doorway, curvaceous bay windows and decorative flourishes, most notably the two frontal columns that frame some skillfully embellished bricks.

DON'T MISS

- ➡ Smith Tower
- ➡ Pioneer Building
- ➡ Grand Central Arcade

PRACTICALITIES

- ➡ Map p234, C1
- ➡ btwn Alaskan Way S, S King St, 5th Ave S, 2nd Ave ext & Columbia St, Pioneer Sq
- ➡ 🚃 First Hill Streetcar

◉ SIGHTS

Pioneer Square is a veritable outdoor museum of late-19th-century red-brick architecture, with several indoor museums thrown in for good measure. Meanwhile, SoDo's sports arenas will be a big draw for sports fans.

The International District is more about street bustle. Its immigrant history and culture are potently summed up in the Wing Luke Museum (p68).

◉ Pioneer Square

PIONEER SQUARE
HISTORICAL DISTRICT   AREA
See p65.

★KLONDIKE GOLD
RUSH NATIONAL
HISTORICAL PARK   MUSEUM
Map p234 (📞206-553-3000; www.nps.gov/klse; 319 2nd Ave S; ⊙9am-5pm Jun-Aug, 10am-5pm Tue-Sun Sep-Feb, 10am-5pm daily Mar-May; 🚋First Hill Streetcar) FREE Eloquently run by the US National Park Service, this wonderful museum has exhibits, photos and news clippings from the 1897 Klondike gold rush, when a Seattle-on-steroids acted as a fueling depot for prospectors bound for the Yukon in Canada. Entry would cost $20 anywhere else; in Seattle it's free!

The best aspect of the museum is its clever use of storytelling. At the outset you are introduced to five local characters who became stampeders (Klondike prospectors) in the 1890s, and you're then invited to follow their varying fortunes and experiences periodically throughout the rest of the museum. Sound effects and interactive exhibits are used to good effect.

The museum, which opened in 2006, is housed in the old Cadillac Hotel (built in 1889), rescued from a grisly fate after nearly being toppled in the 2001 Nisqually earthquake.

OCCIDENTAL PARK   PARK
Map p234 (📞206-684-4075; 117 S Washington St; ⊙6am-10pm; 🚋First Hill Streetcar) Once a rather rough-and-tumble place, Occidental Park has undergone a recent renaissance thanks largely to a partnership between the City of Seattle and a couple of non-profit groups. Following an urban-renewal campaign in 2015, the park has been outfitted with attractive seating, outdoor games (including chess and table football), licensed buskers and a regular posse of food carts.

Add this to what was already there (classic red-brick buildings, Native American art and a firefighting sculpture) and you've got an exceptional place to hang out. Friendly 'park ambassadors' (dressed in yellow vests) handle security, cleanups and tourist information 24/7.

YESLER WAY   STREET
Map p234 (🚋Pioneer Sq) Seattle claims its Yesler Way was the basis for the term 'skid road', which became 'skid row' – logs would 'skid' down the steeply sloped road linking a logging area above town to Henry Yesler's mill.

As for Henry Yesler himself, local historians paint him as an ambitious business zealot who clashed frequently with the wild-and-woolly Doc Maynard. These two men, who by all accounts were equally

---

FIRST THURSDAY ART WALK

Art walks are two a penny in US cities these days, but they were pretty much an unknown quantity when the pioneering artists of Pioneer Square instituted their first amble around the local galleries in 1981. The neighborhood's **First Thursday Art Walk** (📞206-667-0687; www.firstthursdayseattle.com; Occidental Park, Pioneer Sq; ⊙hours vary by venue) claims to be the oldest in the nation and a creative pathfinder for all that followed (and there have been many). Aside from gluing together Pioneer Square's network of 50-plus galleries, the walk is a good excuse to admire creative public sculpture, sip decent coffee (many cafes serve as de facto galleries), browse an array of stalls set up in Occidental Park, and get to know the neighborhood and its people. The Art Walk is self-guided, but you can pick up a map from the information booth in Occidental Park. Free parking is also offered from 5pm to 10pm. Check details on the website.

stubborn, both owned part of the land that would eventually become Pioneer Sq. This resulted in a highly symbolic grid clash, in which Yesler's section of the square had streets running parallel to the river, while Maynard's came crashing in at a north–south angle. Yesler maintained, not unreasonably, that Doc was drunk when he submitted his portion of the plans.

WATERFALL PARK   PARK

Map p234 (☑206-624-6096; 219 2nd Ave S; ⊘8am-3:45pm; ⊠First Hill Streetcar) This unusual park is an urban oasis commemorating workers of the United Parcel Service (UPS), which grew out of a messenger service that began in a basement at this location in 1907. The artificial 22ft waterfall that flows in this tiny open-air courtyard is flanked by tables and flowering plants.

GRAND CENTRAL ARCADE   LANDMARK

Map p234 (☑206-623-7417; 214 1st Ave S; ⊠First Hill Streetcar) Once an opera house and hotel, this stately brick building now contains two floors of commercial businesses, including the excellent Grand Central Baking Co (p70). The facade that faces Occidental Park is covered in creeping ivy.

The businesses are mostly specialty shops, but history buffs will still enjoy strolling the halls of the arcade taking in the photos of old Seattle on the walls.

FOSTER/WHITE GALLERY   GALLERY

Map p234 (☑206-622-2833; www.fosterwhite.com; 220 3rd Ave S; ⊘10am-6pm Tue-Sat; ⊠First Hill Streetcar) FREE The polished Foster/White Gallery, which opened in 1968, features glassworks, paintings and sculpture by mainstream Northwest artists in a beautifully renovated 7000-sq-ft space. Some of the exhibits are for sale (if you're rich), but realistically, this is more a contemporary art gallery – and a fine one too – that deserves half an hour of quiet contemplation.

PIONEER SQUARE PARK   SQUARE

Map p234 (cnr Cherry St & 1st Ave S; ⊠Pioneer Sq) The original Pioneer Square is a cobbled triangular plaza where Henry Yesler's sawmill cut the giant trees that marked Seattle's first industry. Known officially as Pioneer Square Park, the plaza features a bust of **Chief Seattle** (Seattle being an Anglicized version of the Duwamish name

REAL CHANGE

Pioneer Square's large population of unhoused people may give some visitors pause, but it's important to keep in mind that they are citizens of the neighborhood the same as anyone else, and pose no more a threat than their housed neighbors. Other than helping out with spare change, one way to give is buying the weekly newspaper *Real Change*. It's one of the city's largest independent papers and often covers issues surrounding homelessness, gentrification, social services and other related topics. You'll see vendors, many of them unhoused people, selling it on the street for $2 (vendors buy the paper for $0.60 a copy and keep the profit). The paper, founded in 1994, generates nearly $1 million a year for homeless causes.

Si'ahl or Sealth), an ornate pergola and a Tlingit **totem pole**, the first to be erected in Seattle as the Salish people native to the region did not build them.

Some wayward early Seattleites, so the story goes, stole the totem pole from the Tlingit native people in southeastern Alaska in 1890. The tribe successfully sued and received $500 in damages for the stolen art (although they originally demanded $20,000). An arsonist lit the pole aflame in 1938, burning it to the ground, leading the city to request the Tlingit to carve a new one, which you see today.

PERGOLA   LANDMARK

Map p234 (cnr Yesler Way & James St; ⊠Pioneer Sq) This decorative iron pergola in Pioneer Square Park was built in 1909 to serve as an entryway to an underground lavatory and to shelter those waiting for the cable car that went up and down Yesler Way. The reportedly elaborate restroom eventually closed due to serious plumbing problems at high tide. In January 2001, the pergola was leveled by a wayward truck, but it was restored and put back where it belongs the following year, looking as good as new.

PIONEER BUILDING   LANDMARK

Map p234 (606 1st Ave S; ⊠First Hill Streetcar) Elmer Fisher, whose fingerprints are

THE ORIGINAL SKID ROW

Recognized as a byword for decrepit, down-at-heel urban neighborhoods everywhere, the term 'skid row' originated in Seattle in the 1860s, when greased logs were skidded down First Hill to a timber mill on the shores of Elliott Bay owned by a local lumber entrepreneur named Henry Yesler. The mill road – known officially as Yesler Way but colloquially as Skid Row – was punctuated by a strip of bawdy bars that grew up to support a rambunctious population of itinerant mill workers. Famed for its drunken revelry and occasional fistfights, the area quickly acquired an unsavory reputation, causing Seattle's affluent classes to migrate north to the newer, more salubrious streets of what is now the downtown core. Meanwhile, 'Skid Row' was left to slip into a long and inglorious decline, and an infamous nickname was born.

After decades of poverty, Yesler Way turned things around in the 1970s after a vociferous community campaign saved the Pioneer Square Historic District from the demolition ball. Sandwiched amid the handsome red-brick edifices of Seattle's original downtown, it's a gritty but innocuous place these days, where the only log you'll see is the lofty Native American totem pole that towers over nearby Pioneer Square Park.

ubiquitous in Pioneer Square, designed this iconic Pioneer Square building.

SMITH TOWER   LANDMARK
Map p234 (☑206-622-4004; www.smithtower. com; 506 2nd Ave; adult/child $20/16; ⊙10am-11pm Sun-Wed, to midnight Thu-Sat; ⊠Pioneer Sq) Sneak a peak at the beaux arts–inspired lobby while on your way to the 35th-floor **Observatory** of this landmark building. The views aren't as dramatic as taller structures in the city, but it's still picturesque, to be sure.

◉ International District

**WING LUKE MUSEUM OF
THE ASIAN PACIFIC
AMERICAN EXPERIENCE**   MUSEUM
Map p234 (☑206-623-5124; www.wingluke.org; 719 S King St; adult/child $17/12; ⊙10am-5pm Tue-Sun; ⊠First Hill Streetcar) The beautiful Wing Luke museum examines Asia Pacific American culture, focusing on prickly issues such as Chinese settlement in the 1880s and Japanese internment camps during WWII. Recent temporary exhibits include 'A Day in the Life of Bruce Lee.' There are also art exhibits and a preserved immigrant apartment. Guided tours are available; the first Thursday of the month is free (with extended hours until 8pm).

SEATTLE PINBALL MUSEUM   MUSEUM
Map p234 (☑206-623-0759; www.seattlepinball museum.com; 508 Maynard Ave S; adult/child $15/12; ⊙noon-6pm Sun, Mon & Thu, to 8pm Fri & Sat; ⛾; ⊠First Hill Streetcar) Got kids? Got kid-like tendencies? Love the buzzers and bells of good old-fashioned analog machines? Lay aside your iPad apps and become a pinball wizard for the day in this fantastic games room in the International District, with machines from 1960s retro to 2019 futuristic. Admission buys you unlimited games for the day.

KING STREET STATION   LANDMARK
Map p234 (303 S Jackson St; ⊠International District/Chinatown) One of the pillars upon which Seattle built its early fortunes, the old Great Northern Railroad depot, was given a much-needed face-lift in the early 2010s after decades of neglect. Serving as the western terminus of the famous Empire Builder train that runs cross-country between Seattle and Chicago, the station building was designed to imitate St Mark's bell tower in Venice.

It was constructed in 1906 by Reed & Stem, who also designed New York City's Grand Central Station, and is notable for many features, not least a fabulous Italianate plasterwork ceiling in the waiting room that is rich in period detail. The waiting room was covered up by a horrible suspended ceiling in the 1960s but, as part of a $26 million revamp, the entire interior and exterior of the station was returned to its Gilded Age high watermark in 2012.

HING HAY PARK   SQUARE
Map p234 (☑206-684-4075; 423 Maynard Ave S; ⊙6am-10pm; ⊠First Hill Streetcar) If you need a tranquil spot to rest while wandering the

ID, Hing Hay Park lends a little breathing space to this otherwise austere district. The traditional Chinese pavilion was a gift from the people of Taipei. On Saturdays in August you can catch a free outdoor movie here beginning at sunset. Also look out for Asian dance and licensed buskers.

DONNIE CHIN INTERNATIONAL CHILDREN'S PARK
PARK

Map p234 (☑206-684-4075; 700 S Lane St; ⊗6am-10pm; 🚻; 🚊First Hill Streetcar) If your offspring aren't up for exploring the Asian markets or sitting still for a dim-sum brunch, then bring them to this diminutive coming-up-for-air park with a bronze dragon sculpture crying out to be climbed on. It was designed by George Tsutakawa, a Seattle native who spent much of his childhood in Japan, then returned to become an internationally renowned sculptor and painter, and a professor at the University of Washington.

⊙ SoDo

LIVING COMPUTERS: MUSEUM + LABS
MUSEUM

(☑206-342-2020; https://livingcomputers.org; 2245 1st Ave S; adult/child $18/free; ⊗10am-6pm Tue-Sun; 🚊SoDo) Founded by Microsoft co-founder, Paul Allen (1953–2018), this place will evoke heavy nostalgia in anyone who can remember the world pre-internet. Hosted in a nondescript commercial building in industrial SoDo and little known even among locals, it's well worth checking out for its host of antediluvian computers with their blinking green cursors and black, app-free screens. Some of them are large enough to fill an average-sized student bedroom.

Friendly guides give regular tours and you're welcome to 'play' on many of the exhibits.

 EATING

Pioneer Square has changed in recent years with old-school steak and seafood houses being replaced by the kind of chic, rustic restaurants that are more redolent of French kitchens. There's a similar proliferation of gourmet sandwich bars.

The ID can be split into three parts. Japantown, which, while light on sushi, has a few beloved authentic dining and drinking establishments; Chinatown is notable for its dim-sum restaurants and late-night eating options; and Little Saigon, east of 8th Ave S and I-5, is, as you can imagine, a paragon of Vietnamese food.

✖ Pioneer Square

IL CORVO PASTA
ITALIAN $

Map p234 (☑206-538-0999; www.ilcorvopasta. com; 217 James St; pasta $10; ⊗11am-3pm Mon-Fri; 🚊Pioneer Sq) This hole-in-the-wall, pasta-only place has limited seating and a high turnover of office workers on their lunch breaks. Join the perennial queue, order one of three daily pastas with sauces and grab a seat (if there's one available). You have to bus your own table, Seattle-style, at the end. Wine and bread provide welcome accompaniments.

LADY YUM
BAKERY $

Map p234 (www.ladyyum.com; 116 S Washington St; 1/10 macarons $2.25/20; ⊗8am-10pm; 🚊Pioneer Sq) The macarons at this high-femme Pioneer Square bakery are about as good as they get outside of Paris. Flavors like honey-lavender and chili-mango give things a nice touch of Seattle innovation.

★SALUMI ARTISAN CURED MEATS
SANDWICHES $

Map p234 (☑206-621-8772; www.salumicured meats.com; 404 Occidental Ave S; sandwiches $10.50-12.50; ⊗11am-3pm Mon-Sat; 🚊International District/Chinatown) This well-loved deli used to be known for the long lines at it's tiny storefront, and although they've moved to a bigger spot, you can still expect a wait for the legendary Italian-quality salami and cured-meat sandwiches (grilled lamb, pork shoulder, meatballs). You can expect a regular sandwich menu, as well as daily sandwich, soup and pasta specials.

BISCUIT BITCH
SOUTHERN US $

Map p234 (☑206-623-1859; https://biscuit bitch.com; 621 3rd Ave; mains $7-10; ⊗7am-2pm Mon-Fri, 8am-3pm Sat & Sun; 🚊Pioneer Sq) Biscuit Bitch proudly bills itself as trailer-park cuisine, which will only be off-putting to those who haven't experienced the nirvana of tucking into an order of thick, crumbly biscuits and rich gravy. This is one location of a small local chain and things are always busy, but the line moves fast and the staff are a blast.

DELICATUS
SANDWICHES, DELI **$**

Map p234 (☑206-623-3780; www.delicatus seattle.com; 103 1st Ave S; sandwiches $10-13; ☉11am-6pm Mon-Fri; 🚋Pioneer Sq) Delicatus is a new-school Pioneer Square sandwich bar-deli where the sarnies are a bit more deluxe than yesteryear, being both well-stuffed and enlivened with interesting relishes. Go at lunchtime for the best atmosphere.

GRAND CENTRAL BAKING CO
SOUP, SANDWICHES **$**

Map p234 (☑206-622-3644; www.grandcentral bakery.com; Grand Central Arcade, 214 1st Ave S; sandwiches $6-12; ☉7am-5pm Mon-Fri, 8am-4pm Sat; 🚋First Hill Streetcar) Grand Central – located in the eponymous building (p67) – is considered one of the best bakeries in Seattle. Its artisanal breads can be bought whole or sliced up for sandwiches in its cafe and enjoyed in the red-brick confines of the Grand Central mall, or at a Eurochic table in Occidental Park (p66) just outside. Beware the lunchtime queues.

CAFE PALOMA
TURKISH **$**

Map p234 (☑206-405-1920; www.cafepaloma. com; 93 Yesler Way; meze $6-10; ☉10am-6pm Mon, to 9pm Tue-Sat; 🚋Pioneer Sq) Various words spring to mind when thinking of Cafe Paloma: Bistro. Eggplant. Casual. Friendly. Turkish. Meze. Music. Lemonade. Falafel. If any of this sounds interesting, be sure to drop by this jewel of a restaurant in Pioneer Square where small Turkish miracles are concocted.

★LONDON PLANE
CAFE, DELI **$$**

Map p234 (☑206-624-1374; www.thelondon planeseattle.com; 300 Occidental Ave S; small plates $7-19; ☉8am-6pm Mon-Fri, from 9am Sat, 9am-3pm Sun; 🚋First Hill Streetcar) 🥗 Matt Dillon (the Seattle chef, not the Hollywood actor) moved less than a block from his now-closed Bar Sajor to open London Plane, a hybrid cafe, flower shop, deli and breakfast spot that maintains the French country kitchen feel that has become Dillon's trademark.

Sustainability is the overriding theme here. The open prep area is piled high with fresh herbs and myriad foraged plants waiting to be scattered into soups, salads and sandwiches.

INTERMEZZO CARMINE
ITALIAN **$$**

Map p234 (☑206-596-8940; http://intermezzo carmine.com; 409 1st Ave S; small plates $9-14; ☉11:30am-midnight Mon-Thu, to 1am Fri, 4pm-1am Sat; 🚋First Hill Streetcar) Lights that twinkle when they catch your eye, comfy bar seating, high-end furnishings and, of course, delicious pasta give Intermezzo Carmine a plush, New York–Italian restaurant feel. The portions here are small and each dish is priced accordingly: a bonus as you're likely to see a few things on the menu you want to try.

DAMN THE WEATHER
MODERN AMERICAN **$$**

Map p234 (☑206-946-1283; www.damnthe weather.com; 116 1st Ave S; small plates $12-18; ☉11am-11pm Sun-Wed, to midnight Thu-Sat; 🚋First Hill Streetcar) Repeating a mantra that flows freely from the lips of many Seattleites, this well-regarded venture is perhaps best described as a cocktail bar that also serves great food. The interior is typical Pioneer Square – all wooden floors, bare-brick walls and low-lit chandeliers – and the clientele leans heavy toward the younger creative professional crowd.

★NIRMAL'S
INDIAN **$$$**

Map p234 (☑206-388-2196; www.nirmalseattle. com; 106 Occidental Ave S; mains $17-27; ☉11am-2pm & 5:30-10pm Mon-Fri, 5:30-10pm Sat; 🚋Pioneer Sq) In a short period of time Nirmal's has established itself as Seattle's premier Indian fine-dining experience. The menu is a good balance of recognizable curry and tandoori dishes, as well as treats only familiar to those who have been to the subcontinent and exciting fusion plates that nod to its PNW locale (we're looking at you Dungeness crab curry).

✗ International District

TAMARIND TREE
VIETNAMESE **$**

Map p234 (☑206-860-1414; www.tamarindtree restaurant.com; 1036 S Jackson St; mains $10-13; ☉10am-10pm Sun-Thu, to 11pm Fri & Sat; 🚋First Hill Streetcar) Serving upscale food at entry-level prices in a massively popular

GOING UNDERGROUND

It's hard to envisage today, but Pioneer Square's streets were originally 12ft to 30ft lower than their present levels. After the 1889 fire, city planners decided to raise the street level in order to solve long-standing problems with tidal flooding. Hence, the post-fire buildings were constructed with an extra ground floor in anticipation of the impending, but lengthy, regrade. This spooky underground world of abandoned cellars and sidewalks lay forgotten for decades, but was rediscovered and opened to tourists in the 1960s by local historian, Bill Speidel. The tours (p77) are still popular today.

dining room, this legendary place has a nuanced menu that includes everything from satays and salad rolls to *pho* and rice cakes (squid-, prawn- and pork-filled fried crepes). Tamarind Tree donates some of its profits to the Vietnam Scholarship Foundation. It's hidden at the back of an ugly car park.

Where else can you get seven courses of beef (lunch/dinner $35/42) prepared in a variety of Vietnamese styles?

SZECHUAN NOODLE BOWL　　SICHUAN $
Map p234 (☑206-623-4198; 420 8th Ave S; mains $5-10; ◎11:30am-9pm Tue-Sun; ☐First Hill Streetcar) A little more than a hole-in-the-wall, this restaurant is popular with locals for its simple and traditional Chinese dishes ranging from green onion pancakes and spicy pickled cabbage to vegetable dumplings and spicy beef noodle soup. Almost always, you'll see one or two staff members making dumplings at a table in the dining room.

MIKE'S NOODLE HOUSE　　CHINESE $
Map p234 (☑206-389-7099; 418 Maynard Ave S; mains $6-8; ◎9:30am-8pm Sun-Wed, to 9pm Fri & Sat; ☐First Hill Streetcar) Known by local Chinese diners as one of the best wonton noodle houses in Seattle, Mike's Noodle House is a quick and easy way to satisfy your cravings for slurp-worthy noodles and a piping-hot broth.

DOUGH ZONE　　DUMPLINGS $
Map p234 (☑206-285-9999; www.doughzone dumplinghouse.com; 504 5th Ave S; dumplings $5-12; ◎11am-10pm; ☐International District/Chinatown) The gooey soup dumplings at this bright and modern restaurant are quite literally bursting with flavor. They've become a bit of a local sensation – visit in the afternoon to dine with office workers gossiping on their lunch breaks and at

dinner to sit among first dates and other curious tourists.

SHANGHAI GARDEN　　CHINESE $
Map p234 (☑206-625-1688; www.theshanghai garden.com; 524 6th Ave S; mains $10-18; ◎11am-9:30pm Sun-Thu, to 10:30 Fri & Sat; ☐First Hill Streetcar) Hand-shaved barley noodles are the specialty of Shanghai Garden and, frankly, they trounce all expectations you might ordinarily have of a noodle. They're wide and chewy, almost meaty, and just barely dressed with perky spinach and globs of chicken, tofu, beef or shrimp.

JADE GARDEN　　CHINESE $
Map p234 (☑206-622-8181; 424 7th Ave S; dim-sum items $2-4, mains $8-13; ◎10am-2:30am Mon-Sat, to 1am Sun; ☐First Hill Streetcar) Usually mentioned near the top of the list of best places for dim sum in the ID, Jade Garden offers a good range of delicacies with everything from standard, newbie-friendly shrimp dumplings and steamed pork buns to more exotic plates such as black cylinders of sesame-paste gel and, of course, chicken's feet.

PHO BAC　　VIETNAMESE $
Map p234 (☑206-568-0882; www.thephobac. com; 1240 S Jackson St; pho from $9.75; ◎10am-9pm Mon-Fri, from 10:30am Sat, 11am-8pm Sun; ☐First Hill Streetcar) Pho Bac was once the type of dive where your table was always dirty, but the food was absolutely worth it. It's now a bit more spruced up, but excellent *pho* and other Vietnamese dishes can still be found at this bright spot in the heart of Little Saigon.

GREEN LEAF　　VIETNAMESE $
Map p234 (☑206-340-1388; www.greenleaf taste.com; 418 8th Ave S; mains $9-13; ◎11am-10pm; ☐First Hill Streetcar) Popular Green Leaf, located in Chinatown, shoots out

rapid-fire dishes from its tiny kitchen that abuts a dining room not much wider than a railway carriage. Choose the traditional *pho* or go for the excellent rice- or vermicelli-noodle dishes – especially the *bún đắc biệt* (with pork, chicken and shrimp).

★MANEKI
JAPANESE $$

Map p234 (☎206-622-2631; www.maneki restaurant.com; 304 6th Ave S; mains $14-26; ⊗5:30-10:30pm Tue-Sun; ⊡First Hill Streetcar) For an unforgettable dining experience make a reservation for one of Maneki's tatami mat dining rooms (paper and wood lattice private chambers with seating on the floor) and feast on a meal of traditional Japanese cuisine and sake. The fish here is legendarily fresh and the bar (open until midnight) is full of friendly conversation.

Maneki opened in 1904 and in its original iteration was a three-story megarestaurant that served 500 people a night on the weekends. It has downsized quite a bit since, but feels no less authentic and extraordinary.

Reservations for the tatami mat rooms, which hold four to 10 people, should be made at least two weeks in advance.

★7 STAR PEPPER
SICHUAN $$

Map p234 (☎206-568-6446; www.sevenstars pepper.com; 1207 S Jackson St; mains $9-20; ⊗11am-3pm & 5-9:30pm Mon-Wed, 11am-9:30pm Thu, to 10pm Fri & Sat, to 9pm Sun; ⊡First Hill Streetcar) Don't be put off by 7 Star Pepper's location on the 2nd floor of a run-down strip mall: this Szechuan restaurant is one of the best in the city. Everything on the menu is exceptional, but the hand-cut *dan dan* noodles are a must-order. They are thick and flavorful with the just the right amount of chewiness.

TSUKUSHINBO
JAPANESE $$

Map p234 (☎206-467-4004; 515 S Main St; mains $11-30; ⊗5-10pm Mon-Thu, to 11pm Fri, 11am-2pm & 5-11pm Sat, to 9:30pm Sun; ⊡International District/Chinatown) A nondescript Japanese sushi and ramen joint, Tsukushinbo is frequented by locals and tourists alike for its fresh and affordable seafood, which ranges from simple melt-in-your-mouth salmon to sweet *amaebi* (spot prawn), topped with a raw quail egg. A busy, no-frills dining environment, Tsukushinbo somehow feels authentic, comfortable and classy all at the same time. Reservations are highly recommended.

PURPLE DOT CAFÉ
CHINESE $$

Map p234 (☎206-622-0288; www.purpledot seattle.com; 515 Maynard Ave S; mains $9-20; ⊗9am-2am Sun-Thu, to 3:30am Fri & Sat; ⊡First Hill Streetcar) The Purple Dot looks like the inside of an '80s video game (yes, it's actually purple) and draws a late-night, drunken disco crowd on weekends, but most of the time it's a calm, quiet place to get dim sum and Macao-style specialties (meaning you can feast on baked spaghetti and French toast along with your Hong Kong favorites).

✖ SoDo

CAFE CON LECHE
CUBAN $

(☎206-682-7557; www.cafeconlecheseattle.com; 2901 1st Ave S; mains $10-16; ⊗11am-4pm Mon-Wed, to 7pm Thu & Fri; ⊡SoDo) It's worth the trip to SoDo to visit Cafe con Leche in its colorful abode, a former food truck that has sprouted foundations. Sit down and dig into the *ropa vieja* (spicy beef stew) or *puerco asado* (roast pork) accompanied by rice and beans and washed down with a *cafecito* (strong sweet espresso).

🍷 DRINKING & NIGHTLIFE

Though it lends itself more to frenzied clubbing than casual pint-sipping, Pioneer Square is home to some of the city's oldest and most atmospheric bars. If you prefer a saloon to a salon, this historical part of town is your best bet. Beware: things get particularly lively (and crowded) on sports game days.

The lounges inside many of the restaurants in the ID are good haunts for hiding away with a sake any time of day. The ID is also the place to come for all things tea (boba, herbal or otherwise).

★SAKÉ NOMI
SAKE

Map p234 (☎206-467-7253; www.sakenomi.us; 76 S Washington St, Pioneer Sq; flight of 3 $22; ⊗2-10pm Tue, Wed, Fri & Sat, from 5pm Thu, 2-6pm Sun; ⊡First Hill Streetcar) Regardless if you're a sake (Japanese rice wine) connoisseur or casual enjoyer, you're likely to expand your palate and your cultural horizons at this cozy retailer and tasting room in Pioneer Square. The Japanese and

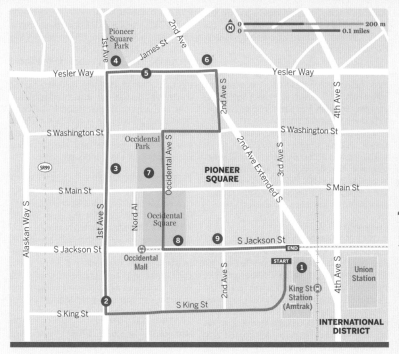

🏃 Neighborhood Walk
Historical Pioneer Square Circuit

START KING STREET STATION
END KING STREET STATION
LENGTH 1 MILE; ONE HOUR

Start at ① **King Street Station** (p68), Seattle's main train terminus, now returned to its Gilded Age glory. Exiting via the side door, walk west along King St in the shadow of CenturyLink Field, home of Seattle's football and soccer teams; the bars and restaurants here are packed with noisy supporters on match days. Turn right onto redbrick ② **1st Ave S**, little altered since it rose in the aftermath of the 1889 fire. Galleries and antique shops will catch your eye, but be sure to drift into the ③ **Grand Central Baking Co** (p70), in the arcade of the same name, for cakes and sandwiches. ④ **Pioneer Square Park** (p67) is usually awash with tourists and unhoused people selling the newspaper *Real Change*. The small triangular park sports an Eiffel-esque iron pergola and the Richardsonian Romanesque Pioneer Building. Leading east,

⑤ **Yesler Way** (p66) holds the distinction of being the nation's original 'skid row.' The appearance of the ugly concrete car park on James St convinced the city to introduce greater conservationist measures in the 1960s. You can divert on the corner with 2nd Ave for a quick glance at the neoclassical ⑥ **Smith Tower** (p68), erected by LC Smith, a man who built his fortune on typewriters (Smith-Corona) and guns (Smith & Wesson). Head south on 2nd Ave S and go right on Washington St S; ⑦ **Occidental Park** (p66), with its ivy-covered edifices and resident food carts and games, quickly opens out on your left. Grab a bite to eat and treat yourself to a game of Cornhole. Cross Main St into Occidental Square before heading left on ⑧ **S Jackson St**. In the 1890s, S Jackson's stores outfitted prospectors heading for the Klondike, Canada. Fill in your historical gaps at the intellectually stimulating ⑨ **Klondike Gold Rush National Historical Park** (p66) before pacing back to King Street Station.

American wife-husband duo who run the place have a clear love for what they do, which shows in their wonderfully educational tasting menu.

★ZEITGEIST COFFEE CAFE

Map p234 (📞206-583-0497; www.zeitgeist coffee.com; 171 S Jackson St, Pioneer Sq; ⏰6am-7pm Mon-Fri, from 7am Sat, 8am-6pm Sun; 🛜; 🚊First Hill Streetcar) Possibly Seattle's best (if also busiest) indie coffee bar, Zeitgeist brews smooth *doppio macchiatos* to go with its sweet almond croissants and other luscious baked goods. The atmosphere is trendy industrial, with brick walls and large windows for people-watching. Soups, salads and sandwiches are also on offer.

PANAMA HOTEL TEA & COFFEE HOUSE CAFE

Map p234 (📞206-515-4000; www.panamahotel. net; 607 S Main St, International District; tea $3-6; ⏰8am-9pm; 🛜; 🚊First Hill Streetcar) The intensely atmospheric teahouse inside the Panama Hotel has such a thoroughly back-in-time feel that you'll be reluctant to pull out your laptop (although there is wi-fi). It's in a National Treasure–designated 1910 building containing the only remaining Japanese bathhouse in the US, and doubles as a memorial to the neighborhood's Japanese residents forced into internment camps during WWII.

BAD BISHOP BAR

Map p234 (📞206-623-3440; www.facebook. com/badbishopbar; 704 1st Ave, Pioneer Sq; ⏰11:30am-10pm Mon & Wed-Sat, from 10am Sun; 🚊Pioneer Sq) This relative newcomer to Pioneer Square offers modern, high-end pub fare without a hefty price tag for their solid craft cocktails and fun small-plate offerings. In fact most items on the menu are $10 and under, making it a great spot to settle in for a few rounds.

CAFFÈ UMBRIA CAFE

Map p234 (📞206-624-5847; www.caffeumbria. com; 320 Occidental Ave S, Pioneer Sq; ⏰6am-6pm Mon-Fri, from 7am Sat, 8am-5pm Sun; 🚊First Hill Streetcar) Started by an Italian immigrant from Perugia, Umbria has a true Italian flavor with its 8oz cappuccinos, chatty clientele, pretty Italianate tiles and breadsticks so fresh they must have been teleported over from the mother country. Ideal for Italophiles and Starbucks-phobes.

PYRAMID ALE HOUSE CRAFT BEER

Map p234 (📞206-682-3377; www.pyramidbrew. com; 1201 1st Ave S, SoDo; ⏰11am-9pm; 🚊Stadium) In SoDo by T-Mobile Park, this brewpub has the cleaned-up-industrial feel – all bricks and brass and designer lighting – that defines modern Pacific Northwest design. It's a nice mainstream (but still appreciably Seattle-ish) place to take your parents or tenderfoot visitors. But don't even try on a game day, unless you want to squeeze into the standing-room-only beer tent outdoors.

ELM COFFEE ROASTERS COFFEE

Map p234 (📞206-445-7808; www.elmcoffee roasters.com; 240 2nd Ave S, Pioneer Sq; ⏰7am-6pm Mon-Fri, from 8am Sat, 8am-2pm Sun; 🛜; 🚊First Hill Streetcar) Currently one of Seattle's freshest coffee 'freshmen,' Elm opened in December 2014 in a spacious cafe-cum-roasting room in Pioneer Square. It's a good indie option if you're after a quick sweet snack and a cup of something home-roasted. The entrance is on Main St.

CENTRAL SALOON PUB

Map p234 (📞206-622-0209; www.central saloon.com; 207 1st Ave S, Pioneer Sq; ⏰11am-2am; 🚊First Hill Streetcar) It may be two years younger than the official 'Oldest Bar in Seattle' (Georgetown's Jules Maes; p171), but the Central isn't exactly modern. More of a locals' hangout than an object of historical interest, this long, narrow joint makes grotty bathrooms and blah food seem charming, by virtue of cheap suds, friendly barkeeps and a comfortable, unfussy vibe. Nirvana, Soundgarden and most of the grunge nobility have played here, and live music still happens regularly.

FUEL SPORTS BAR

Map p234 (📞206-405-3835; www.fuelseattle. com; 164 S Washington St, Pioneer Sq; ⏰3-10pm Mon, to midnight Tue & Thu, to 2am Wed, 11:30am-2am Fri & Sat, to 10pm Sun; 🚊Pioneer Sq) This TV-filled sports bar is the favored spot in Pioneer Square for Mariners and Seahawks fans on game day. Tuck your elbows in and inhale deeply as you enter.

SEATTLE BEST TEA TEAHOUSE

Map p234 (📞206-749-9855; www.seattle besttea.com; 506 S King St, International District; ⏰10:30am-8pm Sun-Thu, to 9pm Fri & Sat; 🚊First Hill Streetcar) This aptly named tea shop has a huge selection of loose-leaf

SODO – A NEIGHBORHOOD ON THE RISE
· ·

The baton for Seattle's most ascendant neighborhood has recently been passed to SoDo, an acronym for the sketchy industrial district SOuth of DOwntown dominated by Seattle's two professional sports stadiums, CenturyLink Field and T-Mobile Park.

A tangled confusion of train tracks, boxy warehouses and concrete overpasses regularly rattled by low-flying airplanes, SoDo is not as homogeneous or community-focused as other Seattle neighborhoods, though this hasn't prevented a number of emerging businesses from setting up shop here. Starbucks was an early convert, moving the company's main headquarters into a vintage red-brick building just off 1st Ave S in 1993. In the last few years, it has been joined by an eclectic mix of newer aspirants, including a micro-distillery (p77); a flagship Filson store (p76), the original Klondike outfitters; a computer museum (p69) created by Microsoft co-founder Paul Allen (1953–2018); and a handful of weed dispensaries. In fact the proliferation of dispensaries has led some to facetiously refer to SoDo as SoDope or 'Little Amsterdam.' Current outlets include the city's first recreational cannabis store, Cannabis City (p77), and Ganja Goddess (p77), another early starter that runs a special shuttle to and from downtown. Aside from its fanatically supported sports teams, SoDo has several downbeat bars and a decent brewpub, the Pyramid Ale House (p74), which is popular with sports fans.

SoDo isn't an obvious walking neighborhood, although many of its sights can be easily accessed from Pioneer Square by strolling south on 1st Ave S. Another entry point is West Seattle, which is linked to SoDo via the 'Duwamish Trail' (a designated biking/hiking path) and bus 21.

blends. It is are also known for having some of the best boba tea in the International District, which is no small distinction.

⭐ ENTERTAINMENT

Entertainment primarily means sport in this neck of the woods: Seattle's two main stadiums overshadow Pioneer Square. There are a few music venues and spots for karaoke as well.

SEATTLE SEAHAWKS   FOOTBALL
Map p234 (www.seahawks.com; 800 Occidental Ave S, SoDo; 🚇Stadium) The Seahawks play at CenturyLink Field and have the loudest supporters in the NFL. Honors remained elusive until the mid-2010s when they won the Super Bowl in February 2014 and were runners-up the following year.

SEATTLE SOUNDERS   SOCCER
Map p234 (📞206-622-3415; www.soundersfc.com; 800 Occidental Ave S, SoDo; 🚇Stadium) Far and away the best supported soccer team in North America with average gates of over 40,000, the Sounders joined the MLS (Major League Soccer) in 2009. They play at CenturyLink Field from March through October.

CENTURYLINK FIELD   STADIUM
Map p234 (www.centurylinkfield.com; 800 Occidental Ave S, SoDo; 🚇Stadium) The late, mostly unlamented Kingdome, long Seattle's biggest eyesore, was once the home field for the city's professional baseball and football franchises. Then it was imploded spectacularly in 2000 and replaced by this 72,000-seat stadium, home of the NFL Seattle Seahawks and Seattle's soccer team, the Sounders.

SEATTLE MARINERS   BASEBALL
Map p234 (www.mariners.org; 1250 1st Ave S, SoDo; 🚇Stadium) Seattle's battling baseball team might not have enjoyed the recent success of the Seahawks (NFL) and the Sounders (MLS), but they're vociferously supported. Even better, local rapper Macklemore once wrote a song about them ('My oh my'). They play at T-Mobile Park from April to September.

COMEDY UNDERGROUND   COMEDY
Map p234 (📞206-628-0303; www.comedy underground.com; 109 S Washington St, Pioneer Sq; 🚋First Hill Streetcar) The best comedy club in Seattle has shows most nights, with a second show common on Friday and Saturday. Talent is mainly local and there's a full bar, plus a pizza-and-burger-style

THE SOUND OF THE SOUNDERS

If you think soccer is a niche sport in the US inspiring little of the passion and noise of American football and baseball, you obviously haven't been to Seattle. The Seattle Sounders (p75), the third incarnation of Seattle's main soccer club that launched in 2008, are the best supported Major League Soccer (MLS) team, garnering more than twice as many home supporters as local baseball team the Mariners. Indeed, their average home gates currently top out at 43,000, higher than many high-ranking English Premier League teams.

Sounders fans, who are organized into half a dozen supporters groups, are famous for their highly musical 'March to the Match' which kicks off from Occidental Park (p66) in Pioneer Square a good couple of hours before the real kickoff. There's plenty to shout about. Since 2009, the team has won an unprecedented four US Open Cups and – perhaps, more importantly – the hallowed Supporter's Shield (the MLS championship) in 2014.

food menu. Monday is open mike, a crapshoot of the surprisingly good or the skin-crawlingly bad. Buy tickets through **TicketWeb** (☑866-468-3399; www.ticketweb. com), preferably in advance.

NORDO'S CULINARIUM
THEATER

Map p234 (☑206-209-2002; www.cafenordo. com; 109 S Main St, Pioneer Sq; ⊡First Hill Streetcar) A theatrical group with culinary inclinations, Cafe Nordo marries two themes in one – food and theater – putting on inspired plays-cum-dinner shows where the performers double as the waitstaff. It's a unique formula first hatched in 2009 when the then-homeless group put on occasional plays in Fremont's Theo Chocolate factory.

SHOWBOX SODO
LIVE MUSIC

Map p234 (www.showboxpresents.com; 1700 1st Ave S, SoDo; ⊡Stadium) The newer sister-club of downtown's Showbox (p58), this SoDo version is actually bigger with a capacity for 1800 in an old warehouse. Touring rock bands play here.

🛍 SHOPPING

Not surprisingly, given its historical importance to the city, Pioneer Square is the place to shop for antiques. It's also a good place to find reasonably priced artwork and crafts by local artists, particularly blown glass and traditional art by coastal Native American artists.

In addition to the behemoth Uwajimaya, it's worth exploring the nooks and crannies of the ID for odd storefronts and imported Asian wares.

SoDo's best shopping is at its weed dispensaries.

⭐ FILSON
SPORTS & OUTDOORS

Map p234 (☑206-622-3147; www.filson.com; 1741 1st Ave S, SoDo; ⊙10am-6pm Mon-Sat, noon-5pm Sun; ⊡Stadium) Founded in 1897 as the original outfitters for prospectors heading for the Klondike, Filson is a long-standing Seattle legend that, in 2015, opened up this hugely impressive flagship store in SoDo. Wall-mounted bison heads and sepia-toned photos evoke the Klondike spirit, while flop-down sofas and literary tomes encourage lingering. Then there's the gear: topquality bags, outdoor jackets and clothing durable enough to survive another gold rush or two. Even better, much of the stuff is designed and made on-site (you can view people working through a glass screen).

UWAJIMAYA
MALL

Map p234 (☑206-624-6248; www.uwajimaya. com; 600 5th Ave S, International District; ⊙8am-10pm Mon-Sat, 9am-9pm Sun; ⊡First Hill Streetcar) Founded by Fujimatsu Moriguchi, one of the few Japanese Americans to return here from the WWII internment camps, this large department and grocery store – a cornerstone of Seattle's Asian community – has everything from fresh fish and exotic fruits and vegetables to cooking utensils and homegoods. It's a terrific place to go gift shopping.

PINK GORILLA GAMES
VIDEO GAMES

Map p234 (☑206-547-5790; www.pinkgorilla games.com; 601 S King St, International District; ⊡First Hill Streetcar) Rare retro games from the old-school Nintendo and Atari days, new releases, toys and collectables – you'll find it all at this neon-pink shop in the International District. Browsing the packed shelves is a fun way to get a nostalgia high, should you have an affinity for the video games of yesteryear.

GANJA GODDESS DISPENSARY
(✆206-682-7220; www.ganjagoddessseattle.com; 3207 1st Ave S, SoDo; ⏰8am-11pm Mon-Sat, 10am-9pm Sun; 🚋SoDo) Ganja Goddess is a popular weed dispensary known for its helpful and unpretentious staff and free shuttle service picking and dropping off clients in and around Seattle's downtown core. It has a great selection and takes debit and credit cards.

SILVER PLATTERS MUSIC
(✆206-283-3472; www.silverplatters.com; 2930 1st Ave S, SoDo; ⏰10am-10pm Mon-Sat, 11am-7pm Sun; 🚋SoDo) Something of a record supermarket bivouacked out in SoDo offering CDs and vinyl. The selection is extremely broad and the staff are pretty knowledgeable.

GLASSHOUSE STUDIO ARTS & CRAFTS
Map p234 (✆206-682-9939; 311 Occidental Ave S, Pioneer Sq; ⏰10am-5pm Mon-Sat, 11am-4pm Sun; 🚋First Hill Streetcar) The Seattle area is known for its Pilchuck School of glassblowing art, and this is the city's oldest glassblowing studio. Stop by to watch the artists in action and pick up a memento right at the source. Demonstrations are held 10am to 11:30am and 1pm to 5pm Monday through Saturday.

CANNABIS CITY DISPENSARY
(✆206-420-4206; www.cannabiscity.us; 2733 4th Ave S, SoDo; ⏰8am-11pm; 🚋SoDo) Seattle's first licensed 'recreational' weed dispensary opened in July 2014 to long queues. Since then it has been joined by quite a few more stores, but it still provides helpful service and a generous selection. Bonus: it takes debit cards.

GLOBE BOOKSTORE BOOKS
Map p234 (✆206-682-6882; 218 1st Ave S, Pioneer Sq; ⏰11am-6pm; 🚋First Hill Streetcar) This small but comfortably cramped shop is an erudite emporium of new and second-hand books, not all of which make it on to the shelves.

KINOKUNIYA BOOKS
Map p234 (✆206-587-2477; www.kinokuniya.com; 525 S Weller St, International District; ⏰10am-9pm Mon-Sat, to 8pm Sun; 🚋First Hill Streetcar) A great source for hard-to-find imported books and magazines in Asian languages (and in English about Asian culture), this bookstore inside Uwajimaya is also one of the few shops in the country where you can buy the lesser-known films of Kinji Fukasaku and other masters of Asian cinema on DVD.

🏃 SPORTS & ACTIVITIES

⭐**WESTLAND DISTILLERY** DISTILLERY
(✆206-767-7250; www.westlanddistillery.com; 2931 1st Ave S, SoDo; tour $17.34; ⏰noon-7pm Tue-Thu, 11am-8pm Fri & Sat, noon-6pm Sun, tours noon-4pm Wed-Sat; 🚌50) On a drizzly day in Puget Sound, the damp essence of Seattle isn't a million miles from the Western Isles of Scotland, a comparison that hasn't been lost on the whiskey-makers of Westland, arguably one of Seattle's finest distilleries. From its plush tasting room and factory in SoDo, this company is breaking seals on some already legendary micro-distilled single malt.

You can taste it in a number of Seattle's burgeoning whiskey bars, or – better still – visit Westland's SoDo headquarters for an informal but informative distillery tour followed by a throat-warming tipple of the 'water of life.'

BILL SPEIDEL'S UNDERGROUND TOUR WALKING
Map p234 (✆206-682-4646; www.undergroundtour.com; 608 1st Ave, Pioneer Sq; adult/senior/child $22/20/10; ⏰departs every hour 10am-6pm Oct-Mar, 9am-7pm Apr-Sep; 🚋Pioneer Sq) This cleverly conceived tour of Seattle's historic 'underground' – the part of the city that got buried by landfill in the 1890s – benefits from its guides, who are excellent, using wit and animation to relate Seattle's unusual early history.

The tour starts at Doc Maynard's Public House with a lighthearted preamble and progresses through a series of subterranean walkways whose shabbiness adds to their authenticity. It is massively popular, especially in prime tourist season, so book ahead via the official website where possible. There are extra tours on the half-hour daily between 9:30am and 4:30pm June through August.

Music & Nightlife

Detroit, New Orleans, Nashville...Seattle! There aren't many cities in the US that can claim to have redirected the path of modern music. But, while the angry firmament of grunge may have faded since the demise of Nirvana et al, the city's rambunctious nightlife scene remains varied and vital.

OSCAR C. WILLIAMS/SHUTTERSTOCK ©

CHECUBUS/SHUTTERSTOCK ©

1. Moore Theatre (p96)
This historic venue is a pillar of Seattle's music scene.

2. Outdoor live music
Al fresco events and street performers abound in summer, particularly around the Seattle Center (p94).

3. Dimitriou's Jazz Alley (p95)
A saxophonist performs at the jazz hotspot.

4. MoPOP's musical foyer (p86)
IF VI WAS IX by sound sculptor Trimpin.

WORLDFOTO/ALAMY ©

Belltown & Seattle Center

Neighborhood Top Five

1 **Chihuly Garden & Glass** (p84) Pondering the shimmering glass art that sprang from the creative mind of Dale Chihuly in Chihuly Garden and Glass underneath the Space Needle.

2 **Olympic Sculpture Park** (p87) Watching the sun slip behind faraway mountains from the grassy slopes of the Olympic Sculpture Park.

3 **Space Needle** (p82) Taking an elevator to the top of the city and marveling at the origins of the innovation and tech boom.

4 **Bars of 2nd Ave** (p92) Stringing together an elongated bar crawl in the dive-y and not-so-dive-y bars of 2nd Ave.

5 **Museum of Pop Culture** (p86) Plugging in a guitar at the Sound Lab and pretending you're Jimi Hendrix.

For more detail of this area see Map p238 ➡

Explore Belltown & Seattle Center

Belltown's compact, relatively flat and easily walkable core is long on dining and entertainment options but relatively short on daytime attractions. The exception is the Olympic Sculpture Park (p87), a grassy art garden that anchors the neighborhood and snares visitors strolling between Pike Place Market and the Seattle Center.

Capitol Hillers might disagree, but Belltown's main nightlife zone (1st and 2nd Aves between Blanchard and Battery Sts) is the best place in the city to string together a bar-hopping evening out. A few of the grunge-era landmarks are still in business, but these days distorted guitars compete with the chatter of the cocktail crowd. Whatever your fashion affiliations, Belltown's after-dark scene is hip and noisy and rarely stands still. Watch out for drunken hipsters and sidewalk vomit.

The Seattle Center, site of the highly successful 1962 World's Fair, is Belltown in reverse; sights and museums abound, but you'll struggle to find any memorable food. The solution: spend most of your sightseeing time in the Seattle Center (Museum of Pop Culture (p86), Chihuly Garden & Glass (p84), and the Space Needle (p82) merit a day between them) and escape to adjacent Belltown for lunch, drinks and dinner.

Local Life

Serious Pie It's all communal tables at Tom Douglas' riotously popular pizza restaurant, where you can discuss weird pizza toppings, microbrews and where Seattle's culinary maestro might open up next.

Dives Belltown hangs onto a few dive bars where bike messengers chat to old rockers and 'feedback' still means a noise that emanates from an electric guitar. Try 5 Point Café (p94) or Shorty's (p94).

Getting There & Away

Bus Dozens of metro buses cross through Belltown, originating from every part of the city.

Monorail It runs every 10 minutes between downtown's Westlake Center, at Pine St and 4th Ave, and the Seattle Center. Tickets cost $2.50/1.25 per adult/child. The journey takes two minutes.

Walking Lacking busy arterial roads and steep hills, Belltown is a highly walkable neighborhood and easily reached on foot from downtown, Pike Place Market, the Seattle Center and Lower Queen Anne.

Lonely Planet's Top Tip

Many people – including a lot of locals – consider the Space Needle to be an expensive tourist trap. If you're on a budget, you might be better off investing your money in tickets for the **Museum of Pop Culture** (p86) or **Chihuly Garden & Glass** (p84). You can get a free nearly-as-good view of Seattle from **Kerry Park** (p103) in the nearby Queen Anne neighborhood.

✖ Best Places to Eat

➝ Top Pot Hand-Forged Doughnuts (p89)

➝ Tavolàta (p91)

➝ Serious Pie (p90)

➝ Macrina (p89)

➝ FOB Poke Bar (p89)

For reviews, see p89.➡

♟ Best Places to Drink

➝ Rendezvous (p92)

➝ Shorty's (p94)

➝ 5 Point Café (p94)

➝ Bedlam (p94)

➝ Queen City (p92)

For reviews, see p92.➡

◉ Best Entertainment

➝ Crocodile (p95)

➝ Dimitriou's Jazz Alley (p95)

➝ McCaw Hall (p95)

➝ Cinerama (p96)

For reviews, see p94.➡

BELLTOWN & SEATTLE CENTER

TOP SIGHT
SPACE NEEDLE

Whether you're from Cincinnati or Shanghai, your abiding image of Seattle will probably be of the Space Needle, a streamlined, modern-before-its-time tower built for the 1962 World's Fair that has been the city's defining symbol ever since. The needle anchors the Seattle Center and persuades over a million annual visitors to ascend to its flying saucer–like observation deck.

Some History

The Space Needle (originally called 'the Space Cage') was designed by Victor Steinbrueck and John Graham Jr, reportedly based on the napkin scribblings of World's Fair organizer Eddie Carlson. Looking like a cross between a flying saucer and an hourglass, and belonging to an architectural subgenre commonly referred to as Googie (futuristic, space age and curvaceous), the Needle was constructed in less than a year and proved to be an instant hit: 2.3 million people paid $1 to ascend it during the World's Fair, which ran for six months between April and October 1962. The lofty revolving dome originally housed two restaurants (they were amalgamated in 2000) and its roof was initially painted a brilliant 'Galaxy Gold' (read: orange). After many color changes, it was repainted in the same shade for its 50th anniversary in 2012. The structure has had two major refurbishments since the '60s: the first in 1982 when the Skyline level was added, and the second in 2000 in a project that cost as much as the original construction. The tradition of holding fantastical New Year's Eve fireworks displays at the Needle

DON'T MISS

→ Observation deck
→ Joint-ticket offers
→ The Loupe
→ Inclined benches

PRACTICALITIES

→ Map p238, C3
→ ☏206-905-2100
→ www.spaceneedle.com
→ 400 Broad St, Seattle Center
→ adult/child $37.50/32.50, incl Chihuly Garden & Glass $49/39
→ ⊙9:30am-11pm Mon-Thu, 9:30am-11:30pm Fri & Sat, 9am-11pm Sun
→ Ⓢ Seattle Center

began in 1992. In 2017 the iconic rotating SkyCity Restaurant was closed, and while there are plans to open another restaurant in the space, no dates have been announced. The closure was part of a larger face-lift, which was unveiled in 2018 and included additions such as the Loupe, a revolving space with glass floors and a wine bar, and an all-glass observation deck with inclined benches that provide nearly heart-stopping vistas of the city below.

Vital Statistics

Standing apart from the rest of Seattle's skyscrapers, the Needle often looks taller than it actually is. On its completion in 1962, it was the highest structure west of the Mississippi River, topping 605ft, though it has since been easily surpassed (it's currently the seventh-tallest structure in Seattle). The part of the Needle that's visible above ground weighs an astounding 3700 tons. Most visitors head for the 520ft-high observation deck on zippy elevators that ascend to the top in a mere 41 seconds. The 360-degree views of Seattle and its surrounding water and mountains are suitably fabulous.

Visiting

To avoid the queues, purchase your ticket from one of the self-service machines outside the Space Base (tourist shop) and proceed up the ramp. You'll undergo a friendly bag search and then enter the gold capsule elevators, where an attendant will give you a quick-fire 41-second précis of the Needle (the time it takes to ascend). The elevators dock at the **observation deck**. The observation deck has a reasonable cafe (with drinks and sandwiches) inside and a newly renovated glass-walled exterior, which is the real reason to make the trip. The view is broad: on clear days, you can see three Cascade volcanoes (Mts Rainier, Baker and St Helen's), the Olympic range, the jagged coastline of Puget Sound and the sparkling surfaces of Lakes Union and Washington fanning out in the haze. Equally interesting is the complex topography of Seattle and its splayed neighborhoods that lie beneath you.

Take the newly opened spiral staircase called the Oculus down to the Loupe, the brand-new rotating glass floored observation space that is not for those afraid of heights. Although, if you get worked up you can always order a glass of liquid courage at the Atmos Wine Bar (open 1pm to close).

JOINT TICKETS

To cut your costs at the Space Needle, you can combine it with a visit to Chihuly Garden & Glass (p84), located at its base, on the same ticket. Joint tickets cost adult/child $49/39. Alternatively, the Needle is part of several package deals, including the $99 Seattle CityPASS that grants access to four other sights (along with the Museum of Pop Culture and the Pacific Science Center). You can check out all the options at www.spaceneedle.com.

If, while standing on the Space Needle's observation deck, you ever wondered what it was like to balance on the structure's outer rim or, perhaps, climb its pointed spire, wonder no more. You can now enjoy these vertiginous views by downloading a free mobile app and watching it on your cell phone through a special virtual reality box. See www.spaceneedle.com/vr for details.

TOP SIGHT
CHIHULY GARDEN & GLASS

This exquisite exposition of the life and work of dynamic local sculptor Dale Chihuly opened in 2012 and is possibly the finest collection of curated glass art you'll ever see. It shows off Chihuly's creative designs in a suite of interconnected rooms and an adjacent garden in the shadow of the Space Needle.

Dale Chihuly

Dale Chihuly born in Tacoma, WA, in 1941, and majored in interior design at the University of Washington before moving to Venice, where he enthusiastically immersed himself in the delicate art of glassblowing. Returning to the Seattle area in 1971, Chihuly founded a glass art school and gradually began to establish a reputation before two successive accidents in the 1970s left him with permanent injuries to his eye and shoulder. Although he was no longer able to contribute directly to the glassblowing process, he remained undeterred by the setback. Instead Chihuly channeled his energies 100% into design, hiring vast teams of glassblowers to enact his lucid artistic visions. It was a highly successful formula. With Chihuly acting as both composer and conductor to a large orchestra of employees, the size and scale of his exhibits soared. Before long, his provocative glass art leaped onto the world stage. By the 1980s, Chihuly's opulent creations were being exhibited all over the globe, inspiring a mixture of awe and controversy in all who saw them, but never failing to get a reaction.

Exhibition Hall

The first standout exhibit is **Sealife Tower**, a huge azure structure of intricately blown glass that looks as if it has sprung straight out of Poseidon's lair. Look out for the small

DON'T MISS

➡ Sealife Tower
➡ Chandeliers
➡ The Sun
➡ Glasshouse

PRACTICALITIES

➡ Map p238, C3
➡ ☎206-753-4940
➡ www.chihulygarden andglass.com
➡ 305 Harrison St, Seattle Center
➡ adult/child $26/17, incl Space Needle $49/39
➡ ⏰10am-8pm Sun-Thu, to 9pm Fri & Sat
➡ Ⓢ Seattle Center

octopuses and starfish melded into the swirling waves and examine Chihuly's early sketches for the work that adorn the surrounding walls. The next exhibit, **Persian Ceilings**, creates a reflective rainbow of light in an otherwise unfurnished room, while the ambitious **Mille Fiori** presents glass as vegetation, with multiple pieces arranged in an ethereal *Wizard of Oz*-like 'garden.' The **Ikebana & Float Boat** consists of several boats overflowing with round glass balls and was inspired by Chihuly's time in Venice: he casually threw luminous glass spheres into the canals and watched as local children enthusiastically collected them in boats. In the adjoining room lie the main objects of the *Chihuly over Venice* project: rich, ornate **chandeliers** of varying sizes and colors that were hung artistically around the city in 1996.

The Glasshouse

Sitting like a giant greenhouse under the Space Needle, the Glasshouse offers a nod to London's erstwhile Crystal Palace, one of Chihuly's most important historical inspirations. You'll notice that the floor space of the glasshouse has been left empty (the area can be hired for wedding receptions), drawing your eye up to the ceiling where a huge medley of flower-shaped glass pieces imitate the reds, oranges and yellows of a perfect sunset. Adjacent to the glasshouse is the **Collections Café**, where numerous collected objects (accordions, bottle openers, toy cars) adorn the ceiling, tables and toilets. Nearby, a **theater** shows several revolving short films including *Chihuly over Venice*.

Practical note: the Glasshouse is occasionally closed for private events during regular museum hours. It's worth checking the schedule on the museum website to make sure you don't miss it when you visit.

The Garden

Seattle's relatively benign climate means glass can safely be displayed outside year-round. Chihuly uses the garden to demonstrate the seamless melding of glass art and natural vegetation. Many of the alfresco pieces are simple pointed shards of glass redolent of luminescent reeds, but the real eye-catcher is **The Sun**, a riot of twisted yellow 'flames' whose swirling brilliance erases the heaviness of the most overcast Seattle sky.

LEARN GLASSBLOWING

In the summer of 1971, Dale Chihuly co-founded **Pilchuck Glass School** (www.pilchuck.com) at a campus in Stanwood, WA, 50 miles north of Seattle on an old tree farm. Inhabiting rustic buildings constructed in typical Northwestern style, the school remains popular 45 years on, especially in the summer, when it offers intensive two-week courses in glassblowing.

If you really fall in love with Chihuly Garden and Glass (warning: it isn't difficult), it's possible to go back and enjoy the art in some novel new ways. Yoga Under Glass is an atmospheric one-hour yoga class held in Chihuly's spectacular glasshouse. Through the Lens is a chance for photographers to make art out of art without a bevy of tourists blocking every frame. There are many one-off opportunities, also. Activities take place either before the museum opens, or after it closes, and cost $26 to $36.

TOP SIGHT
MUSEUM OF POP CULTURE

The Museum of Pop Culture is an inspired marriage between super-modern architecture and legendary rock-and-roll history that sprang from the imagination of Microsoft co-creator Paul Allen (1953–2018). Inside its avant-garde frame, designed by Canadian architect Frank Gehry, you can tune into the famous sounds of Seattle or attempt to imitate the rock masters in an interactive 'Sound Lab.'

Architecture
The highly unusual building with its crinkled folds colored in metallic blues and purples was designed by renowned Canadian architect Frank Gehry, a strong proponent of deconstructivism. Gehry – who designed the equally outlandish Guggenheim Museum in Bilbao, Spain – supposedly used one of Hendrix's smashed-up guitars as his inspiration.

Main Exhibits
The main exhibit hall is anchored by *If VI Was IX,* a tower of 700 instruments designed by German-born artist Trimpin. Many of the permanent exhibits center on Hendrix, including the Fender Stratocaster guitar that he played at Woodstock in 1969. There's also a nostalgic slice of grunge memorabilia in a section entitled 'Nirvana: Taking Punk to the Masses'. Dominating proceedings on level 2 is the **Sky Church**, a huge screen displaying musical and sci-fi films.

Icons of Science Fiction
A permanent 2nd-floor exhibit called 'Infinite Worlds of Science Fiction' displays artifacts from iconic films and TV shows. Expect to come face to face with a *Doctor Who* Dalek, a *Terminator 2* skull and plenty of *Star Wars* life forms and film props.

Sound Lab
Most of the 3rd floor is given over to the interactive **Sound Lab**, where you can lay down vocal tracks, play instruments, fiddle with effects pedals and – best of all – jam in several mini studios. **On Stage** takes things further, allowing you the opportunity to belt out numbers under stage lights with a virtual audience.

Changing Exhibits
MoPOP's generously proportioned galleries are filled with a regularly shuffled pack of exhibits, many of them topical. Some stay for months, while others are so popular they keep going for years. Past exhibits have included the 'We are 12' exhibit in honor of Seattle Seahawks fans following their first Super Bowl victory, and 'Star Trek: Exploring New Worlds,' designed to celebrate the 50th anniversary of Captain Kirk and Co.

At the time of writing, upcoming temporary exhibits included 'A Queen Within,' focusing on the styling of women in contemporary fashion, and one on the immensely popular Minecraft video games.

DON'T MISS
→ Sound Lab
→ 'Nirvana: Taking Punk to the Masses'
→ On Stage
→ Infinite Worlds of Science Fiction

PRACTICALITIES
→ Map p238, D2
→ ☏206-770-2700
→ www.mopop.org
→ 325 5th Ave N, Seattle Center
→ adult/child $28/19
→ ⏱10am-5pm Jan-late May & Sep-Dec, 10am-7pm late May-Aug
→ ⑤Seattle Center

⊙ SIGHTS

The Seattle Center hosts three of Seattle's big-hitter sights within spitting distance of each other. Belltown is more about bars and restaurants, although the Olympic Sculpture Park is a worthy diversion.

⊙ Belltown

MYRTLE EDWARDS PARK   PARK

(☑206-684-4075; 3130 Alaskan Way; ⊙24hr; ◻33) Your best bet for an uninterrupted walk or jog if you're staying downtown is this fringe of lawn and trees along Elliott Bay that starts next to the Olympic Sculpture Park and continues as far as the Interbay area between Queen Anne and Magnolia.

The park (sometimes erroneously called Elliott Bay Park) was named after a Seattle councillor and environmental campaigner in the 1960s, and the path that runs through it is a favorite of joggers and power walkers pursuing lunchtime fitness. In warm weather, the linked paths, with stupendous views over the Sound to the Olympic Mountains, make a good place for a picnic (eagles are sometimes spotted). Halfway through the park a large, distinctive grain terminal bridges the walkway.

PIER 66   PIER

Map p238 (2209 Alaskan Way; ⊙7am-10pm) This elevated pier has a large viewing platform that looks out over downtown and the harbor. It's a good spot to grab a skyline-backed selfie or family photo.

SPHERES   NOTABLE BUILDING

Map p238 (☑206-266-4064; www.seattle spheres.com; 2111 7th Ave, Denny Triangle; ⊙10am-8pm Mon-Sat, 11am-7pm Sun; ◻South Lake Union Streetcar) **FREE** Amazon's latest construction in the Denny Triangle opened January 2018 and is quite different to the Amazon Tower I, which went up in 2015 down the street. Relatively low to the ground with the aesthetic of a sci-fi movie, the name says it all with the Spheres, which are constructed in white metals and glass and contain within them a veritable botanic garden's worth of plants.

You can stop in the atrium (called the 'Understory') for a small exhibit on the building's architecture and ethos. Tours are available as part of a larger tour of Amazon HQ, which can be arranged on the website.

BELLTOWN & SEATTLE CENTER SIGHTS

⊙ TOP SIGHT
OLYMPIC SCULPTURE PARK

The Olympic Sculpture Park, an outpost of the Seattle Art Museum, was inaugurated in 2007 to widespread local approval. The terraced park is landscaped over railway tracks and overlooks Puget Sound with the distant Olympic Mountains winking on the horizon. Along its zigzagging paths are over 20 pieces of modern sculpture that sprout dramatically from the surrounding plants and foliage.

Hard to miss on the shoreline, *Echo* (2011), by Catalan artist Jaume Plensa, is a huge white head that appears to contort depending on which angle you look at it. Another head-turner is Alexander Calder's *The Eagle* (1971), whose curvaceous red arches perfectly frame the nearby Space Needle. Many miss Roxy Paine's *Split* (2003), a stainless-steel tree that draws attention to the sometimes blurry split between art and nature and underlines one of the park's central themes. Infinitely more conspicuous is Claes Oldenburg and Coosje van Bruggen's *Typewriter Eraser, Scale X*, with its weird blue sprouts bristling over Elliott Ave.

DON'T MISS

➡ *Echo* by Jaume Plensa

➡ *The Eagle* by Alexander Calder

➡ *Typewriter Eraser, Scale X* by Claes Oldenburg and Coosje van Bruggen

PRACTICALITIES

➡ Map p238, B4

➡ ☑206-654-3100

➡ 2901 Western Ave, Belltown

➡ admission free

➡ ⊙sunrise-sunset

➡ ◻33

WORTH A DETOUR

THE DENNY TRIANGLE

Once a nondescript no-man's-land shoehorned between South Lake Union and Belltown, the triangle of streets bordered by Denny Way, Olive Way and 6th Ave is positioning itself as Seattle's next big thing with ambitious plans for offices, condo towers and super-modern multi-use buildings. The surge is being led by online retail behemoth Amazon, whose new Seattle headquarters, Amazon Tower I opened in December 2015, with more towers set to follow.

Though it's hard to envisage today, the Denny Triangle sits on some important pioneer history. Seattle's first land claim was staked here by the Denny Party in 1852, though the weary, rain-lashed pioneers probably wouldn't recognize their fledgling settlement now. Until the 1890s, the area was occupied by a steep hill that covered 62 city blocks and had a summit at the intersection of modern-day 4th Ave and Blanchard St. Seen as an impediment to the continued expansion of downtown, the hill was gradually 'demolished' and sluiced into Elliott Bay in a massive public-works project known as the Denny Regrade that began in 1898 and took 32 years to complete.

Devoid of sights per se, the triangle's most recognizable landmark is the gaudy neon **pink elephant sign** outside the Elephant Super Car Wash that has been revolving on the corner of Denny Way and Battery St since 1956. To locals it is as quintessentially Seattle as the Space Needle – and six years older!

TIMES SQUARE BUILDING
LANDMARK

Map p238 (414 Olive Way; ⓢSouth Lake Union Streetcar) This terracotta and granite structure, guarded by eagles perched on the roof, was designed by the Paris-trained architect Carl Gould (who also designed the Seattle Asian Art Museum and the University of Washington's Suzzallo Library). It housed the *Seattle Times* from 1916 to 1931.

AMAZON TOWER I
LANDMARK

Map p238 (2021 7th Ave; ⓢSouth Lake Union Streetcar) The new Seattle HQ of online retail behemoth Amazon opened in December 2015. Officially it's called Amazon Tower I, but it's known colloquially as 'the Doppler.'

◉ Seattle Center

SPACE NEEDLE
LANDMARK

See p82.

CHIHULY GARDEN & GLASS
MUSEUM

See p84.

MUSEUM OF POP CULTURE
MUSEUM

See p86.

SEATTLE CENTER
LANDMARK

Map p238 (☎206-684-8582; www.seattlecenter. com; 400 Broad St; ⓢSeattle Center) The remnants of the futuristic 1962 World's Fair hosted by Seattle and subtitled Century 21 Exposition are still visible over 50 years later at the Seattle Center. Thanks to regular upgrades, the complex has retained its luster and contains Seattle's highest concentration of A-list sights. It's also a superb green space close to downtown.

BILL & MELINDA GATES FOUNDATION DISCOVERY CENTER
VISITOR CENTER

Map p238 (☎206-709-3100; www.discovergates. org; 440 5th Ave N; ⓢ10am-5pm Tue-Sat; ⓢSeattle Center) **FREE** The work of the Bill & Melinda Gates Foundation is celebrated in this suitably high-tech visitor center, part of a larger foundation building located opposite the Space Needle. Spread over five rooms with highly interactive exhibits, the center lays out the Gates' bios and shows examples of their work around the world, including fighting malaria in Africa and notable philanthropic activities inside the US.

It also offers plenty of scope for visitor involvement. Various screens and notepads invite visitors to jot down ideas, help solve tricky problems and lend their own brainpower to the foundation's 'intellectual bank.'

INTERNATIONAL FOUNTAIN
FOUNTAIN

Map p238 (☎206-684-7200; www.seattlecenter. com; 305 Harrison St; ⓢSeattle Center) A remnant of the 1962 World's Fair, the International Fountain was completely rebuilt in

1995. With 272 jets of water (recycled, of course) pumping in time to a computer-driven music system at the heart of the Seattle Center, it's a great place to rest your feet, eat lunch, or have a cold shower on a warm day. On summer nights there's a free light-and-music show. Check the Seattle Center website for more details.

PACIFIC SCIENCE CENTER   MUSEUM

Map p238 (☎206-443-2001; www.pacific sciencecenter.org; 200 2nd Ave N; adult/child $25.95/17.95; ☺10am-5pm Mon-Fri, to 6pm Sat & Sun; ⛲; ⓢSeattle Center) This interactive museum of science and industry once housed the science pavilion of the 1962 World's Fair. Today the center features virtual-reality exhibits, a tropical butterfly house, laser shows, holograms and other wonders of science, many with hands-on demonstrations. Also on the premises is the vaulted-screen **IMAX Theater**, a saltwater tide pool and a planetarium. IMAX movies and special temporary exhibits cost extra.

CHILDREN'S MUSEUM   MUSEUM

Map p238 (☎206-441-1768; www.thechildrens museum.org; 305 Harrison St; $12; ☺10am-5pm Tue-Sun; ⛲; ⓢSeattle Center) In the basement of the Seattle Center Armory near the monorail stop, the Children's Museum is old-school entertainment and a good bet if you want to tear your offspring away from iPads and redirect them toward Lego, fort building and pretending to be a checkout operator. For some it's a little dated; others find it charming and endearing. Best for kids under seven.

 EATING

Belltown has a UN of eclectic restaurants catering to all budgets. Among its rows of bars and cocktail lounges – where condo-clean and dive-dirty often sit right next to each other – is a great variety of cafes, delis, top-of-the-line eateries and budget-friendly hangouts frequented by unpretentious locals. The other advantage of Belltown is that you're more likely to be able to find late-night dining, thanks to an active cocktail scene that encourages many restaurants to serve at least a bar menu until last call.

✖ Belltown

FOB POKE BAR   POKE $

Map p238 (☎206-728-9888; www.fobpokebar. com; 220 Blanchard St; poke bowls from $11; ☺11am-10pm; ⛄13) Ultra-fresh ingredients and bold flavors have made relative Belltown newcomer FOB Poke Bar an instant success in the casual dining scene. This is a make-your-own-bowl place where you can go the simple salmon or tuna route, or mix things up with ingredients like spam and octopus. If you come during lunch hours, be prepared to queue.

MACRINA   BAKERY $

Map p238 (☎206-448-4032; www.macrina bakery.com; 2408 1st Ave; sandwiches $6.50-10.50; ☺7am-6pm; ⛄13) That snaking queue's there for a reason: damned good artisanal bread (you can watch through the window as the experts roll out the dough). There are two options and two lines at Macrina. One is for the fantastic take-out bakery (possibly the best in Seattle); the other's for the sit-down cafe with its so-good-it-could-be-Paris sandwiches, soups and other such snacks.

★TOP POT HAND-FORGED DOUGHNUTS   CAFE $

Map p238 (www.toppotdoughnuts.com; 2124 5th Ave; doughnuts from $1.29; ☺6am-7pm Mon-Fri, 7am-7pm Sat & Sun; ⛄13) Sitting pretty in a glass-fronted former car showroom with art-deco signage and immense bookshelves, Top Pot's flagship cafe produces the Ferraris of the doughnut world. It might have morphed into a 20-outlet chain in recent years, but its hand-molded collection of sweet rings are still – arguably – some of the best in the city. The coffee's pretty potent too.

MAMNOON STREET   MIDDLE EASTERN $

Map p238 (☎206-327-9121; https://mamnoon street.com; 2020 6th Ave, Denny Triangle; mains $8-12; ☺11am-9pm Mon-Sat, to 8pm Sun) Middle Eastern street food doesn't come much better than this casual cafe. There are a few tables inside and on the sidewalk, but most get their *shawarma* (thinly sliced rotisserie meat) and felafel (fried chickpeas) to go.

ASSEMBLY HALL   CAFE $

Map p238 (☎206-812-8413; www.assemblyhall seattle.com; 2121 6th Ave; sandwiches $7-14; ☺6am-8pm Mon-Wed & Fri, 6am-9pm Thu,

7am-6pm Sat & Sun; ⊞South Lake Union Streetcar) Top Seattle chef Tom Douglas owns half a dozen eating places in Belltown these days. His secret: they're all excellent, but none of them are remotely alike. Assembly Hall offers simple but tasty contemporary cafe items (think bacon and egg sandwiches and veggie-filled noodle bowls) in an airy setting. There's a trivia night on Thursdays from 7pm to 9pm.

CYCLOPS   AMERICAN $

Map p238 (☑206-441-1677; www.cyclopsseattle. com; 2421 1st Ave; mains $10-15; ⊙11am-2pm Mon-Fri, from 9am Sat & Sun; ☐13) This off-beat cafe is a neighborhood favorite and does brunchy items (burgers, breakfast burritos and big salads) throughout the day. It makes for a pleasant reprieve from some of the area's swankier offerings.

TILIKUM PLACE CAFE   BISTRO $$

Map p238 (☑206-282-4830; www.tilikumplace cafe.com; 407 Cedar St, Denny Triangle; brunch mains $9-14, dinner mains $23-32; ⊙11am-3pm & 5-10pm Mon-Fri, 8am-3pm & 5-10pm Sat & Sun; ☐3) This charmer of a European-style cafe is beloved by locals for lunch (sardine sandwiches) and brunch (Dutch baby pancakes) and dinner (roasted chicken with Yukon potatoes) and dessert (chocolate polenta cake) – don't make them choose. You'll find it packed no matter the time of day, and it's one of the best dining options within spitting distance of the Space Needle.

SHIRO'S SUSHI RESTAURANT   JAPANESE $$

Map p238 (☑206-443-9844; www.shiros.com; 2401 2nd Ave; 5-piece sashimi $15-20; ⊙5:30-10:30pm; ☐13) A little pricey, but with over 20 years of glowing testimonies about its black cod and deep-fried prawn heads, Shiro's is Belltown's best Japanese option. Although founder Shiro Kashiba no longer runs the restaurant, it has kept its name and reputation for cool, sophisticated food and service.

SERIOUS PIE   PIZZA $$

Map p238 (☑206-838-7388; www.seriouspie seattle.com; 316 Virginia St; pizzas $17-19; ⊙11am-11pm; ⊞South Lake Union Streetcar) In the crowded confines of Serious Pie you can enjoy beautifully blistered pizza bases topped with such unconventional ingredients as clams, potatoes, nettles, soft eggs, truffle cheese and more. Be prepared to share a table and meet a few Seattleites.

PINTXO   TAPAS $$

Map p238 (☑206-441-4042; www.pintxoseattle. com; 2207 2nd Ave; tapas $9-17; ⊙4-10pm; ☐13) Say the word Basque and you might as well be saying 'gourmet' – the Spanish autonomous region has collected a constellation of Michelin stars. *Pintxos* are the Basque version of tapas, and they are served authentically in this ice-cool bar that could have you planning your next vacation to San Sebastián.

LA VITA É BELLA   ITALIAN $$

Map p238 (☑206-441-5322; 2411 2nd Ave; pasta $15-23; ⊙11:30am-3pm & 5-10pm Mon-Thu, to 11pm Fri & Sat, 5-10pm Sun; ☐13) As any Italian food snob will tell you, it's very hard to find authentic home-spun Italian cuisine this side of Sicily. Thus extra kudos must go to La Vita é Bella for trying and largely succeeding in a difficult field. The pizza margherita is a good yardstick, though the *vongole* (clams), desserts and coffee are also spot on.

As in all good Italian restaurants, the owners mingle seamlessly with the clientele with plenty of handshakes and good humor.

BLACK BOTTLE   MODERN AMERICAN $$

Map p238 (☑206-441-1500; www.blackbottle seattle.com; 2600 1st Ave; plates $9-25; ⊙4pm-midnight Sun-Thu, to 2am Fri & Sat; ☐13) This trendy minimalist bar-restaurant specializes in wonderfully shareable small plates, with menu items such as lamb meatballs and sumac hummus, and cauliflower fritters with a Kolkata pepper glaze.

OHANA   HAWAIIAN $$

Map p238 (☑206-956-9329; www.facebook. com/ohanabelltown; 2207 1st Ave; mains $13-19; ⊙11:30am-2am; ☐13) Despite being open until last call, Ohana has the laid-back, friendly feel of a family-run establishment. Many come for the jumbo tiki drinks and interior design to match (think nautical ropes, wooden idols and surf paraphernalia aplenty), but the menu of Hawaiian-Japanese fusion is worth it on its own. The flavors here are fresh as can be.

FARESTART
RESTAURANT   NORTHWESTERN US $$

Map p238 (☑206-443-1233; www.farestart.org; 700 Virginia St, Denny Triangle; 3-course dinner $29.95; ⊙11am-2pm Mon-Fri, 5:30-8pm Thu; ⊞South Lake Union Streetcar) ⊘ FareStart serves substantial meals that benefit the community. All proceeds from lunch and the popular Thursday-night Guest Chef dinners – when FareStart students work with a famous local chef to produce outstanding meals – go to support the FareStart program, which provides intensive job training, housing assistance and job placement for disadvantaged and homeless people.

The constantly changing lunch menu is pretty gourmet for the price – try the hot sandwiches or seafood pasta. Reservations are strongly recommended for dinner.

360 LOCAL   NORTHWESTERN US $$

Map p238 (⌨206-441-9360; www.local360. org; 2234 1st Ave; mains $17-34; ⊘3-9pm Mon, 3-10pm Tue-Fri, 9am-10pm Sat, 9am-9pm Sun; ⬛13) 🖊 Snaring 90% of its ingredients from within a 360-mile radius, this restaurant follows its ambitious 'locavore' manifesto pretty rigidly. The farms where your meat was reared are displayed on the daily blackboard menu and the restaurant's wood-finish interior looks like a rustic barn. With such a fertile hinterland to draw upon, the food is pretty special.

Fresh vegetables supplement most meals, and even the whiskey is local.

CANTINA LEÑA   MEXICAN $$

Map p238 (⌨206-519-5723; www.cantinalena. com; 2105 5th Ave; mains $11-18; ⊘11am-11pm; ⬛13) Small-town Mexican soul food it isn't, but if you fancy hot, smoky chicken tacos and a cooling guacamole dip before a movie at the adjacent Cinerama, this could hit the spot.

★TAVOLÀTA   ITALIAN $$$

Map p238 (⌨206-838-8008; 2323 2nd Ave; mains $18-32; ⊘5-11pm; ⬛13) Owned by top Seattle chef Ethan Stowell, Tavolàta is a dinner-only, Italian-inspired eatery emphasizing homemade pasta dishes and hearty mains like a rack of wild boar with fig *mostarda* (a sweet and spicy mustard and fruit sauce). Many consider it among the best Italian spots in the city.

Get a seat in the mezzanine and you can look down on the chefs spinning their magic in the open kitchen below.

LOLA   GREEK $$$

Map p238 (⌨206-441-1430; www.lolaseattle. com; 2000 4th Ave; mains $19-34; ⊘6am-11pm Mon-Thu, 6am-midnight Fri, 7am-3pm & 4pm-midnight Sat, 4-11pm Sun; ⬛South Lake Union Streetcar) Seattle's ubiquitous cooking maestro Tom Douglas goes Greek in this ambitious Belltown adventure and delivers once again with gusto. Stick in trendy clientele, some juicy kebabs, heavy portions of veg, shared meze dishes, and pita with dips, and you'll be singing Socratic verse all the way back to your hotel.

BAROLO RISTORANTE   ITALIAN $$$

Map p238 (⌨206-770-9000; www.baroloseattle. com; 1940 Westlake Ave; mains $22-44; ⊘11:30am-midnight Mon-Fri, from 3pm Sat & Sun; ⬛South Lake Union Streetcar) An upscale Italian place named after one of Italy's finest vinos, Barolo provides a good excuse to taste the deep, powerful 'king of wines' or – if your budget won't stretch that far – a supporting cast of half a dozen underappreciated Barberas or Dolcettos (there's a generous and popular 'happy hour' that kicks off daily at 3pm).

PALACE KITCHEN   NORTHWESTERN US $$$

Map p238 (⌨206-448-2001; www.palace kitchen.com; 2030 5th Ave; mains $25-38; ⊘4:30pm-1am; ⬛South Lake Union Streetcar) One of Tom Douglas' harder to classify restaurants, the Palace is known for its upscale 'New American' cuisine, late-night happy hour and cool cocktail scene. Foodwise, it's especially good for its Applewood grill items, including trout and rotisserie chicken, although the menu also nurtures some fine Italianate features; try the *plin,* a Piedmontese-style ravioli.

There are two daily happy hours – or as they are known here, Royal Hours – one from 4:30pm to 6pm, and a late night one from 11:30pm to 1am that's perfect for one last drink and some pig-ear poutine.

BUENOS AIRES GRILL   STEAK $$$

Map p238 (⌨206-448-3114; www.buenosaires tangogrill.com; 2328 1st Ave; steaks $39-69; ⊘4-10pm Mon-Sat, to 9pm Sun; ⬛13) On Friday and Saturday evenings at 7:30pm you can dine on Argentinian steak while taking in a live tango performance, all from the comfort of Belltown. Those hankering for massive steaks cooked to perfection should come any night they can get a reservation.

DAHLIA LOUNGE   NORTHWESTERN US $$$

Map p238 (⌨206-682-4142; www.dahlialounge. com; 2001 4th Ave; mains $11:30am-2pm & 5-9pm Mon-Fri, 9am-2pm & 5-10pm Sat, 5-9pm Sun; ⬛South Lake Union Tram) 🖊 Dahlia Lounge specializes in hallmarks of

Tom Douglas restaurants, which caused a boom in Seattle's dining scene in the '90s: locally grown produce, an organic ethos and fusion flavors that lean heavily toward Pacific Northwestern favorites. Luxury mains like Dungeness crab and rotisserie duck fill the menu.

✖ Seattle Center

CÔBA   VIETNAMESE $

Map p238 (☑206-283-6614; www.cobaseattle. com; 530 1st Ave N, Queen Anne; mains $8-15; ☺11am-10pm; ☂; ☒2) While the Mediterranean-inspired stone finishes and overall sleek design touches of CÔBA give this place an expensive feel, the Vietnamese food on offer is affordable and without too many unnecessary twists. Noodles, rice and *banh mi* are joined by more modern small plates like spicy mango tofu salad and kimchi calamari. The Vietnamese coffee is a must.

SEATTLE CENTER ARMORY   FOOD HALL $

Map p238 (☑206-684-7200; www.seattlecenter. com; 305 Harrison St; ☺armory hours 7am-9pm Sun-Thu, to 10pm Fri & Sat; ⓈSeattle Center) Inside the Seattle Center Armory you'll find a bountiful food court with options ranging from Subway to local treats like the Cool Guys Fry Bar. Each restaurant's hours vary; the Seattle Center website has the full breakdown.

TAYLOR SHELLFISH
OYSTER BAR   SEAFOOD $$

Map p238 (☑206-501-4060; www.taylorshellfish farms.com; 124 Republican St; oysters $2.75-3.25; ☺11am-10pm) Bright and airy – and almost within the shadow of the Space Needle – the Taylor Shellfish Oyster Bar is the perfect pit stop on a day of sightseeing. Off the beaten path for a lot visitors, you'll likely see locals slurping freshly shucked bivalves from local farms all owned and operated by Pacific Northwest operator Taylor Shellfish.

🍷 DRINKING &
🍸 NIGHTLIFE

For many people, Belltown remains the pinnacle of Seattle nightlife. While some of the old vanguard will complain **that the scene has been too cleaned up, there's still plenty of sticky-floored establishments to grab a cheap beer and see some bands you've never heard of. If you prefer a more effete drinking experience, you can take yourself to one of the many cocktail bars in the area. Better yet: make a night of it and hit up both.**

★RENDEZVOUS   BAR

Map p238 (☑206-441-5823; www.rendezvous. rocks; 2320 2nd Ave, Belltown; ☺4pm-2am; ☒13) Rendezvous is one of Belltown's oldest heirlooms, starting life in 1927 as a speakeasy and a screening room for early Hollywood talkies. Now on its umpteenth incarnation, the subterranean speakeasy has morphed into 'the Grotto' (with weekly comedy), the screening room has become the diminutive Jewel Box Theater (p96) and the clamorous space upstairs a chic-ish bar and restaurant.

CLOUDBURST BREWING   MICROBREWERY

Map p238 (☑206-602-6061; www.cloudburst brew.com; 2116 Western Ave, Belltown; ☺2-10pm Wed-Fri, noon-10pm Sat & Sun; ☒13) The brainchild of former experimental brewer at Elysian Brewing, Steve Luke, Cloudburst Brewing became an instant Seattle favorite. Replicating the success of Luke's past brewing creations, Cloudburst Brewing features hoppy beers with sassy names, and the bare-bones tasting room is always packed to the gills with beer fans who want to support craft beer in Seattle.

QUEEN CITY   BAR

Map p238 (☑206-402-5095; www.queencity seattle.com; 2201 1st Ave, Belltown; mains $16-28; ☺4-11pm Sun-Thu, to 1am Fri & Sat; ☒13) This longtime Belltown favorite in an old red-brick building was once an old school Seattle restaurant and is now an antique chic bar serving delightful cocktails and a small selection of very tasty bar food (mains $16 to $22); the steak *frites* is especially worth ordering.

NO ANCHOR   BAR

Map p238 (☑206-448-2610; www.noanchorbar. com; 2505 2nd Ave, Belltown; ☺noon-11pm Mon-Thu, noon-midnight Fri, 11am-midnight Sat, 11am-11pm Sun; ☒13) Most things on the menu at No Anchor feel like a big risk, and they often pay off. The cocktails feature ingredients like maple syrup and toasted coconut, while the menu of bar bites has eccentric

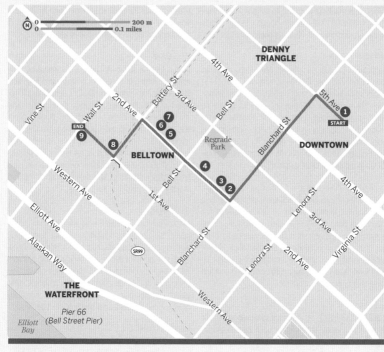

Neighborhood Walk
The Belltown Hustle

START TOP POT DOUGHNUTS
END CYCLOPS
LENGTH 1 MILE; A FULL EVENING

Start the tour by filling up with coffee and sugar at **1 Top Pot Hand-Forged Doughnuts** (p89), whose book-lined cafe in a former car showroom sits under the concrete pillars of the monorail on 5th Ave.

Next wander down Blanchard St to 2nd Ave where, on the corner, you'll spot the snakeskin-green sign of the **2 Crocodile** (p94), a key venue in the rise of grunge. This marks the start of one of Seattle's best nightlife strips that stretches west along 2nd Ave. **3 Tula's** (p96) is a great jazz venue and home to some of Seattle's best improvisers.

Then hop next door to the **4 Lava Lounge** (p94), another groovy nightspot with comfy wooden booths. If you're after more active pursuits and are still thirsty, cross Bell St and pace a few doors down

to **5 Shorty's** (p94), otherwise known as pinball heaven. Grab a cheap beer and head straight to the back room to test your reflexes.

Continue on past bearded lumberjack impersonators and city slickers in Brooks Brothers suits to **6 Rendezvous** (p92), a classy multi-purpose venue dating from the Prohibition era with a curvilinear bar and the adorable **7 Jewel Box Theater** (p96) in the back.

Turn left on Battery St, heading toward the water, then right on 1st Ave: halfway down the block you'll see **8 Macrina** (p89), one of Seattle's best bakeries. If it's past 6pm make menu notes for tomorrow's hangover cure.

Hungry? What – already?! Head toward the corner of 1st Ave and Wall St, where you can procure a substantial snack in **9 Cyclops** (p90), a prime location for observing the street's late-night dramas. Chill at the Cyclops until your eyes match the bleary one hanging over the door, then stumble home.

offerings such as pickled mussels. Beer novices will feel welcomed by the large draft menu featuring a 'what to pick' guide.

WHISKY BAR   BAR

Map p238 (☑206-443-4490; www.thewhiskybar. com; 2122 2nd Ave, Belltown; ☺noon-2am; ☐13) This spot is about more than just the whiskey, though that, of course, is good. If you're sticking to home turf, try the locally made Westland single malt. There are genuine British food treats as well. Where else in Seattle can you get Welsh rarebit – or Scotch eggs for that matter?

STREET BEAN ESPRESSO   COFFEE

Map p238 (☑206-818-2786; www.streetbean.org; 2711 3rd Ave, Denny Triangle; ☺6am-5pm Mon-Fri, 8am-3pm Sat; ☎; ☐3) A commendable community resource and a fine perch to imbibe your morning coffee, Street Bean provides opportunities for disadvantaged youths to find work as baristas. The coffee (roasted on-site) is pretty good too.

RE-BAR   GAY

(☑206-233-9873; www.rebarseattle.com; 1114 Howell St, Denny Triangle; ☺6pm-2am Tue-Sun; ☐70) This storied indie dance club, where many of Seattle's defining cultural events happened (such as Nirvana album releases), welcomes everyone in the LGBTIQ+ rainbow and their allies to its lively dance floor. Also come for its offbeat theater, burlesque shows and poetry slams – among other wacky offerings. Check the website for the nightly offerings.

5 POINT CAFÉ   BAR

Map p238 (☑206-448-9993; www.the5point cafe.com; 415 Cedar St, Denny Triangle; ☺24hr; ☐3) There are Belltown relics and then there's the Five Point whose seedy neon sign and cantankerous advertising blurb ('cheating tourists and drunks since 1929') is practically as iconic as the Space Needle – and 33 years older! Half-diner, half-bar and too worn-in to be mistaken for hip, it's where seasoned Charles Bukowski look-a-likes go to get wasted.

SHORTY'S   BAR

Map p238 (☑206-441-5449; www.shortydog. com; 2316 2nd Ave, Belltown; ☺noon-2am; ☐13) Increasingly shabby but seemingly (hopefully?) eternal, Shorty's is one of the best holdovers from grungy old Belltown. It's all about pinball, hot dogs, cheap beer and loud music. Pinball machines are built into some of the tables, and the back room is basically a church for flipper devotees.

BEDLAM   CAFE

Map p238 (☑202-547-0369; 2231 2nd Ave, Belltown; ☺6am-9pm Mon-Thu, 6am-10pm Fri, 7am-10pm Sat, 7am-9pm Sun; ☐13) There's nothing mad about Bedlam, unless you count the wall-mounted bicycle and the Space Needle sculpture – made out of old junk – that guards the door. Welcome to a one-off coffee bar with no pretensions that specializes in full-bodied drip coffee, decent lattes and ultra-thick slices of wholemeal toast loaded with peanut butter and jam.

ROB ROY   COCKTAIL BAR

Map p238 (☑206-956-8423; www.robroyseattle. com; 2332 2nd Ave, Belltown; ☺4pm-2am; ☐13) A proper cocktail lounge, Rob Roy is dignified yet comfortable – there's a long, dark bar and sophisticated touches such as cologne in the restroom, but there's also puffy wallpaper, squishy leather couches and a boar's head and antlers on the wall.

LAVA LOUNGE   TIKI BAR

Map p238 (☑206-441-5660; 2226 2nd Ave, Belltown; ☺3pm-2am; ☐13) This well-worn, tiki-themed dive has games of all kinds and over-the-top art on the walls. It's more old-school Belltown than new and sits on the agreeably disheveled block on 2nd Ave also inhabited by a handful of other much-loved dives.

☆ ENTERTAINMENT

Seattle Center acts as a huge entertainment nexus with opera, ballet, theater, cinema and live music all concentrated in one campus.

Belltown is the preserve of smaller clubs playing up-and-coming local acts, touring bands and outrageous drag shows.

★CROCODILE   LIVE MUSIC

Map p238 (☑206-441-4618; www.thecrocodile. com; 2200 2nd Ave, Belltown; ☐13) Nearly old enough to be called a Seattle institution, the Crocodile is a clamorous 560-capacity music venue that first opened in 1991, just in time to grab the coattails of the grunge explosion. Everyone who's anyone in

BELLTOWN RELICS

Belltown was a featureless amalgam of dull warehouses and low-rise office blocks in the mid-1980s, and well off the radar of the city's condo-dwelling yuppies. Offering cheap rents and ample studio space, it became an escape hatch for underground musicians and hard-up artists whose arrival heralded a creative awakening and led, in part, to the spark that ignited grunge. But, while the grit and grime of '80s Belltown were crucial components in the rise of the Seattle sound, the music's runaway international success had a catalytic effect: Belltown – much to the chagrin of the hard-up rockers who created it – became cool.

So followed a familiar story: seedy inner-city neighborhood attracts artists, gets creative, becomes cool, attracts hipsters, gentrifies, and loses its edge. Belltown's rise, brief honeymoon and rapid decline largely mirrored that of grunge, which, in the eyes of many purists, died the day Nirvana's *Nevermind* hit No 1. By the 2000s, many locals thought the neighborhood was over. Condos were rising, wine bars were replacing exciting music venues, and the martini-and-cocktail set had suddenly decided it was the ideal place to live. But all was not lost. A handful of Belltown's more tenacious older businesses – despite frequent threats of closure – have put up a brave rearguard action. Bars such as Shorty's continue to attract a loyal clientele, old record shops have benefited from a resurgent interest in vinyl, and the neighborhood's most iconic club, the Crocodile (despite a 2009 clean-up), is still an important part of Seattle's alt-music scene. Add in the general air of excitement among the people that crowd the streets, restaurants and clubs every night, and reports of Belltown's death have clearly been exaggerated. Sure, the bars no longer place cardboard boxes on their toilet floors to soak up the urine, but look hard and you'll see there's life in the old beast yet.

Seattle's alt-music scene has since played here, including a famous occasion in 1992 when Nirvana appeared unannounced, supporting Mudhoney.

Despite changing ownership in 2009 and undergoing a grunge-cleansing refurbishment, the Croc remains plugged into the Seattle scene, though these days aspiring stage divers are more likely to get kicked out than crowd surfed on the arms of an adoring audience. There's a full bar, a mezzanine floor and a no-frills pizza restaurant on-site.

★ DIMITRIOU'S JAZZ ALLEY   JAZZ

Map p238 (✆206-441-9729; www.jazzalley.com; 2033 6th Ave, Belltown; ⊙shows 7:30pm & 9:30pm; 🚋South Lake Union Streetcar) Hidden in an unlikely spot behind a boring-looking office building is Seattle's most sophisticated and prestigious jazz club. Dimitriou's hosts the best of the locals, as well as many national and international acts passing through.

★ MCCAW HALL   OPERA

Map p238 (✆206-684-7200; www.mccawhall.com; 321 Mercer St, Seattle Center; ⓢSeattle Center) Home of the Seattle Opera and Pacific Northwest Ballet, this magnificent structure in the Seattle Center was given a massive overhaul in 2003.

SEATTLE OPERA   OPERA

Map p238 (www.seattleopera.org; 321 Mercer St, Seattle Center; ⓢSeattle Center) Seattle Opera is distinguished and diverse. Based at the McCaw Hall, it has hosted everything from Verdi's *La Traviata* to Pete Townshend's *Tommy*. It's particularly known for its performances of Wagner's *Ring* cycle, first staged in 1973.

PACIFIC NORTHWEST BALLET   DANCE

Map p238 (✆206-441-2424; www.pnb.org; 321 Mercer St, Seattle Center; ⓢSeattle Center) The foremost dance company in the Northwest and one of the most popular in the US puts on more than 100 shows a season from September through June at Seattle Center's McCaw Hall.

SEATTLE REPERTORY THEATRE   THEATER

Map p238 (✆206-443-2222; www.seattlerep.org; 155 Mercer St, Seattle Center; ⊙box office 10am-6pm Tue-Fri; ⓢSeattle Center) The Seattle Repertory Theatre (the Rep) won a Tony Award in 1990 for Outstanding Regional Theater.

The largest non-profit resident theater outfit in the Pacific Northwest, it's known for elaborate productions of big-name dramas and second-run Broadway hits.

TULA'S JAZZ
JAZZ

Map p238 (📞206-443-4221; www.tulas.com; 2214 2nd Ave, Belltown; ⊙music 7:30-8:30pm & 9-10pm Sun-Thu, also 10:30-11pm Fri & Sat; 🚌13) Tula's is an intimate jazz club with live music seven nights a week, from big bands and Latin jazz to up-and-coming names on tour. It focuses mainly on local talent and acts as a non-indie-rock oasis in the booze alley that is Belltown. Before 10pm all ages eight years and older are welcome.

BIG PICTURE
CINEMA

Map p238 (📞206-256-0566; www.thebigpicture.net; 2505 1st Ave, Belltown; tickets $14.50) It's easy to miss Big Picture when exploring Seattle's Belltown neighborhood. For those in the know, it's an 'underground' cinema experience with affordable tickets of first-run screenings in an intimate setting. Order a cocktail from the bar (which you can linger at before your showtime), and then another to be delivered mid-screening.

KEXP
LIVE PERFORMANCE

Map p238 (📞206-520-5800; www.kexp.org; 472 1st Ave N, Seattle Center; 🚌RapidRide D Line) The new KEXP radio headquarters opened in the Seattle Center in December 2015 and provides a central gathering space for live music and parties, a see-through DJ booth and a live recording studio with room for audiences of up to 75 people.

JEWEL BOX THEATER
THEATER

Map p238 (📞206-441-5823; www.therendezvous.rocks; 2320 2nd Ave, Belltown) The restored Jewel Box Theater, tucked away behind the sleek Rendezvous (p92) cocktail bar, has live music and independent theater events including burlesque. It dates from 1927 and was once a screening room for Hollywood movies.

INTIMAN THEATRE
THEATER

Map p238 (📞206-441-7178; www.intiman.org; 201 Mercer St, Seattle Center; tickets from $25; 🚼; 🅂Seattle Center) A beloved theater company based at the Cornish Playhouse in the Seattle Center. Artistic director Jennifer Zeyl curates magnificent stagings of Shakespeare and Ibsen as well as work by emerging artists.

SEATTLE CHILDREN'S THEATER
THEATER

Map p238 (📞206-441-3322; www.sct.org; 201 Thomas St, Seattle Center; tickets from $25; ⊙Thu-Sun Sep-May; 🚼; 🅂Seattle Center) This highly esteemed theater group has two auditoriums in its Seattle Center campus. Friday and Saturday matinees and evening performances run September through May. There's also a Drama School summer season.

MOORE THEATRE
LIVE MUSIC

Map p238 (📞206-443-1744; www.stgpresents.org/moore; 1932 2nd Ave, Belltown; 🚌Westlake) Attached to a stately old hotel, the Moore is the city's oldest surviving theater (from 1907) and a piece of Seattle history. Its 1800-seater auditorium was the recent recipient of a refurbishment and exudes a battered grace and sophistication, whether the act is a singer-songwriter, a jazz phenomenon or a rock band. It mainly hosts music and dance.

Look out for the free theater tours on the second Saturday of each month at 10am.

SIFF FILM CENTER
CINEMA

Map p238 (📞206-464-5830; www.siff.net; 305 Harrison St, Seattle Center; adult/youth $14/13; 🅂Seattle Center) The digs of the famous Seattle International Film Festival (p29) since 2011 runs movies in a small auditorium year-round.

CINERAMA
CINEMA

Map p238 (📞206-448-6680; www.cinerama.com; 2100 4th Ave, Belltown; tickets $17; 🚌13) Possibly Seattle's most popular cinema, and famous for its giant curved three-panel screen, Cinerama is one of only three of its type left in the world and has a cool, sci-fi feel. Sparkling after a 2014 renovation, it has recently acquired a space-age mural, wider seats and a raft of additional extras, including microbrews on tap and Tom Douglas nosh.

🛍 SHOPPING

Belltown's shopping is patchy. Thankfully you can conveniently pop into the few stellar record stores and clothing boutiques on your way to the abundance of options in the adjacent downtown neighborhoods.

★**HERBAN LEGENDS**   DISPENSARY

Map p238 (☑206-849-5596; www.herban
legends.com; 55 Bell St, Belltown; ☺8am-
11:45pm; ☐13) Herban Legends is both a
brilliantly silly pun and one of Seattle's
best dispensaries. It manages to feel very
professionally run while maintaining a
breezy vibe missing from other weed shops
in town. The staff are always ready with a
great recommendation and there is even
a merch shop at the front should you want a
coffee mug.

SINGLES GOING STEADY   MUSIC

Map p238 (☑206-441-7396; 2219 2nd Ave, Belltown; ☺noon-7pm Tue-Thu, to 8pm Fri & Sat,
to 6pm Sun; ☐13) Singles Going Steady –
named after an album by British punk
pioneers the Buzzcocks – is a niche record
store specializing in punk, oi, reggae and
ska, mostly in the form of 7in vinyl singles,
as well as posters, patches and other accessories. There's a good little magazine selection too.

MOOREA SEAL   FASHION & ACCESSORIES

Map p238 (☑206-728-2523; www.mooreaseal.
com; 2523 3rd Ave, Belltown; ☺11am-6pm Mon-
Sat, to 4:30pm Sun) Taking inspiration from
the Pacific Northwest, Moorea Seal is a
three-year-old store that curates accessories and goods that have a rustic-yet-urban
feel. It stocks clothing and accessories,
home decor and personal care products.
Seven percent of all proceeds from sales
benefits local nonprofits.

ALHAMBRA   CLOTHING

Map p238 (☑206-621-9571; www.alhambrastyle.
com; 2127 1st Ave, Belltown; ☺10am-6:30pm
Mon-Sat, noon-5pm Sun; ☐13) A beautifully
laid-out designer boutique showcasing
elegant women's clothing for those with fat
wallets (or envious window-shoppers).

HAVE A HEART   DISPENSARY

Map p238 (☑206-588-2436; www.haveaheartcc.
com; 115 Blanchard St, Belltown; ☺8am-11:45pm)
This dispensary chain is modern and effi-
cient. You'll likely encounter a line snaking through the store no matter the time
of day, but things move quickly and there
are menus to consult and employees buzzing around taking orders and answering
questions. Those in the know order online
and pick up.

🏃 SPORTS & ACTIVITIES

VELO BIKE SHOP   CYCLING

Map p238 (☑206-325-3292; www.velobikeshop.
com; 2151 6th Ave, Denny Triangle; rental per day/
week $35/150; ☺10am-7pm Mon-Thu, 10am-6pm
Fri & Sat, noon-5pm Sun; ☐South Lake Union
Streetcar) Sturdy 'city bikes' with handy
covered back-racks go for $35 a day at
Velo, which is located in the heart of Amazon's new stomping grounds in the Denny
Triangle.

**RIDE THE DUCKS
OF SEATTLE**   TOURS

Map p238 (☑206-441-3825; www.ridetheducks
ofseattle.com; 516 Broad St, Seattle Center;
adult/child $38/23; 👫; ⑤Seattle Center) These
hugely popular tours in amphibious vehi-
cles are partly on land and partly in the
water. From the start point near the Space
Needle, the 90-minute tours encompass the
waterfront, Pioneer Sq and Fremont before
pitching (quite literally) into Lake Union for
half an hour. The guides are renowned for
their humor and the tours are very popular
with families.

**SEATTLE
GLASSBLOWING STUDIO**   ARTS & CRAFTS

Map p238 (☑206-448-2181; www.seattleglass
blowing.com; 2227 5th Ave, Belltown; ☺9am-6pm
Mon-Sat, from 10am Sun; ☐13) If Dale Chihuly's decadent chandeliers have inspired
you, try creating your own modest glass art
at this blow-your-own studio a few blocks
from the master's museum. One-day sessions cost $65 to $395. Alternatively, you
can just watch the fascinating process from
the on-site cafe, which has a viewing window overlooking the workshop.

SEATTLE CENTER ARENA   STADIUM

Map p238 (www.newarenaatseattlecenter.com;
305 Harrison St, Seattle Center; ⑤Seattle Center)
As of 2018, the Seattle Center Arena (formerly known as the Key Arena) is undergoing a massive renovation to prepare the city
for it's upcoming National Hockey League
franchise, beginning with the 2021–22 season. It's home to women's basketball team
Seattle Storm (p140), who will return after
the renovation, and serves as one of the
city's larger music venues.

Art & Culture

You don't have to go to a gallery to see Seattle's art. Creativity is everywhere: on walls, under bridges, in parks and on hatch covers. Join an art walk, organize an 'art attack' or just wait around in neighborhoods like Fremont and Capitol Hill for the local Picassos to show up.

JOHN ELK III/GETTY IMAGES © SAM ARCHITECT: ROBERT VENTURI; HAMMERING MAN, SEATTLE ART MUSEUM, JONATHAN BOROFSKY, 1991

LAWRENCE WORCESTER/LONELY PLANET ©

1. Fremont Solstice Fair (p21)
Stiltwalkers perform in the Solstice Parade.

2. Hammering Man (p48)
The 48ft-high metal sculpture guards the entrance to the Seattle Art Museum (p46).

3. Jimi Hendrix statue (p112)
This 1997 statue immortalizes the guitar god and is something of a shrine for fans.

4. Fremont Rocket (p144)
Created for the Cold War, this zany-looking rocket was adopted by Fremont as a community totem.

5. Waiting for the Interurban (p144)
Seattle's most popular piece of public art.

JIMI HENDRIX BY ARTIST DARYL SMITH, COMMISSIONED BY MICHAEL MALONE, MAX HERMAN/SHUTTERSTOCK ©

Queen Anne & Lake Union

Neighborhood Top Five

1 **Museum of History & Industry** (p102) Riding the streetcar to this fabulous museum for a first-class exposition of Seattle's grunge-playing, aircraft-building, computer-designing history.

2 **Cheshiahud Loop** (p109) Circumnavigating Lake Union on foot (or bike)

on this well-signposted 6-mile route.

3 **Lake Union** (p103) Taking in the tranquil views while you gear up for some outdoor activities at this idyllic urban lake.

4 **Center for Wooden Boats** (p104) Sallying forth on Lake Union on a free

public sailboat ride from this museum and boating enthusiasts' center.

5 **Kerry Park** (p103) Viewing lakes, skyscrapers and the even more sky-scraping Mt Rainier from this spectacular lookout at sunset, amid Beverly Hills–like mansions.

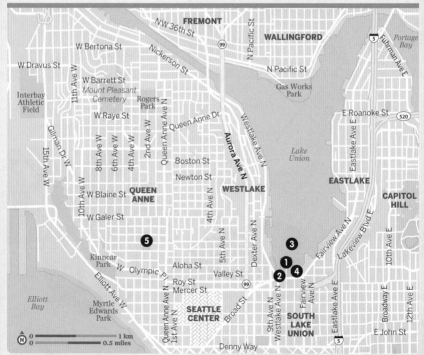

For more detail of this area see Map p240 ➡

Explore Queen Anne & Lake Union

At some point during your Seattle sightseeing sojourn, you'll want to exit the tourist-heavy Seattle Center and be deposited on one of the busy thoroughfares of Lower Queen Anne, a lived-in urban locale good for a cheap meal or an eye-widening dose of Seattle coffee culture. To get a view of the posher side of the neighborhood, take a steep hike (or jump on a bus) up Queen Anne Ave N to a markedly different neck of the woods.

Sitting on a 456ft hill above the Seattle Center, Queen Anne proper is an elegant collection of majestic redbrick houses and apartment buildings with gorgeous views of the city and Elliott Bay. Vistas aside (and, yes, they're worth the energy expenditure), the favorite pastime here is 'mansion-viewing,' ie wandering at will along the traffic-lit streets spying on an opulent array of fin-de-siècle architecture.

To the east, Lake Union – Seattle's watery playground – covers a large area that encompasses several neighborhoods including Fremont and the U District. To get an overview of its famous houseboats and various water-based activities, start in Lake Union Park and circumnavigate the lake on the Cheshiahud Loop (p109), a 6-mile walking circuit. Or head straight for the Museum of History & Industry (p102), one of Seattle's headline sights. Across Mercer St there are enough restaurants and coffee bars in the burgeoning South Lake Union neighborhood to keep you fueled until dinner time. The handy streetcar will zip you back from lakeside to downtown in 10 minutes.

Local Life

Brunch hangout Find out about the party you missed last night while standing in line for a hangover-curing brunch at 5 Spot (p105).

Exercise ritual Take an early-morning jog around Lake Union on the Cheshiahud Loop (p109) and watch the city waking up.

Getting There & Away

Bus Metro buses 2 and 13 run frequently to Queen Anne from downtown and Seattle Center. Buses 62 and 70 serve the Westlake and Eastlake neighborhoods of Lake Union from downtown.

Streetcar One of Seattle's two main streetcar lines runs between South Lake Union and the Westlake Center in downtown every 10 minutes.

Lonely Planet's Top Tip

Hit a Queen Anne supermarket or sandwich bar and take a picnic over to **Kerry Park** (p103), weather permitting, to enjoy what many locals claim is Seattle's finest view.

✖ Best Places to Eat

➡ Toulouse Petit (p105)

➡ How to Cook a Wolf (p104)

➡ Canlis (p106)

➡ Serafina (p106)

For reviews, see p104.➡

🍷 Best Places to Drink

➡ El Diablo Coffee Co (p106)

➡ Uptown Espresso Bar (p107)

➡ Mecca Café (p107)

➡ Hilltop Ale House (p107)

For reviews, see p106.➡

🔒 Best Places to Shop

➡ REI (p108)

➡ Feathered Friends (p109)

➡ Queen Anne Book Company (p108)

For reviews, see p108.➡

 TOP SIGHT
MUSEUM OF HISTORY & INDUSTRY

Almost everything you need to know about Seattle is crammed into the fabulous Museum of History & Industry (MOHAI), located in plush digs on the southern shore of Lake Union. In operation since the 1950s, and with an archive of over four million objects, MOHAI displays its stash of historical booty in an impressively repurposed naval armory building.

Interactive Exhibits

The big eye-catcher as you walk into the huge hangar-sized space is a 1919 **Boeing airplane** hanging from the roof (the first commercial Boeing ever made). Indeed, the name 'Boeing' looms large over the whole museum, along with numerous other Seattle icons (Starbucks, Rainier beer, grunge). In the city that produced Microsoft, there is no shortage of interactive exhibits to enjoy (kids will have a ball), including a photo and comment booth and an opportunity to explore railroad history by banging large mallets on railway sleepers. With so many artifacts to call upon, exhibits can change regularly, although the museum's overriding sentiment remains constant: an unashamed celebration of Seattle's short but action-packed history.

Museum History

MOHAI only moved to its present location in 2012. For the first 60 years of its history, it resided in the more peripheral Montlake neighborhood just north of Capitol Hill. The prestigious collection was initiated in 1914 with the foundation of the Seattle Historical Society, but remained homeless until 1952. Even in its expansive contemporary digs, MOHAI can only display around 2% of its full treasures at any given time.

DON'T MISS

➡ Film and TV exhibit
➡ Main atrium
➡ Periscope

PRACTICALITIES

➡ Map p240, F5
➡ ☎206-324-1126
➡ www.mohai.org
➡ 860 Terry Ave N, South Lake Union
➡ adult/child under 14yr $19.95/free
➡ ⏰10am-5pm
➡ 🚻
➡ 🚊South Lake Union Streetcar

⊙ SIGHTS

Queen Anne and Lake Union host a good selection of small parks beautified with fine city and water views.

Lake Union's southern shore harbors the wonderful Center for Wooden Boats (p104) along with the recently relocated Museum of History & Industry – one of Seattle's big-hitter sights.

⊙ Queen Anne

KERRY PARK
PARK, VIEWPOINT

Map p240 (☎206-684-4075; 211 W Highland Dr; ☺6am-10pm; ☒; ☒2) Amid the glittering Beverly Hills–like homes of Highland Dr, mere commoners can enjoy eagle's-eye views of downtown Seattle and Elliott Bay (and Mt Rainier, should it take its cloudy hat off) from this spectacular lookout.

Binoculars (50¢) are provided, so you can look back at the people at the top of the Space Needle looking over at you. The park is set on a steep incline of Queen Anne Hill (looking south) and is split in two, with a stairway linking to a popular children's playground below. This is a favorite spot to end a romantic date night – or make a proposal!

BHY KRACKE PARK
PARK

Map p240 (☎206-684-4075; 1215 5th Ave N; ☺4am-11:30pm; ☒; ☒3, 4) It would be easy to miss this tiny park, built into a slice of hill surrounded by quiet residential blocks, but it's worth seeking out for its views of downtown Seattle and the Space Needle alone. In addition to plenty of benches and grassy spots to lay out on there's also a kid's play area.

You can access the park either from the main entrance at 5th Ave N or an entrance on Comstock Ave (off Bigelow Ave), which is higher up the hill and easier to access if you're coming from Queen Anne's center.

MARSHALL PARK
PARK

Map p240 (☎206-684-4075; 1191 7th Ave W; ☒2) Atop Queen Anne Hill at the west end of W Highland Dr, this tiny but loftily positioned park has expansive views stretching west across Puget Sound to the Olympic Mountains.

TREAT HOUSE
LANDMARK

Map p240 (1 W Highland Dr; ☒2) This 14-gabled house near the top of Queen Anne Hill was built in 1905 by Harry Whitney Treat, a friend of William F 'Buffalo Bill' Cody. Treat also created Golden Gardens Park (p156) in

⊙ TOP SIGHT
LAKE UNION

Unifying Seattle's various bodies of water, the appropriately named Lake Union is a freshwater lake carved by glacial erosion 12,000 years ago. Native American Duwamish tribes once subsisted on its then-isolated shores, but they wouldn't recognize it today. Twenty-first-century Lake Union is backed by half a dozen densely packed urban neighborhoods and is linked to both Lake Washington and Puget Sound by the Washington Ship Canal, built as part of a huge engineering project in the 1910s. Not surprisingly, the lake attracts water-sports enthusiasts – you'll regularly see kayakers, rowers, sailboats and paddle-boarders negotiating its calm-ish teal waters.

Surrounding the lake on its eastern, western and southern shores respectively are the neighborhoods of **Eastlake** (dominated by the decommissioned City Light Steam Plant – now occupied by a biotech company), **Westlake** and **South Lake Union**, the city's fastest developing neighborhood-in-the-making.

DON'T MISS
➡ Houseboats
➡ Kayaking
➡ South Lake Union

PRACTICALITIES
➡ Map p240, F5
➡ ☒South Lake Union Streetcar

northwest Ballard. After Treat's death in the 1920s, the building was converted into 15 apartments. Built in English arts-and-crafts style, it's worth admiring from the outside.

PARSONS GARDEN   GARDENS

Map p240 (☑206-684-4075; 650 W Highland Dr; ☺6am-10pm; ☐2) A leafy public garden in the posh Queen Anne neighborhood that's especially popular for summer weddings.

☉ Lake Union

MUSEUM OF HISTORY
& INDUSTRY   MUSEUM

See p102.

LAKE UNION PARK   PARK

Map p240 (☑206-684-4075; 860 Terry Ave N, South Lake Union; ☺4am-11:30pm; ♿; ☐South Lake Union Streetcar) Opened in 2010, this welcome green patch occupies ex-navy land on the southern tip of Lake Union and has a wading pond (with model sailboats you can use), an attractive bridge and a boat launch. It hosts the Museum of History & Industry (p102) in the old naval armory building and the Center for Wooden Boats).

Various interpretive panels chronicle Seattle's maritime connections. The South Lake Union streetcar stops outside.

CENTER FOR WOODEN BOATS   MUSEUM

Map p240 (☑206-382-2628; www.cwb.org; 1010 Valley St; sailboat/rowboat/kayak rental per hour $40/40/35; ☺museum 10am-8pm Tue-Sun, rentals from 1pm; ♿; ☐South Lake Union Streetcar) Honoring Seattle's historical, aquatic and Native American antecedents, this one-of-a-kind museum and enthusiasts' center features vintage and replica boats and offers rentals. Best of all, however, are its free Sunday public sailboat rides on Lake Union (first come, first served; sign-ups start 10am).

EATING

Many of the dining options in Lower Queen Anne, just west of Seattle Center (p88), are geared toward the pre- or post-event crowd attending functions at Seattle Center Arena (p97). If you head

up the hill to Upper Queen Anne, you'll find the restaurants have more of the neighborhood's quiet, grown-up, family-friendly atmosphere.

The area around Lake Union used to be a culinary wasteland, but things have changed, especially in South Lake Union, with big-name chefs such as Tom Douglas moving in to cater for the new affluent businesses and residents. Places get busy during weekday lunchtimes and after-work happy hours.

✖ Queen Anne

DICK'S DRIVE-IN   BURGERS $

Map p240 (☑206-285-5155; www.ddir.com; 500 Queen Anne Ave N; burgers from $1.40; ☺10:30am-2am; ☐13) If you're down to your last few dollars and dying for something to eat, don't panic! Dick's is calling you. Welcome to the only fast-food joint in Seattle where you can still buy a burger for $1.40, along with $1.75 fries (hand cut, no less) and $2.50 milkshakes (made with 100% ice cream, of course).

Gourmet it isn't, but as quintessential only-in-Seattle experiences go, it's up there with the Space Needle (and a lot cheaper).

CITIZEN COFFEE   SANDWICHES, BREAKFAST $

Map p240 (☑206-284-1015; www.citizencoffee.com; 706 Taylor Ave N; mains $7-13; ☺7am-9pm Mon-Sat, to 3:30pm Sun; ☐3) Citizen serves breakfast until 4pm and it's a good one. There are plenty of options at this popular red-brick joint near the Space Needle, where you can opt for Greek yogurt and fruit, biscuits and gravy, or huevos rancheros. The slightly tucked-away location means it's less tourist-heavy and more local.

CHACO CANYON   VEGAN $

Map p240 (☑206-402-5173; www.chacocanyoncafe.com; 1525 Queen Anne Ave N; mains $11-16; ☺8am-8pm; ✐; ☐13) Hearty and flavorful vegan fare is served up at this location of the popular local chain, perched on the main drag of Queen Anne proper. The menu is big on grain bowls stuffed with prime ingredients like perfectly roasted sweet potatoes and tangy sauces.

HOW TO COOK A WOLF   ITALIAN $$

Map p240 (☑206-838-8090; www.ethanstowellrestaurants.com; 2208 Queen Anne Ave N; pasta

LOWER QUEEN ANNE

Hungry tourists from the Seattle Center bump into affluent young techies on their lunch breaks in Lower Queen Anne, the thin strip at the bottom of **'the Counterbalance'** (Map p240; Queen Anne Ave N, north of W Roy St, Queen Anne; ☐2) that strikes a less haughty (and more economical) pose than its eponymous neighbor up on the hill. A northern extension of Belltown, Lower Queen Anne – or 'Uptown' as it's sometimes known – is locally renowned for its eclectic mix of restaurants, most of which are quick, casual and, above all, easy on the wallet. Concert-goers and sports fans from the nearby McCaw Hall (p95) and Seattle Center Arena (p97) naturally gravitate here after performances and games (Queen Anne Ave N and Roy St are the main drags), while downtown is only two minutes away on the monorail. As a neighborhood, Lower Queen Anne has more in common with Belltown than Queen Anne, with new condos slowly snuffing out remnants of its unique charms.

$19-23; ☺5-11pm; ☐13) 🍴 Despite its scary name, the Ethan Stowell–run HTCAW has nothing to do with roasting wild fauna over your campfire. Rather it's poached from a book written by MFK Fisher during wartime rationing about how to make the most of limited ingredients. Though times have changed, Stowell embraces the same philosophy.

The food is simple but creative Italian nosh listed on a single sheet of paper and served in a small den-like restaurant. If they ever invent a culinary genre called 'Pacific Northwest Italian,' HTCAW will be its archetype.

★TOULOUSE PETIT   CAJUN, CREOLE $$

Map p240 (☏206-432-9069; www.toulousepetit. com; 601 Queen Anne Ave N; dinner mains $17-45; ☺9am-2am Mon-Fri, from 8am Sat & Sun; ☐13) Hailed for its generous happy hours, cheap brunches and rollicking atmosphere, this perennially busy Queen Anne eatery has the common touch. The menu is large and varied, offering choices such as blackened rib-eye steak, freshwater gulf prawns and house-made gnocchi with artichoke hearts.

PESO'S KITCHEN
& LOUNGE   MEXICAN, BREAKFAST $$

Map p240 (☏206-283-9353; www.pesoskitchen andlounge.com; 605 Queen Anne Ave N; mains $9-17; ☺4pm-2am Mon-Fri, from 10am Sat & Sun; ☐13) Peso's is a trendy Americanized Mexican restaurant and casual hangout that is popular for its lively weekend brunch.

5 SPOT   BREAKFAST $$

Map p240 (www.chowfoods.com; 1502 Queen Anne Ave N; mains $16-25; ☺8am-11pm Mon-Fri, 8am-3pm & 5pm-midnight Sat & Sun; 🏃; ☐2)

Top of the hill, top of the morning and top of the brunch charts: the queues outside 5 Spot at 10am on a Sunday are a testament to its popularity. The crowds inspire a great atmosphere, and the hearty menu, with its perfect French toast, huevos rancheros and plenty more American standards, will shift the stubbornest of hangovers.

🍴 Lake Union

SERIOUS BISCUIT   AMERICAN $

Map p240 (☏206-436-0050; www.seriouspie seattle.com/westlake; 401 Westlake Ave N; biscuits $8-13; ☺7am-3pm Mon-Fri, 9am-3pm Sat & Sun; ☐South Lake Union Streetcar) After Serious Pie (p90) comes Serious Biscuit, Tom Douglas' first bite at the South Lake Union cookie that has lured so many new restaurants into the neighborhood in the last couple of years. The buttery biscuits serve as flaky bases to a variety of brunch-worthy toppings – the 'zach' (fried chicken, gravy, bacon and egg) is a perennial favorite.

Bear in mind that this is a typical Douglas domain with shared tables and limited seating. Upstairs, he operates another of his **Serious Pie** pizza joints in the evenings.

CAFFÈ TORINO   ITALIAN, SANDWICHES $

Map p240 (☏206-682-2099; www.caffetorino seattle.com; 422 Yale Ave N; sandwiches $7-8.50; ☺6:30am-5pm Mon-Fri, from 8am Sat & Sun; 🏃; ☐South Lake Union Streetcar) Those in the know have Turin (Torino) pegged as a temple of good food and coffee, which is why you may want to decamp here for a Lavazza cappuccino, a Nutella cookie and a Caprese sandwich. Best of all is Caffè Torino's honoring of the *aperitivo* tradition, the late-afternoon *pausa* for cheap bites and prosecco.

SWEDISH CLUB
BRUNCH $

Map p240 (☎206-283-1090; http://swedish clubnw.org; 1920 Dexter Ave N; adult/child $11/5; ◉8am-1pm 1st Sun of month; ☒62) Join members of Seattle's Swedish Club on the first Sunday of the month for a buffet of thin pancakes drizzled in lingonberries and served with a hearty slab of ham. Traditional Swedish music and dancing usually accompanies the meal. Come early and grab a seat by the windows for a great Lake Union view.

Don't worry about standing out in the sea of regulars: this brunch is popular with hungover 20-somethings and Seattle foodies – it draws a diverse crowd.

Note the two exceptions to the first Sunday of the month rule: there's no brunch in July and it is held on the second Sunday in September.

SERAFINA
ITALIAN $$

Map p240 (☎206-323-0807; www.serafina seattle.com; 2043 Eastlake Ave E; pastas $16-18, mains $24-36; ◉5-10pm Sun & Mon, 11:30am-2:30pm & 5-10pm Tue-Thu, to 11pm Fri, 5-11pm Sat; ☒70) This lovely neighborhood Italian restaurant in Eastlake specializes in regional Tuscan-style cooking, with simply prepared meat and fish, as well as pastas that can be ordered as a first or main course. A gorgeous leafy deck area behind the restaurant doubles as the entryway to **Cicchetti**, Serafina's sister restaurant, which serves Mediterranean snacks. Reservations are recommended.

EL GRITO
MEXICAN $$

Map p240 (☎206-659-4552; www.elgrito seattle.com; 234 Fairview Ave N; mains $11-16; ◉11am-10pm Mon-Thu, to 1am Fri, 10am-1am Sat, 10am-4pm Sun; ☒South Lake Union Streetcar) El Grito loses a point for its not-entirely authentic taqueria vibe that caters to the lunch appetites of the employees of nearby tech companies, but it's hard to deny: they make a pretty damn tasty burrito. Weekends and lunch are always crowded, so be prepared to grab a spot at the bar.

CANLIS
AMERICAN $$$

Map p240 (☎206-283-3313; https://canlis. com; 2576 Aurora Ave N; 4-course dinner $135; ◉5:30pm-late Mon-Sat; ☒5) One of Seattle's most celebrated restaurants, Canlis is old-school posh and one of the few places in the city where people regularly get dressed up for dinner (as per the restaurant's dress code). The menu is Pacific Northwest traditional (halibut, pork, fresh veg) and the decor's like something out of a 1950s-era Hitchcock movie – all angled glass and sweeping views.

Prices are hefty, ties and jackets required and reservations are pretty much essential. A special-occasion dinner.

RE:PUBLIC
MODERN AMERICAN $$$

Map p240 (☎206-467-5300; www.republic seattle.com; 429 Westlake Ave N; mains $22-33; ◉11am-2:30pm & 5-11pm Mon-Thu, to 1am Fri, 10am-2:30pm & 5pm-1am Sat, 10am-2:30pm Sun; ☒South Lake Union Streetcar) Although the name might read like the sobriquet of an avant-garde play, Re:public (don't forget the colon), situated on the corner of Republican St, is filled with a distinctly South Lake Union type of public – ie young, tech-ish and affluent. It serves modern farm-to-table food – artisanal cheese plates, wild-boar Bolognese – in a neat, minimalist space.

🍺 DRINKING & NIGHTLIFE

When it comes to drinking, this area is all over the map. Pleasantly sleepy Queen Anne has everything from traditional beer halls and dives to swanky jazz bars. South Lake Union is full of new corporate bars catering to the Amazon crowds.

Queen Anne is a breeding ground for coffee shops and many of Seattle's popular coffee chainlets opened their first branches here.

★EL DIABLO COFFEE CO
CAFE

Map p240 (☎206-285-0693; www.eldiablo coffee.com; 1811 Queen Anne Ave N, Queen Anne; ◉6am-6pm; 🛜; ☒13) Anyone for a *café cubano*? This cheerful Queen Anne cafe specializes in Cuban-style coffee – ie strong, short, black and loaded with sugar. Take a cue from the locals and pick up a book from the adjoining Queen Anne Book Company (p108) and dig into it on El Diablo's patio.

CAFFE LADRO
CAFE

Map p240 (206-282-5313; www.caffeladro.
com; 2205 Queen Anne Ave N, Queen Anne;
⏰5:30am-8pm Mon-Fri, 6am-8pm Fri & Sat; 🛜;
🚇13) With an Italian name that trans-
lates as 'coffee thief,' apparently because it
set out to pinch business from Starbucks,
Ladro has subsequently established its own
small Seattle-only chain (16 branches and
counting). This one in Lower Queen Anne
is the original, dating from 1994. Not only
does it roast its own beans, but also does its
own baking.

HOLY MOUNTAIN
BREWING COMPANY
MICROBREWERY

(www.holymountainbrewing.com; 1421 Elliott Ave
W, Queen Anne; ⏰3-9pm Mon-Thu, noon-10pm Fri
& Sat, to 9pm Sun; 🚇RapidRide D Line) A newer
brewery with a handful of years under its
belt, Holy Mountain has developed a serious cult following. Focused on ales aged in
oak barrels and an ever-changing lineup of
new taps, Holy Mountain offers beer lovers
a taste of something a bit different.

Visit the bright and airy taproom to
sample small-batch brews that range from
hoppy pale ales to bright sours and Belgian
ales.

UPTOWN ESPRESSO BAR
CAFE

Map p240 (206-285-3757; https://velvetfoam.
com; 525 Queen Anne Ave N, Queen Anne; ⏰6am-
6pm; 🛜; 🚇13) Foam sets this long-running
local coffee chain apart from its peers. The
foam here is known as 'velvet foam' and has
been bringing people through the doors
since the '80s.

HILLTOP ALE HOUSE
PUB

Map p240 (206-723-5123; www.seattleale
houses.com; 2129 Queen Anne Ave N, Queen
Anne; ⏰11am-11pm Sun-Thu, to midnight Fri &
Sat; 🚇13) Hilltop is a comfy neighborhood
hangout on Queen Anne Hill, sister to the
74th Street Ale House (p149) in Phinney
Ridge. It has a friendly vibe and a large
selection of microbrews, served in proper
20oz pints, and the menu is well above your
standard pub fare (mains $11 to $15).

MECCA CAFÉ
BAR

Map p240 (206-285-9728; http://mecca-cafe.
com; 526 Queen Anne Ave N, Queen Anne; burgers from $10.50; ⏰7am-2am; 🚇13) Half of
the long, skinny room at Mecca Café is a
ketchup-on-the-table diner, but all the fun
happens on the other side, where decades

worth of beer mat scribbles line the walls
and the bartenders know the jukebox songs
better than you do.

A kind of sister-dive to the nearby Five
Point Café, the Mecca was founded at the
tail end of Prohibition (1930) and has been
hailed at many points in its history as the
best bar in Seattle.

MCMENAMINS
QUEEN ANNE
MICROBREWERY

Map p240 (206-285-4722; www.mcmenamins.
com; 200 Roy St, Queen Anne; ⏰11am-midnight
Mon-Thu, to 1am Fri & Sat, noon-midnight Sun;
♿; 🚇13) The McMenamin brothers' microbrewing empire is a product of Portland,
OR, but you can enjoy a comforting out-
of-state taste of the brand's ever-successful
blend of psychedelia meets art nouveau
meets wood-paneled gentleman's club at
this Lower Queen Anne perch. The real
draw, of course, is the beer, including the
classic Hammerhead pale ale, loaded with
Oregon hops. It's kid-friendly.

CAFFÈ FIORE
COFFEE

Map p240 (206-282-1441; www.caffefiore.com;
224 W Galer St, Queen Anne; ⏰6am-6pm; 🚇2)
Queen Anne hosts an abundance of coffee
shops and most of them are good, but Fiore,
which is part of a small four-cafe Seattle chain, has the advantage of being near
Kerry Park (p103) up on the hill and retains
a cozy Queen Anne feel. People rave about
its 'Sevilla' (mocha with orange zest), but its
espressos are pretty potent too.

BRAVE HORSE TAVERN
PUB

Map p240 (206-971-0717; www.bravehorse
tavern.com; 310 Terry Ave N, Lake Union; ⏰11am-
10pm Mon-Thu, to midnight Fri, 10am-midnight
Sat, to 10pm Sun; 🚇South Lake Union Streetcar)
With this place, posing as a kind of German beer hall meets Wild West saloon, Tom
Douglas has made his (inevitable) lunge
into the world of pubs. Brave Horse sports
two dozen draft beers (local amber ales are
well represented) and the place even bakes
its own pretzels in a special oven.

⭐ ENTERTAINMENT

EL CORAZON
LIVE MUSIC

Map p240 (206-262-0482; www.elcorazon
seattle.com; 109 Eastlake Ave E, Lake Union; 🚇70)
Formerly the Off-Ramp, then Graceland,

QUEEN ANNE WHO?

Observant students of history might wonder why the Seattle neighborhood of Queen Anne is named after an undistinguished British queen who reigned between the years 1702 and 1714, 150 years before the city was even founded. The answer is rooted in architecture. The hill on which the Queen Anne neighborhood sits is embellished by a rather nebulous style of revivalist architecture first concocted in the UK in the 1860s and brought to North America in the early 1880s, where it remained in vogue until around 1910 (when the neighborhood was being laid out).

Queen Anne architecture supposedly harked back to the English baroque buildings of the early 18th century (during the reign of Queen Anne), but the name quickly became something of a misnomer, as the revivalist Queen Anne style took on a life of its own, particularly in the US. Typical Queen Anne features in North America include large bay windows, wraparound porches, steep gabled roofs, polygonal towers, shingles and lavish gardens. To see some of the more whimsical examples, wander at will among the large private houses on top of Queen Anne Hill. The mansions along Highland Dr are particularly opulent.

El Corazon has lots of history echoing around its walls – and lots of sweaty, beer-drenched bodies bouncing off them. Save your clean shirt for another night, and don't expect perfect sound quality at every show. The gutsy bands play loudly, presumably to drown out the traffic noise from I-5 just outside the door.

The venue is etched in grunge-era mythology. Pearl Jam, then going under the name of Mookie Blaylock, played their first ever gig here in October 1990.

ON THE BOARDS   DANCE, THEATER
Map p240 (✆206-217-9886; www.ontheboards. org; 100 W Roy St, Queen Anne; tickets from $10; ☐13) *The* place for avant-garde performance art, the non-profit On the Boards makes its home at the intimate Behnke Center for Contemporary Performance and showcases some innovative and occasionally weird dance and music.

SIFF CINEMA UPTOWN   CINEMA
Map p240 (✆206-324-9996; www.siff.net; 511 Queen Anne Ave N, Queen Anne; ☐13) Sister cinema to the nearby SIFF Film Center (p96) in Seattle Center, the SIFF Cinema Uptown is the more public-facing of the two. This three-screen cinema plays a combination of first-run prints, independent films and classic movies that keep seats filled throughout the year. Limited seats create an intimate experience perfect for date night or a family afternoon.

The Uptown is joint HQ for the Seattle International Film Festival (p29), meaning its three screens get an intelligent and varied turnaround of movies.

🛍 SHOPPING

★REI   OUTDOOR EQUIPMENT
Map p240 (✆206-223-1944; www.rei.com; 222 Yale Ave N, Lake Union; ⊗9am-9pm Mon-Sat, 10am-7pm Sun; ☐70) REI is the be-all and end-all of outdoor clothing and equipment, and its Lake Union flagship is no exception. In fact it even comes equipped with some additional perks like an outdoor mountain-bike test track. The store also rents various ski packages, climbing gear and camping equipment, and organizes a ton of courses from map-reading to bike maintenance.

As much an adventure as a shopping experience, the state-of-the-art megastore of America's largest consumer co-op has its own climbing wall – a 65ft rock pinnacle to the side of the store's entryway. The wall offers various climbing options from open climbs to private instruction. Even if you're not in the market for outdoor gear, it's enough of a spectacle to recommend a visit. Check the website for details.

QUEEN ANNE BOOK COMPANY   BOOKS
Map p240 (✆206-283-5624; www.qabookco. com; 1811 Queen Anne Ave N, Queen Anne; ⊗10am-7pm Mon-Fri, to 5pm Sat & Sun; ☐13) This charming little nook is everything a neighborhood bookstore should be, with

frequent poetry readings and book signings. The adjoining El Diablo (p106) coffee shop has a lovely little patio where you can sip a coffee and pore over your latest book purchase.

FEATHERED FRIENDS SPORTS & OUTDOORS
Map p240 (☑206-292-2210; www.feathered friends.com; 119 Yale Ave N, Lake Union; ⊙10am-7pm Mon-Wed, to 8pm Thu & Fri, to 6pm Sat, 11am-5pm Sun; ☐70) Feathered Friends stocks high-end climbing equipment, made-to-order sleeping bags and backcountry ski gear. Products made with down are the specialty.

PATRICK'S FLY SHOP SPORTS & OUTDOORS
Map p240 (☑206-325-8988; www.patricksfly shop.com; 2237 Eastlake Ave E, Lake Union; ⊙noon-6pm Sun & Mon, from 10am Tue-Sat; ☐70) Located near Lake Union, this shop has been around as long as anyone can remember. It offers workshops on fly-fishing, sells equipment and gives advice.

🏃 SPORTS & ACTIVITIES

CHESHIAHUD LOOP WALKING, RUNNING
Map p240 (☑206-684-4075; www.seattle.gov/parks; Westlake Ave N & Valley St, Lake Union; ⊙4am-11:30pm; ☐South Lake Union Streetcar) Inaugurated years ago to tie in with the landscaping of Lake Union Park (p104), this well-signposted 6-mile route circumnavigates Lake Union by gelling together existing trails, sidewalks and paths. Named for a Duwamish chief who once headed a lakeside village, it's a good way to keep away from busy roads while walking/jogging/cycling through at least five Seattle neighborhoods.

The best place to join the trail is at the southern end of the lake at Lake Union Park. You can also download a map from the Seattle Parks Department website.

MOSS BAY ROWING & KAYAK CENTER KAYAKING
Map p240 (☑206-682-2031; www.mossbay.net; 1001 Fairview Ave N, Lake Union; rental per hour kayak/paddleboard $15/16; ⊙9am-8pm summer, 10am-5pm Thu-Mon winter; ☐South Lake Union Streetcar) Moss Bay offers rentals, extensive lessons and tours (from $45 per person) on Lake Union.

NORTHWEST OUTDOOR CENTER KAYAKING
Map p240 (☑206-281-9694; www.nwoc.com; 2100 Westlake Ave N, Lake Union; rental per hr kayak/SUP $18/20; ⊙10am-8pm Mon-Fri, 9am-6pm Sat & Sun Apr-Sep, closed Mon & Tue Oct-Mar; ☐62) Located on the west side of Lake Union, this place rents kayaks and stand-up paddleboards (SUPs) and offers tours and instruction in sea and white-water kayaking.

Capitol Hill & First Hill

Neighborhood Top Five

1 **Pony** (p117) Savoring sunset drinks on the patio that lead to all-night grinding on the dance floor at one of the city's most popular LGBTIQ+ bars.

2 **Neumo's** (p120) Seeing a name band at this legendary live-music venue, one of Seattle's most revered.

3 **Water Tower Observation Deck** (p112) Climbing the water tower in Volunteer Park to admire dazzling vistas of Seattle and Mt Rainier.

4 **Lost Lake Cafe & Lounge** (p114) Enjoying a very late beer or a very early breakfast at the 24-hour *Twin Peaks*–themed Lost Lake Cafe.

5 **Elliott Bay Book Company** (p120) Coming up for air after an afternoon of lazy literary immersion at Seattle's most beloved bookstore.

Explore Capitol Hill & First Hill

To decipher Seattle's most consciously cool neighborhood it's useful to understand a little of its geography. There are three main commercial strips worth exploring in Capitol Hill – Broadway (the main drag), 15th Ave and the ultra-cultural Pike–Pine corridor – all of which are refreshingly walkable (if you don't mind hills). Geographically the strips are gelled together by Capitol Hill's residential grid, a mixture of apartment complexes, large grandiose houses and the green expanse of Volunteer Park. This weird but never caustic juxtaposition of chic and scruffy is one of the neighborhood's biggest allures.

If you're walking up from downtown crossing I-5 on E Pine St, you'll enter the neighborhood at the western end of the Pike–Pine corridor. This stretch of aging brick warehouses and former 1950s car dealerships – made over into gay bars, live-music clubs, coffeehouses, record stores and fashionable restaurants – is Seattle's nightlife central.

Running perpendicular to Pike–Pine is Capitol Hill's main commercial street, Broadway, while several blocks east is the quieter business district of 15th Ave E. This is where some of the city's wealthiest residents live in the grand old mansions that embellish tree-lined streets such as 14th Ave (aka Millionaires Row). Gawp at the opulence as you make your way up to Capitol Hill's peak, Volunteer Park (p112), home to the Seattle Asian Art Museum (p112), a conservatory and a water tower.

More genteel First Hill is best accessed from the bottom of Pike–Pine or by the streetcar line that bears the neighborhood's name.

Local Life

Park play On warm summer evenings, Cal Anderson Park (p112) is the place to come to watch bike polo, office-versus-office baseball games and tattooed bodies picking up a tan.

Meet and greets Make new friends over plates of nachos at C.C. Attle's (p119), known as one of the friendlier and more laid-back LGBTIQ+ bars in the city.

Getting There & Away

Bus Metro bus 10 links Capitol Hill with downtown (Pine and 5th); bus 8 goes to the Seattle Center. To reach First Hill, catch bus 2 on the western side of 3rd Ave downtown and get off at the Swedish Medical Center.

Streetcar The First Hill Streetcar links Capitol Hill and First Hill with the ID and Pioneer Square.

Lonely Planet's Top Tip

Capitol Hill is the epicenter of hour-long waits for a table and packed reservation lists. Avoid this by offering to sit at the bar or dining a little earlier. You'd be surprised at how many places that are booked up at 7:30pm have plenty of tables available at 6pm.

Best Places to Eat

➡ Sitka & Spruce (p116)
➡ Cascina Spinasse (p116)
➡ Poppy (p117)
➡ Coastal Kitchen (p115)
➡ Lost Lake Cafe & Lounge (p114)

For reviews, see p114.➡

Best Places to Drink

➡ Espresso Vivace at Brix (p117)
➡ Unicorn (p117)
➡ Pony (p117)
➡ Optimism Brewing Co (p118)
➡ Capitol Cider (p119)
➡ Victrola Coffee Roasters (p117)

For reviews, see p117.➡

Best Places to Shop

➡ Elliott Bay Book Company (p120)
➡ Ada's Technical Books & Cafe (p121)
➡ Babeland (p121)
➡ Revival (p121)
➡ Glasswing (p121)

For reviews, see p120.➡

CAPITOL HILL & FIRST HILL

◉ SIGHTS

Capitol Hill isn't as chockablock with sights as the nearby downtown neighborhoods, but you'll find parks, churches, stunning real estate and a couple of excellent art museums to catch your eye.

◉ Capitol Hill

VOLUNTEER PARK   PARK

Map p244 (☑206-684-4075; 1247 15th Ave E; ☺6am-10pm; ⊛; ☐10) Seattle's most manicured park sits atop Capitol Hill and is named for US volunteers in the 1898 Spanish-American War. While wandering among its leafy glades, check out the glass-sided Victorian conservatory, filled with palms, cacti and tropical plants; climb the water tower; visit the Asian Art Museum; and don't depart before you've taken in the opulent mansions that grace the streets immediately to the south.

SEATTLE ASIAN ART MUSEUM   MUSEUM

Map p244 (www.seattleartmuseum.org; 1400 E Prospect St; adult/child $14.95/free; ☺10am-5pm Wed, Fri & Sun, to 9pm Thu, 9am-5pm Sat; ☐10) In stately Volunteer Park, this outpost of the Seattle Art Museum houses the extensive art collection of Dr Richard Fuller, who donated this late–art deco gallery (a fine example of Streamline Moderne architecture) to the city in 1932. Spread over one floor and beautifully presented in uncluttered, minimalist rooms, the collection is notable for its **Japanese hanging scrolls**, some of which date from the 1300s and have been skilfully restored (the restoration process is detailed along with the art).

Also of interest are the **Indian stone sculptures** in the foyer and some remarkably intricate **Chinese bronzes** dating from around 1600 BC.

WATER TOWER OBSERVATION DECK   LANDMARK

Map p244 (1400 E Prospect St; ☺10am-dusk; ☐10) FREE It's practically obligatory to climb the 107 steep steps to the top of the 75ft water tower in Volunteer Park. Built in 1907, it provides wonderful vistas of the Space Needle, Elliott Bay and – should it be in the mood – Mt Rainier. Explanatory boards in the covered lookout detail the history and development of Seattle's park system.

GAY CITY LIBRARY   LIBRARY

Map p244 (☑206-860-6969; www.gaycity.org; 517 E Pike St; ☺11am-8pm Mon-Fri, 12:30-5pm Sat; ☐10) This library was set up in 2009 by Gay City, a community organization, and has already collected 6000 volumes on LGBTIQ+ topics. There are regular readings, meditation classes, a lesbian book club and free HIV testing.

JIMI HENDRIX STATUE   MONUMENT

Map p244 (1600 Broadway E; ☐First Hill Streetcar) Psychedelic guitar genius of the late 1960s and Seattle's favorite son, Jimi Hendrix is captured sunk to his knees in eternal rock-star pose in this bronze sculpture by local artist Daryl Smith, created in 1997 and located close to the intersection of Broadway and E Pine St.

Hendrix fans often leave flowers and candles at the statue's base, and it's not unusual to find a half-burnt spliff stuck between his lips.

VOLUNTEER PARK CONSERVATORY   GARDENS

Map p244 (☑206-684-4743; www.volunteerpark conservatory.org; 1400 E Galer St; day pass adult/child $4/2; ☺10am-4pm Tue-Sun; ☐10) The conservatory is a classic Victorian greenhouse built in 1912. Filled with palms, cacti and tropical plants, it features five galleries representing different world environments. Check out the creepy corpse flower.

ROQ LA RUE   GALLERY

Map p244 (☑206-374-8977; www.roqlarue.com; 705 E Pike St; ☺noon-6pm Wed-Sun; ☐First Hill Streetcar) FREE This gallery has secured its reputation by taking risks: the work on view skates along the edge of urban pop-culture. Since opening in 1998, the gallery, which is owned and curated by Kirsten Anderson, has been a significant force in the pop surrealism field and is frequently featured in *Juxtapoz* magazine.

CAL ANDERSON PARK   PARK

Map p244 (☑206-684-4075; 1635 11th Ave; ☺4am-11pm; ☐Capitol Hill) Cal Anderson Park is the active heart of Capitol Hill, where you're sure to bump into locals playing ultimate frisbee, bike polo or soccer as you stroll the paved paths that crisscross the grounds. Pack a picnic and sit in the grass with a view of the cone-shaped water feature that flows into a reflecting pool.

ST MARK'S CATHEDRAL
CHURCH

Map p244 (206-323-0300; 1245 10th Ave E; choir performs 11am Sun; 49) Go north on Broadway (as the dandyish boutiques turn to well-maintained houses with manicured lawns) until it turns into 10th Ave E and you're within a block of Volunteer Park. At the neo-Byzantine St Mark's Cathedral, the Compline Choir performs for free on Sunday, accompanied by a 3944-pipe Flentrop organ.

LAKEVIEW CEMETERY
CEMETERY

(206-322-1582; www.lakeviewcemeteryassoc iation.com; 1554 15th Ave E; 9am-sunset; 10) One of Seattle's oldest cemeteries and the final resting place of many early settlers, Lakeview Cemetery borders Volunteer Park to the north. Arthur Denny and his family, Doc and Catherine Maynard, Thomas Mercer and Henry Yesler are all interred here. This is also the grave site of Princess Angeline, the daughter of Duwamish Chief Sealth, after whom Seattle was named. Most people, however, stop by to see the graves of martial-arts film legends **Bruce and Brandon Lee**.

◉ First Hill

FRYE ART MUSEUM
MUSEUM

Map p244 (206-622-9250; www.fryemuseum. org; 704 Terry Ave; 11am-5pm Tue, Wed & Fri-Sun, to 7pm Thu; P; First Hill Streetcar) FREE This small museum on First Hill preserves the collection of Charles and Emma Frye. The Fryes collected more than 1000 paintings, mostly 19th- and early-20th-century European and American pieces, and a few Alaskan and Russian artworks. Most of the permanent collection is stuffed into a rather small gallery and comes across as a little 'busy'; however, the Frye's tour de force is its sensitively curated temporary shows, which usually have a much more modern bent.

SORRENTO HOTEL
HISTORIC BUILDING

Map p244 (900 Madison St; 64) This grand working hotel on First Hill is a fine example of Italian Renaissance architecture. Built in 1909 by a Seattle clothing merchant, the Sorrento was one of the first hotels designed to absorb the crowds arriving in Seattle for the Alaska-Yukon-Pacific Exposition (p133; the 1909 World's Fair held in Seattle). Don't miss a chance to nose

CAPITOL HILL & FIRST HILL SIGHTS

THE PIKE–PINE CORRIDOR: A VILLAGE WITHIN A VILLAGE

The Pike–Pine corridor, a sinuous urban strip on the eastern edge of Capitol Hill, is Seattle's factory of hip, a village within a village where the city's trend setters set the trends.

Once a huddle of auto showrooms (only a couple remain), the area underwent a metamorphosis in the early 21st century when an influx of artists and young entrepreneurs snapped up the vacant car lots and transformed them into community-run boutiques, cafes, restaurants, clubs and bars.

A fast-evolving scene was quickly established as Pike–Pine garnered a reputation as the best place in Seattle to buy back your grandma's sweaters, bar crawl with Kurt Cobain's ghost, get your hair cut like Phil Oakey from the Human League or merely sit outside with a coffee and a hangover to watch life go by.

And what a colorful life it is. Style in Pike–Pine is edgy, but never shies away from modernity. You're just as likely to stumble into a cafe with a chaotic punk aesthetic as you are one with minimalist white walls, Scandinavian furniture and air plants hanging in terrariums. In the space of half a dozen blocks you'll find a lesbian pub, a *Twin Peaks*–themed restaurant, an apothecary, feminist sex shops, countless indie coffee spots and Seattle's finest bookstore. Tolerance is widespread. This is the historic epicenter of Seattle's LGBTIQ+ community and although gentrification and time have changed things, the friendly, open-hearted vibes are still plentiful.

To experience Pike–Pine in all its glamorous glory, start at Melrose Market (p116) near I-5 in the early afternoon, then walk up E Pike St to Madison Ave and come back down E Pine St. There are enough interesting distractions to keep you occupied until at least midnight – the next day!

around the interior opulence, including the wood-paneled **Fireside Room**, where you can come on Wednesdays for Seattle's least rowdy event: Silent Reading Party (p120).

STIMSON-GREEN MANSION
HISTORIC BUILDING

Map p244 (☑206-624-0474; www.stimson green.com; 1204 Minor Ave; tours $10, registration required; ☺1-2:30pm 2nd Tue each month; ☑64) One of the first homes on First Hill, the baronial Stimson-Green Mansion is an English Tudor–style mansion completed in 1901 by lumber baron and real-estate developer CD Stimson. Built from brick, stucco and wood, this stately home is now owned by Stimson's granddaughter and used for private catered events such as weddings and themed dinners.

 EATING

Ninety-five percent of the best eating choices in this area are in Capitol Hill, one of Seattle's finest culinary neighborhoods. The restaurants along Broadway and 15th Ave and the Pike–Pine corridor offer an impressive range of Seattle dining options, but you'll also find some exciting places popping up further afield as new restaurants vie for space in an already-crowded neighborhood.

Full up with health-care facilities and educational establishments, First Hill doesn't offer much in the way of restaurants, but it's thankfully surrounded by areas that do.

★LOST LAKE CAFE & LOUNGE
AMERICAN $

Map p244 (☑206-323-5678; www.lostlakecafe. com; 1505 10th Ave, Capitol Hill; mains $12-15; ☺24hr; ☑First Hill Streetcar) It would be one thing if Lost Lake was merely a loving homage to David Lynch's hit TV mystery hour *Twin Peaks,* but the food is also fantastic – much better than other gimmick restaurants of its ilk. It specializes in diner grub, but sub in bold flavors and nix the frozen vegetables. Everything here is fresh and tasty.

One half of the restaurant is an Americana diner, while the other looks like a delightfully dim and mysterious roadhouse bar. You can get the full menu at both 24

hours a day. And before you ask: yes, it does indeed serve a damn fine cup of coffee.

BIMBO'S CANTINA
MEXICAN $

Map p244 (☑206-329-9978; www.bimbos cantina.com; 1013 E Pike St, Capitol Hill; burritos $9-11; ☺noon-2am; ☑First Hill Streetcar) Bimbo's slings fat burritos, overstuffed tacos and juicy quesadillas until midnight. The space is bordello kitsch with velvet matador portraits, oil paintings with neon elements and a hut-style thatched awning. The best feature of the restaurant is its subterranean bar, the **Cha-Cha Lounge**, serving drinks until 2am.

ELTANA WOOD-FIRED BAGEL CAFE
CAFE $

Map p244 (www.eltana.com; 1538 12th Ave, Capitol Hill; bagels/sandwiches from $1.75/8.75; ☺7am-4pm; ☑First Hill Streetcar) Although a bagel and a crossword puzzle seems like a quintessentially New York morning, Eltana brought the tradition to Seattle. The bagels are baked in a wood-fired oven (Montreal style) on-site and smeared with heavenly toppings including cream cheese and lox. The crosswords are mounted on the wall and reproduced on paper for the bagel-eating clientele. Clues change regularly.

RUMBA
CARIBBEAN $

Map p244 (☑206-583-7177; www.rumbaonpike. com; 1112 Pike St, Capitol Hill; small plates $8-12, mains $13-17; ☺5pm-1am Sun-Thu, to 2am Fri & Sat; ☑10) With its bright turquoise seating booths and sunny interior, Rumba exhibits a breezy Caribbean vibe. Indeed, you might just think you've died and gone to Jamaica when you taste its plump coconut prawns and rum cocktails. Come for an aperitif and share a plate of something small and tasty as you contemplate a night out in Capitol Hill.

FRANKIE & JO'S
ICE CREAM $

Map p244 (☑206-557-4603; www.frankieandjos. com; 1010 E Union St, Capitol Hill; scoops $4-9; ☺noon-11pm; ☑; ☑First Hill Streetcar) Frankie & Jo's is a 100% vegan ice-cream shop in Capitol Hill that specializes in lux flavors such as chocolate date, gingered golden milk and salty caramel ash, as well as made-from-scratch waffle cones.

MOLLY MOON'S
ICE CREAM $

Map p244 (☑206-708-7947; www.mollymoon icecream.com; 917 E Pine St, Capitol Hill; ice cream

$3-5; ⊙noon-11pm; 🚋First Hill Streetcar) 🔪 So what flavor will it be today? The orange habanero cookie dough, or maybe honey lavender? The seasonal flavors are wild at Molly Moon's, where lines stretch out the door and the whole place smells enticingly of waffle cones. It also has favorites like strawberry. Nursing locavore sensibilities, Molly gets its cream from hormone-free Washington cows.

COASTAL KITCHEN MODERN AMERICAN $$

Map p244 (📞206-322-1145; www.coastalkitchen seattle.com; 429 15th Ave E, Capitol Hill; mains $11-23; ⊙8am-10pm; 🚌10) Coastal Kitchen has become a Capitol Hill legend since its inception in 2012 with its culinary theme (fish) and variations (a different geographical influence is introduced quarterly). Weekend 'Blunch' is mega, as is the recently added oyster bar that complements the favorites: Dungeness crab cakes, Alaskan cod, Taylor shellfish and an epic sardine-heaped pasta.

ODDFELLOWS CAFE MODERN AMERICAN $$

Map p244 (📞206-325-0807; www.oddfellows cafe.com; 1525 10th Ave, Capitol Hill; mains $13-22; ⊙8am-11pm Mon-Fri, to 11pm Sat & Sun, food served 9am-3pm & 5-10pm Mon-Fri, from 8am Sat & Sun; 🚋First Hill Streetcar) 🔪 You can expect a wait for brunch at Oddfellows Cafe, but when you finally do sit down to your smorgasbord of flaky biscuits, fluffy eggs and well-dressed salads you'll realize it was worth it. When it isn't doing meal service you can come for strong coffee and scrumptious pastries.

ADANA JAPANESE $$

Map p244 (📞206-294-5230; www.adanaseattle. com; 1449 E Pine St, Capitol Hill; small plates $10-15; ⊙5-10pm Wed, Thu & Sun, to midnight Fri & Sat; 🚌11) It's hard to find better ambience than at Adana, a slightly subterranean and always dimly lit modern Japanese restaurant known for its extravagant tasting menus (three/five/seven courses $37/62/80), respectable whiskey selection and ramen Wednesdays ($16 a bowl).

ANNAPURNA CAFE NEPALI $$

Map p244 (📞206-320-7770; www.annapurna cafe.com; 1833 Broadway E, Capitol Hill; mains $11-21; ⊙3-9pm Mon-Thu, to 10pm Fri & Sat, 4-9pm Sun; 🖊; 🚊Link light rail) One of the Hill's most engaging dining experiences is this subterranean Nepalese restaurant on Broadway whose extensive menu mixes in a few Indian and Tibetan varietals as well. There are soups, *thalis* (platters of small dishes), curries, breads and plenty of vegetarian options. It's busy (good sign), but service is quick and efficient.

BAR COTO PIZZA $$

Map p244 (📞206-838-8081; 1546 15th Ave, Capitol Hill; pizza $16-18; ⊙5-10pm Sun-Thu, 4-11pm Fri & Sat; 🚌11) Once owned by Seattle restaurant mogul Ethan Stowell, this upscale pizza spot changed ownership in 2018, but the excellent pizza menu and superlative wine remains. The minimalist dining room is just far enough away from Capitol Hill's main drag to not feel picked over. New additions include freshly made pasta dishes and an expanded *salumi* (cured meat) menu.

SUIKA ASIAN $$

Map p244 (📞206-747-9595; www.suikaseattle. com; 611 E Pine St, Capitol Hill; plates $9-15; ⊙5-10:30pm Tue-Thu, to 11:30pm Fri, 4-11:30pm Sat, to 10:30pm Sun; 🚌11) Originally from Vancouver, BC, this Suika izakaya-style bar and restaurant took over a space that was formerly a well-loved restaurant on Capitol Hill. It won over the neighborhood with well-executed traditional and fusion Japanese and Korean dishes, such as its spicy miso ramen with black garlic oil and *unagi bibimbap* (eel over rice with scallion and teriyaki).

CAFÉ PRESSE FRENCH $$

Map p244 (📞206-709-7674; www.cafepresse seattle.com; 1117 12th Ave, Capitol Hill; mains $12-21; ⊙8am-1am; 🚌12) This dreamy cafe, opened by the owners of cute French bistro Le Pichet (p52), specializes in unfussy dishes, the likes of which you'd find once upon a time in a terrace cafe around Saint-Germain-des-Prés. The croque monsieur and madame are huge slabs of creamy goodness, steak *frites* are perfectly cooked and filling, and the vegetables are fresh and crisp.

On Tuesdays there is a popular *prix fixe* menu from 11am to 10pm (two/three courses $19/25).

DINO'S TOMATO PIE PIZZA $$

Map p244 (📞206-403-1742; www.dinostomato pie.com; 1524 E Olive Way, Capitol Hill; pizza $19-27; ⊙4pm-midnight Sun-Wed, to 2am Thu-Sat; 🚌8) With its mirrored walls, wooden

MELROSE MARKET

All glass, metal and greenery, **Melrose Market** (Map p244; ☎206-568-2666; www.melrosemarketseattle.com; 1501–1535 Melrose Ave; ⊙6am-11pm; 🚇10) 🥢 holds court at the bottom of the Pike–Pine corridor. It's always elbow-to-elbow in the afternoon as folks squeeze in for the locavore version of an office lunch break.

The anchor of the market is the peerless Sitka & Spruce (see below), but it's not the only reason to go. There's also a cocktail bar, a couple of specialist cheese and meat sellers, more casual take-out food places and a boutique full of desirable (if a bit overpriced) clothing and home goods. Popular Melrose vendors, all of whom are permanent, include **Homegrown**, the sustainable sandwich shop and **Taylor Shellfish**, which runs a sustainable shellfish farm near Bellingham.

The indoor market is encased in an old 1920s car showroom that balances the industrial glass and metal shell with plenty of wood and plants to achieve that clean-lined neo-industrial finish.

booths and red and yellow stained-glass accents, Dino's strikes a nostalgic chord (water in plastic red tumbler cups, anyone?). Peruse the interesting and sometimes quirky cocktail menu before ordering a Sicilian slice, or get a whole pie in either Sicilian or 'round' style.

Even if you're not in the mood for pizza be sure to check out its wonderfully retro website.

★**SITKA & SPRUCE**   MODERN AMERICAN **$$$**
Map p244 (☎206-324-0662; www.sitkaandspruce.com; 1531 Melrose Ave, Capitol Hill; plates $16-35; ⊙11:30am-2pm & 5-10pm Tue-Thu, to 9pm Mon, to 11pm Fri, 10am-2pm & 5-11pm Sat, to 9pm Sun; 🍴; 🚇10) The king of all locavore restaurants, Sitka & Spruce was the pilot project of celebrated Seattle chef Matt Dillon. It has since become something of an institution and a trendsetter, with its country-kitchen decor and a constantly changing menu concocted with ingredients from Dillon's own Vashon Island farm. Sample items include house-made charcuterie and roasted-asparagus-and-liver parfait. Great choice for vegetarians too.

Stop by at lunch on a weekday for the three-course chef's tasting menu for the very reasonable price of $25 per person. Happy hour is Tuesday through Saturday from 4pm to 6pm and features select small plates, beer, wine and cocktails specials.

OMEGA OUZERI   GREEK **$$$**
Map p244 (☎206-257-4515; www.omegaouzeri.com; 1529 14th Ave, Capitol Hill; small plates $14-18, mains $20-28; ⊙5-10pm Mon-Sat, to 9pm Sun; 🚇11) In an unassuming, square brick building, Omega Ouzeri's doors open to a bright, airy restaurant, pristine in white and baby blue, with metallic and marble accents throughout. Omega celebrates ouzo (a traditional anise-flavored aperitif), and its dishes range from *gigantes* (braised butter beans) to *oktapodi* (grilled octopus) and are prepared thoughtfully and beautifully.

CASCINA SPINASSE   ITALIAN **$$$**
Map p244 (☎206-251-7673; www.spinasse.com; 1531 14th Ave, Capitol Hill; mains $26-45; ⊙5-10pm Sun-Thu, to 11pm Fri & Sat; 🚇11) Successfully re-creating the feel of an Italian trattoria, Spinasse specializes in the cuisine of northern Italy's Piedmont region. This means dishes like hand-cut egg noodles in a variety of appealing ragú sauces and pan-seared trout with Piemontese salsa. The finely curated wine list includes the kings and queens of the region's reds: Barolo and Barbaresco.

MAMNOON   MIDDLE EASTERN **$$$**
Map p244 (☎206-906-9606; www.mamnoonrestaurant.com; 1508 Melrose Ave, Capitol Hill; small plates $7-16, mains $26-37; ⊙11:30am-10pm Mon-Fri, from 11am Sat & Sun; 🚇10) Slink inside Mamnoon for an unusual and wonderfully memorable voyage to the culinary Levant. This Capitol Hill spot specializes in Middle Eastern fusion and you'll find fragrant flatbreads, juicy meat kebabs and flavorful dips you won't be able to wait to get your hands on.

RIONE XIII   ITALIAN **$$$**
Map p244 (☎206-838-2878; www.ethanstowellrestaurants.com; 401 15th Ave E, Capitol Hill; mains $18-29; ⊙5-10pm Sun-Thu, to 11pm Fri &

Sat; 🖥10) The secret of Roman food lies in two words: 'simple' and 'effective.' That's its inherent beauty. Local legend Ethan Stowell probably guessed as much when he opened Rione XIII in 2012. Come here for epic *caccio e pepe* (spaghetti with four ingredients), Roman street pizzas, fried artichokes and mozzarella with fig and arugula.

POPPY   FUSION $$$

Map p244 (☏206-324-1108; www.poppyseattle. com; 622 Broadway E, Capitol Hill; thalis $30; ☺5:30-11pm; 🖥60) A *thali* is an Indian culinary tradition whereby numerous small taster dishes are served on one large plate. At Poppy it has cleverly applied the same principle to a broader list of Seattle/Northwest specialties, meaning that instead of chicken korma you get small portions of halibut, black-eyed peas and orange pickle. It's as good as it sounds.

🍷 DRINKING & NIGHTLIFE

Capitol Hill is *the* place to go out for drinks, whether you want a fancy cocktail, a cappuccino or a beer. It's also where 90% of the city's gay bars are located. Everywhere is crowded on the weekends so arrive ready to muscle your way to the bar.

★PONY   GAY

Map p244 (☏206-324-2854; www.ponyseattle. com; 1221 E Madison St, Capitol Hill; 🖥12) Pony (in a re-purposed car garage from the 1930s) is the type of gay bar that has reached a level of popularity where most denizens of Seattle's LGBTIQ+ nightlife scene either absolutely love or loathe it. Come dance your brains out on a Saturday night or sip a beer on its patio on a sunny afternoon and decide for yourself.

★ESPRESSO VIVACE AT BRIX   CAFE

Map p244 (☏206-860-2722; www.espresso vivace.com; 532 Broadway E, Capitol Hill; ☺6am-11pm; 🛜; 🚊Capitol Hill) Loved in equal measure for its no-nonsense walk-up stand on Broadway and this cafe (a large retro place with a beautiful Streamline Moderne counter), Vivace is known to have produced some of the Picassos of latte art. But it doesn't just offer pretty toppings: many

of Seattle's coffee experts rate its espresso shots as the best in the city.

★VICTROLA COFFEE ROASTERS   CAFE

Map p244 (www.victrolacoffee.com; 310 E Pike St, Capitol Hill; ☺6:30am-8pm Mon-Fri, from 7:30am Sat & Sun; 🖥10) Purveyors of a damned fine cup o' coffee since 2000, Victrola, to its credit, has clung to its grassroots, maintaining only four cafes. You can ponder how small is beautiful with one of its 4oz cappuccinos while watching the action in the roasting room.

Come for the free 'cuppings' (a mix of a demonstration and tasting) with a coffee expert on Wednesday at 11am.

★UNICORN   BAR

Map p244 (☏206-325-6492; www.unicorn seattle.com; 1118 E Pike St, Capitol Hill; ☺2pm-1:45am Mon-Fri, from 11am Sat & Sun; 🖥11) Even if Unicorn's circus theme doesn't exactly tickle your fancy, its commitment to the spectacle makes it worth a visit. Cocktails like the Cereal Killer (made with Fruit Loop–flavored vodka) hark back to the joys of giant lollipops and cotton candy, while the colorful explosion of decoration and pinball machine collection are likely to make even hardened cynics smile.

Check the website for events like drag bingo, cabaret shows and all manner of trivia nights.

ELYSIAN BREWING COMPANY   MICROBREWERY

Map p244 (☏206-860-1920; www.elysian brewing.com; 1221 E Pike St, Capitol Hill; ☺11:30am-11pm Mon-Thu, to midnight Fri, 9:30am-midnight Sat, to 10pm Sun; 🚊First Hill Streetcar) Elysian Brewing's Immortal IPA personifies the strong, bitter 'hop-forward' beers that have become part of craft-beer folklore in the Pacific Northwest. Despite being bought out by Anheuser-Busch in 2015, Elysian maintains several popular Seattle pubs, including this one (its 1996 original) in Capitol Hill, which got a remodel in 2019.

BAR FERDINAND   WINE BAR

Map p244 (☏206-693-2434; www.barferdinand seattle.com; 1424 11th Ave, Capitol Hill; mains $45; ☺1-11pm Tue-Sun) Homey, rustic, cozy, charming and classic all at once, Ferdinand serves locally sourced, Asian-inspired food cooked by fire and paired with a carefully curated wine selection. Bar Ferdinand sits in Chophouse Row (p121) and offers a unique take on a wine bar with its innovative food.

STARBUCKS RESERVE ROASTERY & TASTING ROOM   COFFEE

Map p244 (⚐206-624-0173; http://roastery.starbucks.com; 1124 Pike St, Capitol Hill; coffees $3-12; ⏰7am-11pm; ▣First Hill Streetcar) This high church to the joys of coffee drinking is the antithesis of everything Starbucks-y that has gone before. It's Starbuck's attempt at going back to its roots by emulating its more authentic modern competition. You may still reject it on face value, but the coffee itself is pretty great.

Even the most cynical Starbucks-phobe is likely to find something to like here – be it the tasting menu (three 8oz brews for $15), the coffee library, the huge copper casks, the micro- and small-batch roasters or the custom-made retro furniture.

R PLACE   GAY

Map p244 (⚐206-322-8828; www.rplaceseattle.com; 619 E Pine St, Capitol Hill; ⏰4pm-2am Mon-Fri, from 2pm Sat & Sun; ▣First Hill Streetcar) Weekend cabaret performances, amateur strip shows, go-go boys and DJs – there's something entertaining going on pretty much every night at this three-floor gay entertainment complex. Relax with a beer on the deck or dance your ass off. The ground floor is the lowest key; the top floor is where everything gets turned up a few notches.

WILDROSE   LESBIAN

Map p244 (⚐206-324-9210; www.thewildrosebar.com; 1021 E Pike St, Capitol Hill; ⏰5pm-midnight Mon, 3pm-1am Tue-Thu, 3pm-2am Fri & Sat, 3pm-midnight Sun; ▣First Hill Streetcar) This small, comfortable lesbian bar has theme nights (Taco Tuesdays; karaoke on Wednesday starting at 9pm) as well as a light menu, pool and DJs. On weekends it gets packed so expect a wait.

STUMPTOWN ON 12TH   COFFEE

Map p244 (⚐206-323-1544; www.stumptowncoffee.com; 1115 12th Ave, Capitol Hill; ⏰6am-7pm Mon-Fri, from 7am Sat & Sun; ▣12) 🍃 There's a tug of loyalties with Stumptown, Portland's coffee pioneers founded in 1999 by Duane Sorenson, who originally hails from Puyallup near Seattle. Its Seattle

location may not be the franchise original, but the coffee is still killer and if you're looking to expand your palate you can stop in on Friday at 1pm for a free coffee tasting.

THE LOOKOUT BAR & GRILL   BAR

Map p244 (⚐206-329-0454; www.facebook.com/lookoutseattle; 757 Bellevue Ave E, Capitol Hill; ⏰4pm-2am Mon-Fri, from noon Sat, from 11am Sun) One of the few places left in the area that still feels like old Seattle, The Lookout Bar & Grill sits on the edge of Capitol Hill with a close-up view of the Space Needle and Lake Union. Go for the laid-back atmosphere and happy-hour beers, wines and well drinks, and cheap bar food (plates $7 to $15).

OPTIMISM BREWING CO   MICROBREWERY

Map p244 (⚐206-651-5429; www.optimismbrewing.com; 1158 Broadway, Capitol Hill; ⏰noon-11pm Mon-Thu, to midnight Fri & Sat, to 9pm Sun; ♿🐾; ▣First Hill Streetcar) Capitol Hill has lagged behind Fremont and Ballard beer-wise, but this encouragingly named brewery put froth back on the local pints when it opened in 2015. In the fine style of similarly oriented Fremont Brewing (p148), Optimism offers a tasting room where you can sit at picnic benches on the factory floor and order basically straight from the beer vat.

The brewery, located in a spacious former car showroom, has several huge pros (aside from the beer): large windows, kid- and pet-friendly policies, bring-your-own food and no TVs to distract.

LINDA'S TAVERN   BAR

Map p244 (⚐206-325-1220; www.lindastavern.com; 707 E Pine St, Capitol Hill; ⏰4pm-2am daily, 10am-3pm Sat & Sun; ▣First Hill Streetcar) The back patio here is an excellent place to observe the nocturnal habits of *Hipsterus northwesticus*. Linda's is one of the few joints in town where you can recover from your hangover with an Emergen-C cocktail and a vegetarian brunch while taxidermied moose heads stare at you from the walls.

C.C. ATTLE'S   GAY

Map p244 (⚐206-726-0565; www.ccattles.net; 1701 E Olive Way, Capitol Hill; ⏰3pm-2am Mon-Fri, from 2pm Sat & Sun; ▣10) LGBTIQ+ travelers who prefer catching up over a plate of nachos to blasting EDM will want to post up at this congenial pub. It's known as a bar for bears (slang for stockier, hairier gay men) and their admirers, but anyone looking for a laid-back time will feel welcome. You can also expect friendly bartenders who make strong drinks.

Best of all: no cover ever.

CAFFÉ VITA
CAFE

Map p244 (☏206-712-2132; www.caffevita.com; 1005 E Pike St, Capitol Hill; ⏲6am-11pm Mon-Fri, from 7am Sat & Sun; ⛟First Hill Streetcar) The laptop camper, the first-daters, the radical student, the homeless person, the dreamy philosopher, the business person on their way to work: watch the whole neighborhood pass through this Capitol Hill institution (one of six in Seattle), whose on-site roasting room is visible through a glass partition.

TAVERN LAW
COCKTAIL BAR

Map p244 (☏206-322-9734; www.tavernlaw. com; 1406 12th Ave, Capitol Hill; ⏲5pm-midnight Sun & Tue-Thu, to 2am Fri & Sat; ⛟12) Named for the 1832 law that legalized drinking in public bars and saloons, Tavern Law is one of Seattle's most sought-after high-end cocktail bars (they call them 'libations' here). It's themed like a speakeasy – or, at least, a romanticized version of a speakeasy, as such establishments were never this plush.

CAPITOL CIDER
PUB

Map p244 (☏206-397-3564; www.capitolcider. com; 818 E Pike St, Capitol Hill; ⏲11am-2am Mon-Fri, from 10am Sat & Sun; ⛟First Hill Streetcar) The best cider pub in Seattle is far more than a taproom for apple-infused alcoholic beverages – although the 20-item cider menu is, of course, a big bonus. There's decent food, live music, game nights, craft beer, cocktails and a wonderful 'pub' feel set off by its cozy booths and portrait-bedecked walls.

COMET TAVERN
BAR

Map p244 (☏206-323-9853; www.thecomet tavern.com; 922 E Pike St, Capitol Hill; ⏲noon-2am; ⛟First Hill Streetcar) The Comet 2.0 replaced the dirty, dive-y, older version in 2014 after a brief closure. While not as endearingly disheveled as its predecessor (yet), the place still occupies the grungier end of the Pike–Pine ladder and serves food (mains $7 to $14). Sporadic live bands rock the rafters.

FUEL COFFEE
COFFEE

Map p244 (☏206-329-4700; www.fuelcoffee seattle.com; 610 19th Ave E, Capitol Hill; ⏲6am-7pm Mon-Fri, from 7am Sat & Sun; ⛟10) For once a cafe that doesn't try too hard to be cool. Fuel has a tangible community feel, retro gas-station motifs and great coffee.

CANTERBURY ALE HOUSE
PUB

Map p244 (☏206-322-3130; www.thecanterbury alehouse.com; 534 15th Ave E, Capitol Hill; ⏲2pm-midnight Mon-Thu, to 2am Fri, 10am-2am Sat, to midnight Sun; ⛟10) During a 2014 renovation Capitol Hill's default old-world pub got rid of dark booths and the suit of armor that once guarded the door. These have been replaced with a more open, gastropub feel, which has good points (better food and a fine rendering of Chaucer's *Canterbury Tales* on the wall) and bad (too many TVs).

The Geeks Who Drink trivia night (Wednesdays at 7pm) is legendary.

FIRESIDE LOUNGE
LOUNGE

Map p244 (☏206-622-6400; www.hotel sorrento.com; 900 Madison St, First Hill; ⏲7am-10pm Sun-Wed, to 11pm Thu-Sat) Stop in at this cozy bar in the Sorrento Hotel (p193) for a cocktail or beer while sitting in an over-stuffed leather chair next to the lounge's titular fire. Seating is first come first served.

NEIGHBOURS
GAY

Map p244 (www.neighboursnightclub.com; 1509 Broadway E, Capitol Hill; cover $10; ⏲9pm-2am Sun, Wed & Thu, to 4am Fri & Sat; ⛟First Hill Streetcar) Neighbours is an always-packed dance factory that seems to attract as many straight folks as LGBTIQ+ ones these days, but is still a reliable good time if you're eager to lose yourself in some dance music with the bass turned up high.

It's 18+ on Wednesdays and weekends after 2am, and 21+ all other times.

HIGH LINE
BAR

Map p244 (☏206-328-7837; www.highline seattle.com; 210 Broadway E, Capitol Hill; ⏲5-11pm; ⛟Capitol Hill) Bar, meat-free restaurant, live-music venue, people-watching perch – call it what you will. The High Line is best suited to vegan punk rockers who like playing foosball and arcade games, although all types are welcome.

CAPITOL HILL & FIRST HILL DRINKING & NIGHTLIFE

SILENT READING PARTY

Seattle is a famously literate city with a high quotient of bibliophiles. It is also the inventor of a rather peculiar 'party' that people attend purely to read books.

The Silent Reading Party is held at 6pm on the first Wednesday of every month in the wood-paneled Fireside Room at the Sorrento Hotel (p113). But, this is no conventional book club. Rather it's an excuse to just sit down and read silently, the only distractions being the discreet drinks service, some tinkling background piano music, and perhaps the chance to eavesdrop on other people's whispered book recommendations.

☆ ENTERTAINMENT

NEUMO'S
LIVE MUSIC

Map p244 (☑206-709-9442; www.neumos.com; 925 E Pike St, Capitol Hill; ☐First Hill Streetcar) This punk, hip-hop and alternative-music joint is, along with the Crocodile (p94) in Belltown, one of Seattle's most revered small music venues. Its storied list of former performers is too long to include, but if they're cool and passing through Seattle, they've probably played here. The audience space can get hot and sweaty, and even smelly, but that's rock and roll.

NORTHWEST FILM FORUM
CINEMA

Map p244 (www.nwfilmforum.org; 1515 12th Ave, Capitol Hill; ☐First Hill Streetcar) A film arts organization whose two-screen cinema offers impeccable programming, from restored classics to cutting-edge independent and international films. The snack bar has a nice selection of beer and wine in addition to the regular movie theater offerings.

CHOP SUEY
LIVE MUSIC

Map p244 (www.chopsuey.com; 1325 E Madison St, Capitol Hill; ☉4pm-2am Mon-Fri, 9pm-2am Sat & Sun; ☐12) Chop Suey is a small, dark space with high ceilings and a ramshackle faux-Chinese motif. Reborn under new ownership in 2015, it now serves burger-biased food as well as booze and music. The bookings are as mixed as the dish it's named after – electronica, hip-hop, alt-rock and other creative rumblings from Seattle's music underground.

ANNEX THEATRE
THEATER

Map p244 (☑206-728-0933; www.annextheatre.org; 1100 E Pike St, Capitol Hill; ☐First Hill Streetcar) Seattle's main experimental-fringe theater group is the Annex whose 99-seat theater (with bar) inhabits the Pike–Pine corridor. The highlight for many is the 'Spin the Bottle' nights on the second Thursday of every month (show at 8pm, tickets $10 to $15), a riot of comedy, music and variety.

🛍 SHOPPING

Shopping on Capitol Hill makes you instantly hipper; even just window-shopping is an education in cutting-edge popular culture. This is the place to find great record shops, unusual bookstores, vintage clothing and risqué sex toys.

★ELLIOTT BAY BOOK COMPANY
BOOKS

Map p244 (☑206-624-6600; www.elliottbay book.com; 1521 10th Ave, Capitol Hill; ☉10am-10pm Mon-Thu, to 11pm Fri & Sat, to 9pm Sun; ☐First Hill Streetcar) Seattle's most beloved bookstore offers over 150,000 titles in a large, airy, wood-beamed space with cozy nooks that can inspire hours of serendipitous browsing. In addition to the size, the staff recommendations and displays of books by local authors make this place extra special. Bibliophiles will be further satisfied with regular book readings and signings.

ADA'S TECHNICAL BOOKS & CAFE
BOOKS

Map p244 (☑206-322-1058; www.seattletech nicalbooks.com; 425 15th Ave E, Capitol Hill; ☉8am-9pm; ☐10) Ada's plush interior is done out in clean white wood with royal blue accents. There's a cafe on one side and a well-curated collection of books on the other (tech books are the specialty). Relax at the cafe tables or on a comfy chair in front of an old-fashioned fireplace. It also sells breakfast and sandwiches (mains $8 to $13).

GLASSWING · HOMEWARES

Map p244 (☑206-641-7646; www.glasswing shop.com; 1525 Melrose Ave, Capitol Hill; ☺11am-7pm Mon-Sat, noon-6pm Sun; ☒11) If you have some money to burn and you'd like to outfit your home and yourself in stylish, well-made goods that scream PNW chic, this is your place. It has everything from trendy houseplants to fashionable camping gear on the shelves, and even if you're just browsing, the industrial-meets-nature vibe of the store's design is worth popping in for.

BABELAND · ADULT

Map p244 (☑206-328-2914; www.babeland.com; 707 E Pike St, Capitol Hill; ☺11am-10pm Mon-Thu, to 11pm Fri & Sat, noon-8pm Sun; ☒First Hill Streetcar) Remember those pink furry handcuffs and glass dildo you needed? Well, look no further. Babeland is a national chain made popular by its feminist, LGBTIQ+ inclusive and generally judgment-free environment. The friendly staff at its Capitol Hill outpost can suit you up with anything you may desire in the realm of adult toys.

REVIVAL · VINTAGE

Map p244 (☑206-395-6414; www.revivalshop seattle.com; 233 Broadway E, Capitol Hill; ☺11am-7pm Tue-Sat, noon-6pm Sun; ☒Capitol Hill) Imagine a brick-and-mortar version of eBay with gear chosen by your ultimate personal shopper. This vintage/used clothes shop is far from being a dumping ground for someone else's unwanted clothes. Rather it is a collection of little gems uncovered by skilled and resourceful treasure hunters.

THROWBACKS NW · CLOTHING

Map p244 (☑206-402-4855; www.throwbacksnw. com; 1205 E Pike St, Capitol Hill; ☺11am-7pm Mon-Sat, noon-6pm Sun; ☒First Hill Streetcar) A niche vintage shop that focuses on active-wear clothing that not only evokes nostalgia for sports teams, but also revisits the hip-hop street fashions of the 1980s and '90s.

TWICE SOLD TALES · BOOKS

Map p244 (☑206-324-2421; www.twicesold tales.com; 1833 Harvard Ave, Capitol Hill; ☺10am-9pm; ☒Link light rail) Twice Sold Tales is a cozy den full of very-well-priced used books, stacked haphazardly along narrow aisles. A book 'happy hour' 25% discount kicks in daily after 6pm. A bunch of aloof cats roam the shop, actively ignoring everybody.

CROSSROADS TRADING CO · CLOTHING

Map p244 (☑206-328-5867; www.crossroads trading.com; 325 Broadway E, Capitol Hill; ☺11am-8pm Mon-Sat, to 7pm Sun; ☒First Hill Streetcar) This used-clothing store is less expensive than others in the area but also generally less hipster-chic, which is nice if you just want to shop for basics without having some too-cool clerk stare down their nose at your khaki slacks. There's another branch in the U District (p140).

WALL OF SOUND · MUSIC

Map p244 (☑206-441-9880; www.wosound.com; 1205 E Pike St, Capitol Hill; ☺11am-7pm Mon-Sat, noon-6pm Sun; ☒10) Bedroom-sized Wall of Sound has a civilized, studious air and a penchant for avant-garde sounds. If you're into esoterica or weird musical sub-genres such as 'Japanoise' (aka the noise music scene of Japan), this could be heaven.

CHOPHOUSE ROW · FOOD & DRINKS

Map p244 (☑206-324-0637; www.chophouse row.com; 1424 11th Ave, Capitol Hill; ☺7am-11:30pm; ☒First Hill Streetcar) Hidden among the historical and modern architecture of Capitol Hill, Chophouse Row feels like a locals-only secret. This new-in-2016 establishment features independent shops like facial specialists **Cake Skincare**, farmstead ice cream at **Kurt Farm Shop** and cocktail and wine spot Bar Ferdinand (p118).

The market itself is open 7am to 11:30pm, but individual shop times will vary. Check the website for specifics.

🏃 SPORTS & ACTIVITIES

CENTURY BALLROOM · DANCING

Map p244 (☑206-324-7263; www.centuryball room.com; 915 E Pine St, Capitol Hill; ☒First Hill Streetcar) Dance lessons (drop-in classes from $16) followed by an everyone-out-on-the-floor dance free-for-all (from $9 or included in the price of a class) makes a night at the Century the perfect combination of spectating and participating. Dance nights include everything from the Lindy hop to salsa. Check the website for a schedule of events.

Only in Seattle

Turn your chewing gum into communal art, sneer back at a grimacing statue of Vladimir Ilyich Ulyanov (aka Lenin), watch fishmongers play catch with giant halibut, and meet *Star Trek* nerds in a futuristic museum that's all about sci-fi...and rock and roll. And you thought Seattle was normal?

KELLI HAYDEN/SHUTTERSTOCK ©

FAINA GUREVICH/SHUTTERSTOCK ©

1. Museum of Pop Culture (p86)
The 'Infinite Worlds of Science Fiction' permanent exhibit includes costumes from popular TV shows.

2. Pike Place Market fishmongers (p43)
The piscine purveyors of Pike Place are at the heart of the market.

3. Gum wall (p49)
A bright, unsanitary Seattle icon in Pike Place Market.

4. Lenin statue (p143)
This bronze Bolshevik (created by Emil Venkov) resides among the public art of Fremont.

KENB/SHUTTERSTOCK ©

The CD, Madrona & Madison Park

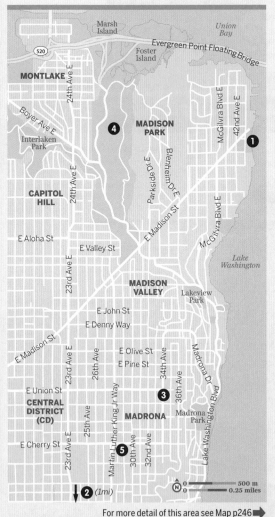

Neighborhood Top Five

1 Madison Park Beach (p127) Following the old trolley route down E Madison St to original Seattle seaside resort Madison Park Beach for a game of Frisbee, a brave dip in the lake and some wholesome food.

2 Northwest African American Museum (p126) Learning about Seattle's long, but often overlooked, history of African American heritage in this Central District museum.

3 European food (p127) Finding French, Italian and other European flavors on the taste-heavy commercial strip of 34th Ave in Madrona.

4 Washington Park Arboretum (p126) Tree-spotting and bird-watching in this wild and lovely park.

5 Little Ethiopia (p128) Seeking out great African food in the CD's 'Little Ethiopia,' especially along E Cherry St.

For more detail of this area see Map p246 ➡

Explore The CD, Madrona & Madison Park

The three neighborhoods sandwiched between Capitol Hill and Lake Washington are somewhat spread out and, while individually distinct, don't really form a coherent whole. Most non-residents come here for a specific reason: the beach at Madison Park, brunch in Madrona, or French food in Madison Valley.

Running down the east slope of First Hill, the Central District (CD), also the center of Seattle's African American community, is relatively easy to reach from downtown. Much of the neighborhood leans residential, but there are commercial stretches along and between 23rd St and Martin Luther King Jr Way. E Union St, particularly at the intersection of 23rd St, has exploded as a commercial corridor in recent years. Elsewhere you'll find quiet streets and the occasional piece of breathtaking public art.

Keep walking east through the CD and you'll hit Madrona, a diverse but rapidly gentrifying neighborhood on a hill above Lake Washington. Things are idyllic down by the water, and up top you'll find the area's unofficial 'Main St' along 34th Ave, roughly between E Pike and E Spring Sts.

If the weather's good, Madison Park merits a separate visit for its cute beach and short strip of glass-fronted cafes. About a mile before you reach the beach it's worth stopping in tree-lined Madison Valley, aka 'Little France,' for buttery croissants and a quiet stroll in the Washington Park Arboretum (p126).

Local Life

For brunch Hi Spot Café (p128) is one of those neighborhood brunch spots that lures in people from all over town; this is where sleepy Madrona wakes up, especially on Sunday.

Cultural education Take in a lecture, music performance or just grab a cup of coffee and browse the community bulletin boards at the CD's historic meeting place, Washington Hall (p126).

Getting There & Away

Bus Metro bus 11 runs from downtown along Pike and E Pine Sts to Capitol Hill and then along E Madison St all the way to Madison Park. Bus 8 goes from the Seattle Center via Capitol Hill to the CD, where it runs north–south through the neighborhood along Martin Luther King Jr Way. Buses 2 and 3 connect downtown with Madrona Beach via Capitol Hill.

Lonely Planet's Top Tip

Madison Valley, the 'other' (fourth) neighborhood in this rather disparate grouping, is worth a visit in its own right. Enjoy some fine French, vegetarian or Southern soul food from one of several eating places before taking a peek at the tree collection in the **Washington Park Arboretum** (p126).

✕ Best Places to Eat

➡ Taco Chukis (p127)

➡ Simply Soulful (p129)

➡ Voila! (p129)

➡ Cafe Soleil (p128)

For reviews, see p127.➡

🍺 Best Places to Drink

➡ Tougo Coffee (p129)

➡ Madrona Arms (p129)

➡ Attic Alehouse & Eatery (p129)

➡ Union Coffee (p129)

For reviews, see p129.➡

◉ Best Parks & Gardens

➡ Washington Park Arboretum (p126)

➡ Madrona Park & Beach (p126)

➡ Japanese Garden (p127)

➡ Madison Park Beach (p127)

◎ SIGHTS

Attractions in Madrona and Madison consist mainly of parks, but they're scattered over a wide area.

The CD hosts a culturally important (but often overlooked) museum, the Northwest African American Museum, as well as a few historic buildings and churches.

◎ The CD

NORTHWEST AFRICAN
AMERICAN MUSEUM   MUSEUM

(NAAM; ☑206-518-6000; www.naamnw.org; 2300 S Massachusetts St; adult/child, student & senior $7/5; ◷11am-5pm Wed & Fri-Sun, 11am-7pm Thu; ▣7) Small, concise and culturally valuable, NAAM opened in 2008 after more than 30 years of planning. It occupies the space of an old school, which, until the 1980s, educated a large number of African American children in the Central District. After the school closed, it was occupied for a while by community activists who prevented it from being demolished. Inside, the museum's main exhibits map the story of black immigration to the Pacific Northwest, especially after WWII.

WASHINGTON HALL   HISTORIC BUILDING

(☑206-322-1151; www.washingtonhall.org; 153 14th Ave; ◷8:30am-6pm Mon-Sat, 11am-3pm Sun; ▣27) Originally built in 1908 by the Danish Brotherhood, Washington Hall has been a meeting place, music venue (hosting Billie Holiday, Jimi Hendrix and Duke Ellington, among others), space for political organizers, and general neighborhood hangout ever since. In 2009 the building was purchased and saved from demolition by an organization called Historic Seattle, which embarked on an ongoing restoration project. It's currently home to a number of community organizations, a politically minded coffee shop and event spaces.

★LANGSTON
HUGHES PERFORMING
ARTS CENTER   HISTORIC BUILDING

(104 17th Ave S) This Byzantium Revival building began life in 1915 as a synagogue for a congregation of Orthodox Jews. By 1969 the demographics of the neighborhood had changed and the building was reintroduced as the Langston Hughes Performing Arts Center and was operated by the city's parks and rec department. More recently, the newly formed non-profit LANGSTON organization has taken over programming events in the space.

◎ Madrona

MADRONA PARK & BEACH   PARK

Map p246 (☑206-684-4075; 853 Lake Washington Blvd; ◷4am-11:30pm; ▮; ▣2) FREE Madrona Park Beach, down a steep hill from the business district in Madrona Park, is one of the nicest along the lake. In clear weather the views of Mt Rainier are fantastic. Swimming is only for hardy souls, however, as the water is icy cold, even in summer. Further south, past the yacht moorage, is **Leschi Park**, a grassy green space with a play area.

There are lifeguards on duty late May to late August (2pm to 7pm Monday to Friday, from 11am Saturday and Sunday late May to late June, noon to 7pm Monday to Friday, from 11am Saturday and Sunday late June to late August).

DENNY BLAINE PARK   PARK

Map p246 (☑206-684-4075; 200 Lake Washington Blvd E; ◷6am-10pm; ▣2) South of Madison Park toward the tail of Lake Washington Blvd is Denny Blaine Park, found at the end of a looping tree-lined lane. The beach is surrounded by an old stone wall that marked the shoreline before the lake level dropped 9ft during construction of the shipping canal. It was once well known as a lesbian hangout, but these days it's more of a mixed crowd. It still has a well-earned reputation for nude sunbathers, though.

VIRETTA PARK   PARK

Map p246 (☑206-684-4075; 151 Lake Washington Blvd E; ◷4am-11:30pm; ▣2) FREE Amid a lakeside nirvana of posh mansions, you'll find two-tiered Viretta Park, from which you can see the large house once owned by Kurt Cobain and Courtney Love – it's the house on the north side of the benches.

◎ Madison Park

WASHINGTON PARK ARBORETUM   PARK

Map p246 (☑206-543-8800; https://botanicgardens.uw.edu; 2300 Arboretum Drive E; ◷dawn-dusk; ▣11) FREE This wild and lovely park stretching from Madison Valley

GENTRIFICATION

As long as Seattle has been around it has been changing and growing, and while that pioneer spirit has propelled the city to become a world leader in tech innovation, it has not always made room for its historically disadvantaged and has discriminated against some communities. At present the Central District is at the fiery center of the city's ongoing gentrification debate. New tech jobs combined with a rising cost of housing has seen condo developers buying up land in the neighborhood, which, in turn, has seen a rapid decrease in the black population that made up its majority in the '60s and '70s as more young, mostly white, upper-middle-class people move in, followed by businesses catering to them and susequently increasing the cost of living for everyone. The debate is very much at the forefront of life in the Central District at present, and one you may experience firsthand while in the neighborhood. If your travels in Seattle do take you here, it's something to be mindful of.

up to Union Bay offers a wide variety of gardens, a wetlands nature trail and 200 acres of mature forest threaded by paths. More than 5500 plant species grow within the arboretum's boundaries. In the spring **Azalea Way**, a meandering trail that winds through the arboretum, is lined with a giddy array of pink- and orange-flowered azaleas and rhododendrons.

Trail guides to the plant collections are available at the **Graham Visitor Center** (Map p246; ⏰9am-5pm). Tram tours ($20 per person) are offered April through October, usually on Saturdays. Check online for the full schedule and to make reservations.

MADISON PARK BEACH   BEACH
Map p246 (☑206-684-4075; 1900 43rd Ave E; ⏰4am-11:30pm; 🚻; 🚌11) **FREE** A riotously popular place in the summer with a grassy slope for lounging and sunbathing, two tennis courts, a swimming raft floating in the lake, and lifeguards on duty from late June to Labor Day (noon to 7pm Monday to Friday, from 11am Saturday and Sunday). The park has been a lure for townies since the early 20th century, when a trolley route was built from downtown to bus everyone in.

JAPANESE GARDEN   GARDENS
Map p246 (☑206-684-4725; www.seattlejapan esegarden.org; 1075 Lake Washington Blvd E; adult/senior & student $8/4; ⏰10am-6pm Tue-Sun, from noon Mon Apr & Sep, 10am-7pm Tue-Sun, from noon Mon May-Aug, reduced hours Oct & Nov, closed Dec-Mar; 🅿🚻; 🚌11) At the southern edge of Washington Park Arboretum, this 3.5-acre formal garden has koi pools, waterfalls, a teahouse and manicured plantings. Granite for the garden's sculptures was laboriously dragged in from

the Cascades. There are often events, such as tea ceremony demonstrations and art exhibits – check the website for listings.

EATING

In recent years, the CD's unpretentious delis, soul food take-out spots and Ethiopian restaurants have been joined by a few trendy (and gentrifying) bistros and burger bars.

Madison Valley has established itself as a gourmet Gallic quarter with several French-run establishments. Other small restaurant huddles punctuate Madison Park and the increasingly upscale business strip on 34th Ave in Madrona. The brunches in the latter neighborhood are legendary.

The CD

⭐**TACO CHUKIS**   TACOS $
Map p246 (www.facebook.com/TacosChukis; 2215 E Union St; tacos $2.20-2.75; ⏰11am-9pm; 🚌2) At the moment in Seattle there are few bites of food better than the signature taco at Taco Chukis. It's a simple design (juicy pork, guacamole, melted cheese and brilliantly tangy grilled pineapple) that's executed so well you're likely to get into line immediately after finishing to order a couple more.

EZELL'S FAMOUS CHICKEN   SOUTHERN US $
Map p246 (☑206-324-4141; www.ezellschicken. com; 501 23rd Ave; mains $9-13; ⏰10am-9pm Mon-Fri, to 10pm Sat, 11am-10pm Sun; 🚌3)

LITTLE ETHIOPIA

The Central District has a history of reinventing itself to incorporate successive waves of new immigrants. In the 1910s it was a primarily Jewish neighborhood, pre-WWII it welcomed Japanese settlers, and postwar it became Seattle's main African American enclave, a characteristic it partly retains. Since the 1970s the neighborhood has welcomed an increasing number of African immigrants moving in, particularly from Ethiopia.

The first Ethiopians arrived in 1974 after the country's Derg takeover provoked a massive exodus. In 1970 there were no more than 20 Ethiopians in Seattle; today the region counts approximately 25,000, one of the biggest communities in the US. The East African flavor is most prevalent along E Cherry St, where you'll see taxi businesses, grocery stores selling local Amharic-language newspapers, and a slew of Ethiopian restaurants (four alone sit along E Cherry St near Martin Luther King Jr Way). Not surprisingly, the name 'Little Ethiopia' is sometimes used to describe the area. In 2013 Joseph W Scott and Solomon A Getahun published a book about the diaspora called *Little Ethiopia of the Pacific Northwest*.

There's fast food and then there's fast food. This is the good kind. Ezell's was started by a transplanted Texan in 1984 right here in the CD. Its crispy, spicy, Southern-style chicken and equally scrumptious side dishes like coleslaw and sweet-potato pie have since spread nationwide and, in 2015, went international when Ezell's opened a restaurant in Dubai.

CAFE SELAM ETHIOPIAN $
Map p246 (☑206-328-0404; www.cafeselam. com; 2715 E Cherry St; mains $11-16; ☺10am-9pm; ☐3) Aptly located in the heart of the CD's 'Little Ethiopia,' Cafe Selam wows with dishes such as *foul* (a fava-bean concoction that's not at all foul) and *fir fir* (*injera* flatbread, yogurt and lamb) – all done to perfection here.

This place is definitely authentic, so expect to scoop up your beans, lamb, okra etc using torn-off bits of bread, not a knife and fork. Selam even roasts its own coffee, the product so beloved by Seattleites, which was first 'discovered,' legend has it, by an Ethiopian goat herder.

FAT'S CHICKEN & WAFFLES SOUTHERN US $
Map p246 (☑206-602-6863; www.fatschicken andwaffles.com; 2726 E Cherry St; mains $12-16; ☺11am-9pm Tue-Fri, 9am-3pm & 5-9pm Sat, 9am-3pm & 5-8pm Sun; ☐3) Occupying the intersection once inhabited by old-school CD institution Catfish Corner, Fat's is considered by most to be a credible replacement. Wisely, it's chosen to continue the long-standing CD tradition for Southern food in an area that has otherwise lost a lot of its old-school grit (and grits).

✖ Madrona

CAFE SOLEIL ETHIOPIAN $
Map p246 (☑206-325-1126; 1400 34th Ave; mains $10-15; ☺5:30-9pm Wed-Fri, 8:30am-2pm & 5:30-9pm Sat, 8:30am-2pm Sun; ☐2) Surprise! It looks like an American diner and serves a hearty American brunch, but Cafe Soleil's real specialty is Ethiopian food – it's like a becalmed offshoot of 'Little Ethiopia' in the CD. The bright, light-filled room is an excellent place to dip your *injera* (flatbread) in spicy African stews.

HI SPOT CAFÉ BREAKFAST $
Map p246 (☑206-325-7905; www.hispotcafe. com; 1410 34th Ave; mains $10-14; ☺7am-4pm Mon-Fri, from 8am Sat & Sun; ☐2) The cinnamon rolls here are bigger than your head, and that's no exaggeration. It's a comfy little space in an old craftsman-style house where you can either get a sit-down meal (only served until 2:30pm daily) or a quick espresso and pastry to go.

RED COW FRENCH $$$
Map p246 (☑206-454-7932; www.ethansto wellrestaurants.com; 1423 34th Ave; mains $27-60; ☺5-10pm Sun-Thu, to 11pm Fri & Sat; ☐2) Welcome to a new endeavor from lauded Seattle chef Ethan Stowell who normally specializes in Italian fare, but for this venture has crossed the Alps into France. The decor is typical Stowell – open kitchen, intimate interior and clean-lined minimalist design – while the menu star is steak (seven different cuts), *frites* and garlic aioli.

✕ Madison Park

★**SIMPLY SOULFUL**　　　SOUTHERN US **$**

Map p246 (📞206-474-9841; www.simply-soulful.
com; 2909b E Madison St, Madison Valley; mains
$13-19; ⊙8am-7pm Tue-Fri, 8am-4pm Sat, 10am-
3pm Sun; 🚌11) If you're hungry for something that will really fill your tank, head
directly to this authentic family-owned
Southern restaurant. The menu is full of
dishes from the Gulf Coast region; it's a riot
of catfish and grits, chicken and waffles,
biscuits and gravy, and banana pudding if
you're still peckish.

CAFÉ FLORA　　　VEGETARIAN **$$**

Map p246 (📞206-325-9100; www.cafeflora.
com; 2901 E Madison St; mains $17-22; ⊙9am-
9pm Sun-Thu, 9am-10pm Fri & Sat; 🖋; 🚌11) A
longtime favorite for vegan and vegetar-
ian food, Flora has a garden-like feel and a
creative menu, with dinner treats like fried
avocado, yam fries, a grilled asparagus
pizza and black-bean burgers. Or go for the
hoppin' John fritters or tomato asparagus
scrambles at brunch.

VOILA!　　　FRENCH **$$**

Map p246 (📞206-322-5460; www.voilabistrot.
com; 2805 E Madison St, Madison Valley; mains
$16-27; ⊙11:30am-9pm Tue-Sat, 5-9pm Sun,
from 4pm Sat; 🚌11) This cozy Gallic bistro
has an old French flag in the window that
looks like it got left behind by some romantic revolutionaries. Half the deal here is in
creating an exotic Euro-flavored atmosphere that is as fine honed as the food. The
menu's *plats* consist of well-known French
standards from pâté and pork chops to
escargot.

🍺 DRINKING & NIGHTLIFE

**Wave goodbye to franchises! Search
around in the CD, Madrona and Madison
Park, and you'll find some of Seattle's
most understated neighborhood pubs
and coffee bars.**

UNION COFFEE　　　COFFEE

Map p246 (📞206-577-7953; www.unioncoffee
seattle.com; 2407 E Union St, CD; ⊙7:30am-
3:30pm; 🚌2) Perfect pour-overs and
expertly pulled espresso are the hallmarks

of this laid-back Central District place that
takes its interior design inspiration from
Berlin and Osaka (think white walls and
homey furniture).

TOUGO COFFEE　　　CAFE

Map p246 (📞206-860-3518; www.tougocoffee.
com; 1410 18th Ave, CD; ⊙6am-6pm Mon-Fri,
from 7am Sat & Sun; 🚌2) Community cafe
par excellence where the skilled barista
doubles as an excellent DJ. It's now part of
a small chain, but retains its locally owned
vibe.

CYPHER CAFE　　　CAFE

(www.facebook.com/CypherCafeWAHall; 153 14th
Ave, CD; ⊙8:30am-6pm Mon-Fri, 8:30am-7pm
Sat, 11am-3pm Sun; 🚌27) Owned by a local
non-profit (Black Power Unlimited), Cypher
Cafe is on the 1st floor of Washington Hall
and aims to function as a modern *salon*
for the CD's African American community.
Everyone is welcome for cups of strongly
brewed coffee, great espresso drinks and a
small, but always tasty, collection of baked
goods.

MADRONA ARMS　　　PUB

Map p246 (📞206-739-5104; www.madronaarms.
com; 1138 34th Ave, Madrona; ⊙11am-midnight
Mon-Fri, from 9am Sat & Sun; 🚌2) A newish
neighborhood pub in Madrona fashioned
in the old British tradition with obvious
nods to Seattle (local draft ales). It's run by
an Irishman so there's Guinness on tap and
some old-country food standards, including bangers and mash, and shepherd's pie.

ATTIC ALEHOUSE & EATERY　　　PUB

Map p246 (📞206-323-3131; www.atticalehouse
seattle.com; 4226 E Madison St, Madison Park;
⊙11am-2am Mon-Fri, 9am-2am Sat & Sun; 🚌11)
A friendly, unpretentious pub that makes
for a great post-beach beer.

MCGILVRA'S　　　IRISH PUB

Map p246 (📞206-325-0834; www.mcgilvras.
com; 4234 E Madison St, Madison Park; ⊙11am-
midnight Mon-Fri, 10am-2am Sat & Sun; 🚌11)
This backdrop to Madison Beach is definitely more pub than bar and has a loyal
local following of drinkers slapping on the
after-sun lotion. You can get your Guinness
in a glass or poured over your beef stew.
The Jameson Irish whiskey, meanwhile,
often ends up in the crab soup. Dozens of
soccer jerseys are hung from the ceiling.

⭐ ENTERTAINMENT

Don't be fooled by the quiet exterior; there's precious history in these neighborhoods. The CD once bebopped with segregated jazz bars, while a decade later Jimi Hendrix played his first gig at the Temple de Hirsch Sinai on the corner of E Pike St and 15th Ave. Some of that spirit still remains at two recently revitalized neighborhood performance spaces, Washington Hall (p126) and the Langston Hughes Performing Arts Center (p126).

LANGSTON   ARTS CENTER
(📞206-323-7067; www.langstonseattle.org; 104 17th Ave S, CD; 🚊27) LANGSTON is a new non-profit arts organization in the CD dedicated to 'cultivating black excellence.' It hosts programs at the Langston Hughes Performing Arts Center, including film festivals and art exhibitions. Check the website for details of upcoming events.

CENTRAL CINEMA   CINEMA
Map p246 (📞206-328-3230; www.central-cinema.com; 1411 21st Ave, CD; 🚊2) Welcome to a bona fide dine-in cinema. What might be par for the course in Portland, OR, is a rare sight in Seattle, which makes this small neighborhood movie house in the CD all the more precious. The food consists of relatively simple pizzas, but it's backed up by some decent local microbrews. Movies range from screwball comedies to Japanese docs and indie hits.

NEW CITY THEATER   THEATER
Map p246 (📞206-271-4430; www.newcity theater.org; 1404 18th Ave, CD; 🚊2) A small but long-standing artist-run theater in the CD with a good back catalog of plays under its belt including excellent stripped-down productions of Shakespeare. *Hamlet, King Lear* and *The Tempest* have all been staged here.

🛍 SHOPPING

⭐TWO BIG BLONDES   CLOTHING
(📞206-762-8620;   www.twobigblondes.com; 2501 S Jackson St, CD; 🕙11am-6pm Tue-Sat, noon-5pm Sun; 🚊8) If you are in the market for women's clothing in a size 14+, Two Big Blondes is the place for you – this plus-size consignment store has thousands of items to pick through. The helpful staff and chatty loyal customers elevate the experience here. Come prepared to make some friends.

CURA   BOUTIQUE
Map p246 (📞206-660-4176; www.thecuraco. com; 2407 E Union St, CD; 🕙noon-5:45pm Wed & Thu, to 6:30pm Fri, 11:30am-6:30pm Sat, to 6pm Sun; 🚊2) Conscientious consumption is the mission of this new jewelry, clothing, art and home-goods store in the CD. Everything for sale here is both gorgeous and ethically sourced from artisans around the world, with a special consideration for women artisans from the global south. One of the store's best features are its price tags: there's tons of great stuff under $20.

TWO OWLS   CHILDREN'S CLOTHING
Map p246 (📞805-617-4252; www.shoptwoowls. com; 3308 E Spring St, Madrona; 🕙11am-5pm Tue-Fri & Sun, from 10am Sat; 🚊2) This delightful children's boutique has jaunty clothing made from organic cotton and a good collection of unique toys.

UNCLE IKE'S POT SHOP   DISPENSARY
Map p246 (www.uncleikespotshop.com; 2310 E Union St, CD; 🕙8am-11:45pm; 🚊2) One of the first recreational weed dispensaries in Seattle is still well known for its well-stocked shelves and friendly budtenders. It courted controversy soon after its 2014 opening as part of a larger conversation around gentrification in the CD.

🏃 SPORTS & ACTIVITIES

FOSTER ISLAND WETLANDS TRAIL   WALKING
Map p246 (Madison Park; 🕙dawn-dusk; 🚊43) The northern edge of Washington Park Arboretum includes this wonderful wood chip–paved trail around Foster Island in Lake Washington's Union Bay, a picnic spot that was once a burial ground for Union Bay Native Americans. The waterfront trail winds through marshlands and over a series of floating bridges to smaller islands and reedy shoals.

U District

Neighborhood Top Five

❶ University of Washington (p133) Reliving (or living) your cerebral undergraduate years on the leafy, architecturally attractive campus of the University of Washington with its art galleries, neo-Gothic library and tree-studded quad.

❷ The Ave (p137) Revisiting the non-cerebral part of your undergraduate days in the pubs, bars and oh-so greasy and good take-out spots of the so-called 'Ave.'

❸ Blue Moon (p137) Reading the graffiti and listening to the latest street poets at this legendary counterculture dive.

❹ Burke Museum (p133) Learning the history of the Pacific Northwest's natural history and indigenous cultures at this campus museum.

❺ University Book Store (p139) Spending a bibliophilic afternoon in Seattle's oldest bookstore, founded in 1900.

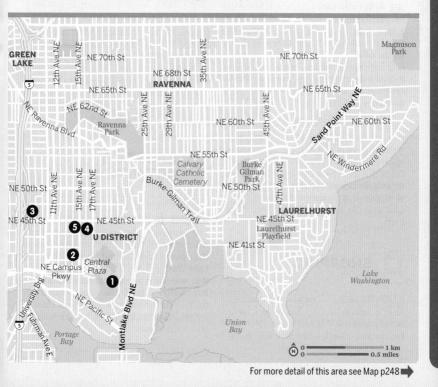

For more detail of this area see Map p248 ➡

Lonely Planet's Top Tip

A great way to explore the university is on a bicycle: the Burke-Gilman Trail (p139) follows the south side of campus, providing easy access. Further exercise can be procured on water: the campus abuts the shores of Lake Union and is one of the best places in Seattle to hire a kayak.

✗ Best Places to Eat

➡ Portage Bay Cafe (p136)
➡ Thai Tom (p136)
➡ Shultzy's Bar & Grill (p136)
➡ Morsel (p136)

For reviews, see p134. ➡

🍷 Best Places to Drink

➡ Blue Moon (p137)
➡ Café Racer (p137)
➡ Boba Up (p137)
➡ Big Time Brewery & Alehouse (p138)
➡ Monkey Pub (p138)

For reviews, see p137. ➡

◉ Best Places to Read

➡ Suzzallo Library (p134)
➡ Zoka Coffee (p138)
➡ Cafe Solstice (p138)
➡ Café Allegro (p137)

Explore U District

Head east off I-5 north of Lake Union and suddenly you'll feel as if you're no longer in Seattle. The U District, named for 'U Dub' (what locals call the University of Washington, or UW), feels like its own little college town. Just like you, most of the people here are visitors – they're merely staying a bit longer (several semesters or more).

Nearly everyone gets oriented in the U District on 'the Ave' (University Way, roughly between 40th and 50th Sts), an atmospheric main drag full of tiny cheap eateries, thrift stores, record stores, secondhand bookstores, tattoo parlors, bars, and coffee shops full of deadline-chasing, laptop-gazing students. Read fly-posters on lampposts, eavesdrop on conversations in coffee bars and follow the action on the Ave and you'll soon feel 23 again (if you aren't already).

The number of cheap places to eat, especially Indian and southeast Asian cuisines, makes the Ave the best place to find an inexpensive meal. If you want to head inside, lose yourself in the cavernous University Book Store (p139), which takes up an entire city block.

Reserve a sunny day to explore the adjacent UW campus, a veritable arboretum/architectural showcase with a couple of top-notch museums focusing on art and natural history. The campus is made for people-watching (or, more specifically, student-watching) and you can enter many of the buildings unannounced, including the Suzzallo Library (p134) and the Hub (student union).

Local Life

Campus life On a warm day in spring or summer, students loaf alfresco under the gnarled cherry trees in the Quad (p134), exchanging gossip, study notes and Instagram photos.

The Ave Hang around on University Way, aka 'the Ave (p137),' anywhere between 40th and 50th Sts and follow the crowds.

Bohemian bar Bump into U Dub's more bohemian demographic at colorful Café Racer (p137).

Getting There & Away

Bus Several Metro buses, including buses 70 and 74, run frequently to the U District from downtown Seattle. Buses 31, 32 and 4 link the U District with nearby Fremont and Ballard.

Link light rail Connects University of Washington to Capitol Hill, downtown and, ultimately, Sea-Tac International Airport.

⊙ SIGHTS

The University of Washington campus, originally laid out as the Alaska-Yukon-Pacific Exposition site in 1909, is a beautiful place to explore, especially when the weather cooperates. Among its regal buildings are two notable museums, the Burke Museum and the Henry Art Gallery.

UNIVERSITY OF WASHINGTON UNIVERSITY
Map p248 (www.washington.edu; ⓡUniversity of Washington) Founded in 1861, Seattle's university is almost as old as the city itself and is highly ranked worldwide (the prestigious *Times Higher Education* magazine listed it 32nd in the world in 2016). The college was originally located in downtown on a 10-acre site now occupied by the Fifth Avenue Theater (the university still owns the land), but with both university and city outgrowing their initial confines, a new site was sought in 1895.

The present-day 700-acre campus that sits at the edge of Lake Union about 3 miles northeast of downtown is flecked with stately trees and beautiful architecture, and affords wondrous views of Mt Rainier framed by fountains and foliage. Roughly 47,000 students and 22,000 staff enjoy the noble setting, making 'U Dub' easily the largest university in the state. The core of the campus is Central Plaza (p134). Close by you can pick up information and a campus map at the **visitor center** (Map p248; ☑206-543-9198; Odegaard Undergraduate Library; ◷8:30am-5pm Mon-Fri).

The university is ideal for gentle strolls, people-watching and lung-stretching exercise on the Burke-Gilman Trail (p139). The campus also hosts two decent museums, fine sports facilities, a theater, a library, and a student-union building where leaflet-filled noticeboards advertise the kinds of outré, spontaneous events that typically color student life.

BURKE MUSEUM MUSEUM
Map p248 (☑206-543-5590; www.burkemus eum.org; 4300 15th Ave NE; check website for details; ◷10am-5pm, to 8pm 1st Thu of month; ☐70) An interesting hybrid museum covering both natural history and indigenous cultures of the Pacific Rim. Inside you'll find, arguably, Washington's best natural-history collection, focusing on the geology and evolution of the state. It guards an impressive stash of fossils, including a 20,000-year-old saber-toothed cat. Also

---

THE ALASKA-YUKON-PACIFIC EXPOSITION

Seattle's 1962 World's Fair wasn't the only time the city has hosted an international 'expo.' Along with five other US cities, Seattle has been bequeathed the honor twice – the first time in 1909 with the so-called Alaska-Yukon-Pacific Exposition (the AYPE).

The AYPE helped transform Seattle from a boom-bust Northwestern backwater into a city of national prestige. Initially inspired by the Klondike gold rush of 1896–97, an event that Seattle both supported and supplied, the expo quickly morphed into a wider celebration of Pacific Rim trade and the nascent vitality of the Pacific Northwest region.

Built on what was then the relatively new campus of the University of Washington, the expo site was designed by influential American landscapers, the Olmsted brothers, who covered 250 acres of formerly virgin forest with a regal cluster of temporary buildings.

While the 1962 World's Fair left behind the Space Needle (p82) and the Seattle Center (p88), the AYPE's legacy was more general. Only two original buildings remain, the university's **Architecture Hall** and **Cunningham Hall**. However, the expo's landscaped gardens, with their trickling fountains and tree-lined Mt Rainier vistas, later became the grand stencil upon which the modern University of Washington developed. The campus today owes much to the Olmsted brothers' inspired vision.

Approximately 3.7 million people attended the AYPE, which was considered a success for the time. Driven by new technologies, the event instigated a car race from New York to Seattle (the winner completed it in 23 days), and was the first time that many Seattleites saw an airplane. Among those impressed by the flying display was a 27-year-old local timber merchant named William Boeing...

not to be missed is an awe-inspiring collection of Kwakwaka'wakw masks from British Columbia.

HENRY ART GALLERY   MUSEUM

Map p248 (☑206-543 2280; www.henryart.org; cnr 15th Ave NE & NE 41st St; adult/senior $10/6, Thu free; ☑11am-4pm Wed & Fri-Sun, 11am-9pm Thu; ☑70) Approaching 90 years of age, the Henry is Seattle's modern-art masterpiece. Set in a sophisticated space on the University of Washington campus, it revolves around a remarkable permanent exhibit created in 2003 by light-manipulating sculptor James Turrell. Backing it up is a full revolving program of high-quality temporary and touring collections. Expos here are modern, provocative and occasionally head-scratching.

There are also regular artist talks, discussion groups and workshops.

RAINIER VISTA   VIEWPOINT

Map p248 (☑University of Washington) What other US university campus has a perfectly framed view of a glacier-drizzled, 14,410ft stratovolcano? This beautiful green corridor of lawns and walkways emanates from the steps of UW's Red Sq and was designed by John Olmsted as the centerpiece for the 1909 Alaska-Yukon-Pacific Expo (p133).

QUAD   LANDMARK

Map p248 (☑University of Washington) The lovely Quad is home to some of the original campus buildings, many of them built in a Collegiate Gothic style reminiscent of New England. On sunny days, you can relax on the grass amid Frisbee throwers, sunbathers dodging seminars, earnest undergraduates discussing international affairs, and young love blossoming under the cherry trees.

SUZZALLO LIBRARY   LANDMARK

Map p248 (☑206-543-0242; www.lib.washi ngton.edu; 4000 15th Ave NE; ☑University of Washington) The architecturally minded will be interested in the University of Washington's Suzzallo Library. Designed by Carl Gould in 1926, this bibliophile's dream was inspired by Henry Suzzallo, UW's president at the time. Suzzallo wanted it to look like a cathedral, because 'the library is the soul of the university.' Unfortunately for him, his bosses disagreed; on reviewing the building, they deemed it too expensive and fired Suzzallo for his extravagance.

However, the dream was partially realized in the grand neo-Gothic entrance lobby and the truly beguiling **reading room** with its massive cathedral-like windows that, on fine days, cast filtered sunlight onto the long reading pews. Hours change with the school year, so it's best to check ahead before visiting if you're interested in peeking inside.

DRUMHELLER FOUNTAIN   FOUNTAIN

Map p248 (☑University of Washington) Drumheller Fountain sits inside what was originally known as Geyser Basin (now 'Frosh Pond'), one of the few remaining pieces left over from the 1909 expo that beefed up the university.

CENTRAL PLAZA (RED SQUARE)   SQUARE

Map p248 (☑University of Washington) The center of campus is more commonly referred to as Red Sq (because of its base of red brick rather than any Bolshevik inclinations). It's not the coziest plaza, but it fills up with students cheerfully sunning themselves on nice days and it looks impressive at night. *Broken Obelisk*, the 26ft-high stainless-steel sculpture in the square, was made by noted color-field painter Barnett Newman.

Just below Red Sq is a wide promenade leading to lovely Rainier Vista, with spectacular views across Lake Washington to Mt Rainier.

RAVENNA PARK   PARK

Map p248 (☑206-684-4075; 5520 Ravenna Ave NE, Ravenna; ☑6am-10pm; ☑; ☑74) Just north of the U District is Ravenna, a residential neighborhood that's home to a lot of professors and university staff. At its heart is Ravenna Park, a lush and wild park with two playgrounds on either side of the foliage-drenched ravine carved by Ravenna Creek. Escape the clamor of the city – briefly.

✖ EATING

This is one of the best districts in Seattle for cheap and authentic ethnic food. Vegan and vegetarian haunts also abound.

When you're browsing for lunch or dinner, don't be put off by unappetizing-looking storefronts; some of the most

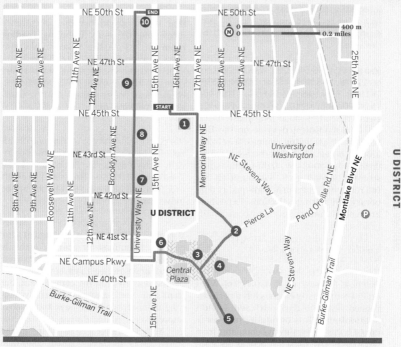

Neighborhood Walk
U District

START BURKE MUSEUM
END THE AVE, OR GRAND ILLUSION CINEMA
LENGTH 2 MILES; ONE HOUR

Start this tour at the ❶ **Burke Museum** (p133), which you may choose to visit now (add an hour to the tour time) or simply note to check it out later. Its collection of indigenous art from around the Pacific is not to be missed. From here, walk along NE 45th St to Memorial Way NE – take a right and amble into campus through the university's north gate.

Keep going down Memorial Way NE and snake a left when you reach the roundabout to continue along Spokane Lane. Take a left when you can and you'll be at the ❷ **Quad** (p134), the campus's prettiest nook. From here a straight path cuts southwest to central ❸ **Red Square** (p134), full of criss-crossing students rushing to lectures.

Red Square is dominated by the cathedral-like ❹ **Suzzallo Library** (p134). Admire it from the inside and out, then take a sharp left when you exit. Descend the stairs and walk straight ahead toward ❺ **Drumheller Fountain** (p134). Along the pathway leading to the fountain, you'll be stunned (if it's a clear day) by the views from what is appropriately named the Rainier Vista.

Head back toward Red Square, and bear left at the library. This will lead you to the ❻ **Henry Art Gallery** (p134), one of the best contemporary galleries in Seattle. After being blinded by modern art, head over to bustling University Way NE, aka 'the Ave.' Duck into ❼ **Café Allegro** (p137), accessed via an alley off NE 42nd St: this (not Starbucks) is Seattle's oldest surviving espresso bar. Continue up the Ave and put your hunger on hold while you investigate the ❽ **University Book Store** (p139), then cross the road and squeeze into ❾ **Thai Tom** (p136) for Bangkok street food. End at the intersection with NE 50th St, where you may want to check out what's showing at the art house ❿ **Grand Illusion Cinema** (p138).

interesting food comes from places that have the outward appearance of run-down hovels. The adventurous will be rewarded.

★PORTAGE BAY CAFE
BREAKFAST $

Map p248 (☑206-547-8230; www.portagebay cafe.com; 4130 Roosevelt Way NE; brunch $10-19; ⊗7am-2pm Mon-Fri, 7:30am-2:30pm Sat & Sun; ☑74) ✦ A hugely popular brunch spot and for good reason. Aside from the usual suspects (eggs, bacon, pancakes), there's a help-yourself breakfast bar loaded with fresh fruit, cream, syrup, nuts and the like (all local, of course), waiting to be spread on your doorstep-thick slices of French toast. Arrive early or after 1pm at weekends to avoid the rush.

THAI TOM
THAI $

Map p248 (☑206-548-9548; 4543 University Way NE; mains $7-10; ⊗11:30am-9pm Mon-Thu, 11:30am-10pm Fri & Sat, noon-9pm Sun; ☑70) About as wide as a train carriage, with permanently steamed-up windows, an open-kitchen lunch counter, and flames leaping up from beneath the constantly busy pans on the stoves, Thai Tom feels like a backstreet Bangkok hole-in-the-wall, and many hail its simple Thai food as the best in the city.

Push in among the elephant heads, dark-brown walls and elbow-to-elbow crowds to find out. Cash only.

ALADDIN GYRO-CERY
MIDDLE EASTERN $

Map p248 (☑206-632-5253; 4143 University Way NE; gyros $6-9; ⊗10am-2:30am; ☑; ☑70) Handy late-night beer soaker-upper or emergency day-after hangover 'cure' on 'the Ave' that is legendary with UDub students. There are plenty of vegetarian options.

MORSEL
CAFE $

Map p248 (☑206-268-0154; www.morsel seattle.com; 4754 University Way NE; biscuits & sandwiches $3-8; ⊗8am-3pm; ☑70) A diminutive cafe that specializes in biscuits – and they're not morsels! Choices include the classic (with gravy), or a formidable leaning tower of bacon, egg and cheese. Enjoy them while making friends at the shared tables.

SHULTZY'S BAR & GRILL
GERMAN $

Map p248 (☑206-548-9461; www.shultzys. com; 4114 University Way NE; hot dogs $9-13; ⊗11:30am-2am Mon-Fri, noon-2am Sat, noon-10pm Sun; ☑70) There are really only two words you need to know about Shultzy's – beer and sausages. The most obvious common denominator between the two is 'German' and it's true, there are good German beers and bratwurst here; but this is also the kind of place you can get a Cajun sausage burger or a chili cheese dog.

Rotating draft beers complement the menu and there's chicken and veggie burgers for those not overly enamored with sausages.

AGUA VERDE CAFÉ
MEXICAN $

Map p248 (☑206-545-8570; www.aguaverde cafe.com; 1303 NE Boat St; 3 tacos $12.50-15.50; ⊗7:30am-9pm Mon-Fri, 9am-9pm Sat, 9am-8pm Sun; ☑70) On the shores of Portage Bay at the southern base of University Ave, Agua Verde Café is a solid restaurant with incredible bay views and a menu full of fat tacos stuffed with lemony cod, catfish or portobello mushrooms, plus other Mexican-inspired favorites.

There's usually a wait for a table, but you can have a drink and linger on the deck, or order from the walk-up window. Kayaks

FARMER'S MARKET

In a city that produced Pike Place Market, it's not surprising that there is a rich cache of other weekly farmers markets where you can sniff out the freshest veg.

The largest and oldest (and best in the eyes of many) is the **U District Farmers Market** (Map p248; 5031 University Way NE; ⊗9am-2pm Sat; ☑70) ✦, which has been held every Saturday in the vicinity of the university year-round since 1993. Faithful to the spirit of farmers markets, the U District is a food-only affair – all of its displayed produce comes from an alliance of 60-plus stall-holding farmers and is grown 100% in Washington State. Products of note include spot prawns (May and June), cheeses, Washington wines and apples (over 30 varieties). **Market Bites** is a collection of small take-out stalls designed for hungry shoppers on the go.

LOCAL KNOWLEDGE

THE AVE

University Way NE, the sometimes seedy, sometimes studious strip that runs north–south through the U District, is known to anyone with even the sketchiest knowledge of Seattle as 'the Ave.' Pretty much anything a penny-counting, beer-guzzling, fashion-craving student might desire can be found on or close to this hallowed urban artery. Tick off Seattle's oldest still-functioning espresso bar, one of the city's earliest brewpubs, its weirdest cinema, its oldest bookstore and copious consignment shops. And all this before you've even tasted the food – a veritable UN of choices hidden, more often than not, behind smudged-glass windows decorated with taped-up, hand-written notices.

Panhandlers, frat parties and seminar-dodging undergraduates all stalk the Ave, though it's not an overly unsavory place. Some deride sporadic attempts to clean it up; others celebrate its eclecticism. University of Washington hip-hop band the Blue Scholars once wrote a song about the Ave, describing its social scene as an essential part of a U-Dub education.

can be rented in the same building, in case you want to work off your dinner.

CEDARS RESTAURANT INDIAN $

Map p248 (☎206-325-3988; www.cedars seattle.com; 4759 Brooklyn Ave NE; mains $10-17; ⊙11am-10pm Tue-Sun, to 9:30pm Mon; ✏; ☐70) Seattle isn't exactly London or Mumbai when it comes to Indian restaurants, but there's some relief for curry-lovers at Cedars, a family-run Indian spot with a few eastern Mediterranean cameos (falafel and gyros mainly). Lentils, *aloo gobi* (spiced potatoes and cauliflower) and *palak masala* (spinach stewed in spices) make the menu vegetarian friendly.

🍷 DRINKING & ⚓ NIGHTLIFE

No surprise. The U District has some of the city's best and most eccentric dive bars, as well as its most student-friendly coffee shops: bank on strong wi-fi, lots of plug-ins and no angry looks if you sit around for more than two hours. 'The Ave' (University Way NE) is a jolly fine place to string together a cheap bar crawl with plenty of late-night greasy-spoon holes-in-the-wall available to soak up the beer afterward.

★BLUE MOON BAR

Map p248 (☎206-675-9116; www.bluemoon seattle.wordpress.com; 712 NE 45th St; ⊙4pm-2am Mon-Fri, from 2pm Sat & Sun; ☐74) A legendary counterculture dive that first opened in 1934 to celebrate the repeal of Prohibition, Blue Moon makes much of its former literary patrons – including Dylan Thomas and Allen Ginsberg. The place is agreeably gritty and unpredictable, with graffiti carved into the seats and punk poets likely to stand up and start pontificating at any moment. Frequent live music.

CAFÉ ALLEGRO CAFE

Map p248 (☎206-633-3030; www.seattle allegro.com; 4214 University Way NE; ⊙6:30am-9pm Mon-Fri, 7:30am-9pm Sat, 8am-9pm Sun; ☐70) Let's dispel a myth: it's this place, not Starbucks, that's the oldest functioning coffee bar in Seattle. Founded in 1975, it was a bona fide espresso bar when Starbucks was still just a store that sold coffee beans and machinery. Stuffed into a back alley between NE 42nd and NE 43rd Sts, the cafe hasn't changed much over the years.

BOBA UP CAFE

Map p248 (☎206-547-8800; www.bobaup seattle.com; 4141 University Way NE; ⊙11am-11pm Sun-Thu, to 2am Fri & Sat) Adopting the 'make your own sundae' model of business, Boba Up is a newer operation on the Ave where you can mix and match jellies, tapiocas and teas to create your own ideal boba tea creation. Make sure to grab a picture with the mascot on the way out.

CAFÉ RACER BAR

(☎206-523-5282; www.caferacerseattle.com; 5828 Roosevelt Way NE; ⊙11am-11pm Tue-Thu,

11am-1am Fri, 9am-1am Sat, 9am-11pm Sun; 🚇67 from UW station) A bohemian beauty tucked away in the northern part of the U District, the Racer is an eclectic headspinner full of crazy little details. It's known for its hearty brunches (the cornbeef hash hits the spot), fine coffee and Sunday 'Racer Sessions' (improv jazz). It's one of the last places that has that distinct old Seattle feel.

Head upstairs to enjoy the truly delightful OBAMA Room (Official Bad Art Museum of Art).

ZOKA COFFEE   CAFE

Map p248 (☑206-527-0990; www.zokacoffee. com; 2901 NE Blakeley St; ☺6am-8pm Mon-Fri, from 7am Sat & Sun; 📶; 🚇74) Aside from its desirable coffee (home-roasted, of course), Zoka is *the* place to go for a marathon laptop session. Don't feel guilty about lingering: the staff actively encourage you to stay, with plenty of plug-in points scattered around a vast wooden interior full of students all seemingly on the same deadline.

MONKEY PUB   BAR

Map p248 (☑206-523-6457; www.themonkey pub.com; 5305 Roosevelt Way NE; ☺5pm-1:45am; 🚇74) This unironic U District dive is one of the few places in town where you can slug pitchers of cheap beer, shoot free pool and sing drunken karaoke on a weekend night on a whim. If the karaoke sucks, there's always the jukebox alleged to be the best in town. And did we mention the beer's cheap?

CAFE SOLSTICE   CAFE

Map p248 (☑206-675-0850; 4116 University Way NE; ☺6:30am-11pm Mon-Thu, to 9pm Fri, 7am-9pm Sat, to 11pm Sun; 📶; 🚇70) This coffee shop on 'the Ave' is large. It needs to be in order to accommodate the armies of laptop campers who seemingly descend here to churn out their own inferior versions of *War and Peace*. There's a nice wooden outdoor patio and a comfy organic vibe with lots of vegetarian and vegan snacks.

BIG TIME BREWERY
& ALEHOUSE   BREWERY

Map p248 (☑206-545-4509; www.bigtimebre wery.com; 4133 University Way NE; ☺11:30am-12:30am Sun-Thu, to 1:30am Fri & Sat; 🚇70) A fun hangout, this expansive brewpub is quiet and casual in the daytime but gets hopping at night. During the school year, it can be crowded with students eager to do some legal drinking. It's been around since 1988 – ancient history by brewpub standards.

FLOWERS   BAR

Map p248 (☑206-633-1903; 4247 University Way NE; ☺4pm-2am; 🚇70) Flowers used to be known as a low-key vegan restaurant, but since a change of ownership it's mostly regarded as a campus adjacent dive-bar. It's location in a historic flower shop make it worth a couple of cheap beers.

☆ ENTERTAINMENT

★GRAND ILLUSION CINEMA   CINEMA

Map p248 (☑206-523-3935; www.grandillusion cinema.org; 1403 NE 50th St; 🚇70) Totally unique! Far from being a reincarnated Gilded Age movie house, the Grand Illusion sits in an old dentist's office. Run by volunteers and passionately not-for-profit, it has a cherished national reputation among independent movie guerrillas for its director retrospectives and other cool, under-the-radar series.

NEPTUNE THEATER   LIVE MUSIC

Map p248 (☑800-982-2787; www.stgpresents. org; 1303 NE 45th St; 🚇70) Providing an ideal pulpit for young indie bands and smirking comedians sharpening their teeth on the university-gig circuit, the Neptune, a historic theater originally dating from the silent-movie era, reopened its doors in 2011 as a performing arts venue (it formerly functioned purely as a cinema).

Run by the not-for-profit Seattle Theater Group, the 800-capacity venue offers a welcome midsize (but relatively intimate) live venue. Alt-rock, hip-hop and alt-comedy predominate.

UNIVERSITY OF
WASHINGTON HUSKIES   SPECTATOR SPORT

Map p248 (☑206-543-2200; www.gohuskies. com; 3800 Montlake Blvd NE; 🚊University of Washington) The nickname of all of the University of Washington's 19 college sports teams. The NFL football team plays at the massive Husky Stadium.

THE BURKE-GILMAN TRAIL

Cutting a leafy, vehicle-free path through multiple north Seattle neighborhoods, including a large segment of the U District, the Burke-Gilman Trail gets busy with human-powered traffic on sunny days at weekends, when cyclists overtake joggers, and skaters weave in and out of walkers and strollers. The asphalt trail was first laid out in 1978 along the path of a former railroad pioneered by two Seattle attorneys, Thomas Burke and Daniel Gilman, in 1885 (the railway ceased operation in 1971). Initially extending for 12 miles, the route has since been lengthened and now runs almost 20 miles from Kenmore on the northeast shore of Lake Washington to Golden Gardens Park in northwest Ballard.

There is a 'missing link' in Ballard between 11th Ave NW and Hiram M Chittenden Locks, though it's easy to navigate through the relatively quiet streets and reconnect. The Burke-Gilman has plenty of pretty sections, many of them surrounded by foliage and close to water, but to get a real taste for the neighborhoods through which it passes (U District, Wallingford, Fremont and Ballard), you need to wander off and explore a little.

Zoka Coffee (p138) in the U District and Fremont Coffee Company (p151) and Milstead & Co (p148) in Fremont make for great coffee pit stops, while for a picnic, try Gas Works Park (p145) in Wallingford, or Hiram M Chittenden Locks (p156) or Golden Gardens Park (p156) in Ballard. The best spots to dine include Agua Verde Café (p136) in the U District, Pie (p147) in Fremont and Lockspot Cafe (p158) in Ballard.

For bike hire, look no further than Recycled Cycles (p140) in the U District.

HUSKY STADIUM
STADIUM

Map p248 (3800 Montlake Blvd NE; ⒭University of Washington) With room for 70,000, the Husky is a scenic giant with splendid water and mountain views. Once Seattle's largest sports stadium, it has undergone four remodels since its inception in 1920; the most recent in 2013 cost a whopping $280 million. It is home to the successful Washington Huskies, which you'll quickly ascertain wears the colors purple and gold.

🛍 SHOPPING

Bookstores and thrift shops are the main thing here and bargains abound. 'The Ave' is the main shopping drag.

★UNIVERSITY BOOK STORE
BOOKS

Map p248 (☑206-634-3400; www.ubookstore. com; 4326 University Way NE; ⊗9am-7pm Mon-Fri, 10am-6pm Sat, noon-5pm Sun; ☏; ☐70) University Book Store is a vast all-purpose book emporium founded in 1900, making it Seattle's oldest. Its huge catalog of tomes is a browser's dream, and helpful staff, a regular program of events and a cozy cafe mean you could quite easily spend a whole afternoon here. There's also a gift shop and free parking on-site.

SCARECROW VIDEO
ELECTRONICS

Map p248 (☑206-524-8554; www.scarecrow. com; 5030 Roosevelt Way NE; ⊗noon-9pm Sun-Tue & Thu, 11am-10pm Wed, noon-10pm Fri & Sat; ☐74) In an era when video stores appear to have befallen the same fate as the *Tyrannosaurus rex,* Scarecrow soldiers on. It's the largest video store in the country, with over 100,000 films in stock, many of them rare. A true community resource.

MAGUS BOOKS
BOOKS

Map p248 (☑206-633-1800; www.magusbooks seattle.com; 1408 NE 42nd St; ⊗10am-8pm Sun-Thu, to 10pm Fri & Sat; ☐70) Magus is a great used-book store, the kind of place where you can literally spend hours getting lost in the crooked, narrow aisles on the hunt for that obscure out-of-print title you're not sure you can even remember any more.

BUFFALO EXCHANGE
CLOTHING

Map p248 (☑206-545-0175; www.buffaloexch ange.com; 4530 University Way NE; ⊗10am-9pm Mon-Sat, to 8pm Sun; ☐70) This secondhand-clothing store is comfortable to browse in, but can be hit-and-miss in terms of good finds (but when it hits, boy does it hit).

Some of its merchandise is on the square side – which doesn't, ironically, make it any easier to sell your old clothes here: staff are notoriously picky.

HARDWICK'S
HARDWARE STORE   HOMEWARES

Map p248 (☎206-632-1203; www.hardwickand sons.com; 4214 Roosevelt Way NE; ⊙8am-6pm Mon-Fri, from 9am Sat; 🚌74) Locals in the know come to Hardwick's to explore the rows and rows of buckets filled with bizarre little gadgets and gizmos. Some people probably know what these objects are for, but most shoppers are looking for things to use in their art projects. It's a hive of a place that's fun just to explore.

CROSSROADS TRADING CO   CLOTHING

Map p248 (☎206-632-3111; www.crossroads trading.com; 4300 University Way NE; ⊙11am-8pm Mon-Sat, to 7pm Sun; 🚌70) This second-hand store is a little trendier and less funky than others in the area. But, as with others, there's a lot of rough before you hit any diamonds.

BULLDOG NEWS & ESPRESSO   BOOKS

Map p248 (☎206-632-6397; 4208 University Way NE; ⊙7am-6:30pm Mon-Sat; 🚌70) The newsstand of choice on 'the Ave,' this place has pretty much every magazine or newspaper you might want, from imports and big glossies to stapled-together zines. There's an excellent street-side espresso window peddling good coffee, croissants and muffins.

🏃 SPORTS &
ACTIVITIES

RECYCLED CYCLES   CYCLING

Map p248 (☎206-547-4491; www.recycled cycles.com; 1007 NE Boat St; rental per day from $40; ⊙10am-7pm Mon-Fri, to 6pm Sat & Sun; 🚌70) Rent bikes here and hit the nearby Burke-Gilman Trail (p139) to explore as far as Fremont, Ballard and Discovery Park

without touching road. Kids' chariots and trail-a-bikes are also available ($20 per day); reserve in summer.

AGUA VERDE PADDLE CLUB   KAYAKING

Map p248 (☎206-545-8570; www.aguaverde. com; 1303 NE Boat St; single kayak/double kay-aks/SUPs per hour $20/26/23; ⊙hours vary Mar-Oct; 🚌70) On Portage Bay, near the university, you can rent kayaks from this friendly place right at the edge of the water. When you get back from your paddle, be sure to visit the cafe (p136) upstairs to eat fish tacos on the covered deck.

Opening hours vary quite a bit depending on the time of year; check the website for a month-by-month breakdown.

SEATTLE STORM   BASKETBALL

Map p248 (☎206-217-9622; http://storm.wnba. com; game tickets $27-200) With the demise of the SuperSonics, local basketball fans have turned to Seattle's female team, the WNBA championship–winning Storm. Boasting several star US and international players, it made the play-offs every year between 2004 and 2014, taking the title in 2004, 2010 and 2018.

Home court has long been the Key Arena, and they are set to return when it reopens as the Seattle Center Arena (p97). At the time of writing, home games were taking place at the University of Washington's Husky Stadium.

UW WATERFRONT
ACTIVITIES CENTER   CANOEING

Map p248 (☎206-543-9433; www.washington. edu/ima/waterfront; 3710 Montlake Blvd NE; kayak/canoe/rowboat per hour $16/12/12; ⊙10am-7pm Mon-Fri, from 9am Sat & Sun May-Aug, reduced hours Sep; 🚇University of Washington) A good way to explore the waters surrounding the university grounds is to rent a canoe or rowboat from the UW facility. You need a current driver's license or passport. The center is in the southeast corner of the Husky Stadium (p139) parking lot.

Green Lake & Fremont

Neighborhood Top Five

❶ Sculpture (p143) Walking around Seattle's most irreverent neighborhood in search of its peculiar public art, as well as keeping an eye out for any spontaneous 'art attacks.'

❷ Woodland Park Zoo (p145) Taking in chimps, giraffes, hippos and more at one of the better zoos in the US.

❸ Green Lake Park (p145) Joining the walking, running, skating, cycling mass of humanity powering around beautiful Green Lake Park.

❹ Fremont Vintage Mall (p151) Diving head first into the search for a perfect secondhand outfit or wacky home wares in the neighborhood's biggest vintage store.

❺ Fremont Brewing Company (p148) Taste-testing locally brewed beers and getting to know the neighborhood's residents (and their dogs).

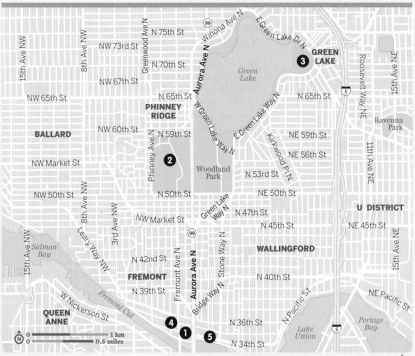

For more detail of this area see Map p250 and p251 ➡

Lonely Planet's Top Tip

If you've had your fill of the noise and frenetic pace of downtown Seattle, consider staying over in Fremont – the affordable **Hotel Hotel Hostel** (p194) is a dependable bet – for a more laid-back, under-the-radar look at one of the city's most interesting neighborhoods.

✖ Best Places to Eat

➡ The Whale Wins (p148)

➡ Paseo (p147)

➡ Nuna Ramen (p147)

➡ Pam's Kitchen (p149)

For reviews, see p146.➡

🍷 Best Places to Drink

➡ Fremont Brewing Company (p148)

➡ Milstead & Co (p148)

➡ Outlander Brewery & Pub (p151)

➡ Schilling Cider House (p149)

For reviews, see p148.➡

🔒 Best Places to Shop

➡ Fremont Vintage Mall (p151)

➡ Hashtag Cannabis (p152)

➡ Brooks Sports Inc (p152)

➡ Uncommon Cottage (p152)

For reviews, see p151.➡

Explore Green Lake & Fremont

Weirder than Ballard and more self-deprecating than Capitol Hill, Fremont's essential business is its public sculpture. Most of its outlandish statues and monuments lie clustered around a few square blocks on the southern edge of the neighborhood close to the bridge, roughly between the water and NW 36th St, stretching to Aurora Ave N and Phinney Ave N. Here you'll also find the bulk of the notable eating places, offbeat boutiques and Fremont's best situated hotel.

Fremont's a great neighborhood for getting a taste for local life, especially in summer, when festivals and regular outdoor movies send the locals positively delirious. With good bus connections and a bike-friendly intra-urban trail, it can easily be incorporated with visits to the adjacent neighborhoods of Ballard and Wallingford.

Just north of Fremont lies Green Lake, a small natural lake that's the hub of a large park complex and a pleasant low-key neighborhood punctuated by detached craftsman-style houses. The lake is packed with crowds in summer, but it's even better in fall, when the leaves are changing, or on a rare rain-free day in winter.

Below Green Lake, Woodland Park Zoo (p145) is eternally popular. And don't neglect to head further up to Phinney Ridge, the hilltop neighborhood north of the zoo along Phinney Ave N, for some quiet everyone-knows-everyone-else pubs and restaurants.

Local Life

Green Lake Park exercisers Meet 75-year-old marathon runners, whole packs of kids on leashes, contemporary in-line skaters, and lawyers getting bullied by their personal trainers at this well-kept park (p145).

Fremont Solstice Fair Any attempt to fully understand Seattle has to incorporate this crazy **summer celebration** (📞20 6-649-6706; www.fremontfair.com; N 34th & N 35th Sts; ⏱Jun) of life, the universe...and Fremont.

Getting There & Away

Bus Three different metro buses link Fremont to central Seattle. Bus 62 runs from downtown to Fremont and then onto Green Lake Park. Bus 5 runs from downtown via Fremont to Phinney Ridge and Woodland Park Zoo. Bus 40 originates in downtown and makes stops along Fremont's N 36th St before breezing off to Ballard. For cross-town connections, buses 31 and 32 link Fremont with the U District.

TOP SIGHT
FREMONT PUBLIC SCULPTURE

Long known for its wry contrarianism, Fremont does bizarre like the rest of the world does normal. For proof, look no further than its public sculpture, an eclectic amalgamation of the scary, the political and the downright weird. The five most famous pieces are scattered around four square blocks in the southern part of the neighborhood abutting the Lake Washington Ship Canal, between N 34th St, N 36th St, Aurora Ave N and Evanston Ave N.

Statue of Lenin

Fremont's provocative bronze **statue of Lenin** (Map p250; cnr N 36th St & Fremont Pl N; 🚌40) was salvaged in 1993 from the people of Poprad, Czechoslovakia, who, given their resounding rejection of Soviet rule, were probably glad to see the back of the bearded curmudgeon. It was unearthed by a resident of Issaquah, WA, named Lewis Carpenter, who found it unloved and abandoned in a junkyard while working in Czechoslovakia as an English teacher soon after the Velvet Revolution. Carpenter forked out $13,000 to purchase the fierce 16ft-tall re-creation of the wily Bolshevik leader and then put up another $41,000 (by remortgaging his home) to ship it to the US. After Carpenter's death in 1994, the statue turned up – where else? – in Fremont.

Fremont Troll

Just when you thought you had returned to planet earth, up sprouts the **Fremont Troll** (Map p250; N 36th St & Troll Ave; 🚌62), a 13,000lb steel and concrete sculpture of a troll crushing a Volkswagen Beetle in its hand, which resides under the Aurora Bridge. The sculpture was the winner of a 1989 Fremont Arts Council competition to design

ART ATTACKS

There are two types of art attack in Fremont. The first targets existing monuments: decorating the *Interurban* is one example; sticking drag on the Lenin statue is another. The second type of attack is to concoct brand new urban art exhibits. Most of these pieces are temporary and appear anonymously overnight. There have been many classics over the years, including papier-mâché cows, an 8ft-long steel pig, and an enormous spider suspended over a parking lot. The bulk of these inspired creations are quickly removed, though some have entered local folklore and been allowed to stay.

Dedicated in 2008, the life-sized statue of two clowns (Map p250; N 34th St; 🖵62), **arms interlinked, striding off in opposite directions, honors the characters JP Patches and Gertrude, who appeared daily on the children's *JP Patches Show* on Seattle TV during the 1960s and '70s. Located a mere 250yd east of *Waiting for the Interurban*, it has been humorously christened *Late for the Interurban*.**

some thought-provoking public art and has since appeared in films like 1999's *10 Things I Hate About You*. It took seven weeks to make.

Fremont Rocket

Fremont has adopted the phallic and zany-looking **Fremont Rocket** (Map p250; Evanston Ave & N 35th St; 🖵40), grafted onto the corner of a shoe shop, as its community totem. Constructed in the 1950s for use in the Cold War, the rocket was plagued with engineering difficulties and never actually went anywhere, leaving its constructors with the unfortunate problem of not being able to get it up. Before coming to Fremont, it was temporarily affixed to an army surplus store in Belltown. When the store went out of business in 1993, the Fremont Business Association snapped it up.

Waiting for the Interurban

Seattle's most popular piece of public art, **Waiting for the Interurban** (Map p250; N 34th St & Fremont Ave N; 🖵62), sculpted in recycled aluminum, depicts six people waiting for a train that never comes. The train that once passed through Fremont stopped running in the 1930s, and the people of Seattle have been waiting for a new train – the Interurban – ever since (a new train connecting Seattle with Everett opened in 2003 but doesn't stop in Fremont). Take a look at the human-faced dog peeking out between the legs of the people. That face belongs to Armen Stepanian, one of the founders of today's Fremont and its excellent recycling system. Sculptor Richard Beyer and Stepanian had a disagreement about the design of the piece, which resulted in Beyer's spiteful yet humorous design of the dog's face.

The Guidepost

The whimsical **guidepost** (Map p250; Fremont Ave N & Fremont Pl N; 🖵5) that points in 16 different directions – including toward the Troll, the Lenin statue and the Milky Way – appeared anonymously on Fremont Ave in 1995, the result of one of the neighborhood's periodic art attacks. Unlike other ephemeral sculptures, the guidepost stayed put and quickly became a neighborhood symbol. Originally made out of cedar wood, the rotting signpost was replaced in 2009 by a better-quality one made out of pressure-treated wood. At the same time, the artist revealed himself to be Maque DaVis, a resident of nearby Ballard, but a Fremonter in spirit. The signpost advertises itself as 'the center of the known universe,' a phrase that has since been adopted as a popular Fremont slogan.

◉ SIGHTS

◉ Green Lake

★WOODLAND PARK ZOO   ZOO

Map p251 (☎206-548-2500; www.zoo.org; 5500 Phinney Ave N; adult/child May-Sep $22.95/13.95, Oct-Apr $15.50/10.50; ⊙9:30am-6pm May-Sep, to 4pm Oct-Apr; ♿; ☐5) In Woodland Park, up the hill from Green Lake Park, the Woodland Park Zoo is one of Seattle's most popular tourist attractions. Consistently rated as one of the top 10 zoos in the country, it was one of the first in the nation to free animals from their restrictive cages in favor of ecosystem enclosures, where animals from similar environments share large spaces designed to replicate their natural surroundings.

GREEN LAKE AQUA THEATER   LANDMARK

Map p251 (W Green Lake Way N; ☐Rapid Ride E-Line) The lonely-looking grandstand at the southern end of Green Lake is all that remains of the former 5500-capacity Green Lake Aqua Theater, an outdoor auditorium overlooking the lake (where the stage once was) that stood here from 1950 to 1970.

◉ Fremont

FREMONT PUBLIC SCULPTURES   MONUMENT

See p143.

GAS WORKS PARK   PARK

(☎206-684-4075; 2101 N Northlake Way; ⊙6am-10pm; ♿; ☐62) Urban reclamation has no greater monument in Seattle than Gas Works Park. The former power station here produced gas for heating and lighting from 1906 to 1956. The gas works was thereafter understandably considered an eyesore and an environmental menace. But the beautiful location of the works, with stellar views of downtown over Lake Union, sailboats and yachts sliding to and from the shipping canal, induced the city government to convert the former industrial site into a park in 1975.

APATOSAURS   SCULPTURE

Map p250 (NW Canal St at Phinney Ave N; ☐40) Along the banks of the ship canal and abutting the Burke-Gilman Trail at the bottom of Phinney Ave N, you'll see two life-size 'apatosaurs' fashioned out of ivy. The adult dino measures 66ft long, making it the

GREEN LAKE & FREMONT SIGHTS

◉ TOP SIGHT
GREEN LAKE PARK

Scenic Green Lake Park surrounds Green Lake, a small natural lake created by a glacier during the last ice age. In the early 1900s, city planners lowered the lake's water level by 7ft, increasing the shoreline to preserve parkland around the lake. After the lowering, however, Ravenna Creek, which fed the lake, no longer flowed through. Green Lake became stagnant and filled with stinky green algae. Massive dredging efforts to keep Green Lake a navigable lake continue, although the lake remains prone to algae blooms.

Two paths wind around the lake, but these aren't enough to fill the needs of the hundreds of joggers, power-walkers, cyclists and in-line skaters who throng here daily. In fact, competition for space on the trails has led to altercations between speeding athletes; the city government now regulates traffic on the paths.

Green Lake also has a soccer field, bowling green, baseball diamond, basketball and tennis courts, plus boat, bike and in-line skate rentals. Two sandy swimming beaches line the lake's northern end.

DON'T MISS

➡ Walking path
➡ Green Lake Aqua Theater
➡ Green Lake Boat Rental

PRACTICALITIES

➡ Map p251, D2
➡ ☎206-684-4075
➡ 7201 E Green Lake Dr N, Green Lake
➡ ⊙24hr
➡ ☐62

FREEDOM TO BE PECULIAR

Coined the 'Artistic Republic of Fremont' by irreverent locals who once symbolically voted to secede from the rest of Seattle, the neighborhood of Fremont has always marched eccentrically to its own bongo – albeit with its tongue stuck firmly in its cheek. Where else in the US can you find an un-desecrated statue of Vladimir Lenin, an antediluvian Cold War rocket, an annual nude cyclists parade, and a sculpted troll crushing a Volkswagen Beetle under a bridge? Even Fremont's vandals are creative. The neighborhood's famous statue *Waiting for the Interurban,* a study of six commuters waiting for a train that never comes, is regularly decorated by audacious art guerrillas who dress the figures up in clothes, hats and ties, or cover them with amusing placards.

Some of Fremont's countercultural spirit comes from its history: it was a separate city until 1891, and still is in the minds of many of its residents. 'Set your watch back five minutes' reads a sign on Fremont Bridge as you cross over from the stiffer, less self-deprecating neighborhood of Queen Anne. Fremont's idiosyncratic personality resurfaced in the 1970s, when community activism attempted to offset years of economic decline. The Fremont Public Association, today the envy of every neighborhood association in Seattle, was created in 1974 to provide shelter, food and help to disadvantaged residents. Its formation spawned a number of other thriving community associations, including the Fremont Arts Council, and, in 1994, irked by bureaucratic planning and boundary laws, the neighborhood made its token and somewhat humorous secession.

These days, Fremont is showing signs of creeping gentrification. Various software companies including Google have opened up offices since the mid-2000s, and trendy boutiques are starting to compete with the area's legendary junk shops. But the spirit of ludicrousness still resounds, enshrined in the neighborhood's libertine motto: *De Libertas Quirkas* (Freedom to be Peculiar). Enough said.

world's largest known topiary (ornamental shrub). The apatosaurs were originally displayed in the Pacific Science Center, but were picked up by the Fremonters in 1999.

EATING

Fremont's restaurant scene has a frustrating number of bland offerings for a neighborhood so known for its commitment to culture, but there are enough steady favorites and exciting newcomers to satisfy.

Green Lake has an everybody-knows-each-other neighborhood feel to it, and the cafes and restaurants consequently tend to be welcoming and casual.

Green Lake

BETH'S CAFÉ
BREAKFAST $

Map p251 (📞206-782-5588; www.bethscafe.com; 7311 Aurora Ave N; omelets $13.95-17.25; ⏰24hr; 🚌RapidRide E Line) The best – or at least biggest – hangover breakfast in the world is at

Beth's, and you can get it all day long in an agreeably greasy space decorated with the amateur scribblings of former diners. You have your choice between a staggering six-egg or truly shocking 12-egg omelet. Still hungry? Bottomless hash browns!

The cafe is on down-at-heel Aurora Ave, which sits in ironic juxtaposition between the salubrious suburbs of Green Lake and Phinney Ridge.

RED MILL BURGERS
BURGERS $

Map p251 (📞206-783-6362; www.redmill burgers.com; 312 N 67th St, Phinney Ridge; burgers $4.25-9.25; ⏰11am-9pm Tue-Sat, noon-8pm Sun; 🚌5) You can find what is possibly Seattle's most popular burger in this urban legend in Phinney Ridge, the second incarnation of a restaurant that originally opened in 1937. The key is in the burger's simplicity...plus the crispy onion rings, which act as the de rigueur side dish. There's usually a line out the door, but it moves along quickly.

COOKIE COUNTER
BAKERY $

Map p251 (www.seattlecookiecounter.com; 7415 Greenwood Ave N, Phinney Ridge; cookies from

$3; ⊙noon-10pm Tue-Sun; ✐; 🖵5) Everything at this well-loved bakery and ice-cream shop is totally vegan and incredibly delicious. It does a number of fun pastries, but even the basic chocolate chip cookies are exceptional.

WINDY CITY PIE PIZZA $
Map p251 (✐206-486-4743; www.windycitypie. com; 5918 Phinney Ave N, Phinney Ridge; pizza $22-29; ⊙4-10pm Sun, Wed & Thu, to 11pm Fri & Sat; 🖵24) This much talked about (and adored) deep-dish pizza joint made the move to Phinney Ridge after some time in a permanent location limbo. Drop in for a giant pizza and a fun cocktail or a pop (soda, for those not from the Midwest).

SHELTER LOUNGE AMERICAN $$
Map p251 (✐206-420-7452; www.shelterlounge. com; 7110 E Green Lake Dr N; mains $14-20; ⊙11am-11pm Mon-Fri, 9am-midnight Sat & Sun; 🖵45) Shelter's wood and glass facade is pleasingly modern, while also calling back to the days of '60s-cocktail-bar cool. Inside you'll find serene views of Green Lake, cozy fireplaces and a menu of upscale bar food that doesn't sacrifice flavor for sophistication. Obviously the drink menu is ace, as well.

IVAR'S SALMON HOUSE SEAFOOD $$$
(✐206-632-0767; www.ivars.com/locations/salmon-house; 401 NE Northlake Way; mains $20-37; ⊙11am-9pm Sun-Thu, to 10pm Fri & Sat; 🖵26) Perfecting a Pacific Northwest–cabin vibe, Ivar's Salmon House features various alderwood-smoked salmon dishes and a bevy of seafood-focused starters, but the chowder and fish-and-chips are the traditional favorite. Northwest art and images adorn the rich wood walls and a fireplace crackles by the bar.

✕ Fremont

★PASEO CARIBBEAN $
Map p251 (✐206-545-7440; www.paseo restaurants.com; 4225 Fremont Ave N; sandwiches $9.95-12.50; ⊙11am-9pm Tue-Fri, to 8pm Sat, to 7pm Sun; 🖵5) A glorified food shack whose overflowing Cuban sandwiches (which are a lot more generously stuffed than they are in Cuba) have long prompted plenty of Seattleites to re-route their daily commute in order to savor them. If you've

come this far, you shouldn't overlook the exquisitely simple rice and beans either.

NUNA RAMEN RAMEN $
Map p250 (✐206-258-3612; www.nunaramen. us; 501 N 36th St; ramen from $9.50; ⊙11am-3pm & 5-9pm Mon-Thu, to 10pm Fri, 11am-10pm Sat, noon-9am Sun; 🖵40) Some of the best ramen in Seattle's northern neighborhoods can be enjoyed at modern, but unpretentious, Nuna. There are nine varieties to choose from (including a veggie broth option) and lots of add ins, such as kimchi and garlic oil. Most importantly: the broth is silky and perfectly seasoned and it gives you a whole egg instead of half.

SEATTLE BISCUIT COMPANY SOUTHERN US $
(www.seattlebiscuitcompany.com; 4001 Leary Way NW; mains $8-14; ⊙8am-3pm Mon, Wed & Thu, to 4:30pm Fri-Sun; 🖵40) Bring your appetite to this brick-and-mortar location of the beloved local food cart Seattle Biscuit Company. The biscuits are giant and it doesn't skimp on the toppings. Imagine mudslides of gravy, saucer-sized fried eggs and whole links of andouille sausage.

PIE PIES $
Map p250 (✐206-436-8590; www.sweetand savorypie.com; 3515 Fremont Ave N; pies from $5.95; ⊙11am-7pm Mon-Wed, 11am-9pm Thu & Fri, 10am-9pm Sat, 11am-5pm Sun; 🖵5) Locals and visitors alike rave about the sweet and savory pies on offer at this single-minded bake shop in Fremont.

REVEL KOREAN $$
Map p250 (✐206-547-2040; www.revelseattle. com; 403 N 36th St; small plates $12-19; ⊙check website; 🖵40) This modern Korean-American crossover restaurant (with a bit of French influence thrown in) has quickly established itself as a big name on the Seattle eating scene thanks, in part, to its simple, shareable plates. Of note are the pork-belly pancakes, the short-rib dumplings and the various seasonal hot pots, all of which go down well with a cocktail or two. At the time of writing it was temporarily closed, with plans to reopen in fall 2019, and a new location was open in South Lake Union at 513 Westlake Ave N.

KAMONEGI JAPANESE $$
Map p250 (✐206-632-0185; www.kamonegi seattle.com; 1054 N 39th St; mains $9-20;

GREEN LAKE & FREMONT EATING

◎4-10pm Tue-Thu, to 11pm Fri & Sat; ⚟; 🔲62) Tiny Kamonegi and its head chef and owner Mutsuko Soma are currently all the rage on the Fremont dining scene. The specialties here are soba noodles and tempura, and on the very vegetarian-friendly menu you'll find a satisfying selection of both. The restaurant feels refreshingly authentic down to its Tokyo side-street sized dining area (reservations strongly recommended).

BRIMMER & HEELTAP
MODERN AMERICAN $$

(☑206-420-2534; www.brimmerandheeltap. com; 425 NW Market St; mains $13-18; ◎5-10pm Wed-Sun, also 9am-2pm Sat & Sun) One of only two Seattle restaurants that made 2016's 'Best Bars in America' list by *Food & Wine*, Brimmer & Heeltap proffers creative drinks. Quaff one before partaking in a satisfying meal featuring Asian influences and fermented and pickled ingredients.

★THE WHALE WINS
EUROPEAN $$$

Map p250 (☑206-632-9425; www.thewhalewins. com; 3506 Stone Way N; small plates $12-16, mains $28-33; ◎5-10pm Mon-Sat, 5-9pm Sun; 🔲62) 🖉 Forget the whale: it's the sardines that are the main winners at this eccentrically named fish-biased restaurant that shares trendy Euro-style digs with the equally hip Joule restaurant next door. The sardines arrive on thick crispy bread spread with a heavenly mayo concoction and zesty veg. Indeed, the 'Whale' excels in veg. Have carrots and fennel ever tasted this good?

WESTWARD
SEAFOOD $$$

(☑206-552-8215; www.westwardseattle.com; 2501 N Northlake Way; mains $27-37; ◎5-9pm Mon,5-9:30pm Tue & Wed, 5-10pm Thu & Fri, 10am-10pm Sat, 10am-9pm Sun; 🔲31) With Lake Union lapping at your feet and the city skyline as a backdrop, it's no surprise that Westward is a favorite local haunt. The menu combines bold Mediterranean flavors with seasonal ingredients from local purveyors, which are served up while you're lounging in the Adirondack chairs next to fire pits made from oyster shells.

ROCKCREEK SEAFOOD & SPIRITS
SEAFOOD $$$

Map p251 (☑206-557-7532; www.rockcreek seattle.com; 4300 Fremont Ave N; small plates $14-17, mains $27-33; ◎4-11pm Mon-Fri, 9am-11pm Sat & Sun; 🔲5) Chef Eric Donnelly's seafood-focused restaurant in Fremont features an extensive menu that uses seasonal ingredients throughout. The space feels like a place to eat rustic seafood dishes – woodsy with a touch of industrial, with high ceilings, raw timber, dark metal accents and, true to its name, a large mural of a riverbed overlooking the space.

🍷 DRINKING & NIGHTLIFE

You'll find an excellent array of bars, taverns and brewpubs in Fremont. It's a good place to uncover what's trending in Seattle's booze-soaked zeitgeist. The less bohemian Green Lake area specializes in relaxing family-oriented neighborhood pubs.

★FREMONT BREWING COMPANY
BREWERY

Map p250 (☑206-420-2407; www.fremont brewing.com; 1050 N 34th St, Fremont; ◎11am-9pm; 🚼🐾; 🔲62) 🖉 This microbrewery, in keeping with current trends, sells its wares via an attached tasting room rather than a full-blown pub. Not only is the beer divine (try the seasonal bourbon barrel-aged Abominable), but the industrial-chic tasting room and 'urban beer garden' are highly inclusive spaces, where pretty much everyone in the 'hood comes to hang out at communal tables.

A liberal policy on pets and minors keeps things congenial, meaning you'll see more dogs and kids than hardened drinkers as you work your way through trays of small samplers. Although there's no food service, bowls of free pretzels help soak up any light-headedness. (You're welcome to bring in your own food too.)

★MILSTEAD & CO
CAFE

Map p250 (☑206-659-4814; www.milstead andco.com; 900 N 34th St, Fremont; ◎6am-6pm Mon-Fri, from 7am Sat & Sun; ☎; 🔲62) This fabulous neighborhood coffee bar in Fremont prefers to carefully select other people's beans rather than roast its own, but chooses them with the skill and precision of a French sommelier. The 'bean menu' changes daily, but, thanks to the expertise of owner Andrew Milstead, it rarely disappoints.

WALLINGFORD

Residential Wallingford, sandwiched like a tangy relish in between Fremont and the U District, is a neighborhood slowly gaining a reputation as 'cool,' but for the time being it's still not entirely on the map and you can still while away an afternoon slumped in an unpretentious cafe and quietly imbibe a side of Seattle that one million annual visitors to the Space Needle never get to see. Wallingford's arterial road, NE 45th St, supports an eclectic parade of local businesses ranging from the homespun to the bizarre, with dedicated bookstores, an enlightening Afghan restaurant and a handful of small Seattle 'chains' including an Uptown Espresso and the original Dick's Drive-In (p104). About a mile to the south, the car-free Burke-Gilman Trail (p139) bisects the neighborhood east–west along the northern shores of Lake Union. Stop, if you have time, amid the post-industrial landscape of Gas Works Park (p145), where a rusting disused power plant contrasts sharply with the surrounding greenery. It remains a favorite spot for lakeside kite-flyers and rock album cover shoots.

A wander along NE 45th St rewards with lots of interesting places to eat, drink and browse. Don't miss the following:

Pam's Kitchen (Map p251; ☑206-696-7010; www.pams-kitchen.com; 1715 N 45th St; mains $10-19; ☉5-10pm Tue-Thu & Sun, 11am-3pm & 5-11pm Fri & Sat; ☐62) Discover the spices hidden in the wonderful Trinidadian flavors of this Caribbean restaurant, recently relocated from the nearby U District.

Kabul (Map p251; ☑206-545-9000; www.kabulrestaurant.com; 2301 N 45th St; mains $18-26; ☉5-9:30pm Mon, Wed, Thu & Sun, to 10pm Fri & Sat; ☐62) Fine-tune your international tasting palate with Afghan food, including stewed eggplant, lamb kebabs, yogurt, and mild, creamy curry.

TNT Taqueria (Map p251; ☑206-322-0124; www.chowfoods.com/tnt-taqueria; 2114 N 45th St; mains $7-11; ☉8am-10pm; ☐44) Dive into some tasty Mexican fare with a bomb selection of homemade salsas.

SCHILLING CIDER HOUSE   BAR

Map p250 (☑206-420-7088; www.schillingcider. com; 708 N 34th St, Fremont; ☉noon-11pm; ☐62) Continuing a tradition that began with the Pilgrim Fathers (who allegedly smuggled a barrel of cider onto the *Mayflower*), Schilling is at the forefront of Seattle's craft cider scene, offering 32 of its fruity concoctions on draft at this woody Fremont taproom. Get a flight of as many ciders as you like for $2 per pour to whet your palate.

Take-out cans are also available.

74TH STREET ALE HOUSE   PUB

Map p251 (☑206-784-2955; www.74thst.com; 7401 Greenwood Ave N, Phinney Ridge; ☉11am-11pm Sun-Thu, to midnight Fri & Sat; ☐5) A sibling to the Hilltop Ale House (p107) in Queen Anne, this is the kind of place that, if you lived nearby, you'd find yourself in several times a week. It's as comfortable as a British country pub, with an ambience that will make you feel like an instant regular – plus there are dozens of outstanding beers on tap.

BROUWER'S CAFE   BAR

Map p250 (☑206-267-2437; 400 N 35th St, Fremont; ☉11am-midnight Sun-Thu, to 2am Fri & Sat; ☐40) Rather than producing its own beer, Brouwer's stocks the brews of others – lots of them. Indeed, it, arguably, offers the finest beer selection in the city: an astounding 64 brews on tap along with over 400 bottled varieties. Its collection of Scotch and American whiskey is no slouch, either.

HALE'S ALES BREWERY   BREWERY

(☑206-782-0737; www.halesbrewery.com; 4301 Leary Way NW, Fremont; ☉11am-9pm Sun-Thu, to 10pm Fri & Sat; ☐40) A relative old-timer, Hale's was only the third microbrewery in Washington State when it opened in 1983. Its large, contemporary brewery and pub on the cusp of the Ballard and Fremont neighborhoods mixes seasonal brews with old favorites including its flagship tipple, Hale's Pale Ale, a good entry-point beer for beginners keen to learn how to differentiate their malt from their hops.

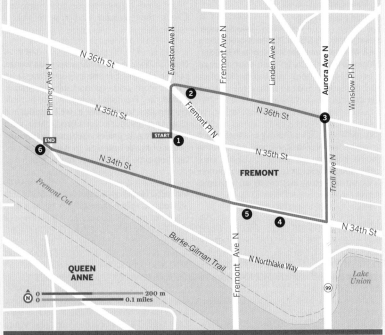

Neighborhood Walk
Center of the Universe

START FREMONT ROCKET
FINISH APATOSAURS
LENGTH 0.75 MILES; ONE HOUR

Start this surreal walk on the corner of Evanston Ave N and N 35th St, at the rather conspicuous **1 Fremont Rocket** (p144) before walking north (away from the water) up Evanston Ave N to N 36th St. Take a right onto Fremont Place N. On N 36th St at Fremont Place N, you'll see a bronze, 16ft statue of former communist leader **2 Vladimir Lenin** (p143) weighing 7 tons.

Turn right to go east on N 36th St, which you'll follow until you're underneath the giant Aurora Bridge. Turn left and head for the dark, shadowy space where the bridge meets the ground. Here lies the **3 Fremont Troll** (p143), an 18ft concrete figure busily munching on a VW Beetle, a reference to the children's story *The Three Billy Goats Gruff*. Back away slowly, turn around and behold the sight of the concrete bridge supports that descend down Troll

Ave before you. Their elegant arches resemble the nave of a Gothic cathedral. Walk down the 'nave' and turn right on N 34th St.

Follow N 34th St west, toward the Fremont Bridge, passing a life-size statue of two clowns pulling in opposite directions, jokingly known as **4 Late for the Interurban** (p144). A couple of minutes later you'll fall upon what they're late for; namely Seattle's most popular piece of public art, **5 Waiting for the Interurban** (p144), showing people waiting for a train that never comes.

Go west past Fremont Bridge and along N 34th St for a couple of blocks until you get to Phinney Ave N. Along the banks of the ship canal, Fremont Canal Park extends west following the extension of the Burke-Gilman Trail. Right at the start of the park, at the bottom of Phinney Ave N, look for two giant, life-sized **6 apatosaurs** (p145), giant topiaries given to Fremont by the Pacific Science Center.

OUTLANDER BREWERY & PUB
MICROBREWERY

Map p250 (☑206-486-4088; www.outlander brewing.com; 225 N 36th St, Fremont; ⊙4-10pm Tue & Wed, 4pm-midnight Thu, 4pm-1am Fri & Sat, 2-10pm Sun; ☑40) Cozier than your average brewery, but certainly not lacking in selection, Outlander makes for an ideal stop on any drinking tour of Fremont.

FREMONT COFFEE COMPANY
CAFE

Map p250 (☑206-632-3633; www.fremont coffee.net; 459 N 36th St, Fremont; ⊙6am-8pm Mon-Fri, from 7am Sat & Sun; ☎; ☑40) This coffee shop's location in a craftsman home dials up the cozy factory to an extreme degree.

GEORGE & DRAGON PUB
PUB

Map p250 (☑206-545-6864; www.georgeand dragonpub.com; 206 N 36th St, Fremont; ⊙11am-2am; ☑40) If you're British, or just an Anglofile, head straight to George & Dragon Pub, where you'll find more than a few tastes of the cold isles.

EL CHUPACABRA
BAR

Map p251 (☑206-706-4889; www.elchupacabra. com; 6711 Greenwood Ave N, Phinney Ridge; ⊙11:30am-midnight Sun-Thu, 11am-2am Fri & Sat; ☑5) This Phinney Ridge bar is known for its front patio (great for sipping margaritas), kitschy decor (let's call it punky Mexican) and San Francisco–style burritos ($9 to $12). Be warned: service can be slow when the place is crowded.

☆ ENTERTAINMENT

Rock-and-roll dives, comedy clubs and open-air cinemas – Fremont has its own self-contained and characteristically quirky entertainment scene. For Green Lake's best entertainment options, hop on a bus and head back down to Fremont.

ATLAS THEATER
COMEDY

Map p250 (☑425-954-5618; www.seattlecom edygroup.com; 3509 Fremont Ave N, Fremont; adult/discounted $15.50/14; ⊙shows 8pm & 10pm Fri & Sat, also 4pm Sun; ☑5) Spend more than five minutes in Fremont and you'll quickly glean that it's got a healthy sense of humor. So it'll come as no bombshell to discover this tiny theater specializing in improv comedy with the odd adult-only

'blue' show thrown in for good measure. Check the calendar and reserve tickets online.

NECTAR LOUNGE
LIVE MUSIC

Map p250 (☑206-632-2020; www.nectarlounge. com; 412 N 36th St, Fremont; ⊙8pm-2am; ☑40) This small and comfortable live-music venue in Fremont outgrew its humble beginnings to become a well-established club that includes a covered patio with stage views. It prides itself on hosting any genre of music and was an early refuge for hip-hop acts. Macklemore has played here.

HIGH DIVE
LIVE MUSIC

Map p250 (www.highdiveseattle.com; 513 N 36th St, Fremont; ⊙7pm-2am; ☑40) A bit of a dive – but not an unpleasant one – this is one of two local live-music stalwarts in Fremont. It hosts rock primarily for small-name bands on their way up. Strong drinks and BBQ food provide the accompaniment.

LITTLE RED HEN
LIVE MUSIC

Map p251 (☑206-522-1168; www.littleredhen. com; 7115 Woodlawn Ave NE, Green Lake; ⊙9am-2am; ☑62) This is Seattle's only real venue for pure live country music. Nightly entertainment includes country karaoke and good-time honky-tonk bands – or you can don a cowboy hat for the free line-dancing lessons held on Mondays at 8pm. There's a small food menu touting cheap Tex-Mex.

🛍 SHOPPING

Fremont's junk and craft-supply shops might not be as ubiquitous as they once were, but they're still fun places to browse.

Green Lake and Phinney Ridge shops are less unique; it's not the area for window shopping.

★ FREMONT VINTAGE MALL
ANTIQUES

Map p250 (☑206-329-4460; www.fremontvint agemall.com; 3419 Fremont Pl N, Fremont; ⊙11am-7pm Mon-Sat, to 6pm Sun; ☑5) Descending into this subterranean antique mall is like diving down to a sunken Spanish galleon full of plundered treasure. Who knows what you might bring to the surface? An old 1950s vending machine? A clownish unicycle? An Afghan coat that looks exactly like something Hendrix once wore? It's worth the trip to find out!

FREMONT ON FOOT

With its tree-lined waterfront and offbeat statues, Fremont is a highly walkable neighborhood. A group of enterprising locals have instituted the Fremont Tour, but if you'd rather not contemplate loquacious superheroes accosting innocent passersby with zany humor, you can go it alone. Nearly every local business stocks a handy free *Walking Guide to Fremont* leaflet (with map) or you can download it from the community's official website (www.fremont.com).

FREMONT SUNDAY MARKET   MARKET

Map p250 (www.fremontmarket.com; N 34th St, btwn Phinney Ave N & Fremont Ave, Fremont; ⊗10am-4pm Sun; 🚇5) People come from all over town for this huge market. It features fresh fruit and vegetables, arts and crafts, and all kinds of people getting rid of junk.

BROOKS SPORTS INC   SPORTS & OUTDOORS

Map p250 (🕾425-488-3131; www.brooksrunning. com; 3400 Stone Way N, Wallingford; ⊗10am-7pm Mon-Sat, to 6pm Sun; 🚇62) One of the greenest buildings in Seattle (LEED platinum status), super-modern Stone 34 was finished in 2014 and sits beside the Burke-Gilman running/cycling trail in Fremont. Appropriately, its first tenants are running-shoe company Brooks Sports Inc, which has made Fremont its new global headquarters.

OPHELIA'S BOOKS   BOOKS

Map p250 (🕾206-632-3759; www.ophelias books.com; 3504 Fremont Ave N, Fremont; ⊗11am-7pm Mon-Sat, to 6pm Sun; 🚇5) Like an indie record store for bibliophiles, Ophelia's is full of rare, yellowing, story-filled tomes that possess bags more character than electronic readers.

HASHTAG CANNABIS   DISPENSARY

Map p250 (🕾206-946-8157; www.seattlehash tag.com; 3540 Stone Way N, Fremont; ⊗9am-11pm; 🚇62) As with other dispensaries in the city, you won't want for selection at Hashtag Cannabis. This bright and friendly shop does have a more robust selection of weed accessories than most others, so if you're looking for a tricked-out vaporizer, this is the place to come.

UNCOMMON COTTAGE   GIFTS & SOUVENIRS

Map p250 (🕾206-483-7949; www.theuncommon cottage.com; 711 N 35th St, Fremont; ⊗11am-6pm Tue-Fri, from 10am Sat, 11am-5pm Sun) Uncommon Cottage is a newer addition to Fremont's shopping scene, but one that harks back to the neighborhood's heyday as an offbeat trend setter. There's a great selection of clothing, gifts and accessories that is well calibrated to be quirky, but not clichéd or overbearing.

JIVE TIME RECORDS   MUSIC

Map p250 (www.jivetimerecords.com; 3506 Fremont Ave N, Fremont; ⊗11am-9pm Mon-Sat, 10am-7pm Sun; 🚇5) A vinyl collector's dream come true full of rarities and secondhand bargains stuffed into a diminutive interior.

🏃 SPORTS & ACTIVITIES

FREMONT TOUR   WALKING

Map p250 (🕾800-838-3006; www.thefremont tour.com; cnr N 34th St & Fremont Ave N, Fremont; adult/child $20/free; ⊗Jun-Sep; 🚇62) To help outsiders infiltrate Fremont's wacky underbelly, some local 'Fremonsters' started the Fremont Tour, a 90-minute neighborhood stroll accompanied by outlandishly costumed guides with names such as Rocket Man and Crazy Cat Lady.

GREEN LAKE BOAT RENTAL   BOATING

Map p251 (🕾206-527-0171; www.greenlakeboat rentals.net; 7351 E Green Lake Drive N, Green Lake; per hour $24; ⊗9am-7pm May-Sep, weekends only Mar-Apr; 🚇; 🚇62) You can rent kayaks, canoes, paddleboats and stand-up paddleboards from March to October from the kiosk on the eastern shore of the Green Lake (where there's also a cafe). In March and April it opens weekends only.

THEO CHOCOLATE FACTORY   FOOD & DRINK

Map p250 (🕾206-632-5100; www.theochocolate. com; 3400 Phinney Ave N, Fremont; tours $12; 🚇40) Adding a bit of Willy Wonka to Fremont's atypical street life is this chocolate factory on the site of the old Redhook Brewery (now moved to Woodinville, WA). The chocolate micro-producer makes organic chocolate and the detailed factory experience is both witty and interesting (if you don't mind donning the obligatory hairnet). And, yes, there are tastings!

Ballard & Discovery Park

Neighborhood Top Five

❶ Hiram M Chittenden Locks (p156) Feeling the breeze on your face and watching birds, fishing boats, motor yachts, kayaks and salmon negotiating the locks on a sunny summer's evening.

❷ Nordic Museum (p156) Learning about the history and culture of Ballard's most well-known immigrant community at this museum that got a major update in 2018.

❸ Discovery Park (p155) Feeling like you've left the city far, far behind in this verdant ocean-side oasis.

❹ Populuxe Brewing (p160) Making the first (but not last) stop on your tour of the neighborhood's record number of breweries.

❺ Ballard Farmers Market (p164) Enjoying Sunday brunch and shopping on Ballard Ave NW during the neighborhood's weekly outdoor market.

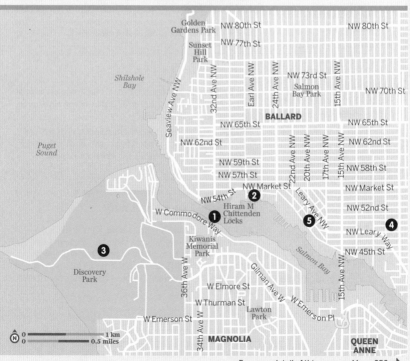

For more detail of this area see Map p252 ➡

Lonely Planet's Top Tip

Don't miss the unconnected western section of the recreational Burke-Gilman Trail (p139) that stretches from Hiram M Chittenden Locks out to Golden Gardens Park (1.75 miles) and takes in a different, quieter side of Ballard that faces the open Sound.

✕ Best Places to Eat

➡ La Carta de Oaxaca (p158)

➡ Staple & Fancy (p159)

➡ Bastille Cafe & Bar (p159)

➡ Stoneburner (p159)

➡ Walrus & the Carpenter (p159)

➡ Un Bien (p157)

For reviews, see p157.➡

🍷 Best Places to Drink

➡ Populuxe Brewing (p160)

➡ Noble Fir (p162)

➡ Hattie's Hat (p162)

➡ Sunset Tavern (p163)

➡ Little Tin Goods & Apothecary Cabinet (p162)

For reviews, see p160.➡

🛍 Best Places to Shop

➡ Ballyhoo (p163)

➡ Bop Street Records (p164)

➡ Lucca Great Finds (p164)

➡ Gold Dogs (p164)

➡ Buffalo Exchange (p164)

For reviews, see p163.➡

Explore Ballard & Discovery Park

The commercial heart of Ballard stretches out on either side of NW Market St between roughly 14th Ave NW and 32nd Ave NW, which is lined with an expanding selection of restaurants, boutiques, a couple of bars and plenty of coffee options. From NW Market St head south on Ballard Ave NW, Leary Ave NW or 20th Ave NW for more of the same. These blocks closer to the water contain many of the neighborhood's most charming historic buildings, now home to a bevy of modern offerings, including some of the best shopping in the city.

If you keep going south things become much more industrial. Many beloved pubs and music venues thrive here and have been joined by some excellent new offerings. Be aware that at night parts of this area can feel deserted.

North of NW Market St you'll find miles and miles of some of the city's nicest single family homes. There are a few small, but thriving, commercial districts here as well: NW 70th Ave between 15th Ave NW and 14th Ave NW has a high concentration of laudable restaurants and bars; 15th Ave NW itself is also home to some notable establishments.

The neighborhood's far west side is bordered by the Puget Sound and has staggering views of the water and Olympic Peninsula to match. On the southwestern edge you'll find the historic Hiram M Chittenden Locks (p156), from where you can continue south over the water to the hiking trails of Discovery Park.

Local Life

Old Ballard Pay your respects to one of Ballard's most beloved establishments at Hattie's Hat (p162) before hitting a live-music gig in the Sunset Tavern (p163).

Hidden eats Leave the main commercial drag and you'll find some of the neighborhood's best restaurants, such as Bushwick & Hunt (p159) and Un Bien (p157), in its most residential enclaves.

Getting There & Away

Bus RapidRide D Line, which runs down 15th Ave NW, is the fastest direct bus into downtown. Metro bus 40 travels from downtown via Fremont to Ballard stopping at multiple places in the neighborhood. For Golden Gardens Park (p156) and the western waterfront, you can take bus 44 originating from the U District.

TOP SIGHT
DISCOVERY PARK

A former military installation ingeniously transformed into a wild coastal park, Discovery Park is a relatively recent addition to the city landscape; it wasn't officially inaugurated until 1973. The largest green space in Seattle at 534 acres, its compact cornucopia of cliffs, meadows, dunes, forest and beaches stands as a healthy microcosm of the surrounding Pacific Northwest ecosystems.

Orientation & Trails

For a map of the park's trail and road system, stop by the **Discovery Park Environmental Learning Center** (Map p252; ☎206-386-4236; 3801 W Government Way; ⏰8:30am-5pm Tue-Sun; 🚌33) near the Government Way entrance. The main walking trail is the 3-mile-long **Loop trail**, part of a 12-mile network of marked paths. Branch off onto the **South Beach trail** descending down a steep bluff if you want to view the still-functioning **West Point Lighthouse**, a great spot for panoramic views of the Sound and mountains to the west. You can circumnavigate back round to the Loop Trail via North Beach.

Seventeen acres in the north of the park are Native American land and home to the Daybreak Star Indian Cultural Center (p157), a community center for the United Indians of All Tribes Foundation (UIATF), a confederation of the many Native American tribes in the Seattle area.

Wildlife

Wildlife is abundant in Discovery Park, particularly birdlife: 270 different species have been logged. At ground level, coyote, chipmunks and raccoons inhabit the woods, while offshore a marine park shelters sea lions and harbor seals.

DON'T MISS

➡ Loop Trail
➡ West Point Lighthouse
➡ South Beach
➡ Daybreak Star Indian Cultural Center

PRACTICALITIES

➡ Map p252, D4
➡ ☎206-386-4236
➡ 3801 Discovery Park Blvd, Magnolia
➡ admission free
➡ ⏰4am-11:30pm
➡ 🅿 ♿ 📷
➡ 🚌33

◉ SIGHTS

Majestic views of the Puget Sound and the snowcapped mountains of the Olympic Peninsula can be found all along the Burke-Gilman Trail (p139), which runs on the shore along Seaview Ave NW. Sunsets should be taken in at the aptly named **Sunset Hill Park** (Map p252; NW 77th St & 34th Ave, Ballard; 🚌45 from U-District), which is on a bluff looking out over the waterfront. There are also plenty of historic buildings and antique remnants of a bygone industrial age to be found along the southern edge of the waterfront. If you want to keep things wild head over to Discovery Park (p155).

◉ Ballard

★ NORDIC MUSEUM   MUSEUM
Map p252 (📞206-789-5707; www.nordic
museum.org; 2655 NW Market St; adult/child
$15/10; ⊙10am-5pm Tue, Wed & Fri-Sun, to 8pm
Thu; 🅿; 🚌44) Reason alone to come to Ballard – if the culinary scene and waterside parks weren't enough – is this delightful surprise of a museum dedicated to Nordic history and culture. In 2018 the museum upgraded in size from its original location in a historic schoolhouse to a newly constructed and fjord-inspired building. Its collections and temporary exhibits (usually an additional $5) represent a hugely accomplished collection of stories, artifacts and other assorted treasures from the recent and distant past.

CARL ENGLISH JR BOTANICAL GARDENS   PARK
Map p252 (⊙7am-9pm; 🚌44) On the northern bank of Hiram M Chittenden Locks is this charming arboretum and specimen garden. Trails wind through gardens filled with flowers and mature trees, each labeled. Flanking the gardens is a **visitor center** (Map p252; 📞206-783-7059; www.ballardlocks.org; 3015 NW 54th St; ⊙10am-12:30pm & 1:30-4pm Thu-Mon Oct-Apr, 10am-6pm May-Sep) **FREE** containing a small museum documenting the history of the locks.

GOLDEN GARDENS PARK   PARK
(📞206-684-4075; 8498 Seaview Pl NW; ⊙4am-11:30pm; 🚌45 from U District) Golden Gardens Park, established in 1904 by Harry W Treat, is a lovely 95-acre beach park with sandy

---

◉ TOP SIGHT
HIRAM M CHITTENDEN LOCKS

Seattle shimmers like an impressionist painting on sunny days at the Hiram M Chittenden Locks. Here, the freshwater of Lake Washington and Lake Union that flows through the 8-mile-long Lake Washington Ship Canal drops 22ft into salt-water Puget Sound. Construction of the canal and locks began in 1911; today 100,000 boats a year pass through.

On the southern side of the locks, the **fish ladder** was built in 1976 to allow salmon to fight their way to spawning grounds in the Cascade headwaters of the Sammamish River. Visitors can watch the fish from underwater glass-sided tanks or from above (there are nets to keep salmon from overleaping). The best time to visit is during spawning season, from mid-June to September.

On the northern entrance to the lock area is the **Carl English Jr Botanical Gardens**, a charming arboretum and specimen garden. Trails wind through gardens filled with flowers and mature trees, each labeled. Flanking the gardens is a **visitor center** containing a small museum documenting the history of the locks.

DON'T MISS
➡ Locks
➡ Fish ladder
➡ Carl English Jr Botanical Gardens

PRACTICALITIES
➡ Map p252, D3
➡ 3015 NW 54th St, Ballard
➡ admission free
➡ ⊙7am-9pm
➡ 🚌44

beaches north of Shilshole Bay Marina. There are picnic facilities, restrooms, basketball hoops, volleyball nets, gangs of Canadian geese, lots of parking and plenty of space to get away from all the activity. The Burke-Gilman Trail (p139) effectively ends here.

Rising above Golden Gardens is Sunset Hill Park, a prime perch for dramatic sunsets and long views.

BERGEN PLACE PARK · LANDMARK

Map p252 (☑206-684-4075; 5420 22nd Ave NW; ☺4am-11:30pm; ☒40) In case you forget where you are or the origin of the settlers to whom Ballard owes its existence, a quintet of flags fly over diminutive Bergen Place Park: those of Norway, Sweden, Denmark, Iceland and Finland, the five so-called Nordic countries. The park was inaugurated by King Olaf V of Norway in 1975 and sports five 'Witness Tree' sculptures.

SHILSHOLE BAY MARINA · MARINA

Map p252 (7001 Seaview Ave NW; ☒44 from U District) The Shilshole Bay Marina, about 2 miles northwest of the Hiram M Chittenden Locks along Seaview Ave NW, offers pleasant views across Puget Sound framed by multiple masts. As Seattle's primary sailboat moorage it also has a glittery collection of boats – millions of dollars worth. Inside the marina, you can rent sailboats or take classes at Windworks (p164).

LEIF ERIKSON STATUE · STATUE

Map p252 (Seaview Ave NW; ☒44) Looking out over the modern yachts in the Shilshole Bay Marina is this magnificent statue of the Icelandic explorer and 'discoverer' of America, Leif Erikson, surrounded by a stone circle. The statue is an important reminder of Seattle's (and Ballard's) Nordic heritage: the city claims more Icelandic Americans than anywhere else in the US.

◎ Discovery Park

DAYBREAK STAR INDIAN CULTURAL CENTER · CULTURAL CENTER

Map p252 (☑206-285-4425; www.unitedindians. org; 5011 Bernie Whitebear Way; donations encouraged; ☺9am-5pm Mon-Fri) FREE Inside Discovery Park (p155) you'll find this cultural center that displays a permanent collection of Native American artwork, special

exhibitions and hosts events (check the online calendar). It's also a great place to pick up gifts – the on-site **Sacred Circle Gift Shop** (10am-5pm Wednesday to Friday) is full of incredible indigenous art and crafts.

FISHERMEN'S TERMINAL · PIER

Map p252 (3919 18th Ave W, Magnolia; ☒RapidRide D Line) Seattle's fishing fleet resides at Fishermen's Terminal, in a wide recess in the ship canal called Salmon Bay on the south side of the Ballard Bridge. Fishermen's Terminal is a popular mooring spot because the facility is in freshwater, above the Chittenden Locks; freshwater is much less corrosive to boats than salt water.

✕ EATING

Ballard's restaurant scene is exemplary and always growing. Yes, the food is consistently impressive across the board, but it's the neighborhood's diverse dining options that really put it over the top. New American gastropubs, Mexican brunch spots, trendy Thai eateries and more crowd the neighborhood's commercial blocks. You won't want for a good meal while you're here.

UN BIEN · CUBAN $

Map p252 (☑206-588-2040; www.unbien seattle.com; 7302 ½ 15th Ave NW, Ballard; mains $11-16; ☺11am-9pm Wed-Sat, to 8pm Sun; ☒RapidRide D Line) Lines can get long at this Cuban take-out spot far from Ballard's commercial center, but the wait is worth it to finally sink your teeth into a perfectly juicy and tangy pork sandwich. The restaurant is owned by brothers working from family recipes and you can taste the affection in every bite.

There's a covered patio area with very limited seating next to the food stand.

CAFE BESALU · BAKERY, CAFE $

Map p252 (☑206-789-1463; www.cafebesalu. com; 5909 24th Ave NW, Ballard; pastries from $2.50; ☺6:30am-2pm Mon-Fri, to 3pm Sat & Sun; ☒40) Slightly away from Ballard's 'downtown' streets, Besalu lures visitors to its isolated perch on 24th Ave with its French-style baked goods (in particular the croissants and quiches), which some bloggers have hailed as 'better than Paris.'

BALLARD & DISCOVERY PARK EATING

SEATTLE'S NORDIC HERITAGE

Seattle, like many US cities, is ethnically diverse, its population concocted from a complex melange of natives and immigrants, from the original Duwamish tribe to the Hmong flower-sellers of Pike Place Market. In common with the USA's Upper Midwest, much of the city's early history was forged by Nordic immigrants from the countries of Norway, Sweden, Finland, Denmark and Iceland. Their arrival in such large numbers wasn't coincidental. The rain-sodden fjords, forests and mountains of Puget Sound coupled with the dominant industries of fishing and logging reminded 19th-century Scandinavian settlers of home; and home it quickly became.

The bulk of Seattle's Nordic immigrants arrived in the late 19th and early 20th centuries, pushed out of their native lands by a lack of good farmland and lured to America by cheap homesteads, higher wages and religious tolerance. Nordics were instrumental in rebuilding Seattle after the 1889 Great Fire and were equally important in the early evolution of Ballard, then a separate city, but redolent of a Norwegian fishing settlement with its burgeoning salmon industry.

Famous Seattle Nordics during this era included John Nordstrom, a Swede, who struck it rich in the Klondike gold rush before turning his nascent Seattle shoe shop into a chain of high-end department stores that now bears his last name; Nils Johanson, who founded Seattle's famous nonprofit Swedish Medical Center; and Ivar Haglund, the son of Norwegian-Swedish immigrants who made his name with a still-popular fish-and-chip shop called Ivar's Acres of Clams (p53).

Generational cultural assimilation has blunted some of Seattle's Nordic identity in recent years, but thanks to Ballard's fine Nordic Museum (p156) and its affiliated events and festivals, the culture can still be tasted, if you know where to look.

PORTAGE BAY CAFE
BREAKFAST $

Map p252 (206-783-1547; www.portagebay cafe.com; 2821 NW Market St, Ballard; mains $10-15; ⊙8am-2pm Mon-Fri, to 2:30pm Sat & Sun; 44) This bright, cheery location of the popular local cafe chain serves an extensive brunch menu made with mostly organic, sustainable ingredients. It's known for its breakfast bar: order from its menu of waffle and pancake varieties, then take your plate up to the bar and dress it up with fresh fruit, nuts and other goodies.

LOCKSPOT CAFE
SEAFOOD $

Map p252 (206-789-4865; www.facebook. com/thelockspotcafe; 3005 NW 54th St, Ballard; mains $10-15; ⊙8am-late; 44) The Lockspot is a throwback to old Ballard, before the attempted gentrification and you're likely to see some actual boat-faring folks grumbling over coffee and eggs. Grab a spot next to them for classic greasy-spoon fare. Even better, order fish-and-chips from the walk-up window outside and take them to the Hiram M Chittenden Locks (p156) to watch the boats go by.

★LA CARTA DE OAXACA
MEXICAN $$

Map p252 (206-782-8722; www.lacartade oaxaca.com; 5431 Ballard Ave NW, Ballard; mains $11-18; ⊙5-11pm Mon, 11:30am-3pm & 5-11pm Tue-Thu, to midnight Fri & Sat; 40) La Carta de Oaxaca is easily one of Seattle's best lunch and brunch spots. Those who crave authentic Oaxacan-style cooking will swoon at the *birria* (braised leg of lamb) or the house special *mole negro Oaxaqueño* (chicken or pork in a chocolate and chili sauce). Whatever you order, expect serious flavors.

This place is always crowded, especially on Saturdays, so expect a wait or try to slip into one of the spots at the bar, from where you can also see the master chefs in action.

★BITTERROOT
BARBECUE $$

Map p252 (206-588-1577; www.bitterrootbbq. com; 5239 Ballard Ave NW, Ballard; mains $11-19; ⊙11am-2am; 40) People come to Bitterroot for two things: smoked meat and whiskey. Thankfully this restaurant with a pleasing modern roadhouse vibe does both exceptionally well. You can get your meat in sandwich form, or by itself with sides like cast-iron cornbread and roasted cauliflower. Likewise, the extensive whiskey menu comes neat or as an expertly mixed craft cocktail.

You can hang out in the bar at the back until late and food is served until 1am.

★**BASTILLE CAFE & BAR** FRENCH $$

Map p252 (www.bastilleseattle.com; 5307 Ballard Ave NW; mains $16-38; ⊘4:30-10pm Mon-Thu, to midnight Fri & Sat, 10am-3pm & 4:30-9pm Sun; 🖵40) ✈ French but not at all faux, Bastille could easily pass for a genuine Parisian bistro if it weren't for the surfeit of American accents. First there's the decor: beautiful white tiles juxtaposed with black wood, mirrors and chandeliers. Then there's the menu: *moules* (mussels), *frites* (real French fries), rabbit pâté, oysters and steak (all sourced locally).

SAN FERMO ITALIAN $$

Map p252 (✆206-342-1530; www.sanfermo seattle.com; 5341 Ballard Ave NW, Ballard; mains dinner $19-32, brunch $14-17; ⊘5-10pm Mon-Thu, to 11pm Fri, 10am-3pm & 5-11pm Sat, 10am-3pm & 5-9pm Sun; 🖵40) San Fermo makes great use of its location in a historic single family home on Ballard Ave NW. It serves hearty Italian fare (think thick homemade noodles, buttery sauces and grilled branzino) for dinner and weekend brunch. While some changes have been made to the home's interior, the rustic charm remains in the minimalist decorations and old-world design.

WALRUS & THE CARPENTER SEAFOOD $$

Map p252 (✆206-395-9227; www.thewalrusbar. com; 4743 Ballard Ave NW, Ballard; small plates $14-18; ⊘4-10pm; 🖵40) Puget Sound waters practically bleed oysters and – arguably – there isn't a better place to knock 'em back raw with a glass of wine or two than the Walrus, a highly congenial oyster bar named not after a Beatles song but a poem by Lewis Carroll in *Through the Looking-Glass*. The accolades (like the customers) keep flying in.

PESTLE ROCK THAI $$

Map p252 (✆206-466-6671; https://pestlerock. com; 2305 NW Market St, Ballard; mains $13-19; ⊘11:30am-9:30pm Mon, Wed & Thu, to 10pm Fri, noon-10pm Sat, to 9pm Sun; 🖵40) This swanky Thai restaurant is a neighborhood favorite. Its large menu caters to casual Thai food fans and adventurous eaters alike, and features a choose-your-own spiciness system. Make sure to order a minty cocktail to complement your meal.

SEÑOR MOOSE MEXICAN $$

Map p252 (✆206-784-5568; www.senormoose. com; 5242 Leary Ave NW, Ballard; mains $12-19; ⊘8am-3pm daily, 4:30-9pm Mon-Thu, 5-10pm Fri & Sat, to 9pm Sun; 🖵40) Reading the menu at Señor Moose is like a mini lesson in Mexican culinary geography. Each of the traditional dishes is described along with the region it originated from, which makes narrowing down what to eat a challenge, but rest assured there are no wrong answers here.

BRUNSWICK & HUNT AMERICAN $$

Map p252 (✆206-946-1574; www.brunswick andhunt.com; 1480 NW 70th St, Ballard; mains $18-28; ⊘4-9pm Tue & Wed, to 10pm Thu & Fri, 9am-2pm & 5-10pm Sat, 9am-2pm Sun; 🖵Rapid-Ride D Line) Brunswick & Hunt is synonymous with one thing: its incredible fried chicken, smothered in Dijon mustard cream and served on a soft bed of mashed potatoes and collard greens. If you're not in the mood for fowl, you'll find plenty else to enjoy, especially if you're a cocktail enthusiast.

★**STAPLE & FANCY** ITALIAN $$$

Map p252 (✆206-789-1200; www.ethanstowell restaurants.com; 4739 Ballard Ave NW, Ballard; mains $23-38, tasting menu $60; ⊘5-11pm; 🖵40) There's much to be said about Staple & Fancy's pedigree as another of Ethan Stowell's many hip Seattle eateries, but the bottom line is the food at this moody Italian restaurant is simply exquisite. Everything, from the seasonal cocktails to the perfectly al dente pasta, is imbued with well-balanced flavors and keen attention to detail.

STONEBURNER MEDITERRANEAN $$$

Map p252 (✆206-695-2051; www.stoneburner seattle.com; 5214 Ballard Ave NW, Ballard; mains $18-34; ⊘3-10pm Mon-Thu, to 11pm Fri, 10am-11pm Sat, to 10pm Sun; 🖵40) Come and see homemade pasta prepared before your eyes in this popular restaurant affiliated with the swanky Hotel Ballard (p194). Pasta-rollers massage dough at workstations in full view of the diners waiting to enjoy the fruits of their labor in Stoneburner's vaguely Parisian-style bistro. Pasta aside, the brunch breakfast pizza and creative vegetable dishes stand out.

RAY'S BOATHOUSE SEAFOOD $$$

Map p252 (✆206-789-3770; www.rays.com; 6049 Seaview Ave NW, Ballard; mains $28-46; ⊘5-9pm; 🖵44) Out in western Ballard near the Shilshole Bay Marina (p157), Ray's is all about placid Olympic Peninsula views, nautical decor and an exhaustive fresh-fish menu. It offers tourists everything they imagine when they think about a nice dinner out in Seattle.

Reservations are required and it isn't cheap, but if you can't get in for dinner, at least come for a drink on the sundeck.

CHINOOK'S AT SALMON BAY   SEAFOOD **$$$**
Map p252 (206-283-4665; 1900 W Nickerson St, Magnolia; mains $15-40; 11am-10pm Mon-Fri, 8am-10pm Sat & Sun; RapidRide D Line) Across the Ballard Bridge in the Fishermen's Terminal (p157), Chinook's is where fish practically leap out of the water and into the kitchen. You can't get it much fresher than this, and the selection of fish and range of preparations is vast. Watch the fishing fleet coming in from the massive restaurant windows.

🍺 DRINKING & NIGHTLIFE

Ballard is Seattle's beer capital – which is saying something in a city that helped kick-start North America's microbrewing obsession in the 1980s. There are micro and nano-breweries aplenty, and hopping between them on a sunny afternoon is a favorite neighborhood activity of locals and tourists alike. You'll also find plenty of great wine around, as well as a growing number of inventive cocktail-centric lounges.

Those seeking cheap beer and sticky floors will also be in heaven: the neighborhood has no shortage of dive bars and live music venues full of character.

⭐**POPULUXE BREWING**   BREWERY
Map p252 (206-706-3400; www.populuxe brewing.com; 826 NW 49th St, Ballard; 3-9pm Mon-Thu, to 10pm Fri, noon-10pm Sat, to 9pm Sun; RapidRide D Line) Microbreweries too large for you? Move down a notch to a nanobrewery. The menu of nine ever-changing brews is impossible to predict; just bank on it being made with skill, know-how and a whole lotta love. Food carts park outside in the small 'garden,' where you can sit, sup and play cornhole on warm summer evenings.

🏃 Neighborhood Walk Old Ballard & Beyond

START CONOR BYRNE
END GOLDEN GARDENS PARK
LENGTH 2.5 MILES; 1½ TO TWO HOURS

Redbrick old Ballard is a diminutive low-rise version of Pioneer Square and dates from the same era (1890s to 1910s), when Ballard was a separate city with Ballard Ave NW as its 'downtown.' Most of the historic buildings lie in and around this thoroughfare.

To get acquainted with the neighborhood's historic side, warm up in **1 Conor Byrne** (p162) – today an Irish pub – one of Seattle's oldest still-operating taverns. The establishment's first liquor license was granted in 1904, when it was called the Owl, a name that endured through Prohibition, when it was briefly re-branded as a 'cafe.' Name changes aside, it still has its original mahogany bar.

When you're done with your drink hang a right out of the building and walk up to the intersection of 20th Ave NW. On your right is the **2 Cors & Wegener Building**. Once the offices of the early local broadsheet *Ballard News*, this is one of the most impressive buildings in the area, dating from 1893. An early recipient of Ballard's historical revitalization program, it's now mostly shops, apartments and office space.

Older still is the **3 Junction Building** (1890) just across the street. Now lacking its decorative 3rd-floor corner turret, the narrow edifice has had any number of reincarnations in its 125-year history, from community hall to theater, shop and saloon. It currently houses Macleod's (p162) Scottish pub.

Continue on Ballard Ave NW. At the next junction (with Vernon Pl) is the Second Empire baroque–style **4 Scandinavian American Bank Building**, a fine example of the early-1900s tendency to flatter by imitation: its concrete surface is treated to look like stone. You can still see the 'Bank Building' sign embedded in the top corner. It once housed the flophouse Starlight Hotel but, since 2011, has been home to the more salubrious Ballard Inn.

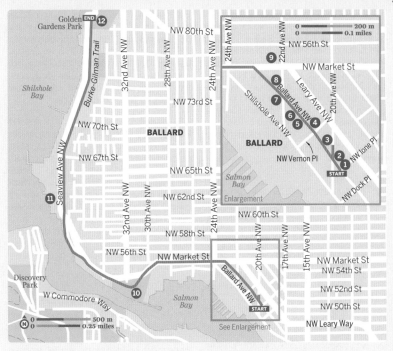

Continue northwest along Ballard Ave. Of note on the left is the **5 GS Sanborn Building**, Ballard's only example of Richardsonian Romanesque architecture, a style that was popular on the East Coast in the 1880s. It has a sandstone face and a 3rd-story arch, and housed some of Ballard's key businesses in the early 1900s.

A little further on is a small wood-frame **6 house** at No 5341. Predating the 1889 Great Fire, this is one of the oldest surviving buildings in Seattle, rescued and brought here from the International District in the 1970s. Rumor says it was once a bordello. Currently it houses the excellent Italian eatery San Fermo (p159).

A great example of the attractive brickwork that embellishes many of the buildings along Ballard Ave, the **7 Portland Building** has housed all kinds of businesses since its construction, including taverns and dry-goods stores. It was given a historically sympathetic face-lift in 1985.

Opposite the Portland Building on the corner of 22nd Ave NW is a **8 Commemorative Bell Tower**. This corner is the original location of Ballard City Hall, sometimes called 'Hose Hall,' which also contained the jail and the fire-department hose company

(hence the nickname). Weakened by a series of earthquakes, the building was demolished in 1965, but the columns and bell were saved and made into this little landmark.

Ballard Ave NW ends at the intersection with NW Market St. Just to the right on the north side of the street stands the **9 Ballard Building**. Ballard's only major terracotta structure, it was built in the 1920s by the Fraternal Order of Eagles and once housed a community hospital.

To truly understand Ballard, you have to tear yourself away from its historic core and digest a bit of its seafaring spirit. Continue west on NW Market St for a bit over half a mile before veering left on NW 54th St. Here you'll find the entrance to the **10 Hiram M Chittenden Locks** (p156), as much an engineering marvel as a waterside attraction. Back outside, you can pick up the western segment of the Burke-Gilman Trail (p139) and follow it to where the ship canal opens out into Puget Sound. If hunger pangs attack, stop at **11 Ray's Boathouse** (p159) for excellent seafood and equally good views. Pass Shilshole Bay Marina on the Burke-Gilman and head toward this walk's end point, **12 Golden Gardens Park** (p156), with its gorgeous sandy beach.

NOBLE FIR
BAR

Map p252 (✆206-420-7425; www.thenoblefir. com; 5316 Ballard Ave NW, Ballard; ✆4-11pm Wed & Thu, to midnight Fri, 1pm-midnight Sat, to 6:30pm Sun; ▣40) Almost qualifying as a travel bookstore as well as a bar, Noble Fir's highly curated, hops-heavy beer list might fill you with enough liquid courage to plan that hair-raising trip into the Amazon, or even just a trek around Ballard. The bright, laid-back bar has a nook given over to travel books and packing cases on which to rest drinks.

HATTIE'S HAT
BAR

Map p252 (✆206-784-0175; www.hatties-hat. com; 5231 Ballard Ave NW, Ballard; ✆10am-2am Mon-Fri, 9am-2am Sat & Sun; ▣40) As long as there's a Hattie's Hat, a bit of old Ballard will always exist. This classic old divey bar has been around in some guise or other since 1904. It was last revived with new blood in 2009 but hasn't lost its charm – a perfect storm of stiff drinks, fun-loving staff and cheap, greasy-spoon food.

LITTLE TIN GOODS & APOTHECARY CABINET
COCKTAIL BAR

Map p252 (✆808-635-6516; www.littletinballard. com; 5335 Ballard Ave NW, Ballard; ✆5-11pm Wed & Thu, to midnight Fri & Sat year-round, noon-5pm Sun Apr-Oct, 4-10pm Sun Nov-Mar; ▣40) Even if you're not bowled over by the cutesy name you'll want to drop in for a unique and – most importantly – tasty cocktail at this Ballard hideaway. The interior is tastefully whimsical and feels like a secret garden miles away from the city outside.

Seasonal hours are subject to change; check the website.

JOLLY ROGER TAPROOM
BAR

Map p252 (✆206-782-6181; www.maritime brewery.com; 1111 NW Ballard Way, Ballard; ✆4-10pm Mon & Tue, 11:30am-11pm Wed-Sat, to 9pm Sun; ▣RapidRide D Line) Maritime Pacific Brewing's Jolly Roger Taproom is a tiny, pirate-themed bar with a nautical chart painted onto the floor. These days it's less scurvy-barnacle and more placid-yachtie, but the beer's still tops – and served in 20oz pints. There are about 15 taps, all serving Maritime Pacific brews, including Jolly Roger Christmas Ale when it's in season.

NO BONES BEACH CLUB
BAR

Map p252 (✆206-453-3233; www.nobones beachclub.com; 5410 17th Ave NW, Ballard; ✆4-9pm Mon, Wed & Thu, 11am-10pm Fri & Sat, to 9pm Sun; ▣40) At the time of writing No Bones Beach Club was the only vegan tiki-themed bar and restaurant in Seattle, but even if it wasn't it would still be worth a visit to sip a Banana Killer (dark rum, banana, coconut milk and spice) while snacking on fried avocado tacos.

MACLEOD'S
PUB

Map p252 (✆206-687-7115; www.macleods ballard.com; 5200 Ballard Ave NW, Ballard; ✆4pm-midnight Sun-Thu, to 2am Fri & Sat; ▣40) This Scottish-style pub sells the inevitable phone book's worth of whiskey varietals in a bar overlooked by the framed countenances of notable Scots. However, Macleod's trump card might just lay in its adjacent eating room where it does *real* British fish-and-chips with mushy peas, or – for the ultimate Scottish touch – curry sauce (mains $10 to $16).

KING'S HARDWARE
BAR

Map p252 (✆206-782-0027; www.kingsballard. com; 5225 Ballard Ave NW, Ballard; ✆3pm-2am Mon-Fri, from noon Sat & Sun; ▣40) King's Hardware is a true dive: the walls are loaded with taxidermy, the scuffed wooden benches reek of marinated beer and the best in-house art is on people's bodies. You can soak up the hard liquor with some tangy chicken wings. Bonus: it's a popular spot for people to bring their dogs.

CONOR BYRNE
PUB

Map p252 (✆206-784-3640; www.conorbyrne pub.com; 5140 Ballard Ave NW, Ballard; ✆4pm-midnight Mon-Thu, to 2am Fri-Sun; ▣40) A bit of old Ballard they chose to leave behind (or perhaps just forgot about), Conor Byrne is a raffish Irish pub bivouacked in an old terracotta-brick building that has been a bar of some sort since its inception in 1904. It's best known for its Guinness and regular live music.

BAUHAUS
CAFE

Map p252 (✆206-453-3068; www.bauhaus strong.coffee; 2001 NW Market St, Ballard; ✆6am-9pm Mon-Fri, from 7am Sat & Sun; ▣40) Right in the heart of Ballard's commercial center, this large, vaguely art deco–inspired cafe serves great drip coffee and espresso pulls, and usually has an open table or two if you're looking for a place to sit with a book or laptop.

BALLARD BREWERY DISTRICT

If you've come to Seattle in search of good beer (smart move!) head directly to Ballard, where the beer-brewing industry commands a level of economic importance once reserved for boat-building and fishing. There is even a name for the slice of neighborhood that most beer-makers inhabit (roughly between 15 Ave NW and 8th Ave NW below NW Market St): the Ballard Brewery District.

At last count Ballard had 11 breweries, many of them conceived and ignited in the post-recessionary 2010s. Some breweries maintain on-site pubs (known as brewpubs), others merely host tap or tasting rooms. This boom created a new class of even further downsized microbreweries aptly named nano-breweries. These tiny local operations prefer to ferment high-quality, small-batch beers that emphasize fun and creativity over huge profit margins. Run by beer-lovers and hobbyists, sometimes operating out of garages and warehouses, their modus operandi is subtly different from well-established microbrewers. Instead of knocking out big-hitting flagship beers, the nanos rely on eternally changing seasonal menus of experimental brews and esoteric one-offs producing one or two barrels at a time. Nanos have been known to attract rock-band-like followings of committed beer lovers eager to share in their latest creative endeavors, be it a British-style IPA or a dark, chocolatey stout. With a tangible potluck feel, taprooms are known for their incredibly laid-back atmosphere. Typical nanos might allow bring-your-own food, and usually have liberal policies on pets and kids.

Since the initial movement, some nano-breweries, like the venerated Populuxe Brewing (p160), have moved from former pint-sized homes to larger venues with more seating and better food options. However, the spirit of the nano-brewery is much more about the attention to quality and playful experimentation than the size of the tasting room, and that spirit is very much still alive across the Ballard Brewery District.

☆ ENTERTAINMENT

TRACTOR TAVERN   LIVE MUSIC
Map p252 (✆206-789-3599; www.tractortavern. com; 5213 Ballard Ave NW, Ballard; tickets $8-20; ⊙8pm-2am; 🚌40) One of Seattle's premier venues for folk and acoustic music, the Tractor books local songwriters and regional bands, plus quality touring acts. Music runs toward country, rockabilly, folk, bluegrass and old-time. It's an intimate place with a small stage and great sound; occasional square dancing is frosting on the cake.

SUNSET TAVERN   LIVE MUSIC
Map p252 (✆206-784-4880; www.sunsettavern. com; 5433 Ballard Ave NW, Ballard; 🚌40) One of the two pillars of Ballard's thriving live-music scene along with the Tractor, the Sunset has been spruced up since its grungy heyday and sports a riotously red front bar (no cover) complete with an old-fashioned photo booth (that works) and a small but sizzling music space out back that books great dirty-rock shows of local and touring bands.

🛍 SHOPPING

There is tons of shopping to be done in Ballard, regardless if you're looking to beef up your wardrobe, add to your record collection, or get your home decor on trend. The NW Market St area is home to most of these stores and it's not to be missed for those with retail therapy on the itinerary.

★BALLYHOO   ANTIQUES
Map p252 (✆206-268-0371; www.ballyhoo seattle.com; 5445 Ballard Ave NW, Ballard; ⊙11am-8pm Mon-Thu, to 9pm Fri & Sat; 🚌40) Even if you think you've been to every oddities shop worth a two-headed calf, Ballyhoo is worth a visit. What it lacks in space it makes up for in the breadth of its merchandise. On one side of the store you'll find fun trinkets in the $1 to $10 range and on the other a fossilized woolly mammoth tooth.

★LUCCA GREAT FINDS   GIFTS & SOUVENIRS
Map p252 (✆206-782-7337; www.luccagreat finds.com; 5332 Ballard Ave NW, Ballard; ⊙11am-6pm Mon-Fri, to 7pm Sat, 10am-5pm Sun) One of

the best things about this Ballard boutique is that it offers two shopping experiences: in the front is a chic PNW themed homewares store that will have you redesigning your apartment in your head while you browse, and in the back is a stationery shop with reams of enviably stylish wrapping paper and rows of charming greeting cards.

★ BOP STREET RECORDS   MUSIC

Map p252 (⏹206-297-2232; www.bopstreet records.com; 2220 NW Market St, Ballard; ⏲noon-8pm Tue-Wed, noon-10pm Thu-Sat, noon-5pm Sun; ⏹40) Probably the most impressive collection of vinyl you're ever likely to see lines the heavily stacked shelves of Bop Street Records. The collection of half a million records covers every genre – it even has old-school 78s. No wonder rock stars and other serious musicians make it their first Seattle port of call.

GOLD DOGS   CLOTHING

Map p252 (⏹206-499-1811; www.shopgolddogs. com; 5221a Ballard Ave NW, Ballard; ⏲11am-7:30pm Mon-Thu, to 9pm Fri & Sat, 10am-6pm Sun; ⏹40) City slickers looking to add a little *yee-haw* to their wardrobe should stop at Gold Dogs. The vibe is very outlaw country, so expect to find distressed dungarees, leather jackets layered in fringe, rock-and-roll tees and cowboy boots from its extremely Instagramable Boot Wall. Everything is a mix of vintage and contemporary and feels very thoughtfully selected.

BUFFALO EXCHANGE   CLOTHING

Map p252 (⏹206-297-5920; www.buffalo exchange.com; 2232 NW Market St, Ballard; ⏲11am-8pm Mon-Sat, to 7pm Sun; ⏹40) Come to this location of the popular vintage clothing chain to dig through the chic discarded threads of Ballard's trendsetters. The store is small, but the trash-to-treasure ratio is weighed much more heavily in favor of treasure than other vintage shops in the area.

CARD KINGDOM   TOYS

Map p252 (⏹206-523-9605; www.cardkingdom. com; 5105 Leary Ave NW, Ballard; ⏲11am-midnight Mon-Fri, from 10am Sat & Sun; ⏹40)

Attracting poker players, *Magic: The Gathering* enthusiasts, kids and table top game lovers, Card Kingdom is a fantastic games emporium. There are plenty of organized activities here, including an on-site games parlor, but you can drop by any time it's open to browse the shelves or play a hand.

BALLARD FARMERS MARKET   MARKET

Map p252 (www.sfmamarkets.com; 22nd Ave NW & Ballard Ave NW, Ballard; ⏲10am-3pm Sun; ⏹40) Seattle's most popular Sunday market is open year-round, rain or shine, every Sunday on Ballard Ave NW.

WILD SALMON SEAFOOD MARKET   FOOD

Map p252 (⏹206-283-3366; www.wildsalmon seafood.com; 1900 W Nickerson St, Magnolia; ⏲8:30am-6pm Mon-Sat, to 5pm Sun; ⏹Rapid-Ride D Line) At Wild Salmon Seafood Market – in the Fishermen's Terminal (p157) on the south side of the Ballard Bridge, which is technically Magnolia, but still – you can buy fresh salmon and shellfish directly from the fisherfolk who caught it. The market will also ship fresh fish at reasonable prices.

🏃 SPORTS & ACTIVITIES

ELECTRIC & FOLDING BIKES NORTHWEST   CYCLING

Map p252 (⏹206-547-4621; www.electric vehiclesnw.com; 4810 17th Ave NW, Ballard; regular/electric bike rental per hour $15/25, per day $60/100; ⏲11am-6pm; ⏹40) As the name suggests, this popular retail store specializes in both electric and easy-to-carry folding bikes. You can rent either by the hour or day.

WINDWORKS   SAILING, BOAT RENTAL

Map p252 (⏹206-784-9386; www.windworks sailing.com; 7001 Seaview Ave NW, Ballard; classes from $148; ⏹44) Inside the Shilshole Bay Marina (p157), you can rent sailboats or take classes at Windworks.

Georgetown & West Seattle

Neighborhood Top Five

1 Museum of Flight (p167) Seeing how *Homo sapiens* got from the Wright Brothers to the Concorde in the space of just 66 years at this illustrious, entertaining and subtly educational museum.

2 Alki Beach Park (p168) Slowing down the rhythm a couple of notches on a week-end summer's afternoon on Alki Beach.

3 Georgetown (p171) Going on a pub crawl, or a vintage store crawl – or both – amid the red-brick bars and beer-stained history of this bohemian enclave.

4 Alaska Junction (p168) Strolling West Seattle's commercial hub and explor-ing the area's underrated restaurants and shops.

5 Art Attack (p169) Investigating surreal and abstract art creations in George-town's fabulous monthly arts event.

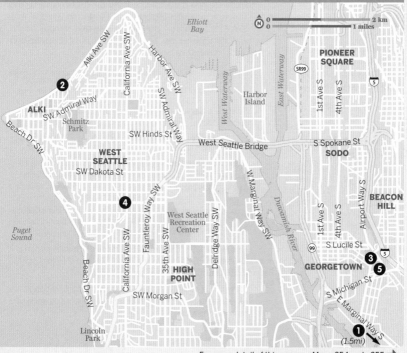

For more detail of this area see Map p254 and p255

Lonely Planet's Top Tip

Even Seattle's most rain-hardened brethren would admit that West Seattle is best saved for a sunny day. Visit this hilly, beach-embellished neighborhood in spring or summer and join in the high jinks on ebullient Alki Beach. Make sure you stay for the incredible sunsets.

✖ Best Places to Eat

➡ Bakery Nouveau (p169)
➡ Ma'Ono (p170)
➡ Fonda la Catrina (p169)
➡ Arthur's (p170)
➡ Sunfish (p170)

For reviews, see p169. ➡

🍷 Best Places to Drink

➡ West Seattle Brewing Co (p171)
➡ Machine House Brewery (p171)
➡ Outwest Bar (p171)
➡ Jules Maes Saloon (p171)

For reviews, see p171. ➡

🔒 Best Places to Shop

➡ Easy Street Records & Café (p172)
➡ Susan Wheeler Home (p172)
➡ Antique Mall of West Seattle (p173)
➡ Fantagraphics Bookstore & Gallery (p173)

For reviews, see p172. ➡

Explore Georgetown & West Seattle

Located south of downtown and its industrial extension, SoDo, the neighborhoods of Georgetown and West Seattle feel detached from the center by the glassy expanse of Elliott Bay and SoDo's utilitarian warehouses. Since transportation connections to downtown are better than those between the neighborhoods, they're often visited separately. Georgetown can be incorporated with a visit to the Museum of Flight, while West Seattle works as a summer-weekend beach getaway.

Georgetown is an old neighborhood with a scrappy yet independent artistic sensibility whose reputation as a bastion of coolness is on the rise. Once you get here (regular buses from downtown take 20 minutes), navigation is easy. Most of Georgetown's pubs, bars, funky shops and restaurants are clustered on Airport Way S.

Plenty of Seattleites would more likely visit Hawaii than spend a day catching rays in West Seattle. But, although this island-like haven is distinctly peripheral in the minds of many urbanites, it's actually only – ahem – 15 minutes from downtown by water taxi. Not that everyone dismisses it. Indeed, for a certain type of Seattleite, West Seattle beckons like a proverbial Coney Island, courtesy of sandy Alki Beach (p168).

Spread over a hilly peninsula, the neighborhood spins on two hubs: the de-facto downtown called 'the Junction' at the intersection of California Ave SW and SW Alaska St, and the aforementioned famous beach and its promenade. Free shuttles from the water-taxi dock connect with both.

Local Life

Seattle's backyard When the sun's out, Alki Beach (p168) and its adjacent promenade become Seattle's communal backyard and a fabulous spot to hunker down with a beer and enjoy people-watching.

Arty inclinations Mingle with minstrels, painters, poseurs and beer aficionados as Georgetown exhibits its playful side during its monthly Art attack (p169).

Getting There & Away

Bus Metro buses 106 and 124 run frequently from downtown to Georgetown. The 124 carries on to the Museum of Flight. RapidRide C Line runs from downtown to West Seattle.

Water taxi Hourly water taxis leave Pier 50 from the downtown waterfront to Seacrest Park in West Seattle. There's no weekend service in the winter.

ELENA_SUVOROVA/SHUTTERSTOCK ©

TOP SIGHT
MUSEUM OF FLIGHT

Chronicling flight history from Kitty Hawk to Concorde, the city that spawned Boeing unsurprisingly houses one of the nation's finest aviation museums. It's a multifarious affair gluing together a broad sweep of flying-related memorabilia in several hangar-sized galleries. Exhibits include some of the most ingenious gravity-defying human-made objects: picture nefarious V2 rockets, Apollo lunar modules and aerodynamic gliders.

Great Gallery

The centerpiece of the museum is a humongous gallery filled with historic aircraft that overhang chronological exhibits on the history of flight. If you're short on time, jump-cut to the **Tower**, a mock-up of an air-traffic-control tower overlooking the still operational Boeing Field. Another must-see is a replica of the Wright Brothers' original 1903 *Wright Flyer*. Nearby, **X-Pilot simulators** pitch you into a WWII dogfight; they cost an extra $9 per person.

Aviation Pavilion & Space Gallery

The Aviation Pavilion opened in 2016 and is accessible via a modernist bridge over E Marginal Way. It displays half a dozen iconic planes that you can look inside, including a British Airways **Concorde**; the first jet-powered **Air Force One**, used by presidents Eisenhower, Kennedy, Johnson and Nixon; and a **Boeing 727** prototype. The adjacent Space Gallery houses the decommissioned **Full Fuselage Trainer** of the Space Shuttle. It costs an extra $30/25 per adult/child to explore the crew compartment.

DON'T MISS

➡ Aviation Pavilion
➡ X-Pilot simulators
➡ Full Fuselage Trainer
➡ 1903 *Wright Flyer*

PRACTICALITIES

➡ Map p254, A3
➡ ☏206-764-5720
➡ www.museumof flight.org
➡ Boeing Field, 9404 E Marginal Way S, Georgetown
➡ adult/child $25/16, 5-9pm 1st Thu of month free
➡ ⊘10am-5pm, to 9pm 1st Thu of month
➡ ⧖
➡ ▣124

◉ SIGHTS

◉ Georgetown

MUSEUM OF FLIGHT   MUSEUM
See p167.

FOGUE STUDIOS & GALLERY   GALLERY
Map p254 (☑206-717-5900; www.foguestudios.
com; 5519 Airport Way S; ⊘11am-6pm Wed-Sat,
noon-5pm Sun; ☐124) **FREE** This large gallery space is dedicated to the work of artists over the age of 50 and features a wide
breadth of mediums (painting to pottery to
abstract installations) on display.

HAT 'N' BOOTS   LANDMARK
Map p254 (☑206-684-4075; 6427 Carleton Ave
S; ⊘4am-11:30pm) These two sculptures of
a giant cowboy hat and boots originally
embellished a Georgetown gas station in
the 1950s – the hat was the pay kiosk, and
the boots were the toilets. Obsolete by the
1990s, they lay rotting until foresighted
community activists rescued and relocated
them to this small local park. Full refur-
bishments were completed in 2010, meaning the comical cowboy behemoths now
look as kitschy as they did in 1954.

KRAB JAB STUDIO   GALLERY
Map p254 (☑206-456-4035; www.krabjab
studio.com; 5628 Airport Way S; ⊘11am-6pm
Wed-Sun) You never know what you're going
to get at this small gallery inside the old
red-brick Rainier beer factory in Georgetown, which leans heavily toward 'fantasy
art.' Krab Jab opens extended hours during
Georgetown's Art Attack (p169). Check the
website for details.

GEORGETOWN STEAM PLANT   LANDMARK
Map p254 (☑206-763-2542; 6605 13th Ave S;
⊘10am-2pm 2nd Sat of month; ☐124) **FREE**
The Georgetown Steam Plant, built in
1906, has one of the last working examples
of the large-scale steam turbines that dou-
bled the efficiency of electricity production
and shifted the public's view of electricity
from a luxury to a standard part of modern
living. The plant ceased operations in 1972
and in 1980 was declared a Historic American Engineering Record site. It's now an
education-oriented museum.

Free tours are offered at 11am and 1pm
when the plant is open to visitors. Reservations are recommended.

◉ West Seattle

ALKI BEACH PARK   BEACH
Map p255 (☑206-684-4075; 1702 Alki Ave SW;
⊘4am-11:30pm; ☐37) Alki Beach has an
entirely different feel from the rest of Seattle: on a sunny day this 2-mile stretch of
sand could be confused for California.
There's a bike path, volleyball courts on the
sand, and rings for beach fires.

Look for the **miniature Statue of Lib-
erty**, donated by the Boy Scouts. There's
also a **pylon** marking Arthur Denny's landing party's first stop in 1851, which for
some reason has a chip of Massachusetts'
Plymouth Rock embedded in its base.

LINCOLN PARK   PARK
(☑206-684-4075; 8011 Fauntleroy Way SW,
Fauntleroy; ⊘4am-11:30pm; 🚻; ☐RapidRide C
Line) Forest trails, an outdoor swimming
pool and scenic beaches make this one of
Seattle's most underrated parks.

**DUWAMISH LONGHOUSE
& CULTURAL CENTER**   CULTURAL CENTER
(☑206-431-1582; www.duwamishtribe.org;
4705 W Marginal Way SW; ⊘10am-5pm Tue-Sat;
☐RapidRide C Line) This Duwamish tribal
cultural center takes the form of a traditional longhouse built out of cedar wood
and located beside the Duwamish River. It's
used mainly for cultural events (check the
website for more information), but it does
display some historical information and
indigenous artifacts.

LOG HOUSE MUSEUM   MUSEUM
Map p255 (☑206-938-5293; www.loghouse
museum.info; 3003 61st Ave SW, Alki Beach; suggested donation adult/child $3/1; ⊘noon-4pm
Thu-Sun; ☐775 from Seacrest Dock) **FREE** A
historical curiosity in Seattle's oldest neighborhood, this museum was built in 1903
from Douglas fir trees as a carriage house
for the currently disused Homestead Restaurant a block away. When all around it
was moved or demolished to lay out West
Seattle, the house miraculously survived
and now sits amid a dense grid of modern single family homes rather than dense
forest. It serves as a small museum with
revolving historical exhibitions.

ALASKA JUNCTION   AREA
Map p255 (cnr California Ave SW & SW Alaska St;
☐RapidRide C Line) You'll see Alaska Junction

GEORGETOWN SECOND SATURDAY ART ATTACK

Georgetown's industrial art scene pulls together on the second weekend of each month at the Georgetown Second Saturday Art Attack. This is the best time to visit the neighborhood's myriad galleries, some of which have rather sporadic opening hours. Almost the entire commercial strip takes part in the monthly event, which runs from 6pm and 9pm and exhibits work in cafes, pubs, galleries and studios. Complimentary drinks and snacks are often laid on.

A unique Georgetown feature is its free 'art ride' bus that runs up and down Airport Way S every 15 minutes between 6pm and 9:30pm. Many of the best galleries inhabit the former Rainier Brewery, including Krab Jab Studio (p168), a shared work space, gallery and shop specializing in fantasy art. Other places worth visiting are the Fogue Studios & Gallery (p168), which celebrates artists aged over 50, **Miller School of Art** (☏206-861-9265; www.millerschoolart.com; 1226a S Bailey St; ☒124) and **Georgetown Arts & Cultural Center** (☏206-851-1538; 5809 Airport Way S; ☒124).

referenced often around West Seattle, as it functions as the de facto commercial center for the mostly suburban neighborhoods that orbit it. The surrounding blocks are where you'll find most of the noteworthy restaurants, bars and boutiques in the area.

EATING

While lighter on restaurant options than the city-center neighborhoods, you'll find more than a few pleasant dining surprises in both areas.

West Seattle has two separate eating nexuses: the seaside boulevard backing Alki Beach and the businesses spread along California Ave SW around the so-called 'Junction' with SW Alaska St. Nearly all of Georgetown's eating joints are on or adjacent to Airport Way S.

✗ Georgetown

★FONDA LA CATRINA   MEXICAN $

Map p254 (☏206-767-2787; www.fondalacatrina. com; 5905 Airport Way S; mains $9-14; ☺11am-10pm Mon-Thu, to 11pm Fri, 10am-11pm Sat, to 10pm Sun; ☒124) You'll find a number of things in the busy confines of Fonda la Catrina, a shockingly good Mexican restaurant in industrial Georgetown. There's the colorful Day of the Dead decorations and the Diego Rivera–inspired murals, strong drinks and – most importantly – fabulous food.

HANGAR CAFE   CAFE $

Map p254 (☏206-762-0204; www.thehangar cafe.com; 6261 13th Ave S; mains $8-13; ☺7am-3pm Mon-Fri, 8am-3pm Sat, to 2pm Sun; ☒60) No matter where you fall in the great 'sweet or savory' crepe debate, you're likely to enjoy the ones at Hangar Cafe. This extremely popular Georgetown eatery specializes in the French delicacy, but also has a large menu of sandwiches and salads.

VIA TRIBUNALI   PIZZA $$$

Map p254 (☏206-464-2880; www.viatribunali. net; 6009 12th Ave S; pizza $15-20; ☺11am-11pm Mon-Thu, to midnight Fri, 4pm-midnight Sat, 3-10pm Sun; ☒124) This small Seattle-founded chain operates in four of the city's hipper sanctums (including Capitol Hill and Fremont) plus a couple of foreign enclaves (NYC and Portland, OR). It deals not in pizzas but *pizze:* crisp-crusted Italian pies that are true to the food's Neapolitan roots.

✗ West Seattle

★BAKERY NOUVEAU   BAKERY $

Map p255 (☏206-923-0534; www.bakery nouveau.com; 4737 California Ave SW; baked goods from $2; ☺6am-7pm Mon-Fri, 7am-7pm Sat, 7am-6pm Sun; ☒RapidRide C Line) No discussion of Seattle's best bakery omits Bakery Nouveau. The crumbly, craggy almond and chocolate croissants are as good as they get this side of the Atlantic. Don't take our word for it: the bakery consistently wins awards for its excellent pastries.

SUNFISH SEAFOOD **$**

Map p255 (☎206-938-4112; 2800 Alki Ave SW, Alki Beach; fish & chips $6-14; ☺11am-9pm Wed-Sun; 🖶; 🚌775 from Seacrest Dock) You haven't really been to Alki until you've tried the fish-and-chips. Options include cod, halibut, salmon, fried oysters and clam strips – or combinations thereof. Sit at one of the outdoor tables and enjoy the boardwalk feel.

SPUD FISH & CHIPS SEAFOOD **$**

Map p255 (☎206-938-0606; www.alkispud.com; 2666 Alki Ave SW, Alki Beach; fish & chips $7-16; ☺11am-9pm; 🚌775 from Seacrest Dock) Spud is as much a piece of West Seattle history as the Log House Museum or the Alki Point Lighthouse, having been in the fish-and-chip business since 1935. Two pieces of battered cod and hand-cut fries is the default dinner, although it also does oysters, clams, prawns and halibut. The downstairs lobby is an intriguing photo-museum of local history.

EASY STREET CAFE DINER **$**

Map p255 (☎206-938-3279; www.easystreet online.com/Cafe; 4559 California Ave SW; mains $7.25-9.50; ☺7am-3pm; 🚌RapidRide C Line) Attached to Easy Street Records (p172), this friendly cafe is the best place in the area for a cheap, hearty breakfast. It has tons of specials under $10 that are actually quite tasty and filling. Best of all, you can drift right into the shop to browse LPs when you're done eating.

★MA'ONO HAWAIIAN **$$**

Map p255 (☎206-935-1075; www.maonoseattle. com; 4437 California Ave SW; mains $12-17; ☺5-10pm Wed & Thu, 5-11pm Fri, 9am-3pm & 5-11pm Sat, 5-10pm Sun; 🚌55) The fried chicken sandwich – served on a King's Hawaiian roll with cabbage and a perfectly spicy sauce – at this West Seattle spot is one of the best things between two slices of bread currently available in Seattle. Treat yourself to one during the always-packed brunch with a guava mimosa and side of roasted sweet potato with caramelized lime.

ARTHUR'S AUSTRALIAN **$$**

Map p255 (☎206-829-8235; www.arthurs seattle.com; 2311 California Ave SW; mains $10-14; ☺9am-10pm Mon-Thu, 9am-11pm Fri, 8am-11pm Sat, 8am-10pm Sun; 🖉; 🚌55) Drop in at this sunny cafe in rainy Seattle for a taste of modern Aussie brunch food. We're talking big hunks of sourdough bread smothered in smashed avocado, thick-cut bacon and poached eggs, and marinated lamb sandwiches served with pints of local beer.

ITTO'S TAPAS **$$**

Map p255 (☎206-420-6676; www.ittostapas. com; 4160 California Ave SW; tapas $4-15; ☺4pm-midnight Mon-Fri, from 2pm Sat & Sun; 🖉; 🚌RapidRide C Line) Settle in at this tiny and well-decorated restaurant and get ready to taste plate after plate of authentic Mediterranean and North African food, such as Moroccan lemon chicken and grilled squid steak in Romesco sauce. Sundays and Mondays, when bottles of wine are half off with purchase of food, are especially popular.

EL CHUPACABRA MEXICAN **$$**

Map p255 (☎206-933-7344; www.elchupacabra seattle.com; 2620 Alki Ave SW, Alki Beach; burritos $10-12; ☺11:30am-midnight Mon-Thu, to 2am Fri, 11am-2am Sat, to midnight Sun; 🚌775 from Seacrest Dock) While the burritos and tacos at El Chupacabra probably wouldn't be described as authentic, they are still pretty darned good, especially when combined with a margarita and eaten on the patio overlooking the water. On Saturday nights this place is buzzing with 20-somethings chatting over drinks and guacamole. Expect a wait, and to make friends at the bar while waiting.

NEW LUCK TOY CHINESE **$$**

Map p255 (☎206-971-0698; www.newlucktoy. bar; 5905 California Ave SW; mains $9-19; ☺4pm-2am) New Luck Toy serves up Chinese food with cocktails like boozy slushies and activities such as Skee-Ball and karaoke in a bar fully decked out in decorations and atmosphere. Named after a Chinese-American restaurant that used to be on the same street, this old-meets-modern establishment is headed by chef Mark Fuller.

SALTY'S ON ALKI STEAK **$$$**

Map p255 (☎206-937-1600; www.saltys.com; 1936 Harbor Ave SW; mains $32-55; ☺11am-3pm Mon-Fri, 9:30am-1:30pm Sat, 8:45am-1:30pm Sun, 4:30-9pm daily; 🚢Seacrest Dock) Salty's isn't actually on Alki Beach; rather it is on the other side of Duwamish Head facing Elliott Bay. In any case, the view of the Seattle skyline combined with the deluxe steak-and-seafood menu make this a big enough lure for people all over Seattle. Eschewing the fish-and-chips frugality of the rest of West Seattle, this place is distinctly upscale.

CHRISTO'S ON ALKI
PIZZA $$$

Map p255 (206-923-2200; www.christos onalki.com; 2508 Alki Ave SW, Alki Beach; mains $16-26; 3-11pm Mon-Thu, from 11am Fri, 8am-11pm Sat & Sun; 775 from Seacrest Dock) This family-run Mediterranean restaurant that specializes in pizzas and calzones with thick, garlicky crusts is the definition of a neighborhood institution. It is right on the waterfront and does a very popular brunch on the weekends. For the best Alki Beach gossip, sit at the bar while you eat.

DRINKING & NIGHTLIFE

Head to Georgetown, former home of the Rainier beer factory, for a fine selection of red-brick drinking houses, most of which give at least a passing nod to the neighborhood's gritty industrial past.

West Seattle has the beachy charm of a vacation community and is *the* place to go in summer for an ice-cold beer with a beach view. It also has a great record store (p172) where you can sup a beer while you browse.

WEST SEATTLE BREWING CO
MICROBREWERY

Map p255 (TapShack; 206-420-4523; www.westseattlebrewing.com; 2536 Alki Ave SW, Alki Beach; 3-9pm Tue-Fri, 1-9pm Sat & Sun; 775 from Seacrest Dock) The beer at the promenade-adjacent Alki Beach location of this popular microbrewery is fantastic, but it's the experience of sitting on one of the many lounge chairs facing the water and watching bikers and dog walkers go by that brings the crowds. You'll have to fight for a spot outside on weekends; come on a weekday afternoon for maximum relaxation.

OUTWEST BAR
GAY & LESBIAN

Map p255 (206-937-1540; 5401 California Ave SW, West Seattle; 4-10pm Sun-Tue, to midnight Wed & Thu, to 2pm Fri & Sat; RapidRide C Line) Proof that you don't need to gravitate to Capitol Hill to enjoy a good gay-friendly neighborhood bar is this laid-back place with cocktails, burgers, DJs and regular karaoke. The vibe is friendly and casual and there are regular theme nights, such as

WEST SEATTLE MURALS

Following a noble city tradition of free public art, West Seattle's Diego Rivera–like murals have become an important part of the neighborhood fabric. The 11 giant paintings are scattered over a relatively small area around the Junction commercial zone and do a good job of relating the important chapters of the neighborhood's pioneer history, depicting lively scenes of old streetcars, ferries, beach gatherings and esoteric parades. The murals were commissioned in 1989 and painted by artists from around the country. All are etched onto the sides of buildings, including a post office and a bank. They're kept colorful with periodic touch-ups.

Martini Monday and Lez Sing Wednesday (lesbian karaoke, natch).

JULES MAES SALOON
BAR

Map p254 (206-957-7766; 5919 Airport Way S, Georgetown; 11am-11pm Sun-Thu, to 1am Fri & Sat; 124) You could almost absorb the beer off the wallpaper in Seattle's oldest surviving pub: it's been serving since 1888, when the city was a youthful 37 years old. Once a speakeasy and allegedly haunted, it's a well-worn, comfortable, old-fashioned saloon with just the right contemporary touches: tattooed millennials at the bar, better-than-average food and a killer tap list of local microbrews.

MACHINE HOUSE BREWERY
MICROBREWERY

Map p254 (206-432-6025; www.machinehouse brewery.com; 5840 Airport Way S, Georgetown; 3-9pm Wed-Fri, noon-9pm Sat, to 6pm Sun; ; 124) If you want to enjoy a beer in Georgetown's erstwhile red-brick Rainier beer factory, head to this minimalist taproom and microbrewery where old-fashioned hand pumps dispense classic British-style ales that are big on taste but not too high in alcohol per volume. Bonus: it's kid-friendly.

ELLIOTT BAY BREWERY & PUB
BREWERY

Map p255 (206-932-8695; www.elliottbay brewing.com; 4720 California Ave SW, West Seattle; 11am-11pm Sun-Thu, to midnight Fri & Sat; RapidRide C Line) All of the beers at this

WORTH A DETOUR

FAUNTLEROY

South of West Seattle you'll find the Fauntleroy neighborhood, a quiet stretch of leafy suburban sprawl with a few features that should entice those looking for a slower-paced vacation experience. This isn't a tourist neighborhood at all. Instead, it offers a chance to get some rest and relaxation away from the noise of downtown or the wait for tables at restaurants in the increasingly popular neighborhoods around the city center's periphery. Stay a night or two in the stunning Gatewood B&B (p194), a restored craftsman house with a palatial common room complete with overstuffed chairs and a grand fireplace, as well as plenty of porch space for reading. Take your meals at **Endolyne Joe's** (☑206-937-5637; www.chowfoods.com/endolyne-joes; 9261 45th Ave SW; mains $16-25; ☺8am-10pm Sun-Thu, to 11pm Fri & Sat; ☒RapidRide C Line), a favorite with the locals for its ever-changing menu and commitment to exceptional preparations. During the day you can explore Lincoln Park (p168), one of the city's best, which boasts forested trails and a pretty stretch of beach that has breathtaking views, usually without the crowds. For a more adventurous day, hop on the ferry (p179) to nearby Vashon Island to enjoy a foray into rural Seattle.

congenial brewery are organic and range from the light Luna Weizen to the heavy-hitting Demolition IPA. The food goes way outside the conventional 'pub grub' box with a pan-seared tofu sandwich and a quinoa garbanzo salad.

FLIP FLIP DING DING   BAR
Map p254 (☑206-508-0296; www.flipflip dingding.com; 6012 12th Ave S, Georgetown; ☺2pm-2am; ☒124) If golf can qualify as a sport, then so can pinball. The game has become a popular dive-bar amenity and its popularity is exemplified in places such as this wonderfully named bar and pinball emporium in Georgetown. Grab a beer and some quarters and join in. Boisterous tournaments kick off most weekends.

SMARTY PANTS   BAR
Map p254 (☑206-762-4777; www.smartypants seattle.com; 6017 Airport Way S, Georgetown; ☺11am-midnight Mon-Fri, 9am-midnight Sat, 9am-4pm Sun; ☒124) This red-brick industrial hangout for scooterists and sport-bike riders has vintage motorcycles propped up in the windows, a hearty sandwich menu (around $12), a popular weekend brunch and an obvious fondness for two-wheeled mischief of all types. Wednesday is Bike Night, when fans watch the week's recorded races.

BROTHER JOE   CAFE
Map p254 (☑206-588-2859; www.brotherjoegt. com; 5629 Airport Way S, Georgetown; ☺7am-3pm Mon-Fri, 8am-2pm Sat & Sun; ☒124) This trendy coffee shop mixes ultra-cool

interior design (check out the giant gold faux-taxidermied rhino head and cat portraits on the wall) with a menu of interesting coffee drinks, such as the egg coffee (drip coffee, egg yolk and condensed milk).

🔒 SHOPPING

West Seattle's shopping district is clustered around 'the Junction' (corner of SW Alaska St and California Ave SW). Georgetown's art and antique shops line Airport Way S, especially between Corson Ave S and S Lucille St, where there's a small hub of incredible vintage furniture and home-wares stores.

★SUSAN WHEELER HOME   VINTAGE
Map p254 (☑360-402-5080; www.susanwheeler home.com; 5515 Airport Way S, Georgetown; ☺11am-6pm Wed-Sun; ☒124) This newer addition to Georgetown's small vintage row manages to find a perfect balance of pleasingly cluttered yet artfully refined. There are shelves precariously stacked full of antique plates, tables covered in crystal glassware sets and an entire corner devoted to towels and linens from around the world. Somehow there isn't an item that doesn't feel specially selected.

★EASY STREET RECORDS & CAFÉ   MUSIC
Map p255 (☑206-938-3279; www.easystreet online.com; 4559 California Ave SW, West Seattle; ☺9am-9pm Mon-Sat, to 7pm Sun; ☒RapidRide C Line) Pearl Jam once played at Easy Street,

arguably Seattle's most multifarious record store, and the business continues to sponsor regular events. Inside, young kids with elaborate tattoos mingle with graying ex-punks under a montage of retro parking signs and Nirvana posters. Proving itself to be an invaluable community resource, Easy Street has its own cafe selling food, coffee and beer.

ORIGINS CANNABIS

DISPENSARY

Map p255 (☑206-922-3954; www.origins cannabis.com; 4800 40th Ave SW, West Seattle; ⊗8am-11:30pm Mon-Sat, 9am-9pm Sun) Most dispensaries in Seattle have great customer service, but at this low-key West Seattle weed shop everyone is just an extra bit more friendly and attentive. If that weren't enough, it has a large selection with fun items like locally made edibles.

ANTIQUE MALL
OF WEST SEATTLE

ANTIQUES

Map p255 (☑206-935-9774; 4516 California Ave SW, West Seattle; ⊗noon-6pm Mon-Fri, 10am-6pm Sat, to 5pm Sun; 🚌55) This friendly antique mall wastes no space: there is stuff covering every surface and spilling out of every corner. Not all of it is worth your money, but the dedicated hunter will uncover lots of incredible finds.

FANTAGRAPHICS
BOOKSTORE & GALLERY

BOOKS

Map p254 (☑206-658-0110; www.fantagraphics. com; 1201 S Vale St, Georgetown; ⊗11:30am-8pm Mon-Sat, to 5pm Sun; 🚌124) Founded in the 1970s on the East Coast, this cool alt-comic and graphic-book publisher moved to Seattle in the late '80s and opened this one-of-a-kind bookstore-gallery in 2006. Stocked with quirky books, comics and magazines, and furnished in an exhibition space that hosts monthly shows and readings, it's well worth making a pilgrimage out to Georgetown to visit.

GEORGETOWN RECORDS

MUSIC

Map p254 (☑206-762-5638; www.georgetown records.net; 1201 S Vale St, Georgetown; ⊗11:30am-8pm Mon-Sat, to 5pm Sun; 🚌124) This amazing record store had the guts to open in 2004 when vinyl sales were close to an all-time low. With the format now

returning to its pre-1990s glory, it's an excellent place to go to score rare picture-cover 45in singles from obscure British 1970s punk bands (and plenty more besides).

Bonuses: it hosts in-store performances and is part of the Georgetown Art Attack (p169).

KIRK ALBERT
VINTAGE FURNISHINGS

HOMEWARES

Map p254 (☑206-762-3899; www.kirkalbert. com; 5517 Airport Way S, Georgetown; ⊗11am-6pm Wed-Sat; 🚌124) Not so much stocked as curated, this funky, beautiful store represents the obsessions and tastes of its owner, a designer with a strongly original aesthetic. Come to browse and leave inspired, or come ready to part with a large chunk of change and leave with some truly original art.

🏃 SPORTS & ACTIVITIES

RAINIER GLASS STUDIO

ARTS & CRAFTS

Map p254 (☑206-557-7883; www.rainierglas sstudio.com; 6006 12th Ave S, Georgetown; classes from $125; ⊗11am-7pm Thu-Sun; 🚌124) Glass art is quickly becoming synonymous with Seattle (thank Dale Chihuly) and this new nook is a good place to browse, participate or watch the masters in action. It's run by an ex-student of the famous Pilchuck Glass School near Seattle and offers classes in glassblowing as well as an opportunity to fashion your own glass art with an expert.

ALKI KAYAK TOURS

ADVENTURE SPORTS

Map p255 (☑206-953-0237; www.kayakalki.com; 1660 Harbor Ave SW, Alki Beach; kayaks/SUPs/bikes per hour $20/20/10; ⊗noon-6pm Mon-Fri, 10am-7pm Sat & Sun Apr-Oct; 🚤Seacrest Dock) You can rent bicycles, stand-up paddleboards and kayaks from this outlet whose boathouse is right next to West Seattle's water-taxi dock should you wish to explore Alki by human-powered means. It also offers instruction in water activities and guided kayak excursions, including a very popular four-hour excursion to the Alki Lighthouse ($89 per person).

Seattle Outdoors

Maybe it's the lure of lofty snowcapped Mt Rainier or the sight of calm, kayak-able Lake Union – Seattle has the unnerving habit of turning traditionally sedentary office stiffs into fleece-donning, Lycra-wearing athletes. Wake up and smell the pine needles. They don't call it the Emerald City for nothing.

STEVE ESTVANIK/SHUTTERSTOCK ©

ADAM HESTER/GETTY IMAGES ©

1. Mt Rainier National Park (p183)
Beguiling Mt Rainier offers bountiful activities and views in all seasons.

2. Gas Works Park (p145)
A former power station, repurposed as green space.

3. Rowing on Lake Union (p103)
Take to the water to explore a different side of Seattle.

4. Running (p32)
There are good trails for runners, in the urban landscapes and the many city parks alike.

BILL HINTON PHOTOGRAPHY/GETTY IMAGES ©

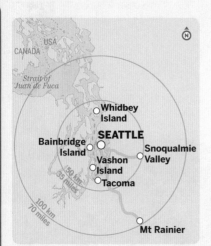

Day Trips from Seattle

Bainbridge Island p177
The ferry ride to this bucolic island off the coast of downtown Seattle is almost as good as the destination itself.

Snoqualmie Valley p178
Verdant woods, snaking rivers and pastoral farmland mark the landscape east of Seattle where the iconic TV series *Twin Peaks* was partially filmed.

Vashon Island p179
The unpretentious atmosphere and slower pace of life on Vashon Island is just a short ferry ride from Seattle.

Tacoma p180
Tacoma isn't large or as full of attractions as it's bigger sister city, Seattle, but a handful of choice museums make it worth the drive down.

Whidbey Island p181
Fishing villages and stunning state parks wait for you on this island long beloved by vacationing Seattleites.

Mt Rainier p183
Instead of waiting for a clear day to sneak a view of this massive peak, make the 90-mile trip and see it up close.

Bainbridge Island

Explore

Bainbridge Island is a favorite vacation destination for Seattleites and visitors from further afield, but the island is close enough to the city that it contains a healthy full-time population, many of whom commute to Seattle by ferry. It's the quickest and easiest way to get out on the water from the big city, and the ride over provides stunning views of both Seattle and the Sound. Prepare to stroll around lazily, tour some waterfront taverns, taste wines, and maybe rent a bike and cycle around the invitingly flat countryside.

The Best...

Activity Bainbridge Vineyards

Place to Eat Blackbird Bakery

Place to Drink Harbour Public House

Getting There & Away

Washington State Ferries (p214) run several times a day from Pier 52 (adult/car and driver $8.50/19.15, bicycle surcharge $1, 30 minutes).

Need to Know

Area Code ⌨206

Location About 9 miles (35-minute ferry ride) off the coast of downtown Seattle

Tourist Office Can be found in town at the **Bainbridge Island Chamber of Commerce** (⌨206-842-3700; www.visitbainbridge.com; 395 Winslow Way E; ⊘9am-5pm Mon-Fri, 10am-3pm Sat).

⊗ EATING & DRINKING

There are tons of places to eat including upscale restaurants, cafes and delis, and some very special ice-cream shops. When it comes to having a drink, lively pubs and great Washington wines are the order of the day on Bainbridge. The island doesn't stay up very late, but you won't go thirsty when it comes to happy hour or leisurely cocktails in the evening.

BLACKBIRD BAKERY BAKERY $
(⌨206-780-1322; www.blackbirdbakery.com; 210 Winslow Way E; baked goods $2-5; ⊘6am-6pm Mon-Fri, from 6:30am Sat, from 7am Sun) This lauded bakery is always crowded in the mornings. Queue up for a sweet (killer muffins and croissants) or savory (cheesy biscuits and bialys) treat.

STREAMLINER DINER DINER $
(⌨206-842-8595; http://streamlinerdiner.com; 397 Winslow Way E; mains $8-13; ⊘7am-2pm Mon-Sat, from 7:30am Sun) As the name suggests, space is tight in this diner made out of a reclaimed Streamline trailer. It's worth it to squeeze in for the fluffy omelets and pancakes, and the strong coffee on offer. Expect a wait on weekends.

MORA ICED CREAMERY ICE CREAM $
(⌨206-855-1112; www.moraicecream.com; 139 Madrone Lane; single scoop $4.50; ⊘11:30am-9:30pm Sun-Thu, to 10pm Fri, 10am-10pm Sat) Luscious ice creams and sorbets made locally on Bainbridge Island come in cones, cups or pints – and, as a bonus, it's all low-fat. You can also splash out for a sundae, banana split or root-beer float.

HARBOUR PUBLIC HOUSE PUB FOOD $$
(⌨206-842-0969; www.harbourpub.com; 231 Parfitt Way SW; mains $11-17; ⊘11am-10pm Mon-Sat, from 10am Sun) After a bike ride or boating excursion, sit back and sample microbrews and hearty pub food at this lively bar and restaurant near the water. It has been an island favorite since it opened in the '90s.

🏃 ACTIVITIES

BAINBRIDGE VINEYARDS WINE
(⌨206-842-9463; www.bainbridgevineyards.com; 8989 NE Day Rd; tasting of 4 wines $5; ⊘tasting room noon-5pm Thu-Mon) Bainbridge Vineyards is a quaint and certified organic winemaker within spitting distance from Seattle. It's about 4 miles north of the ferry dock off Hwy 305: perfect for a bike ride on a sunny day.

Snoqualmie Valley

Explore

East of Seattle's Eastside, the Snoqualmie Valley has long been a photogenic backwater of dairy farms, lush orchards and produce gardens surrounded by steep alpine peaks. Although suburbs are quickly taking over the valley, there's still enough of a rural, small-town ambience to make for a beautiful drive or bike ride.

The Best...

Sight Snoqualmie Falls

Place to Eat Herbfarm

Place to Drink Salish Lodge & Spa

Top Tip

The region is accessible by bus, but to properly explore you'll want to have your own car. It's about 40 minutes to an hour outside the city off I-90 east.

Getting There & Away

King's County Metro (p216) bus 208 runs from Seattle to North Bend on weekdays. The trip takes 1½ hours.

Need to Know

Area Code ☑425

Location About 30 miles east of Seattle

Tourist Office In the town of Snoqualmie you'll find the **Snoqualmie Valley Visitor Center** (☑425-888-6362; www.snovalley.org; 38767 SE River St, Snoqualmie; ⊘9am-5pm Mon-Fri).

◉ SIGHTS

The following sights are arranged south to north.

NORTH BEND   AREA

North Bend, on Hwy 202 just off I-90, is quite literally *Twin Peaks* country. The town was used as the setting for David Lynch's surreal TV series from the early 1990s.

SNOQUALMIE   AREA

Along Hwy 202 you'll find the little town of Snoqualmie, with its antique shops and a store devoted to Northwest wines.

NORTHWEST RAILWAY MUSEUM   MUSEUM

(www.trainmuseum.org; 38625 SE King St, Snoqualmie; ⊘10am-5pm) **FREE** This museum, housed in a Victorian-era train depot, displays the history of rail in the area.

★SNOQUALMIE FALLS   WATERFALL

(www.snoqualmiefalls.com; 6501 Railroad Ave SE, Snoqualmie) Whether or not you recognize this wide and powerful waterfall from the opening credits of *Twin Peaks,* it's more than worth it to pull over and take in this stunner from one of the many view points at Snoqualmie Falls park. When you've picked your jaw up off the floor and gotten your pictures, embark on one of several trails that start from the parking lots.

There are two parking lots: one at the upper observation deck next to the falls, which has paid parking starting at $7, and one across the street, which is free but requires you to cross a bridge to reach the falls side.

If you want to get to know the falls, intimately spend a few nights in the ultra-luxe **Salish Lodge & Spa** (☑info 425-888-2556, reservations 800-272-5474; www.salishlodge.com; 6501 Railroad Ave, Snoqualmie; d from $459; P❄☺), which was used for the fictional Great Northern Hotel in *Twin Peaks* (although it has since been remodeled).

CARNATION   AREA

Hwy 203 branches off from 202 at Fall City; follow it north to Carnation, where the Snoqualmie and Tolt Rivers meet at **Tolt-MacDonald Park** (31020 NE 40th St). This is a great place for a riverside picnic, swim or hike. Carnation was once the center of the valley's dairy industry, and several farms here sell fruit and vegetables at roadside stands.

✗ EATING

TWEDE'S   AMERICAN $

(☑425-831-5511; www.twedescafe.com; 137 W North Bend Way, North Bend; mains $8-11; ⊘8am-8pm Mon-Fri, from 6:30am Sat & Sun) The former Mar T's Cafe, now called Twede's, was the diner with the famous cherry pie and cups of joe in *Twin Peaks;* a fire gutted it in 2000, but it has been rebuilt. Sadly these days the coffee, food and service are all mediocre, so this one is for fans of the TV show only.

★**HERBFARM**   AMERICAN $$$
(☑425-485-5300;   www.theherbfarm.com; 14590 NE 145th St, Woodinville; dinner $205-280; ⊘7-11:30pm Thu-Sat, 4:30-9pm Sun) At this legendary, very, very, upscale restaurant, nine-course dinners are created around a specific theme (at the time of writing it was Salmon Nation) and are drawn from the gardens, the farm itself and small local growers, and matched with locally produced wines.

While it does have the occasional last-minute table, reservations are required and should be made well in advance.

Vashon Island

Explore

More rural and countercultural than Bainbridge, Vashon Island has resisted suburbanization – a rare accomplishment in the Puget Sound area (locals attribute the success to their opposition to letting the state build a bridge). Much of Vashon is covered with farms and gardens; the small community centers double as commercial hubs and artists' enclaves. Cascade views abound, with unencumbered vistas of Mt Rainier and north to Baker.

Vashon is a good island to explore by bicycle or car, lazily stopping to pick berries or fruit at a 'U-pick' garden or orchard. You can also hike in one of the county parks.

The Best

Sight Vashon Heritage Museum

Places to Eat Hardware Store (p180)

Places to Shop SAW-Starving Artist Works (p180)

Top Tip

The ferry dock on the island is about 4 miles from the main commercial hub.

Getting There and Away

King County Water Taxi (Map p234; www.kingcounty.gov/depts/transportation/water-taxi/vashon; Pier 50, Seattle; one way $6.75) This passenger-only ferry leaves from Pier 50 downtown six times each weekday for Vashon Island ($6.75, 25 minutes).

Washington State Ferries (☑20 6-464-6400; www.wsdot.wa.gov; 4829 SW Barton St, Fauntleroy; per person/bike/car $5.55/6.55/19.20) From Fauntleroy in West Seattle, a car ferry leaves more than 30 times daily for Vashon (passenger $5.55, car and driver $19.60, 15 minutes). Fares are collected only on the journey to the island.

Getting Around

Metro bus 118 traverses the island, picking up right on the ferry dock and passing through the island's main drag. However, service is very limited, only coming once every few hours in the afternoon, so make sure you plan accordingly. The schedule can be found on the King County Metro's website (www.kingcounty.gov).

Need to Know

Area Code ☑206

Location Four miles off the coast of the Fauntleroy neighborhood of West Seattle

Tourist Office The island's chamber of commerce has a **tourist office** (www.vashonchamber.com; 17141 Vashon Hwy; ⊘9am-4pm Mon-Fri Jun-Sep, 10am-3pm Mon-Fri Oct-May).

◉ SIGHTS

VASHON HERITAGE MUSEUM   MUSEUM
(☑206-463-7808; www.vashonheritagemuseum.org; 10105 Bank Road SW; ⊘1-4pm Wed-Sun; ☐118) **FREE** Veer off Vashon's main drag and immerse yourself in the island's history at this small but lovingly tended museum in a historic house. Permanent exhibits detail the island's history, from its original indigenous inhabitants to the early European colonists and the community of Japanese immigrants whose legacy on the island stretches back generations.

BLAKE ISLAND STATE PARK

Seattle's parks offer a welcome reprieve from the city's dazzling, yet exhausting, industrialization. Those looking for a wilder slice of nature should head to **Blake Island State Park** (☑360-731-8330; www.parks.state.wa.us/476/blake-island; ⊗8am-dusk). The 475-acre island is the birthplace of Seattle's namesake Chief Sealth and has stunning views of the city's skyline and the Olympic Mountains, as well as countless hiking trails, miles of shoreline and tributes to the area's original inhabitants, the Native American tribes who call the Puget Sound home.

All of Blake Island is a state park and the only way to get there is by private boat or on a tour with **Argosy Cruises** (Map p232; ☑206-443-1244; www.argosycruises.com; Pier 55, Seattle; tours adult/child $92/36; ⊗daily summer, Sat & Sun only Apr, May & Sep). The tour lasts four to five hours and includes a traditional salmon bake, a visit to a recreated indigenous village and a show featuring Native American storytelling.

✕ EATING & DRINKING

There's a cluster of restaurants in the island's commercial center, around Vashon Hwy SW and SW Bank Road. You'll find them elsewhere on the island in smaller numbers.

HARDWARE STORE　　　AMERICAN **$$**
(☑206-463-1800;　www.thsrestaurant.com; 17601 Vashon Hwy SW; mains $12-20; ⊗8am-9pm Mon-Thu, to 10pm Fri & Sat, to 8pm Sun; ▯118) Occupying a historic building oozing '50s Americana charm, Hardware Store's menu aims for 'upscale diner favorites' and knocks it out of the park. Many ingredients are sourced locally, giving you the chance to sample produce and meat from some of the island's prominent farms.

WILD MERMAID　　　　　CAFE
(☑206-408-7424;　10824 Vashon Hwy SW; ⊗6am-3pm Wed-Sat, from 9am Sun) Wild Mermaid has the distinction of being the only ferry-adjacent establishment on the island and it doesn't abuse the privilege. You can find a solid cup of coffee and giant pastries in this charming house with enviable water views. If you have a bigger appetite there's a very limited daily menu of lunch items ($6 to $9).

🅰 SHOPPING

**SAW – STARVING
ARTIST WORKS**　　　　HOMEWARES
(☑206-979-4192;　www.facebook.com/saw starvingartistworks; 9922 SW Bank Rd; ⊗noon-5pm Wed-Fri, from 11am Sat, noon-4pm Sun) A one-stop shop for island souvenirs; SAW's storefront is small but the shelves are crammed full of art and home wares of all varieties made by Vashon locals.

Tacoma

Explore

Tacoma gets a bad rap as a beleaguered mill town known mostly for its distinctive 'Tacom-aroma,' a product of nearby paper mills. Its nickname, 'City of Destiny' – because it was Puget Sound's railroad terminus – once seemed a grim joke. But destiny has started to come through – renewed investment in the arts and significant downtown revitalization make it a worthy stop on the Portland–Seattle route. It's also a popular hub for all manner of corporate conventions.

The Best

Sight Point Defiance
Museum Museum of Glass
Place to Eat Pacific Grill

Getting There and Away

Bus A number of services including SoundTransit (www.soundtransit.org) and Amtrak (www.amtrak.com) run regular buses between Seattle and Tacoma ($3.75 to $12, 90 minutes).

Car I-405 connects Seattle with Tacoma

and, depending on traffic, the trip takes 40 minutes to an hour.

Train Five Amtrak trains run daily connecting Seattle with Tacoma (from $15, 40 minutes).

. . . .

Need to Know

Area Code ✍253

Location On Commerce Bay about 30 miles south of Seattle

Tourist Office In the Greater Tacoma Convention Center you'll find the **Tacoma Visitor Information Center** (✍253-284-3254; www.traveltacoma.com; 1516 Commerce St; ☺10am-4pm Mon-Fri, to 3pm Sat Jun-Aug, 10am-4pm Tue-Fri Sep-May).

 SIGHTS

MUSEUM OF GLASS   MUSEUM
(✍866-468-7386; www.museumofglass.org; 1801 Dock St; adult/child $17/5; ☺10am-5pm Wed-Sat, noon-5pm Sun) The Museum of Glass, with its slanted tower called the Hot Shop Amphitheater, is Tacoma's tribute to native son Dale Chihuly. It has art exhibits and glassblowing demonstrations. Chihuly's characteristically elaborate and colorful Bridge of Glass walkway connects the museum with the enormous copper-domed neobaroque 1911 Union Station.

On the third Thursday of the month the museum is open late and admission is free from 5pm to 8pm.

POINT DEFIANCE   PARK
(✍253-305-1088; www.pdza.org; 5400 N Pearl St; zoo adult/child $19/15; ☺zoo hours vary) Take Ruston Way out to Point Defiance, a 700-acre park complex with free-roaming bison and mountain goats, a logging museum, a zoo, an aquarium and miles of trails.

TACOMA ART MUSEUM   MUSEUM
(✍253-272-4258; www.tacomaartmuseum. org; 1701 Pacific Ave; adult/student/under 5yr $15/13/free; ☺10am-5pm Tue-Sun) For a look at his small-scale work, don't miss Dale Chihuly's permanent collection at the Tacoma Art Museum. While there you can also check out exhibitions of art from Washington and the rest of the Pacific Northwest, including contemporary Native American

work, as well as historic pieces from Japan, Europe and the rest of the Americas.

FEDERAL COURTHOUSE   NOTABLE BUILDING
(1717 Pacific Ave) The Tacoma Federal Courthouse is a grand government building that features glass pieces by beloved local artist Dale Chihuly.

✖ EATING

No one drives to Tacoma to eat, but you definitely don't have to leave Tacoma to find a great meal. There are lots of grab-and-go lunch spots in the downtown area catering to the business crowds where you can get a solid sandwich before or after you hit the museums.

PACIFIC GRILL   AMERICAN $$
(✍253-627-3535; www.pacificgrilltacoma.com; 1502 Pacific Ave; mains $15-36; ☺11am-2pm & 4:30-9pm Mon-Thu, to 10pm Fri, 10am-2pm & 4:30-10pm Sat, to 9pm Sun) Pacific Grill serves lunch and dinner to office workers, museum tourists and conference attendees. The interior is cozy, if a bit generic, but the food is exceptional, elevating clubhouse favorites turkey sandwiches and Caesar salads with bold flavors and fun ingredients like artichoke heart tapenade and white anchovies.

Whidbey Island

. . . .

Explore

Whidbey Island is an idyllic emerald escape beloved of stressed-out Seattleites. While it's not as detached or nonconformist as the San Juans (there's a bridge connecting it to adjacent Fidalgo Island at its northernmost point), life is certainly slower, quieter and more pastoral here. Having six state parks is a bonus, and there's also a plethora of B&Bs, two historic fishing villages (Langley and Coupeville), famously good mussels and a thriving community of artists and artisans. Of less interest to travelers is the US Naval Air base that dominates Oak

WORTH A DETOUR

FUTURE OF FLIGHT: AVIATION CENTER & BOEING TOUR

You don't need to be an aviation enthusiast to enjoy a trip to the **Future of Flight Aviation Center & Boeing Tour** (☑800-464-1476; www.futureofflight.org; 8415 Paine Field Blvd, Mukilteo; adult/child $25/15; ⊗8:30am-5:30pm, tours 9am-3pm) in the city of Everett, 25 miles north of Seattle. The center is the world's largest building by volume and houses both a museum and the real working Boeing factory where the famous airplanes are made.

Harbor. At 41 miles long, Whidbey is the longest island on the US west coast.

The Best

Sight Deception Pass State Park

Place to Eat Christopher's

Place to Drink Useless Bay Coffee Roasters

Getting There and Away

Washington State Ferries (WSF; ☑888-808-7977; www.wsdot.wa.gov/ferries) Services run between Clinton and Mukilteo (passenger/car and driver $5.10/11.40, 30 minutes) and between Coupeville (formerly called Keystone) and Port Townsend ($3.45/14.80, 30 minutes).

Getting Around

Island Transit (☑360-678-7771; www.islandtransit.org) is a community-financed scheme offering the ultimate encouragement for people to get out of their cars and onto the buses. Buses run the length of Whidbey daily except Sunday, from the Clinton ferry dock to Greenbank, Coupeville, Oak Harbor and Deception Pass. Other routes reach the Keystone ferry dock and Langley on weekdays. Service is hourly and free – yes, free!

Need to Know

Area Code ☑360

Location The southern tip of the island is 30 miles (1½-hour drive) north of Seattle

Tourist Office Several towns on the island have visitor centers.

⊙ SIGHTS

DECEPTION PASS STATE PARK　　　PARK

(☑360-675-2417; www.parks.state.wa.us/497/deception-pass; 41229 N State Hwy 20; day pass $10; ⊙dawn-dusk) Deception Pass State Park straddles the eponymous steep-sided water chasm that flows between Whidbey and Fidalgo Islands, and incorporates lakes, islands, campsites and 27 miles of hiking trails. This area is also one of the best places in Washington to spot orcas from the shore, so keep an eye out to sea!

GREENBANK FARM　　　FARM

(☑360-222-3797; 765 Wonn Rd, Greenbank; ⊙11am-4pm Mon-Thu, to 5pm Fri & Sat, to 4:30pm Sun) Go 10 miles south of Coupeville to find this park-style farm that's open daily for shopping at the food stands on-site, strolling the bucolic fields and picnicking. Don't miss a stop in the cafe for the island's best fruit pies.

✗ EATING & DRINKING

If you love mussels, you're in for a treat: Whidbey Island has some of the best. Otherwise you'll find everything from great coffee and fruit pies to Mediterranean fare and outstanding American-style breakfasts.

CHRISTOPHER'S　　　SEAFOOD $$

(☑360-678-5480; www.christophersonwhidbey.com; 103 NW Coveland St; lunch mains $12-16, dinner mains $16-26; ⊙11:30am-2pm & 5-8pm Sun, Mon, Wed & Thu, to 8:30pm Fri & Sat) The mussels and clams are the best in town (no mean feat in Coupeville), and the seafood Alfredo pasta is wonderfully rich. Try the Penn Cove seafood stew – prawns, scallops, mussels and clams in a tomato broth – or just go for the huge plate of mussels in a white-wine cream sauce.

EBEY'S LANDING NATIONAL HISTORICAL RESERVE

This National Historical Reserve was the first of its kind in the nation when it was created in 1978 in order to preserve Whidbey Island's historical heritage from the encroaching urbanization that had already partly engulfed Oak Harbor. Ninety per cent privately owned, **Ebey's Landing** (☑360-678-6084; www.nps.gov/ebla; 162 Cemetery Rd, Coupeville) **FREE** comprises 17,400 acres encompassing working farms, four historic blockhouses, two state parks and the town of Coupeville itself. A series of interpretive boards shows visitors how the patterns of croplands, woods (or the lack of them) and even roads reflect the activities of those who have peopled this scenic landscape, from its earliest indigenous inhabitants to 19th-century settlers.

The **Island County Historical Society Museum** (908 NW Alexander St; ⊙10am-4pm Mon-Sat, from 11am Sun) **FREE** in Coupeville distributes a brochure on suggested driving and cycling tours through the reserve. Highly recommended is the 3.6-mile **Bluff Trail** that starts from a small parking area at the end of Ebey Rd. The energetic can walk or cycle here from Coupeville (approximately 2.5 miles along a quiet road), thus crossing the island at one of its narrowest points.

Other recreational activities here include scuba diving, boating and bird-watching – best along Keystone Spit on the southwestern tip of Crockett Lake.

USELESS BAY COFFEE ROASTERS
CAFE

(☑360-221-4515; https://uselessbaycoffee.com; 121 2nd St; ⊙7:30am-4:30pm) You'll smell the rustic scent of roasting beans long before you see this place. The vast, industrial-meets-1950s diner interior spills out to outdoor picnic tables, and the coffee is great, as are the burgers and sandwiches (mains $8 to $13). Any food preferences from gluten-to dairy-free are very well catered to.

TOBY'S TAVERN
PUB FOOD $$

(☑360-678-4222; www.tobysuds.com; 8 Front St NE; mains $10-18; ⊙11am-9pm Sun-Thu, to 10pm Fri & Sat) A quintessential dive bar housed in a vintage mercantile building dating from the 1890s; even the polished back bar was originally shipped here from around Cape Horn in 1900. Sip home-produced microbrews and enjoy a menu spearheaded by local classics such as tasty mussels, clam strips, and halibut and chips, while listening to the jukebox or shooting pool.

 **ACTIVITIES**

DECEPTION PASS TOURS
WILDLIFE

(☑888-909-8687; www.deceptionpasstours. com; 1hr Deception Pass tour adult/child $40/35) This company offers tours of Deception Pass and whale-watching excursions.

ANACORTES KAYAK TOURS
KAYAKING

(☑360-588-1117; www.anacorteskayaktours. com; tours from $39) Hour-long to multi-day long kayak tours in Deception Pass State Park are available from this popular and professional company.

Mt Rainier

Explore

Emblazoned on every Washington license plate and visible throughout much of the western state, Mt Rainier is the contiguous USA's fifth-highest peak and, in the eyes of many, its most awe-inspiring. Part of a 368-sq-mile national park (inaugurated in 1899), the mountain's snowcapped summit and forest-covered foothills boast numerous hiking trails, swaths of flower-carpeted meadows and an alluring peak that presents a formidable challenge for aspiring climbers.

The park website (www.nps.gov/mora) includes downloadable maps and descriptions of 50 park trails, plus links to current weather and road conditions. The driving loop around the mountain is 147 miles (driving time is about five hours without stops) and the main roads are usually open mid-May through October.

The Native Americans called the mountain Tahoma or Tacoma, meaning the 'mother of waters'; George Vancouver named it Rainier in honor of his colleague and friend Rear Admiral Peter Rainier. Most Seattleites refer to it reverently as 'the Mountain' and forecast the weather by its visibility.

The Best...

Sight Paradise

Places to Eat Copper Creek Inn

Places to Drink Mountain Goat Coffee

Top Tip

This southwestern portion of Mt Rainier National Park is its most developed (and hence most visited) corner. It's massively busy on summer weekends, so visit on a weekday if you can, or arrive early to avoid waiting in line at the entrance station.

Getting There & Away

For the most part you're best off driving yourself, but there are also tour options out of Seattle. If driving, do some research before you leave to find out which entrance you want to head to. Check for road closures at www.nps.gov/mora or call park headquarters at ☑360-569-2211.

Need to Know

Area Code ☑360

Location 92 miles (2 hour drive) southeast of Seattle

Tourist Office Help can be found at the **Henry M Jackson Visitor Center** (☑360-569-6571; ☺10am-5pm daily May-Oct, Sat & Sun Nov-Apr) in Paradise or various visitor centers throughout the park.

⊙ SIGHTS

★ PARADISE   AREA

(Paradise Valley Rd) Home to numerous trailheads and the starting point for most summit hikes, Paradise also holds the iconic Paradise Inn (built in 1916) and the massive, informative Henry M Jackson Visitor Center, where a cutting-edge museum has hands-on exhibits on everything from flora to glacier formation, and shows a must-see 21-minute film entitled *Mount Rainier: Restless Giant*. Park naturalists lead free interpretive hikes from the visitor center daily in summer, and snowshoe walks on winter weekends.

The daughter of park pioneer James Longmire unintentionally named this high-mountain nirvana when she exclaimed what a paradise it was on visiting the spot for the first time in the 1880s. Suddenly, the place had a name, and a very apt one at that. One of the snowiest places on earth, 5400ft-high Paradise remains the park's most popular draw, with its famous flower meadows backed by dramatic Rainier views on the days (a clear minority annually) when the mountain decides to take off its cloudy hat.

LONGMIRE INFORMATION
CENTER & MUSEUM   HISTORIC BUILDING

(☑360-569-6575; Hwy 706, Longmire; ☺museum 9am-4:30pm year-round, info center May-Oct) FREE The tiny, free **Longmire Museum** describes the history of Longmire, originally the park's headquarters. James Longmire first came here in 1883 and noticed the hot mineral springs that bubbled up in a lovely meadow opposite the present-day National Park Inn. The next year he established Longmire's Medicinal Springs, and in 1890 he built the **Longmire Springs Hotel** (☑360-569-2275; Hwy 706, Longmire; r with shared/private bath from $138/203; ⊛). Across from the museum is a Wilderness Information Center (closed in winter).

 EATING & DRINKING

★ COPPER CREEK INN   AMERICAN $$

(☑360-569-2326; www.coppercreekinn.com; 35707 SR 706 E, Ashford; breakfast $9-14, burgers $11-15, dinner mains $12-28; ☺11am-8pm Mon-Fri, 8am-9pm Sat, 8am-8pm Sun, opens earlier summer) Forget the historic inns. This is one of the state's great rural restaurants, and breakfast is an absolute must if you're heading off for a lengthy hike inside the park. Situated just outside the Nisqually entrance, the Copper Creek has been knocking out pancakes, wild-blackberry pie and its own home-roasted coffee since 1946.

MOUNTAIN GOAT COFFEE   CAFE $

(☑360-494-5600; 105 E Main St, Packwood; pastries from $2; ☺7am-5pm) While cops eat doughnuts, park rangers seem to prefer muffins. Stop in at this cozy morning spot for the best coffee in town (they roast their own beans), baked goods and perhaps an informative chat with a friendly, khaki-clad officer. Show up early, though: the pastries often sell out before noon.

WHITTAKER'S CAFÉ & ESPRESSO   CAFE $

(☑360-569-2439; www.whittakersbunkhouse. com; 30205 SR 706 E, Ashford; breakfast from $3; ☺6:45am-8pm, weekends only winter) If you've ever pondered huckleberry ice cream for breakfast (why not?), this is the place for it. The cute little cafe attached to a **bunkhouse** (dm $40, d $90-145; ☎) also serves good coffee, breakfast burritos and breakfast sandwiches.

🏃 ACTIVITIES

Close to Puget Sound's urban areas and unobstructed by other peaks, Mt Rainier has an overwhelming presence, set off by its 26 glaciers, and it has long enraptured the millions of inhabitants who live in its shadow. Though it's an iconic peak to bag, climbing Rainier is no picnic; old hands liken it to running a marathon in thin air with crampons stuck to your shoes. Approximately 9000 people attempt it annually, but only half of them make it to the top.

There are plenty of trails in the foothills, for short or medium-sized walks. When the clouds magically disappear during long, clear days in July and August, the whole area around Mt Rainier becomes one of Washington's most paradisiacal playgrounds. If you have the time, plan a hike all the way around it on the 93-mile **Wonderland Trail**.

SKYLINE TRAIL   HIKING

Starting behind the Paradise Inn, the 5-mile Skyline Trail climbs approximately 1600ft to **Panorama Point**, with good views of Mt Rainier and the neighboring Tatoosh Range.

SOURDOUGH RIDGE TRAIL   HIKING

(Sunrise Park Rd, Sunrise; ☺late Jun-Sep) This 1-mile ridge climb heads from the north side of the Sunrise parking area on the park's eastern side and takes you out into pristine subalpine meadows for stunning views over Washington's volcanic giants: namely, Mt Rainier, Mt Baker, Glacier Peak and Mt Adams.

TRAIL OF THE SHADOWS LOOP   HIKING

Before you hit the exposed mountain splendor of Paradise, warm up in the forests of Longmire on this 0.8-mile interpretive trail that begins across the road from the Longmire hotel and museum. The hike includes a replica homestead cabin and easily digestible information on the local plant life. It's wheelchair accessible for the first 0.4 miles.

GROVE OF THE PATRIARCHS TRAIL   HIKING

(Stevens Canyon Rd) Starting off Hwy 123 just north of the **Ohanapecosh Visitor Center,** (☑360-569-6581; Hwy 123; ☺9am-5pm Jun–mid-Oct) this 1.5-mile trail is one of the park's most popular short hikes and explores a small island (the grove) in the middle of the Ohanapecosh River replete with soaring Douglas fir, cedar and hemlock trees, some of which are over 1000 years old.

WHITE PASS SKI AREA   SKIING

(☑509-672-3100; www.skiwhitepass.com; 48935 US 12, White Pass; day pass adult/child $69/49) A small ski area with a view of Mt Rainier, accommodations at the base, and a mid-mountain lodge for refreshments.

Sleeping

In common with many US cities, Seattle's sleeping options are plentiful and varied. Want to drive up to a motel and park your car where you can see it through the window? You can do that. Rather toss your keys to the valet while a bellhop whisks your bags to your suite? You can do that too, as well as everything in between.

Finding Deals

Hotel prices in Seattle vary considerably; don't be put off by quoted rack rates. For the best deals, search around online. Room prices can vary wildly depending on season (up to 50% off the rack rates from November to March; peak season is generally May through August); day of the week (weekends are usually cheaper); time of booking (earlier is usually better); hotel capacity (the fuller the hotel, the more expensive it is); whether there are festivals or events going on in town; and luck (are they throwing a deal?). Most places offer special AAA (auto club) rates. Some offer a third night for free. For more details on hotels, see the website www.visitseattle.org.

Choosing to stay outside of popular tourist areas such as downtown, Capitol Hill and anywhere near Pike Place Market will also be a great help at keeping costs down. Options in neighborhoods further afield, such as Ballard, West Seattle and Fremont, are considerably cheaper throughout the year.

Note that Seattle hotel rooms are subject to a room tax of 15.6% (less for most B&Bs and historical properties), which will be tacked onto the final bill.

Hotel Types

Seattle has a quartet of good economical hostels: one in downtown, one in Belltown, one in the International District, and one a little further out in Fremont. Aside from dorms, they also offer economical private rooms. You'll find few good hotels for under $120 a night unless you're willing to share a bathroom/toilet. For some good bargains in the $120 to $200 range, including a raft of reliable Holiday Inns, Best Westerns and Quality Inns, look around Belltown and Lower Queen Anne, especially near the Space Needle. There has been a recent increase in boutique hotels, especially those run by Pineapple Hospitality and the Kimpton Group. Capitol Hill has some excellent B&Bs. Big chains and more expensive options, many of which are encased in their own mini-skyscrapers, are spread around downtown.

Apartment Rentals

If you're planning to stay for more than a couple of nights, are traveling with a large group, or are extremely budget conscious, going the route of an apartment rental through a service like Airbnb (www.airbnb.com) is an option worth exploring. In many neighborhoods that lack lots of traditional hotels (Ballard, Fremont and West Seattle, for instance) you can find incredible deals for apartments starting at around $60 a night for a one-bedroom rental.

Be mindful that gentrification is a huge issue in Seattle and some neighborhoods have been harder hit than others. There's tons of cheap, newly constructed rentals in the Central District, but when you arrive you might find yourself in the crossfire of that neighborhood's battle against rising housing costs that are displacing longtime residents. Doing research before you book is essential.

Lonely Planet's Top Choices

Edgewater (p191) A piece of rock-and-roll history jutting out over Puget Sound.

Hotel Monaco (p189) In the heart of downtown; no two rooms are exactly the same.

Maxwell Hotel (p192) Free cupcakes, bike-lending, pool, gym, mosaics and jolly comfortable beds.

Fairmont Olympic Hotel (p189) Seattle's grande dame is a perfect mix of comfort, tradition and good taste.

Best by Budget

$

Moore Hotel (p190) Cheap, historic and perfectly comfortable option on the cusp of downtown.

Hotel Hotel Hostel (p194) Fremont's only non-B&B accommodations – a kind of hipster hostel.

City Hostel Seattle (p191) Hostel with private options and good wall art.

Green Tortoise Hostel (p189) Seattle's favorite backpacker haunt.

$$

Hotel Max (p191) Boutique hotel with an art-and-music theme.

Moxy (p192) Newer boutique catering to tech business travelers with fun amenities and personable service.

University Inn (p193) Close to the university, but a long way from austere student digs.

Palladian Hotel (p191) Big boutique hotel with funky rock-star wall art.

$$$

Edgewater (p191) Pier-top hotel that is steeped in history.

Hotel Monaco (p189) Lavish hotel with refreshingly down-to-earth service.

Fairmont Olympic Hotel (p189) This jazz-age giant rolls out the red carpet.

Arctic Club (p189) Commodious throwback to the age of the gold rush.

Best B&Bs

Bacon Mansion B&B (p192) Lovely Tudor-style house in Capitol Hill.

11th Avenue Inn (p193) Two blocks from Broadway, Capitol Hill's strip of hip.

Gaslight Inn B&B (p193) Something of a Capitol Hill institution.

Gatewood B&B (p194) Stunning renovated craftsman far from downtown.

Best Pet-Friendly Hotels

Alexis Hotel (p190) No size limits and dog-sitting services are available.

Hotel Monaco (p189) Pets are welcomed at no extra charge and with no size restrictions.

Graduate Seattle (p193) Such big dog fans they offer freebies to canine guests.

Best Neighborhood Accommodations

Hotel Ballard (p194) Positively grandiose hotel and reason alone to visit Ballard, if you can afford it.

Watertown Hotel (p194) Boutique hotel in the U District that's a big step up from standard student digs.

Georgetown Inn (p194) Motel-style accommodations with personal touches in arty Georgetown.

NEED TO KNOW

Price Ranges

The following price ranges refer to a standard double room in high season, not including tax or extra fees such as parking and breakfast.

$	less than $100
$$	$100–$250
$$$	more than $250

SLEEPING

Tipping

It's standard practice to tip your housekeeper by leaving $2 to $5 in your room every morning.

Parking

Essentially all downtown hotels charge extra for parking. Usual parking rates start at around $35 a night, but check when booking as you can end up paying up to $55 a night just for your car.

Useful Websites

Lonely Planet (lonelyplanet.com/usa/seattle/hotels) Recommendations and bookings.

Visit Seattle (www.visitseattle.org) Deals available through the 'Lodging' page of the official Seattle/King County website.

Seattle Bed & Breakfast Association (www.lodginginseattle.com) Portal of the city's 20 best B&Bs; navigate to the 'Specials' page for info on packages and deals.

Where to Stay

Neighborhood	For	Against
Downtown, Pike Place & Waterfront	Highest concentration of hotels of all types. Best neighborhood for absolute luxury. Fantastic central location.	Many places are expensive. Driving can be a nightmare and parking usually costs extra.
Pioneer Square, International District & SoDo	Close to sports grounds, downtown and the waterfront.	A noisy, rambunctious neighborhood at night that's a bit edgy for some. There's a dearth of non-chain economical hotels.
Belltown & Seattle Center	Plenty of economical hotel options within close walking distance of all Seattle's main sights.	Noisy at night with a boozy bar scene.
Queen Anne & Lake Union	Some great midrange options in Lower Queen Anne a stone's throw from the Seattle Center.	Lacking options in Queen Anne proper. Lake Union has a lot of noisy building construction that has no end date.
Capitol Hill & First Hill	Excellent selection of high-quality, well-run B&Bs. Adjacent to Seattle's most exciting nightlife.	Lack of hotel choices in Capitol Hill. A little removed from downtown.
The CD, Madrona & Madison Park	Quiet and inexpensive.	Despite their proximity to downtown, these largely residential districts are bereft of decent accommodations options.
U District	Three fantastic affordable boutique hotels adjacent to the pulsating life of 'the Ave.'	A little isolated from the downtown core and other major sights; caters to college students and their families.
Green Lake & Fremont	Fun neighborhoods to hang out in with plenty of eating options and good bus and walking-trail access.	Options are limited to one budget hotel-hostel and the odd B&B.
Ballard & Discovery Park	Lovely boutique hotel, engaging but laid-back nightlife and great restaurants.	Dearth of choices. Isolated from downtown and other neighborhoods.
Georgetown & West Seattle	Cheap, motel-style places close to a hip strip.	Few options and it's close to nowhere – except Georgetown.

🛏 Downtown, Pike Place & Waterfront

GREEN TORTOISE HOSTEL
HOSTEL $

Map p232 (📞206-340-1222; www.greentortoise.net; 105 Pike St, Downtown; dm from $44; @🛜; 🚇Westlake) Seattle's backpacker central – and what a location right across the street from Pike Place Market! Green Tortoise Hostel got its start in the '70s and while it still retains a bit of that era's crustiness, the 30 bunk rooms and 16 European-style rooms (shared bath and shower) are clean and comfortable. Free breakfast includes waffles and eggs.

The hostel offers a free dinner three nights a week and there are weekly events such as open-mike nights.

PENSIONE NICHOLS
GUESTHOUSE $$

Map p232 (📞206-441-7125; www.pensionenichols.com; 1923 1st Ave, Pike Place; d/apt $200/300; 🛜🍴; 🚇Westlake) For a homey stay right near Pike Place, this cozy guesthouse is hard to beat. Interior rooms are quiet, but still bright with skylights, while deluxe rooms offer street views. Apartment suites sleep four to six and boast full kitchens. There are great water views from the common room, where continental breakfast is served.

CROWNE PLAZA SEATTLE
HOTEL $$

Map p232 (📞206-464-1980; www.cphotelseattle.com; 1113 6th Ave, Downtown; r/ste from $170/218; P❄@🛜🍴; 🚇University St) This 34-floor downtown skyscraper is more business-like than ostentatious, although a 2014 renovation has upped its ante somewhat. Get a room on one of the higher floors and enjoy broad Seattle vistas while swanning around in your bathrobe using the free wi-fi. The hotel is pet-friendly and has the obligatory (for downtown) gym. It sometimes offers good online deals.

⭐FAIRMONT OLYMPIC HOTEL
HOTEL $$$

Map p232 (📞206-621-1700; www.fairmont.com/seattle; 411 University St, Downtown; d from $424; P❄@🛜🏊; 🚇University St) With 450 rooms and every imaginable service, this place is certainly a splurge, but it's worth exploring even if you don't stay here – have an oyster at Shuckers (p56), the oak-paneled hotel bar, or pose like royalty on the Versailles-worthy main staircase.

⭐PALIHOTEL
BOUTIQUE HOTEL $$$

Map p232 (📞206-596-0600; www.palisociety.com; 107 Pine St, Downtown; r from $298; ❄🛜) The rare new hotel that isn't a utilitarian business tower, Palihotel is an understated boutique (part of a small, but expanding, chain) whose early-20th-century 'forest green walls and overstuffed leather chairs' aesthetic is as chic as it is cozy. Although the theme is antique, the building's remodel ensures 21st-century luxuries like air-conditioning and rain showers.

Rooms tend to be on the small side, and you'll get some street noise, but it's a small price to pay considering the hotel is located two blocks from Pike Place Market (p42), among other Seattle highlights.

⭐HOTEL MONACO
BOUTIQUE HOTEL $$$

Map p232 (📞206-621-1770; www.monaco-seattle.com; 1101 4th Ave, Downtown; d/ste $293/406; P@🛜🍴; 🚇University St) 🐾 Whimsical and with dashes of European elegance, the downtown Monaco is a classic Kimpton hotel whose rooms live up to the hints given off in the illustrious lobby. Bed down amid the bold, graphic decor and reap the perks (complimentary bikes, fitness center, free wine tasting, in-room yoga mats).

ARCTIC CLUB
HOTEL $$$

Map p232 (📞206-340-0340; www.thearcticclubseattle.com; 700 3rd Ave, Downtown; r $316-436; P@🛜; 🚇Pioneer Sq) This plush hotel is housed in a downtown building renowned for its carved walrus heads, the former home of an association for 1897 Klondike gold-rush vets. Currently under the ownership of Doubletree hotels, it has been upgraded to lure in equally rich contemporary clients with a wood-paneled private-club feel not far removed from its original incarnation.

FOUR SEASONS HOTEL SEATTLE
LUXURY HOTEL $$$

Map p232 (📞206-749-7000; www.fourseasons.com/seattle; 99 Union St, Downtown; r/ste from $949/4500; P❄@🛜🏊; 🚇University St) 🐾 You can expect swish, five-star luxury from the Four Seasons with exemplary beyond-the-call-of-duty service to go with it;

indeed, the personal touches are more akin to an intimate B&B than a 147-room hotel. The look is contemporary Northwest and is complemented by the setting – downtown and close to the water.

ALEXIS HOTEL
HOTEL $$$

Map p232 (✆206-624-4844; www.alexishotel.com; 1007 1st Ave, Downtown; d/q/ste from $389/414/447; P❄@☎✖; ❲Ꭱ❳University St) Run by the Kimpton Hotel group, the Alexis is a boutique hotel that is positively lavish, with huge rooms, thick carpets, gleaming bathrooms and some luxury extras – a steam room and fitness center, for instance. The hotel's pet-friendly moniker is taken seriously; visiting dogs get bowls of distilled water on arrival.

Thick double-glazed windows keep out the cacophony of downtown just outside the front door. If you're thirsty you can head downstairs to the Bookstore Bar (p54) for a fireside cocktail.

THOMPSON SEATTLE
HOTEL $$$

Map p232 (✆206-623-4600; www.thompsonhotels.com/hotels/thompson-seattle; 110 Stewart St, Pike Place; d/ste from $399/760; P❄☎; ❲Ꭱ❳University St) The Thompson Hotel has been a hot spot among tourists and locals alike since it opened early in the summer of 2016. Designed by the famed local Olson Kundig architects, the boutique hotel is sleek and modern, and offers expansive views of Puget Sound. The rooms have a cozy blue-and-white color scheme with minimalist furniture and comfy beds.

Its restaurant, **Scout**, specializes in Pacific Northwest cuisine by local restaurateur Josh Henderson, and a rooftop bar called the Nest (p54) offers a perfect place to enjoy artisanal cocktails high above the city, looking out onto the water.

INN AT THE MARKET
BOUTIQUE HOTEL $$$

Map p232 (✆206-443-3600; www.innatthemarket.com; 86 Pine St, Pike Place; d/ste from $414/752; P❄@☎✖; ❲Ꭱ❳Westlake) Right in the heart of Pike Place Market, this boutique hotel has elegant, good-sized rooms, many with large windows or small balconies. There's an awesome communal terrace offering views onto market activity and Puget Sound. A swimming pool is available at a nearby gym.

🛏 Pioneer Square, International District & SoDo

HI AT THE AMERICAN HOTEL
HOSTEL $

Map p234 (✆206-622-5443; www.americanhotelseattle.com; 520 S King St, International District; dm $37-42, private r $80; @@☎; ❲Ꭱ❳International District/Chinatown) Seattle's HI hostel is handily positioned next to King Street Station and other transportation hubs, though it's a 1.25-mile walk to Pike Place Market. Set in an old building in the disheveled ID, it fits the bill if you don't mind the edgy – sometimes noisy – street life. Rooms are clean, if utilitarian, and staff are eager to please.

SILVER CLOUD HOTEL
HOTEL $$$

Map p234 (✆206-204-9800; www.silvercloud.com; 1046 1st Ave S, Pioneer Sq; r from $349; P❄@☎✖; ❲Ꭱ❳Stadium) Sports fans are in luck – this relatively new hotel is smack in the middle of the action, across the street from T-Mobile Park and next to CenturyLink Field (p75). Rooms are spacious and modern, with refrigerator and microwave, an iPhone dock on the alarm clock, and Aveda bath products.

A free shuttle service takes guests practically anywhere within 2 miles. And in warm weather you can splash around in the rooftop pool.

BEST WESTERN PIONEER SQUARE HOTEL
HOTEL $$$

Map p234 (✆206-340-1234; www.pioneersquare.com; 77 Yesler Way, Pioneer Sq; r from $275; P@☎; ❲Ꭱ❳First Hill Streetcar) Rooms and common areas at this historical hotel feature period decor and a comfortable atmosphere. The only hotel in the historical heart of Seattle, it can't be beaten for location – nightlife, restaurants, shopping and the city's scenic waterfront are just steps from the door.

🛏 Belltown & Seattle Center

MOORE HOTEL
HOTEL $

Map p238 (✆206-448-4851; www.moorehotel.com; 1926 2nd Ave, Belltown; d with/without bath from $165/117; ☎; ❲❳13) Old-world and allegedly haunted, the hip and whimsical Moore is undoubtedly central Seattle's most reliable bargain, offering fixed annual prices for its large stash of simple but cool rooms. Bonuses – aside from the dynamite location – are the cute ground-floor cafe, and zebra- and leopard-skin patterned carpets.

CITY HOSTEL SEATTLE — HOSTEL $

Map p238 (☎206-706-3255; www.hostelseattle.com; 2327 2nd Ave, Belltown; dm/d from $36/125; ❦@🛜; 🚇Westlake) This well-located, boutique 'art hostel' has colorful murals painted by local artists splashed on the walls of every room. There's also a common room, hot tub, in-house movie theater and all-you-can-eat breakfast. Dorms have four or six beds and some are women only. There are also several private rooms, some with shared bathroom. Guests consistently praise the friendly staff.

★HOTEL MAX — BOUTIQUE HOTEL $$

Map p238 (☎206-441-4200; www.hotelmaxseattle.com; 620 Stewart St, Belltown; r from $263; P❦@🛜🐾; 🚇South Lake Union Streetcar) It's tough to get any hipper than a hotel that has a whole floor dedicated to Seattle's indie Subpop record label (that unleashed Nirvana on an unsuspecting world). The 5th floor pays homage to the music with giant grunge-era photos and record-players with vinyls in every room. The art theme continues throughout the hotel (there's a Warhol in the lobby).

Other bonuses include a fully equipped gym, special offers on Zip cars, free bike rental and a pet-friendly policy.

ACE HOTEL — HOTEL $$

Map p238 (☎206-448-4721; www.acehotel.com; 2423 1st Ave, Belltown; r with/without bath from $239/139; P❦❦🛜🐾; 🚇13) The original locale of the highly stylized Ace Hotel chain, this place sports nouveau-industrial decor, sliding-barn-door bathrooms and Pendleton wool blankets. True to its original ethos, the hotel is economical but trendy, especially if you don't mind sharing a bathroom.

BELLTOWN INN — HOTEL $$

Map p238 (☎206-529-3700; www.belltown-inn.com; 2301 3rd Ave, Belltown; r from $234; ❦❦@🛜; 🚇RapidRide D Line) The reliable Belltown Inn is a popular midrange place to stow your suitcase – good on the basics, if a little light on embellishments. That said, there's a roof terrace, free bike rentals and some rooms have kitchenettes. Both downtown and the Seattle Center are within easy walking distance.

★EDGEWATER — HOTEL $$$

Map p238 (☎206-728-7000; www.edgewaterhotel.com; 2411 Alaskan Way, Belltown; r/ste from $349/466; P❦@🛜; 🚇13) Fame and notoriety have stalked the Edgewater. Perched over the water on a pier, it was once the hotel of choice for every rock band that mattered, including the Beatles, the Rolling Stones and, most infamously, Led Zeppelin, who took the 'you can fish from the hotel window' advertising jingle a little too seriously and filled their suite with sharks.

HOTEL ÄNDRA — BOUTIQUE HOTEL $$$

Map p238 (☎206-448-8600; www.hotelandra.com; 2000 4th Ave, Belltown; r from $299; P❦❦🛜; 🚇South Lake Union Streetcar) It's in Belltown (so it's trendy) and it's Scandinavian-influenced (so it has lashings of minimalist style), plus the Ändra's fine location is complemented by attractive woody decor, subtle color accents, well-stocked bookcases, fluffy bathrobes, Egyptian-cotton bed linen and a complimentary shoe-shine. The Lola (p91) restaurant next door handles room service. Say no more.

HOTEL FIVE — BOUTIQUE HOTEL $$$

Map p238 (☎206-448-0924; www.hotelfiveseattle.com; 2200 5th Ave, Belltown; r from $260; P❦❦🛜; 🚇RapidRide C Line) This trendy hotel mixes retro '70s furniture with sharp color accents to produce something dazzlingly modern. The ultra-comfortable beds are a valid cure for insomnia, while the large reception area invites lingering, especially when complimentary cupcakes and coffee are on offer in the late afternoon.

Look out for regular deals, including 'stay two nights and get the third night free.'

PALLADIAN HOTEL — BOUTIQUE HOTEL $$$

Map p238 (☎206-448-1111; www.palladianhotel.com; 2000 2nd Ave, Belltown; r/ste from $290/410; ❦🛜🐾; 🚇13) Run by the Kimpton Group as an upscale boutique hotel, the Palladian's vintage neoclassical facade lives up to its name. The interior decor is more whimsical. The biggest eye-catchers are the portraits of cultural icons – Bill Gates and Jimi Hendrix among them – depicted in imperial garb on the walls (they're also reproduced on pillowcases).

Ultra-cool rooms come with armoires, yoga mats, retro phones and flat-screen TVs mounted on easels. Even better are the free-to-borrow bikes, boozy social hour (daily at 5pm) and speakeasy-style cocktail bar called **Penny Royal**.

🛏 Queen Anne & Lake Union

MARQUEEN HOTEL
HOTEL **$$**

Map p240 (📞206-282-7407; www.marqueen. com; 600 Queen Anne Ave N, Queen Anne; r $240-270, ste $280-320; 🅿♨@🛜; 🚉RapidRide D Line) A classic old-school apartment building (built in 1918), the MarQueen has hardwood floors throughout and a variety of rooms, all with kitchenettes (left over from the building's days of housing apartments). The neighborhood is an under-visited gem, handy to various attractions.

INN AT QUEEN ANNE
HOTEL **$$**

Map p240 (📞206-282-7357; www.innatqueen anne.com; 505 1st Ave N, Queen Anne; r from $209; 🅿♨@🛜; 🚉RapidRide D Line) The Inn at Queen Anne is a 1929 apartment building turned hotel in a cool neighborhood. Its 68 rooms come with kitchenettes, complimentary internet access and a free continental breakfast. Weekly and monthly rates are available. Note that there are no elevators in this three-story building.

⭐MAXWELL HOTEL
BOUTIQUE HOTEL **$$$**

Map p240 (📞206-286-0629; 300 Roy St, Queen Anne; r/ste from $311/371; 🅿♨@🛜🏊; 🚉RapidRide D Line) Located in Lower Queen Anne, the Maxwell has a huge designer-chic lobby with a floor mosaic and colorful furnishings that welcomes you with aplomb. Upstairs the slickness continues in 139 gorgeously modern rooms with hardwood floors and Scandinavian bedding. There's a small pool, a gym, free bike rentals and complimentary cupcakes.

MOXY
HOTEL **$$$**

Map p240 (📞206-708-8200; http://moxy-hotels. marriott.com; 1016 Republican St, Lake Union; r $265-371; 🛜🏊; 🚉South Lake Union Streetcar) A chain (or rather, a Marriott-branded property) with enough goofy charm to take the corporate edge off, Moxy is a relatively new hotel in the South Lake Union area, opened to cater to the neighborhood's booming tech industry. The lobby is a fantasia of PNW design, and the rooms have both pleasant cleanliness and quirky amenities in droves.

Other perks include a hotel bar you'll actually want to hang out at, a cocktail at check-in, friendly staff, and a fitness room.

MEDITERRANEAN INN
HOTEL **$$$**

Map p240 (📞206-428-4700; www.mediterra nean-inn.com; 425 Queen Anne Ave N, Queen Anne; r from $254; 🅿♨♨@🛜; 🚉RapidRide D Line) There's something about the surprisingly un-Mediterranean Med Inn that just clicks. Maybe it's the handy Lower Queen Anne location, or the genuinely friendly staff, or the kitchenettes in every room, or the small downstairs gym, or the surgical cleanliness in every room. Don't try to define it – just go there and soak it up.

SILVER CLOUD INN LAKE UNION
HOTEL **$$$**

Map p240 (📞206-447-9500; www.silvercloud. com; 1150 Fairview Ave N, Lake Union; r from $250; 🅿♨♨@🛜🏊; 🚉South Lake Union Streetcar) Silver Cloud is a pleasant Pacific Northwest chain (with 10 hotels in Seattle and Portland, OR). This branch with 184 rooms overlooking Lake Union is stuffed with cost-saving extras such as a gym, indoor and outdoor pools, complimentary laundry facilities and complimentary breakfast, free shuttle service to downtown and (unusually for Seattle) free parking.

🛏 Capitol Hill & First Hill

⭐BACON MANSION B&B
B&B **$$**

Map p244 (📞206-329-1864; www.baconmans ion.com; 959 Broadway E, Capitol Hill; r with shared/private bath $189/244, ste from $269; 🅿@🛜; 🚉49) A 1909 Tudor-style mansion whose imposing exterior belies the quirky charm of its friendly hosts, this four-level B&B on a quiet residential street just past the Capitol Hill action is one of the best in the area. Among its charming amenities are a pleasant garden and a grand piano in the main room that guests are invited to play.

GASLIGHT INN B&B
B&B **$$**

Map p244 (☑206-325-3654; www.gaslight-inn.
com; 1727 15th Ave, Capitol Hill; d with shared/pri-
vate bath from $158/178; P@🖙🏊; 🖵10) Set
in a landmark-listed craftsman-style house
in Capitol Hill, the Gaslight Inn has eight
rooms available, six of which have private
baths. In summer, it's refreshing to dive
into the outdoor pool or just hang out on
the sun deck. No pets: the B&B already has
a cat and a dog.

11TH AVENUE INN
B&B **$$**

Map p244 (☑206-720-7161; www.11thavenueinn.
com; 121 11th Ave E, Capitol Hill; d from $212;
P🅿@🖙; 🚋First Hill Streetcar) Formerly a
boarding house and a dance studio, this
1906 home has been a B&B since 2003.
Its facade is not the grandest of Seattle's
B&Bs, but you know what they say about
judging a book by its cover. The 11th Avenue Inn has nine rooms, each with eclectic
Victorian furnishings, grand rugs, handsome headboards and hand-pressed Egyptian cotton sheets.

You won't go hungry here: breakfast
(included in the rates) is a full-course
sit-down affair in the Victorian dining
room, and you're invited to help yourself
to snacks and drinks throughout the day.
Bg bonus – parking is free. There's a three-
night minimum stay.

SORRENTO HOTEL
HOTEL **$$$**

Map p244 (☑206-622-6400; www.hotelsorr
ento.com; 900 Madison St, First Hill; d from $319;
P🅿@🖙🏊; 🖵64) William Howard Taft,
27th US president, was the first registered
guest at the Sorrento, an imposing Ital-
ianate hotel known since its birth in 1909
as the jewel of Seattle. The combination
of luxurious appointments, over-the-top
service and a pervasive sense of class add
up to a perfect blend of decadence and
restraint.

The beautiful on-site Fireside Lounge
(p119) is one of the coziest places in Seattle
to flop down with a stiff drink.

Oh – and it's allegedly haunted.

SILVER CLOUD HOTEL
– SEATTLE BROADWAY
HOTEL **$$$**

Map p244 (☑206-325-1400; www.silvercloud.
com/seattlebroadway; 1100 Broadway, Capitol
Hill; r from $279; P🅿@🖙🏊; 🚋First Hill Street-
car) Capitol Hill's only conventional hotel is
a slick abode that is part of a small regional

chain. Coming with a pool, restaurant,
excellent location and modern rooms, it's
a steal if you can nab a decent room rate
outside of peak season.

🛏 U District

COLLEGE INN
HOTEL **$**

Map p248 (☑206-633-4441; www.collegeinn
seattle.com; 4000 University Way NE; s/d from
$122/137; @🖙; 🖵70) This pretty, half-
timbered building in the U District, left
over from the 1909 Alaska-Yukon-Pacific
Exposition, has 25 European-style guest
rooms with sinks and shared baths. Think
'student digs' and you won't be disap-
pointed. There's no elevator.

⭐UNIVERSITY INN
BOUTIQUE HOTEL **$$**

Map p248 (☑206-632-5055; www.universityinn
seattle.com; 4140 Roosevelt Way NE; r from
$226; P🅿@🖙🏊; 🖵74) This spotless, mod-
ern, well-located place is good – especially
when you factor in the waffles served with
the complimentary breakfast. The hotel is
four blocks from campus and just three
from the bustle of 'the Ave.' The 102 rooms
come in three levels of plushness. All of
them offer such basics as a coffee maker,
hair dryer and wi-fi; some have balconies,
sofas and BlueTooth docking stations.

There's a hot tub, an outdoor pool, laun-
dry facilities and a guest computer in the
lobby. Attached to the hotel is the recom-
mended Portage Bay Cafe (p136), and
there's also a free shuttle to various sight-
seeing areas.

GRADUATE SEATTLE
HOTEL **$$**

Map p248 (☑206-634-2000; www.graduate
hotels.com; 4507 Brooklyn Ave NE; r from $237;
P🅿🖙) This new kid on the block brings
hip sophistication to the U District's hotel
scene. Eclectic furniture and walls full of
framed photographs almost make this
place feel more like a passed-down vacation home than a new hotel, but then
amenities like a 24-hour gym and incredible rooftop bar bring it all back into focus.

Pets are now allowed; they stay for free
and get a BarkBox. There's also a $35 a
night valet parking service.

The same architect who designed the
Old Faithful Lodge in Yellowstone National
Park built this place in 1931, which has
been a variety of hotels ever since.

WATERTOWN HOTEL　　BOUTIQUE HOTEL **$$$**

Map p248 (☑206-826-4242; www.watertown
seattle.com; 4242 Roosevelt Way NE; r/ste from
$262/312; P✴@☎✖☎; ☐74) Easy to miss
because it looks like one of those crisp new
modern apartment buildings, the Water-
town has an arty-industrial feel. Bare con-
crete and high ceilings in the lobby make
it seem stark and museum-like, but that
translates to spacious and warmly fur-
nished rooms with giant beds and huge
windows.

There's a seasonal pool, an on-site cafe
and an exercise room. Guests can borrow
bicycles or use the hotel's free shuttle to
explore the area.

Green Lake & Fremont

HOTEL HOTEL HOSTEL　　HOTEL, HOSTEL **$**

Map p250 (☑206-257-4543; www.hotelhotel.
co; 3515 Fremont Ave N, Fremont; dm $34-
36, d with/without bath $140/120; ☎; ☐5)
Fremont's only real hotel is a good one,
encased in a venerable old building replete
with exposed brick and chunky radiators.
In true Fremont fashion, Hotel Hotel is
technically more of a hostel (with dorms),
but it also passes itself off as an economi-
cal hotel on account of its private rooms
with an assortment of shared and en-suite
bathrooms.

CHELSEA STATION INN　　B&B **$$$**

Map p251 (☑206-547-6077; www.chelsea
stationinn.com; 4915 Linden Ave N, Fremont; ste
$323-367; P✴☎; ☐44) A bit of a walk from
Fremont's commercial center, but a short
one to the fabulous Woodland Park Zoo
and Green Lake, the Chelsea Station Inn
has a collection of stylish and comfortable
guest apartments that include full kitchens. Other luxe amenities include complimentary beer and wine in the afternoons
and a patio with a gas grill and hot tub.

Ballard & Discovery Park

BALLARD INN　　BOUTIQUE HOTEL **$$**

Map p252 (☑206-789-5011; www.ballardinn
seattle.com; 5300 Ballard Ave NW, Ballard; s/d
from $119/149; ☎; ☐40) This small, inti-
mate hotel with a European feel (the Scan-
dinavian influence?) offers a far cheaper

alternative to the nearby Hotel Ballard.
The building, dating from 1902, is right on
Ballard's main drag. The rooms are simple,
but clean and well appointed, and most
share baths. It's in the historic **Scandina-
vian American Bank Building** (Map p252;
5300 Ballard Ave, Ballard; ☐40).

★**HOTEL BALLARD**　　BOUTIQUE HOTEL **$$$**

Map p252 (☑206-789-5012; www.hotelballard
seattle.com; 5216 Ballard Ave NW, Ballard; d/
ste $399/499; P☎; ☐40) Ballard's glit-
tering designer hotel, which opened in
May 2013, exemplifies the neighborhood's
upward rise. The seduction begins outside:
Hotel Ballard has a lovely street profile,
with its wrought-iron balconies blending in with the red-brick edifices of yore.
Inside, it's even more opulent (upholstered
headboards, funky chandeliers, super-
streamlined bathtubs), but stays faithful to
the neighborhood's Scandinavian heritage
with Nordic murals.

Guests get free use of the equally fancy
Olympic Athletic Club next door.

Georgetown & West Seattle

GEORGETOWN INN　　HOTEL **$$**

Map p254 (☑206-762-2233; www.georgetown
innseattle.com; 6100 Corson Ave S, Georgetown;
r from $149; P➡✴☎; ☐124) For a more
diverse look at Seattle, it's worth spending
a night or two in Georgetown, especially
during Art Attack (second Saturday of
the month). This modest but comfortable
hotel provides an ideal base. Rooms are
pretty standard (mini fridge, flat-screen
TV, desk), but there's free on-site parking,
an excellent breakfast and 24/7 coffee and
cookies.

★**GATEWOOD B&B**　　B&B **$$$**

(☑206-938-3482; www.gatewoodwestseattle.
com; 7446 Gatewood Rd SW, Fauntleroy; r $229-
285; ☐22) Ease into a totally cozy getaway
in this beautifully restored home on Seattle's leafy outer edges. Each room is different, but they all have early-20th-century
craftsman touches (think tasteful wood
paneling and black and white tile bathrooms), comfy beds and luxurious linens
and toiletries. Guests also rave about the
personable staff.

Understand
Seattle

Seattle Today

The most unchanging thing about Seattle is that it keeps on changing. Fueled by an Amazon-led building frenzy and inspired by a new generation of technological wizards, it remains, economically speaking, one of the fastest-growing cities in the USA. But skyrocketing housing costs, rampant inequality and gentrification threaten to snuff out what makes Seattle Seattle, and locals are worried about what kind of city they will have in the future.

Best on Film

Sleepless in Seattle (1993) Meg Ryan and Tom Hanks are irresistibly adorable in this riff on An Affair to Remember.

Singles (1992) Attractive slackers deal with apartment life and love.

Hype! (1996) An excellent time capsule of the grunge years.

10 Things I Hate About You (1999) Teen Shakespeare adaptation set in the city.

Battle In Seattle (2007) A fictional account of the 1999 World Trade Organization protests that rocked the city.

Best in Music

Axis As Bold As Love (Jimi Hendrix; 1967) Godfather of Seattle's rock scene.

Nevermind (Nirvana; 1991) Helped launch Seattle into the cultural conversation.

Posse On Broadway (Sir Mix-a-Lot; 1988) Describes the Seattle geography of the future 'Baby Got Back' singer's youth.

By the Way, I Forgive You (Brandi Carlile; 2018) Multi-Grammy-nominated sixth album from Carlile, who got her start in Seattle's music scene.

The Sweet Smell of Success

Seattle has been riding the digital wave since the 1990s and the city has seen another recent boom in tech jobs that has meant construction round the clock. Housing is being built to accommodate the tens of thousands who flock here each year as the unemployment rate falls. In the latter half of the 2010s the tech industry began to reshape the city itself, essentially creating the South Lake Union neighborhood and the new streetcar that services it, constructing corporate buildings that have become iconic in just a few short years and spurring grassroots action against the negative effects of that growth that has influenced the politics of the entire nation.

Tackling Inequalities

Landmark legislation on marijuana and same-sex marriage has proved that Seattle doesn't lack progressive credentials. But while the economy has boomed for some, that boom has created struggles for others. In an attempt to stall widening inequalities and address the rising cost of living, the city council approved a new law in 2014, raising the minimum wage to $15 an hour, the highest rate in the US. With a roll-out spread over seven years, the full impact of the law won't be felt until 2021. Meanwhile, homelessness and gentrification are still major concerns for Seattle, phenomena that cast a dark pall on the sparkling new tech towers of South Lake Union (SLU) and the adjacent Denny Triangle.

By the end of 2018 homelessness in the city had risen by 4%, well above the national average growth of 0.3%. Even those who are housed face uncertainty, as the rapid expansion of new condos is making once affordable neighborhoods like the Central District, the historic home to Seattle's African American population, unlivable for those who have called it home for generations.

Transportation Revolution

The surge of new residents has brought traffic snarls, overcrowded public transportation and strain on the city's already aging infrastructure. For its part, Seattle has been tackling these issues head on. In the past decade the city has expanded its light rail system twice, opened a new streetcar line and introduced a failed bike-share system that was later taken over by the private sector. In February 2019 the long-delayed SR 99 tunnel was opened, replacing the above-ground eyesore that was the Alaskan Way Viaduct. It's too early to tell if it will help alleviate the city's worsening traffic problems, but the tear down of the viaduct has already spurred a revitalization of downtown's long-blighted waterfront.

Grassroots Trends

While Seattle's macro-businesses count their millions, its micros continue to quietly set trends at the grassroots level. Sales of physical books in the US increased by 1.3% in 2018 after increasing by 2% in 2017. Those numbers aren't all Seattle's doing, but the city's dozens of thriving independent bookstores (and 2017 UNESCO recognition as a City of Literature) were no doubt a large contribution. The city's other legacy industry, coffee, also keeps growing thanks to continued proliferation of its many local chains, almost all of which opened new locations in 2017 and 2018. But the boldest retail trend of the 2010s, grassroots or otherwise, is weed dispensaries, which have proliferated after a slow start following the 2014 legalization of recreational marijuana use. Once just a handful of shops spread out across the city, they are now as common as hardware stores, with local chains opening multiple locations and garnering intense loyalties, reminiscent of the coffee boom decades earlier.

Changing Cityscape

All cities naturally evolve over time, but in the past several years Seattle has seen a period of expedited metamorphosis. Construction cranes mingle among the skyscrapers downtown, and in the further-out neighborhoods lazy thoroughfares have been suddenly transformed into commercial stretches lined with new metal-and-glass buildings housing residents and businesses that weren't there a year ago. There's a mile of new construction going up on the eastern shore of Lake Union, near the recently booming neighborhood of South Lake Union, which is itself getting new restaurants and hotels by the week. In the Denny Triangle, Amazon's newest building – the low, futuristic and aptly named Spheres – opened in January of 2018, next to the Doppler, which opened in 2015, and near more offices under construction.

if Seattle were 100 people

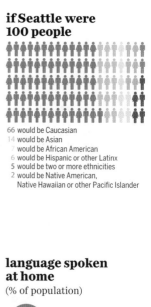

66 would be Caucasian
14 would be Asian
7 would be African American
6 would be Hispanic or other Latinx
5 would be two or more ethnicities
2 would be Native American, Native Hawaiian or other Pacific Islander

language spoken at home
(% of population)

79 English
10 Asian languages
5 Spanish
4 other European languages
2 other

population per sq mile

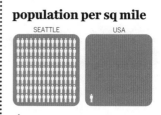

SEATTLE   USA

≈ 85 people

History

In the pantheon of world cities, 168-year-old Seattle is still in its kindergarten years. Native Americans have lived in and around Puget Sound for 10,000 years, living mostly in cooperation with the thick forests and rolling waters of the region.The first colonial settlers bushwhacked their way through to present-day Seattle in 1851, beginning a historical trajectory marked by a mixture of great injustices, pioneering ideas, fires, booms, busts and an explosion of urban growth almost unparalleled in US history.

Native Peoples of Puget Sound

Archaeologists theorize that the area we know today as Seattle has been inhabited since at least 8000 BC by the Duwamish people. Unlike the Plains tribespeople living further inland, who were primarily nomadic hunter-gatherers, the first inhabitants of the Pacific Northwest were intimately tied to the rivers, lakes and sea. They and other tribal groups along Puget Sound – notably the Suquamish, Coast Salish and Chinook – depended on catching salmon, cod and shellfish. On land, they hunted deer and elk, more for their protective hides than for their flesh. Though each group had its own dialect, coastal tribes communicated through a language called Lushootseed, which indigenous people today struggle to keep from extinction.

Summer and fall were dedicated to harvesting the bounty of the sea and forest. Food was stored in massive quantities to carry the tribes through the long winter months, when the most important ancient legends and ceremonies were handed down to the younger generations. In terms of artistic, religious and cultural forms, the Northwest coastal tribes possessed a remarkable richness. Ornately carved cedar canoes served as transportation, and extensive trading networks evolved between the permanent settlements that stretched up and down the coast and along the river valleys.

Extended family groups lived together in cedar longhouses, which were constructed over a central pit-like living area. The social structure

TIMELINE	8000 BC	1700s	1792
	The ancestors of the Duwamish, Suquamish, Coast Salish and Chinook tribes arrive in Puget Sound.	At the time of European contact and colonization there are 13 prominent Duwamish villages in the area that is to become metropolitan Seattle.	British sea captain George Vancouver sails through the Straits of Juan de Fuca and Georgia.

in these self-sustaining tribal villages was quite stratified, with an aristocratic class of chiefs holding the majority of wealth and power. Social and religious rituals were dominated by a strict clan system. Wealth was measured in goods such as blankets, salmon and fish oil. Such commodities were consumed and to some degree redistributed in ceremonial feasts in which great honor accrued to the person who gave away these valued items.

Puget Sound tribespeople evolved complex cultural, social and economic structures, which the invasion of Euro-American settlers in the mid-1800s almost erased. Today native pride is strong in Seattle, as the fight for indigenous rights, reparations and visibility has ushered in a new era of activism and progress.

Early White Exploration

The first white expedition to explore the Puget Sound area arrived in 1792, when the British sea captain George Vancouver sailed through the inland waterways of the Straits of Juan de Fuca and Georgia. In the same year, the USA entered the competition to claim the Northwest when Captain Robert Gray reached the mouth of the Columbia River.

The first permanent European settlers in the region straggled overland to the Pacific Northwest in the 1830s on the rough tracks that would become the Oregon Trail. Following in the footsteps of Lewis and Clark, they founded the cities of Portland (1843) and Tumwater (1846) near present-day Olympia and began to look further north.

'New York Pretty Soon'

Arthur and David Denny were New Yorkers who, in 1851, led a group of settlers across the Oregon Trail with the intention of settling in the Willamette Valley near Portland. On the way, they heard stories of good land and deep-water ports along Puget Sound. When the Denny party arrived in Portland in the fall, they decided to keep going north. The settlers landed on Alki Point, in present-day West Seattle, in November 1851 and staked claims. The group named their encampment Alki-New York (the Chinookan word *alki* means 'pretty soon' or 'by and by'). After a winter of wind and rain, the group determined that their fledgling city needed a deeper harbor and moved the settlement a couple of miles northeast to the mudflats across Elliott Bay. The colony was renamed Seattle for the Duwamish chief Sealth, who was the friend of an early merchant.

Seattle's ornately carved totem poles are part of the city's image, but the practice is not native to the area. You have to go north to tribes such as the Haida of British Columbia and Tlingit of Alaska to see them in their original habitat.

Luther Collins staked a land claim near Georgetown on September 14, 1851, two weeks before the Denny party arrived at Alki. Technically, it is he, not Denny, who was Seattle's first European colonist.

1851	1889	1897	1910
The Denny party arrives at Alki Point and settles in Puget Sound, already home to the Duwamish people.	The Great Fire sweeps through the city, gutting its core and destroying the mostly wooden storefronts and log homes on stilts.	The Klondike gold rush is sparked by the arrival of the ship *Portland*. The city's population doubles by 1900.	Seattle begins to grow up. Its population reaches a quarter million, making it a clear contender for the preeminent city of the Pacific Northwest.

Birth of the City

The heart of the young city beat in the area now known as Pioneer Square. Although there was a small but deep harbor at this point in Elliott Bay, much of the land immediately to the south was mudflats, ideal for oysters but not much else. The land to the north and east was steep and forested. The early settlers (whose names now ring as a compendium of street names and landmarks: Denny, Yesler, Bell, Boren) quickly cleared the land and established schools, churches, civic institutions and Seattle's first industry – Yesler's sawmill. From the start, the people who settled Seattle never doubted that they were founding a great city. The original homesteads were quickly plaited into city streets, and trade, not farming or lumbering, became the goal.

Since it was a frontier town, the majority of Seattle's male settlers were bachelors. One of the town's founders (and sole professor at the newly established university), Asa Mercer, went back to the East Coast with the express purpose of inducing young, unmarried women to venture to Seattle. Fifty-seven women made the journey and married into the frontier life.

Fremont, Ballard and Georgetown were once rival cities to Seattle that were absorbed by their bigger rival in 1891, 1907 and 1910 respectively.

The Great Fire & the Regrading of Seattle

Frontier Seattle was a thrown-together village of wooden storefronts, log homes and lumber mills. Tidewater lapped against present-day 1st Ave S, and many of the buildings and the streets that led to them were on stilts. No part of the original downtown was more than 4ft above the bay at high tide, and the streets were frequently a quagmire.

On June 6, 1889, an apprentice woodworker accidentally let a pot of boiling glue spill onto a pile of wood chips in a shop on 1st Ave and Madison St. The fire quickly spread through the young city, with boardwalks providing an unstoppable conduit for the flames. By the end of the day, 30 blocks of the city had burned, gutting the core of downtown.

What might have seemed a catastrophe was in fact a blessing, as the city was rebuilt immediately with handsome structures of brick, steel and stone. This time, however, the streets were regraded and ravines and inlets filled in. This raised the new city about a dozen feet above the old. In some areas the regrading simply meant building on top of older ground-level buildings and streets. People had to cross deep trenches to get from one side of the street to another. Buildings were constructed around the notion that the first floor or two would eventually be buried when the city got around to filling in the trenches.

The sense of transformation inspired by the Great Fire also fueled another great rebuilding project. One of Seattle's original seven hills, Denny Hill, rose out of Elliott Bay just north of Pine St. Its very steep

1932	1942	1954	1962
A shantytown called 'Hooverville,' after President Hoover, forms south of Pioneer Square. Made up of lean-tos and shacks, it houses hundreds of unemployed squatters.	Japanese Americans are ordered to evacuate Seattle; they are detained under prison conditions in a relocation center for the duration of the war.	Boeing Air Transport, launched 40 years prior and already a pioneer in commercial airline flight, announces production of the 707.	The World's Fair takes place. The headliner on opening night is singer John Raitt. His 12-year-old daughter, Bonnie, holds his sheet music.

face limited commercial traffic, though some hotels and private homes were perched on the hilltop. City engineers determined that if Seattle's growth were to continue, Denny Hill had to go. Between 1899 and 1912, the hill was sluiced into Elliott Bay. Twenty million gallons of water were pumped daily from Lake Union and sprayed onto the rock and soil. Under great pressure, the water liquefied the clay and dislodged the rock, all of which was sluiced into flumes. Existing homes were simply undercut and then burned.

The War Years

Seattle's boom continued through WWI, when Northwest lumber was in great demand. The opening of the Panama Canal brought increased trade to Pacific ports, which were free from wartime threats. Shipyards opened along Puget Sound, bringing the shipbuilding industry close to the forests of the Northwest.

WWII brought other, less positive, developments to Seattle. About 7000 Japanese residents in the city and the nearby areas were forcibly removed from their jobs and homes. They were sent to the nearby 'relocation center,' or internment camp, in Puyallup, then on to another camp in Idaho where they were detained under prison conditions for the duration of the war. This greatly depleted the Japanese community, which up to this point had built a thriving existence farming and fishing in Puget Sound. In all, an estimated 110,000 Japanese across the country, two-thirds of whom were US citizens, were sent to internment camps. Upon their release, many declined to return to the homes they'd been forced to abandon.

Boeing & Postwar Seattle

The Boeing Airplane Company was founded and named by William E Boeing and his partner Conrad Westervelt in 1916. Boeing tested his first plane, the *B&W,* in June 1916 by taking off from the middle of Lake Union. For years, Boeing single-handedly ruled Seattle industry. After WWII, the manufacturer diversified its product line and began to develop civilian aircraft. In 1954 Boeing announced the launch of the 707, and the response was immediate and overwhelming. The world found itself at the beginning of an era of mass air travel, and Boeing produced the jets that led this revolution in transportation. By 1960, when the population of Seattle topped one million, one in 10 people worked for Boeing, and one in four people worked in jobs directly affected by Boeing.

But the fortunes of Boeing weren't always to soar. A combination of overstretched capital (due to cost overruns in the development of the

Seattle's Boom Industries

Lumber: 1852–89

Gold: 1897–1905 (Klondike)

Shipbuilding: 1911–18

Airplanes: 1945–70 (Boeing)

Dot com: 1995–2000 (Microsoft)

Online retail: 2008–present (Amazon)

1975	1991	1992	1999
Bill Gates and Paul Allen start Microsoft, a move that helps power the Seattle economy into the 21st century and beyond.	The formerly underground style of music known as grunge goes mainstream, with Pearl Jam's *Ten* and Nirvana's *Nevermind* hitting record-store shelves.	The following year Seattle hip-hop artist Sir Mix-a-Lot's single 'Baby Got Back' goes to number one on the Billboard Hot 100 chart and wins the Grammy for Best Rap Solo Performance.	Seattle is rocked by the World Trade Organization riots. Microsoft is declared a monopoly and enters into lengthy negotiations over the future of its business.

INDIGENOUS PEOPLE'S DAY

As part of a larger national campaign, in 2014 Seattle's city council voted to do away with Columbus Day (second Monday in October), which had been a celebration of Christopher Columbus, who sailed to the present-day West Indies in 1492. In its place Indigenous People's Day, which celebrates the true 'discoverers' of the United States, its Native American population, was instated.

747) and a cut in defense spending led to a severe financial crisis in the early 1970s, known as the 'Boeing Bust.' Boeing was forced to cut its workforce by two-thirds; in one year, nearly 60,000 Seattleites lost their jobs. The local economy went into a tailspin for a number of years.

In the 1980s increased defense spending brought vigor back to aircraft production lines, and expanding trade relations with Pacific Rim nations brought business to Boeing too. But, in September 2001, the world's largest airplane manufacturer, the company as synonymous with Seattle as rain, relocated 50% of its HQ staff to digs in Chicago. However, the Boeing factory has stayed put in Seattle, where the company remains the city's biggest employer with a workforce of 80,000.

Nisqually Earthquake

On February 28, 2001 the city of Seattle was rocked by a magnitude 6.8 earthquake, which struck at 10:54am. The only reported death was due to a heart attack, but around 400 people were injured and billions of dollars of property damage resulted. The quake was a wake-up call for the city and its citizens. In the years after there was a push to make Seattle's disaster-response systems stronger and more dynamic.

Progressive Fights

Although Seattle has long been a bastion of liberal politics, in the 2010s the city became a true beacon for progressive action. The decade saw Washington State beat the US federal government to legalizing both same-sex marriage and recreational marijuana usage in 2012. In 2013 Seattle itself elected Kshama Sawant as its first socialist city council member in a century, and in 2014 that city council raised the city's minimum wage to $15 an hour, a first for any city in the US. During the presidency of Donald Trump the city has been a hotbed of protests and clashes between far right and leftist groups, as well as political action attempting to address homegrown issues like gentrification, homelessness and the rising cost of living.

2001	2012	2015	2018
On February 28, an earthquake measuring 6.8 on the Richter scale hits Seattle, toppling several historical buildings and causing more than $2 billion in damage.	Washington State passes landmark laws legalizing the limited sale and use of marijuana, and permitting same-sex marriage.	A tech-job boom sees Seattle's population soar by tens of thousands per year, cementing its status as a world tech leader, but exacerbating the city's inequality problems.	Pike Place's famous fish market is sold to four employees, the first time the operation has changed hands since 1965.

Way of Life

Surprisingly elegant in places and coolly edgy in others, Seattle is notable for its technological know-how, passion for books, and long-standing green credentials. Although it has fermented its own pop culture in recent times, it has yet to create an urban mythology like Paris or New York. But it is the future rather than the past that's more important here. Seattle's lifestyle is organic. Rather than trying to live up to its history, it's scanning the horizon for what's next.

What is a Seattleite?

Every city has its stereotypes and Seattle is no different. Those who have never been here imagine it as a metropolis of casually dressed, latte-supping urbanites who drive Priuses, vote Democrat, consume only locally grown food, and walk around with an unwaveringly hip diet of music streaming from their ear pods. To the people who live here, the picture is a little more complex. Seattle has a rich multicultural history and is home to Native American, African American, Asian American and growing Ethiopian American populations. The city's African American population is 7.9% – higher than every West Coast city except Los Angeles – and its Asian American population (14%) is even higher, 10% above the national average.

Living beneath overcast skies for much of the year, the locals have brightened the mood by opening up cafes, reasoning that drinking liberal doses of caffeine in a cozy social environment is more fun than hiking in the rain. Seattleites have reinvented coffee culture, sinking into comfortable armchairs, listening to Ray Charles albums on repeat and nurturing mega-sized locally made coffee mugs large enough to last all day.

Seattle's geographic setting, a spectacular combination of mountains, ocean and temperate rainforest, has earned it the moniker 'Emerald City.' When you look out of your office window on sunny days and see broccoli-green Douglas fir trees framing a giant glacier-covered volcano, it's not hard to feel passionate about protecting the environment. The green culture has stoked public backing for Seattle's rapidly expanding public-transportation network and an almost religious reverence for local food.

In contrast to the USA's hardworking eastern seaboard, life out west is more casual and less frenetic. Idealistically, westerners would rather work to live than live to work. Indeed, with so much winter rain, Seattleites will dredge up any excuse to shun the nine-to-five treadmill and hit the great outdoors. The first bright days of summer prompt a mass exodus of hikers and cyclists making enthusiastically for the wilderness areas for which the region is justly famous.

Creativity is a long-standing Northwestern trait, be it redefining the course of modern rock music or reconfiguring the latest Microsoft operating system. The city that once saw one in 10 of its workforce employed at aviation giant Boeing has long been obsessed with creative engineering – and this skill has been transferred to other genres. Rather than making do with hand-me-downs, Seattle's mechanically minded coffee geeks took apart imported Italian coffee machines in the early 1990s

Don'ts

To avoid faux pas, don't compare Seattle with Portland, tread carefully when talking about Amazon, don't belittle or bemoan unhoused people, and don't disparage the Seahawks.

and reinvented them for better performance. Similarly, they have experimented boldly with British-style beer, using locally grown hops, and have opened up their own whiskey distilleries. More recently, techies with taste have turned their hand to craft cider, small-batch gin and ice-cream micro-creameries.

Dealing with Success

Despite its achievements and importance to the region, Seattle still has the mellow sense of modesty and self-deprecation that characterizes the Northwest. The attitude peaked in the 1950s and '60s, with the wild anti-boosterism of newspaper columnist Emmett Watson, an opponent of Seattle's rapid urban growth plan who invented a series of tongue-in-cheek aphorisms that played down Seattle's lures in the hope that the city would remain small. Such wryness colored the way the nation perceives Seattle, and the popularization of the anti-glamorous continued into the 1990s with grunge, a trend whose success still seems to mortify the city.

Seattle has long made a habit of turning its clever homemade inventions into global brands. But the city has always had an uncomfortable relationship with the success it has struggled to achieve. Ask an average Seattleite how they rate Starbucks and they might express barely concealed pride one minute and tell you they never drink there the next. Similar sentiments are reserved for business behemoths Microsoft, Boeing and Amazon.

Two of Seattle's most successful citizens, Bill and Melinda Gates, also happen to be two of its largest public figures. And they symbolize a certain aspect of the city's contradictory attitude toward its own success: on one hand they are viewed as points of civic pride, especially for their philanthropy, and on the other as irresponsible capitalists who played a part in the city's current crisis of wealth gaps, homelessness and the skyrocketing cost of living.

Seattle Brands That Went Global
....
Amazon
....
Starbucks
....
Microsoft
....
REI
....
Costco
....
Nordstrom
....
Boeing

Environment

Seattle sits right alongside the Cascadia Subduction Zone, one of the earth's most active seismic regions. Beneath the Strait of Juan de Fuca, two tectonic plates – the North American Plate and the Juan de Fuca Plate – struggle against each other, grinding away as the North American Plate slides underneath, causing pressure to build and the earth to rumble. The most recent of these rumblings happened on February 28, 2001, when an earthquake measuring 6.8 on the Richter scale rocked the Seattle area. Scientists have recently concluded that the entire Pacific Northwest is due for a massive earthquake, which the region has seen every 300–500 years (the last was in 1700).

The region's most recent volcanic activity drew worldwide attention in 1980 when Mt St Helens, just 150 miles south of Seattle, blew its top, killing 57 people and spreading ash through five states and three Canadian provinces. Volcanic activity continues in the region.

The land on which Seattle now stands was once dense forest, and the waters of Puget Sound and the freshwater lakes that surround the city once teemed with wildlife. While metropolitan Seattle hardly accounts for a natural ecosystem, you don't have to go far from the center of the city to find vestiges of the wild Pacific Northwest.

Beer & Coffee

Seattle is home to over 50 microbreweries and close to 200 coffee shops. Seattleites are the biggest coffee consumers in the US.

Architecture

Architecturally, Seattle is as notable for what is missing as for what remains. The Great Fire of 1889 ravaged the old wooden storefronts of downtown, which were replaced by the stone and brick structures

POLITICS & SOCIAL ISSUES

Washington is one of the most socially progressive states in the US and has been a progressive leader on fights for same-sex marriage, doctor-assisted suicide and the decriminalization of marijuana. King County, where Seattle makes up the bulk of the population, has voted Democrat in presidential elections since the 1980s, with Barack Obama enjoying 70% of the popular vote in 2012. Similarly, Seattle has had a Democratic mayor since 1969. The city elected the first female mayor of a major American city in history, Bertha Knight Landes, who served from 1926 to 1928. Seattle has also long been one of the more LGBTIQ+ friendly cities in the country.

Seattle has often stood at the forefront of the push for 'greener' lifestyles, in the form of car clubs, recycling programs, organic restaurants and biodiesel whale-watching tours. Former mayor Greg Nickels (2002–10) was an early exponent of eco-friendly practices and advocated himself as a leading spokesperson on climate change. Another recent mayor, Michael McGinn (2010–14), was also an environmental activist and former state chair of the Sierra Club.

In recent years radical activists of all stripes have continued the fight for issues like rights for transgender and gender nonconforming people, gentrification displacement of communities in historically black neighborhoods, larger environmental issues and problems affecting the working class.

around the city's old center in Pioneer Square. Architect Elmer Fisher is responsible for more than 50 buildings erected immediately after the fire. Any Victorian places that escaped the Great Fire did not escape the Denny Regrade (1899–1912), which flattened a steep residential hill in order to make room for more downtown commercial properties.

More recent additions to the downtown skyline include the West Coast's tallest building, the Columbia Center (p48), a monolith with no other distinction than its 76-story shadow. Six others rise higher than 50 stories. Only the Washington Mutual Building, with its plaid-like facade and turquoise glass, makes a pleasant impression.

As the architectural icon of Seattle, no other modern structure comes close to the Space Needle (p82). Built for the 1962 World's Fair, its sleek but whimsical design has aged amazingly well. Perhaps the most controversial addition to Seattle architecture is the Frank Gehry–designed Museum of Pop Culture (p86; 2000), which has a curvy metallic design that caused quite a commotion. The city's sparkliest architectural jewel at the moment, though, is the almost universally admired Seattle Central Library building (p48; 2004). The city's newest architectural wonder, Amazon's aptly named Spheres (p87), opened in 2018 and suggested a shift from utilitarian skyscrapers to buildings that take shape organically and incorporate eco-minded features.

Seattle's Mini Coffee Chains

Caffe Ladro

Caffè Fiore

Uptown Espresso

Top Pot Hand-Forged Doughnuts

Fuel Coffee

Zoka Coffee

Caffè Vita

Espresso Vivace

Victrola Coffee Roasters

Arts

Visual Arts

Museums and galleries in Seattle offer a visual-arts experience as varied as the rest of the city's culture. The three-site Seattle Art Museum (p46) has a substantial European art collection, a range of modern art that's well suited to its new exhibition spaces, and an impressive collection of native artifacts and folk art, especially carved wooden masks. There are also several exhibition spaces around the city devoted to contemporary Native American carvings and paintings. A considerable Asian art collection is located at the Seattle Asian Art Museum (p112) in Volunteer Park. More experimental and conceptual art is displayed at the University of Washington's Henry Art Gallery (p134) and at the Frye Art Museum (p113).

A specialty of the Puget Sound area is glassblowing, led by maverick artist Dale Chihuly, whose flamboyant, colorful and unmistakable work is now on display at a beautiful suite of galleries and gardens in the Seattle Center (p88).

Pushing the envelope of contemporary art is the specialty of several younger galleries around town, notably Pioneer Square's Roq La Rue (p112) and Georgetown's Krab Jab Studio (p168). These unconventional spaces display provocative, boundary-distorting artwork of all kinds, usually by unknown or underground artists.

Monthly art walks are as common as Starbucks in Seattle. You can wise up on the galleries in Pioneer Square, Georgetown, Fremont or Ballard.

Seattle is also known for its interesting and plentiful public art. A King County ordinance, established in 1973, stipulates that 1% of all municipal capital-improvement project funds be set aside for public art. The 'one percent for art' clause, which other cities across the nation have since adopted, has given Seattle an extensive collection of artworks ranging from monumental sculpture and landscape design to individualized sewer hole covers.

> Several Native American languages are spoken and taught in Seattle, such as the Duwamish dialect Lushootseed, a branch of the Salishan language family.

Literature

Seattle is an erudite city of enthusiastic readers with more bookstores per capita than any other US city. It has also, somewhat ironically, produced – and remains HQ to – the world's biggest online retailer, Amazon.com, founded in 1995 as an online bookstore. In the 1960s and '70s, western Washington attracted a number of counterculture writers. The most famous of these is Tom Robbins, whose books, including *Another Roadside Attraction* (1971) and *Even Cowgirls Get the Blues* (1976), are a perfect synthesis of the enlightened braininess, sense of mischief and reverence for beauty that add up to the typical mellow Northwest counterculture vibe.

Having, among other things, a fondness for the Blue Moon tavern in common with Robbins, poet Theodore Roethke taught for years at the University of Washington, and along with Washington native Richard Hugo he cast a profound influence over Northwest poetry.

Raymond Carver, the short-story master whose books include *Will You Please Be Quiet, Please?* (1976) and *Where I'm Calling From* (1988), lived near Seattle on the Olympic Peninsula. Carver's stark and grim vision of working-class angst profoundly affected other young writers of his time. He later married the novelist and poet Tess Gallagher, also from Port Angeles and a UW alumnus, whose books include *At the Owl Woman Saloon* (1997).

> Seattle's regularly praised KEXP (90.3FM) radio used to be the University of Washington station but has become internationally known online, particularly for its promotion of world music and alternative rock.

Sherman Alexie is a Native American author whose short-story collection *The Lone Ranger and Tonto Fistfight in Heaven* (1993) was among the first works of popular fiction to discuss reservation life. In 1996 he published *Indian Killer*, a chilling tale of ritual murder set in Seattle, to great critical acclaim. His 2009 short story and poetry collection *War Dances* won the 2010 PEN/Faulkner Award for fiction.

The misty environs of western Washington seem to be a fecund habitat for mystery writers. Dashiell Hammett once lived in Seattle, while noted writers JA Jance, Earl Emerson and Frederick D Huebner currently call the Northwest home.

One peculiar phenomenon is the relatively large number of cartoonists who live, or have lived, in the Seattle area. Lynda Barry *(Ernie Pook's Comeek, Cruddy)* and Matt Groening (creator of *The Simpsons*) were students together at Olympia's Evergreen State College. Gary Larson, whose *Far Side* animal antics have netted international fame and great fortune, lives in Seattle. A good number of underground comic-book artists live here too, among them the legendary Peter Bagge *(Hate),* Jim

Woodring *(The Frank Book),* Charles Burns *(Black Hole)* and Roberta Gregory *(Naughty Bits).* It could well have something to do with the fact that Fantagraphics, a major and influential publisher of underground comics and graphic novels, is based here.

Cinema & TV

Seattle has come a long way as a movie mecca since the days when Elvis starred in the 1963 film *It Happened at the World's Fair,* a maudlin chestnut of civic boosterism. There are many films with Seattle as their backdrop, but two famous examples came at the peak of the city's cultural cachet in the '90s: *Singles* (1992), with Campbell Scott, Kyra Sedgwick, Matt Dillon and Bridget Fonda, captured the city's youthful-slacker vibe; and then there was *Sleepless in Seattle,* the 1993 blockbuster starring Tom Hanks, Meg Ryan and, perhaps more importantly, Seattle's Lake Union houseboats. As a Seattle-based film phenomenon, however, nothing tops the tween-vampire soap opera *Twilight* (2008) and its sequels, set in the town of Forks, WA; followed by the fan fiction spin-off *Fifty Shades of Grey* (2015).

TV's *Northern Exposure,* filmed in nearby Roslyn, WA, and *Frasier* both did a lot to boost Seattle's reputation as a hip and youthful place to live. The creepy, darker side of the Northwest was captured in the moody *Twin Peaks,* which returned to a few of its Seattle-adjacent locations for it's long-awaited third season in 2017. And let's not forget ABC's phenomenally popular hospital drama, *Grey's Anatomy.*

Theater

Seattle has one of the most dynamic theater scenes in the country. There are reportedly more equity theaters in Seattle than anywhere in the US, except New York City. This abundance of venues provides the city with a range of classical and modern dramatic theater.

In addition to quality professional theater hosting touring Broadway shows, the city offers a wide array of amateur and special-interest troupes, including LGBTIQ+ theater groups, puppet theaters, children's theater troupes, cabarets and plenty of alternative theaters staging fringe plays by local playwrights. Of particular esoteric interest are Pike Place's Market Theater (p58) and Fremont's Atlas Theater (p151; both showing improv comedy), Belltown's Jewel Box Theater (p96; burlesque) and the CD's artist-run New City Theater (p130; stripped-down Shakespeare and the like).

Seattle has two daily newspapers, the *Seattle Post-Intelligencer,* founded in 1863, and the *Seattle Times,* founded in 1993. The *Post-Intelligencer* ended print publication in 2009 but still runs an active website (www.seattlepi.com).

Dance

Seattle is home to the nationally noted and famously well-attended Pacific Northwest Ballet (p95), considered one of the nation's five best ballet companies. It's justifiably renowned for its performance of *The Nutcracker,* which it has been doing since 1983.

Seattle is a springboard for dancers. The modern dance pioneer Merce Cunningham was born and raised in nearby Centralia and was trained at Cornish College in Seattle. Choreographer Mark Morris, known for his fusion of classical and modern dance, is native to Seattle and has worked everywhere from small opera houses to Broadway, and now works mostly in Europe. New York–based avant-garde dancer Trisha Brown is originally from Aberdeen, WA, and classical ballet choreographer Robert Joffrey hailed from Seattle.

Among Seattle's smaller dance groups is On the Boards (p108), which performs at the Behnke Center for Contemporary Performance in Lower Queen Anne. It brings an exciting, experimental edge to the city's dance scene.

Music

Music is as important to Seattle as coffee, computers or airplanes. The jazz era produced soul pioneer Ray Charles, rock delivered Hendrix, the '70s introduced Heart
and hip-hop simmered in the '80s. Then, in the early 1990s, a generation of flannel-
shirted urban slackers produced a whole new genre: grunge. Today in Seattle you can
have a musical moment any night of the week, from checking out an indie rock band
to taking in the Seattle Symphony Orchestra.

The Jazz Age

At its peak in the 1940s, when many GIs were based in Seattle, S Jackson St – in what is now 'Little Saigon,' an eastern outpost of the International District – and its environs had more than 20 raucous bars with
music, dancing and bootleg liquor. Although the city never rewrote the
jazz songbook with its own genre or style, it provided a fertile performance space for numerous name artists. Charlie Parker, Lester Young
and Duke Ellington all passed through and, in 1948, a young, unknown,
blind pianist from Florida named Ray Charles arrived to seek his fortune. Later that year, the 18-year-old Charles met 15-year-old trumpeter
and Seattle resident Quincy Jones in the Black Elk's Club on S Jackson
and the creative sparks began to fly.

Seattle's jazz scene had died down by the 1960s, when S Jackson
embraced tight-lipped sobriety, and the young and hip turned their
attention to rock and roll (enter Hendrix stage left). Benefiting from
regular revivals in the years since, a small jazz scene lives on in Belltown, where two venues – Dimitriou's Jazz Alley (p95) and Tula's (p96)
– still attract international talent.

From Hendrix to Heart

Born in Texas
in 1928, jazz
singer Ernestine
Anderson moved
to Seattle at age
16 and became
a product of the
fertile jazz scene
spearheaded by
Ray Charles and
Quincy Jones.

Seattle lapped up rock and roll like every other US city in the late '50s
and early '60s, but it produced few rockers of its own, save the Fleet-
woods (from nearby Olympia), who had a string of hits from 1959 to
1966. No one took much notice when a poor black teenager named
Johnny Allen Hendrix took to the stage in the basement of a local synagogue in the Central District (CD) in 1960. Hendrix' band fired him
mid-set for showing off – a personality trait he would later turn to his
advantage. Ignored and in trouble with the law, Hendrix served briefly
in the US army before being honorably discharged. After a stint in
Nashville, he gravitated to New York, where he was 'discovered' playing
in a club by Keith Richards' girlfriend. Encouraged to visit London, the
displaced Seattleite was invited by bassist Chas Chandler to play in a
new nightclub for his mates Eric Clapton and the Beatles, whose jaws
immediately hit the floor.

Heart was another band that had to travel elsewhere – in its case,
to Canada – to gain international recognition. The band recorded its
first album in Vancouver and followed it up with a second, which produced the hard-rock million-seller 'Barracuda.' Female-fronted rock

bands weren't exactly shocking at the time, but the mix of Ann Wilson's powerhouse vocals and Nancy Wilson's ability to shred as good as any of the guys instantly garnered them massive amounts of attention.

Grunge

Synthesizing Generation X angst with a questionable approach to personal hygiene, the music popularly categorized as 'grunge' first stage dived onto Seattle's scene in the early 1990s. The anger had been fermenting for years – not purely in Seattle but also in its sprawling satellite towns and suburbs. Some said it was inspired by the weather, others cited the Northwest's geographic isolation. It didn't matter which. Armed with dissonant chords and dark, sometimes ironic lyrics, a disparate collection of bands stepped sneeringly up to the microphone to preach a new message from a city that all of the touring big-name rock acts serially chose to ignore. There were Screaming Trees from collegiate Ellensburg, the Melvins from rainy Montesano and Nirvana from the timber town of Aberdeen, while Hole frontwoman Courtney Love had ties to Olympia and the converging members of Pearl Jam came from across the nation.

Historically, grunge's roots lay in West Coast punk, a musical subgenre that first found a voice in Portland, OR, in the late 1970s, led by the Wipers, whose leather-clad followers congregated in legendary dive bars such as Satyricon. Another musical blossoming occurred in Olympia, WA, in the early 1980s, where DIY musicians Beat Happening invented 'lo-fi' and coyly mocked the corporate establishment. Mixing in elements of heavy metal and scooping up the fallout of an itchy youth culture, Seattle quickly became alternative music's pulpit, spawning small, clamorous venues where boisterous young bands more interested in playing rock music than 'performing' could lose themselves in a melee of excitement and noise. It was a raucous, energetic scene characterized by stage diving, crowd-surfing and barely tuned guitars, but driven by raw talent and some surprisingly catchy tunes, the music filled a vacuum.

A crucial element in grunge's elevation to superstardom was Sub Pop Records, an independent Seattle label whose guerrilla marketing tactics created a flurry of hype to promote its ragged stable of cacophonous bands. In August 1988, Sub Pop released the seminal single 'Touch Me I'm Sick' by Mudhoney, a watershed moment. The noise got noticed, most importantly by the British music press, whose punk-savvy journalists quickly reported the birth of a 'Seattle sound,' later christened grunge by the brand-hungry media. Suitably inspired, the Seattle scene began to prosper, spawning literally hundreds of new bands, all cemented in the same DIY, anti-fashion, audience-embracing tradition. Of note were sludgy Soundgarden, who later went on to win two Grammys; metal-esque Alice in Chains; and the soon-to-be-mega Nirvana and Pearl Jam. By the dawn of the 1990s, every rebellious slacker with the gas money was coming to Seattle to hit the clubs. It was more than exciting.

What should have been grunge's high point came in October 1992, when Nirvana's second album, the hugely accomplished *Nevermind*, knocked Michael Jackson off the number-one spot, but the kudos ultimately killed it. After several years of railing against the mainstream, Nirvana and grunge had been incorporated into it. The media blitzed in, grunge fashion spreads appeared in *Vanity Fair* and half-baked singers from Seattle only had to cough to land a record contract. Many recoiled, most notably Nirvana vocalist and songwriter Kurt Cobain, whose drug abuse ended in suicide in his new Madison Park home in

---

Alumni of Garfield High School

Jimi Hendrix

Quincy Jones

Ernestine Anderson

Ben Haggerty (Macklemore)

Songs About Seattle

'Frances Farmer Will Have Her Revenge on Seattle,' Nirvana (1993)

'Aurora,' Foo Fighters (1999)

'Belltown Ramble,' Robyn Hitchcock (2006)

'Posse On Broadway,' Sir Mix-a-Lot (1988)

MUSIC GRUNGE

INDIE MUSIC SINCE THE 1990S

Seattle has moved on from the '90s and so has its music. The alternative scene dissipated slightly in the mid-'90s, moving south to Olympia, where it embraced feminist punk movement Riot Grrrl, with bands like Bikini Kill and Bratmobile, and north to Bellingham, home of the Posies and Death Cab for Cutie. Post 2000, electronica band the Postal Service gained fresh success for the Sub Pop label, and the advent of rebranded KEXP radio in 2001 gave alternative music a fresh shot of adrenaline. Today Seattle still produces some interesting musical talent and remains an excellent place to catch up-and-coming live indie acts. Arguably, the most well-known contemporary band is the indie rock sextet The Head and the Heart, which emerged out of Ballard's pub scene in 2009. Formerly signed to Sub Pop Records, its most recent album *Let's Be Still* was released in 2013. At the 2018 Grammy awards the most nominated female artist was singer-songwriter Brandi Carlile, who got her start playing at clubs in Seattle.

1994. Other bands soldiered on, but the spark – which had burnt so brightly while it lasted – was gone. By the mid-1990s, grunge was officially dead.

Best Pike Place Market Buskers

Johnny Hahn
Alfresco pianist since 1986

Emery Carl *Hula-hooping guitarist*

Morrison Boomer
Acoustic band

Jim Page *Folk and protest singer*

Ronn Benway
Guitar-playing troubadour

Hip-Hop

Seattle's earliest hip-hop proponent was a DJ rather than a group. 'Nasty Nes' Rodriguez used to air a show called *Fresh Tracks* on KKFX radio in the early 1980s, which pushed the then-unfashionable local rap talent to in-the-know kids with their ears tuned to New York. On his early playlist was the Emerald Street Boys, a rap trio from the CD neighborhood, and Sir Mix-a-Lot (real name Anthony Ray), whose breakthrough song 'Posse on Broadway,' released in 1987, gave a Seattle spin to the region's hip-hop by describing the intimate geography of Capitol Hill and the CD. Sir Mix-a-Lot went on to have a massive number-one hit with 'Baby Got Back' in 1992, a bright if brief explosion on the national stage that wasn't immediately followed up.

Nonetheless, by the 2000s, hip-hop had successfully infiltrated Seattle's indie-rock universe and begun to have a more all-round impact. This was partly thanks to influential radio station KEXP, which added local hip-hop artists into its airplay at all hours. But it was mostly due to the fact that the work coming out of the Pacific Northwest was overwhelmingly high quality and, as befits the region, generally positive and socially conscious. The probing intelligent lyrics of U-Dub (University of Washington) band the Blue Scholars were an important link to massive popularization of Northwest hip-hop in the 2010s, a process that culminated in the unprecedented Macklemore fad that began in 2012 and lasted a few years.

Survival Guide

Transportation

ARRIVING IN SEATTLE

Sea-Tac International Airport

Sea-Tac International Airport (SEA; ☑206-787-5388; www.portseattle.org/Sea-Tac; 17801 International Blvd; ☎), shared with the city of Tacoma, is the arrival point for nearly 50 million people annually.

There are Smarte Carte baggage-storage facilities in the airport as well as currency-exchange services and car-rental agencies, all in the baggage-claim area.

You can dial 55 from any of the traveler-information boards at the base of the baggage-claim escalators for on-the-spot transportation information. For further details on ground transportation to and from the airport, check the Sea-Tac website.

Light Rail

The best option for making the 13-mile trek from the airport to downtown Seattle is with the Central Link light-rail line. It's fast and cheap and takes you directly to the heart of downtown as well as a handful of other stops along the way. In 2016, the line was extended to Capitol Hill and the U District.

Sound Transit (www.sound transit.org) runs the Central Link service to the airport. Trains go every 15 minutes or better between 5am and 1am. Stops in town include the University of Washington, Capitol Hill, Westlake Center, Pioneer Square and SoDo. The ride between the two furthest points, the University of Washington and Sea-Tac, takes 44 minutes and costs $3.25.

Shuttle Bus

Shuttle Express (☑425-981-7000; www.shuttleexpress.com) has a help desk, and pickup and drop-off point on the 3rd floor of the airport garage. It offers ride-share services that are more comfortable than public transit, but less expensive than a cab.

Taxi

Taxis are available at the parking garage on the 3rd floor. Fares to downtown start at around $55.

Seattle Orange Cab (☑206-522-8800; www.orangecab.net)

Seattle Yellow Cab (☑206-622-6500; www.seattle yellowcab.com)

STITA Taxi (☑206-246-9999; www.stitataxi.com)

Private Vehicle

Rental-car counters are located in the baggage-claim area. Some provide pick-up and drop-off services from the 1st floor of the garage, while others provide a shuttle to the airport. Ask when you book your car.

Driving into Seattle from the airport is fairly straight-forward – just take I-5 north. It helps to find out whether your downtown exit is a left-hand or right-hand one, as it can be tricky to cross several lanes of traffic at the last minute during rush hour.

Ride Share

There are dedicated pick-up spots for ride-share services like Uber and Lyft in terminal 1. Fares will range from about $35 to $50 from the airport to downtown Seattle depending on the time of day.

Using a pooling service like Uber Pool or Lyft Line, where you share the ride with others going a similar route, is cheaper, but takes longer and may be uncomfortable when luggage is taken into account. Prices will vary quite a bit for each ride, but they are usually at least $5 to $10 lower than a solo trip.

King Street Train Station

Amtrak serves Seattle's **King Street Station** (☑206-296-0100; www.amtrak.com; 303 S Jackson St, International District). Three main routes run through town: the Amtrak Cascades (connecting Vancouver, Seattle,

CLIMATE CHANGE & TRAVEL

Every form of transport that relies on carbon-based fuel generates CO_2, the main cause of human-induced climate change. Modern travel is dependent on airplanes, which might use less fuel per kilometer per person than most cars but travel much greater distances. The altitude at which aircraft emit gases (including CO_2) and particles also contributes to their climate change impact. Many websites offer 'carbon calculators' that allow people to estimate the carbon emissions generated by their journey and, for those who wish to do so, to offset the impact of the greenhouse gases emitted with contributions to portfolios of climate-friendly initiatives throughout the world. Lonely Planet offsets the carbon footprint of all staff and author travel.

Portland and Eugene), the very scenic Coast Starlight (connecting Seattle, Oakland and Los Angeles) and the Empire Builder (a cross-continental roller coaster to Chicago).

The station is situated between Pioneer Square and the International District, right on the cusp of downtown, and has good, fast links with practically everywhere in the city.

Streetcar

The First Hill streetcar runs from near King Street Station through the International District and First Hill to Capitol Hill every 15 minutes. Fares are $2.25/1.50 per adult/child.

Light Rail

King Street Station is adjacent to the International District/Chinatown Central Link light-rail station, from where it is three stops (seven minutes) to the Westlake Center in downtown. Fares are $2.25/1.50 per adult/child.

Bus Stations

Various inter-city coaches serve Seattle and there is more than one drop-off point – it all depends on which company you are using.

Bellair Airporter Shuttle (Map p232; ☑866-235-5247; www.airporter.com; 705 Pike St, Downtown) Runs buses to Yakima, Bellingham and Anacortes and stops at King Street Station (for Yakima) and the Washington State Convention Center (for Bellingham and Anacortes).

Cantrail (Map p234; www. cantrail.com; adult/child $45/23) Amtrak's bus connector runs four daily services to Vancouver (one way from $42) and picks up and drops off at King Street Station.

Greyhound (Map p234; ☑206-628-5526; www. greyhound.com; 503 S Royal Brougham Way, SoDo; ®Stadium) Connects Seattle with cities all over the country, including Chicago (from $157 one way, two days, three daily), San Francisco ($91, 20 hours, two daily) and Vancouver (Canada; $18, four hours, three daily). The company has its own terminal just south of King Street Station in SoDo, accessible on the Central Link light rail (Stadium Station).

Quick Shuttle (Map p232; ☑800-665-2122; www. quickcoach.com; tickets $29-59; ☎) Fast and efficient, with five to six daily buses to Vancouver ($43). Picks up at the Best Western Executive Inn in Taylor Ave N near the Seattle Center. Grab the monorail or walk to downtown.

The Docks

Nearly 200 cruise ships call in at Seattle annually. They dock at either Smith Cove Cruise Terminal (Pier 91), in

LONG-HAUL TRAIN ROUTES

Three main rail routes fan out from Seattle, serving the following cities:

DESTINATION	COST ($)	DURATION (HR)	FREQUENCY (PER DAY)
Chicago, IL	401	45	1
Los Angeles, CA	238	35	1
Oakland, CA	226	23	1
Portland, OR	63	3-4	5
Spokane, WA	125	8	2
Vancouver, BC	77	3-4	2

the Magnolia neighborhood 2 miles north of downtown, or Bell Street Cruise Terminal (Pier 66). The latter is adjacent to downtown and far more convenient. Many cruise lines pre-organize land transportation for their passengers. Check ahead.

The **Victoria Clipper** (Map p238; ☎206-448-5000; www.clippervacations.com; 2701 Alaskan Way, Belltown) ferry from Victoria, BC (Canada), docks at Pier 69 just south of the Olympic Sculpture Park in Belltown. **Washington State Ferries** (Map p232; www.bainbridgeisland. com; 801 Alaskan Way, Pier 52, Waterfront; walk-on/bike/car $8.50/9.50/19.15) services from Bremerton and Bainbridge Island use Pier 52.

Bus

Metro buses 24 and 19 connect Pier 91 in Magnolia with downtown via the Seattle Center. Fares are a flat $2.75.

Shuttle Bus

Shuttle Express (☎425-981-7000; www.shuttleexpress. com) links the piers with Sea-Tac airport ($34) or downtown ($25).

Private Vehicle

If you are driving to Pier 52 for the car ferries, leave I-5 at exit 164A (northbound) or exit 165B (southbound).

Car & Motorcycle

Seattle's main road highway is mega-busy I-5, which flows north–south along the west coast. Points east are best served by cross-continental I-90, which crosses the Cascade Mountains via Snoqualmie Pass.

To avoid the downtown gridlock, rent a car at Sea-Tac International Airport.

GETTING AROUND

Bus

Buses are operated by **King County Metro Transit** (☎206-553-3000; http://king county.gov/depts/transport ation/metro.aspx), part of the King County Department of Transportation. The website prints schedules and maps and has a trip planner.

To make things simple, all bus fares within Seattle city limits are a flat $2.75. Those aged six to 18 pay $1.50, kids

under six are free, and seniors and travelers with disabilities pay $1. Most of the time you pay or show your transfer when you board. Your transfer ticket is valid for three hours from time of purchase. Most buses can carry two to three bikes.

There are six RapidRide bus routes (A to F). Of interest to travelers are lines C (downtown to West Seattle) and D (downtown to Ballard). RapidRide buses are faster and more frequent (every 10 minutes).

Be aware that very few buses operate between 1:30am and 5am, so if you're a long way from home when the bars close, plan on calling a cab instead.

Streetcar

The revival of the **Seattle Streetcar** (www.seattlestreet car.org; $2.25) was initiated in 2007 with the opening of the 2.6-mile South Lake Union line that runs between the Westlake Center and Lake Union. There are nine stops and fares cost a standard $2.25/1.50 per adult/child. Streetcars breeze by every 15 minutes from 5am to 1am (10am to 8pm Sundays and holidays). A second 10-stop line opened in 2016 running from Pioneer Square via the International District and First Hill to Capitol Hill.

Roll-out plans for future streetcar lines are extensive, with links earmarked for Fremont, Ballard and the U District.

Train

Sound Transit (www.sound transit.org) operates trains connecting Seattle to outlying communities to the north and south. It's set up more for commuters than travelers, but if you happen to want to visit, for example, Everett ($5, 40 minutes, several daily), Mukilteo ($4.50, one hour, several daily) or,

---

THIS CITY WAS MADE FOR WALKING

Yes, the monorail was highly revolutionary in 1962, and the streetcar will bring back pleasant memories of the 1930s (if you're old enough to remember), but on a pleasant clear spring day in Seattle, you can't beat the visceral oxygen-drinking act of walking. Because most of Seattle's through-traffic is funneled along one of three main arteries – I-5, SR 99 and Aurora Ave N – the central streets aren't as manic as you'd imagine. In Belltown and Pioneer Square your worst hassle might be sports fans hanging out by the nearby stadiums, in downtown the hills might slow your progress slightly, while on the waterfront you'll need to watch out for the seagulls – and the tourists! Seattle's most walkable neighborhoods are leafy Capitol Hill and Queen Anne. If you're really adventurous, ditch the car/bus/train and explore the U District, Fremont and Ballard on that entertaining alfresco people-watching bonanza, the Burke-Gilman Trail (p139).

STREETWISE

Seattle street addresses are confusing, and few visitors will have time to figure out how the system works. It's easier to use neighborhoods to indicate where things are found: '10th Ave in Queen Anne' indicates which 10th Ave is being referred to; likewise '1st Ave in Wallingford' as opposed to 1st Ave downtown. So it's important to get a working knowledge of Seattle's neighborhoods. With so many different numbering systems, it's the only easy way to make sense of the city.

Downtown is in the middle of the hourglass part of Seattle; Pioneer Square is to the south of it. Capitol Hill lies to the northeast, and the Central District/Madrona area to the east. The U District is north of Capitol Hill, across Lake Washington. Belltown, Seattle Center and Queen Anne are slightly northwest of downtown. Fremont, Wallingford and Green Lake are north, across Lake Union, and Ballard is off to the northwest. Georgetown is south, and West Seattle – well, that's easy.

Generally speaking, avenues run north and south, and streets run east and west. Usually Seattle's avenues have a directional suffix (6th Ave S), while its streets have directional prefixes (E Pike St); however, downtown streets and avenues have neither. Yesler Way near Pioneer Square is where avenues start taking on their 'S' and Denny Way is downtown's northern border.

more realistically, Tacoma ($5.25 to $5.50, one hour, several daily), the trains are new and clean and schedules run smoothly. Sound Transit also runs the light-rail service to Sea-Tac airport.

Although it doesn't exactly count as a train, the **Monorail** (☑206-905-2620; www.seattlemonorail.com; adult/youth $2.25/1.25; ☉7:30am-11pm Mon-Fri, 8:30am-11pm Sat & Sun) was originally intended as public transportation. It only goes 1 mile, from Westlake Center straight to Seattle Center and back every 10 minutes, but it's a fun if kitschy way to get between these two places.

Bicycle

Bike lanes in Seattle have been improved in the past few years. They are painted green and usually separated from traffic lanes. Pick up a copy of the *Seattle Bicycling Guide Map*, published by the City of Seattle's Transportation Bicycle & Pedestrian Program (www.cityofseattle.net/transportation/bikemaps.htm) and available at bike shops (or downloadable from the website). The website also has options for ordering delivery of the printed map (free of charge).

The best route is the scenic Burke-Gilman Trail (p139), which passes through the northern neighborhoods of the U District, Wallingford, Fremont and Ballard. Other handy bike paths are the Ship Canal Trail on the north side of Queen Anne, Myrtle Edwards Park, Green Lake Park and the Cheshiahud Loop around Lake Union.

Seattle and all of King County require that cyclists wear helmets. If you're caught without one, you can be fined $30 to $80 on the spot. Most places that rent bikes will rent helmets to go with them, sometimes for a small extra fee.

The city's bike-sharing program was officially shuttered in 2017, but several commercial bike-sharing operations have sprung up in the meantime.

Boat

The most useful inter-neighborhood boat route is the water taxi that connects the downtown waterfront (Pier 50) with West Seattle (Seacrest Park). The water taxi runs hourly every day in the summer and weekdays only in the winter. The fare is $5.75 for the 10-minute crossing.

Car & Motorcycle

Seattle traffic is disproportionately heavy and chaotic for a city of its size, and parking is scarce and expensive. Add to that the city's bizarrely cobbled-together mishmash of skewed grids, the hilly terrain and the preponderance of one-way streets and it's easy to see why driving downtown is best avoided.

TOURS

Seattle excels in first-rate city tours undertaken by various means of transportation including buses, boats and amphibious bus-boats. Non-daunting tours on foot are similarly popular. Some tours are neighborhood-specific, while others cover a particular topic; several pull together the city's best sights.

Not surprisingly, the city has abundant food tours, many of them centered on its proverbial larder, Pike Place Market. The culinary theme also extends to liquid refreshment, with tours specializing in beer and coffee.

A couple of companies run tours of Seattle's spooky but historically significant 'underground' buried beneath the streets of Pioneer Square. Calling on a well-established team of witty guides, they are riotously popular.

Directory A–Z

Accessible Travel

All public buildings (including hotels, restaurants, theaters and museums) are required by law to provide wheelchair access and to have appropriate restroom facilities available. Telephone companies provide relay operators for the hearing impaired. Many banks provide ATM instructions in braille. Dropped curbs are standard at intersections throughout the city.

Around 80% of Metro's buses are equipped with wheelchair lifts. Timetables marked with an 'L' indicate wheelchair accessibility. Be sure to let the driver know if you need your stop to be called and, if possible, pull the cord when you hear the call. Service animals are allowed on Metro buses. Passengers with disabilities qualify for a reduced fare, but first need to contact **Metro Transit** (206-553-3000; http://kingcounty.gov/depts/transportation/metro.aspx) for a permit.

Most large private and chain hotels have suites for guests with disabilities. Many car-rental agencies offer hand-controlled models at no extra charge. Make sure you give at least two days' notice. All major airlines, Greyhound buses and Amtrak trains allow guide dogs to accompany passengers and often sell two-for-one packages when attendants of passengers with serious disabilities

are required. Airlines will also provide assistance for connecting, boarding and disembarking. Ask for assistance when making your reservation.

Download Lonely Planet's free Accessible Travel guides from http://lptravel.to/AccessibleTravel.

Resources

The following organizations and tour providers specialize in the needs of travelers with disabilities:

Access-Able Travel Service (www.access-able.com) Packed full of information, with tips on scooter rental, wheelchair travel, accessible transportation and more.

Easter Seals of Washington (206-281-5700; www.easterseals.com/washington) Provides technology assistance, workplace services and camps for individuals with disabilities and special needs.

Society for Accessible Travel & Hospitality (212-447-7284; www.sath.org) Provides info for travelers with disabilities.

Customs Regulations

US Customs allows each person over the age of 21 to bring 1L of liquor, 100 cigars and 200 cigarettes duty-free into the USA. US citizens are

allowed to import, duty-free, up to $800 worth of gifts from abroad, while non-US citizens are allowed to import $200 worth. If you're carrying more than $10,000 in US and foreign cash, traveler's checks, money orders etc, you need to declare the excess amount. There is no legal restriction on the amount that may be imported, but undeclared sums in excess of $10,000 will probably be subject to investigation. If you're bringing prescription drugs, make sure they're in clearly marked containers. For updates, check www.cbp.gov.

Discount Cards

If you're going to be in Seattle for a while and plan on seeing its premier attractions, consider buying a Seattle CityPASS (p83) (www.citypass.com/seattle; $99/79 per adult/child aged five to 12). Good for nine days, the pass gets you entry into five sights: the Space Needle, Seattle Aquarium, Argosy Cruises Seattle Harbor Tour, Museum of Pop Culture or Woodland Park Zoo and Pacific Science Center or Chihuly Garden & Glass. You wind up saving about 49% on admission costs and you never have to stand in line. You can buy one at any of the venues or online.

Electricity

120V/60Hz

120V/60Hz

Emergency

Health and Human Services Info	211
Police, Fire & Ambulance	911
Seattle Police	20 6-625-5011
Washington State Patrol	360- 596-4000

Etiquette

In true West Coast tradition, Seattle is a casual city.

Attire Dressing up for dinner is the exception rather than the rule. In the birthplace of grunge, shirts and ties aren't common and you'll rarely be turned away from somewhere for being inappropriately dressed.

Conversation For a large city, Seattle is a noticeably friendly place. Expect to strike up conversations in bars or lines.

Road rules Aggressive driving is frowned upon and Seattleites only honk their horns for emergencies. Even jaywalking is likely to attract some dirty looks.

Insurance

No matter how short or long your trip, make sure you have adequate travel insurance purchased before departure. At a minimum, you need coverage for medical emergencies and treatment including hospital stays and an emergency flight home if necessary. Medical treatment in the USA is of the highest caliber, but the experience of receiving even basic healthcare could end up costing thousands or tens of thousands of dollars.

You should also consider getting coverage for luggage theft or loss and trip cancellation. If you will be driving, it's essential that you have liability insurance.

Worldwide travel insurance is available at www. lonelyplanet.com/travel-insurance. You can buy, extend and claim online anytime – even if you're already on the road.

Internet Access

Seattle seems to be one big wi-fi hot spot. It's free nearly everywhere: in most hotels, many bars and all but a handful of coffee shops. You'll also find free wi-fi on some Sound Transit trains, all Rapid Ride buses and Washington State Ferries services (for the latter you must subscribe through Boingo).

Legal Matters

If you're arrested, you have the right to remain silent. There is no legal reason to speak to a police officer if you don't wish to – especially since anything you say 'can and will be used against you' – but never walk away from an officer until given permission. If you don't have a lawyer or a family member to help you, call your consulate. The police will give you the number upon request.

Seattle Police (206-625-5011; www.seattle.gov/police) has precincts in most neighborhoods and should be contacted if you are the victim of a robbery or any other crime.

TIPPING

Tipping is a way of life in the US and not optional.

Waitstaff 18% to 25%

Bartenders $1 per drink, more for cocktails

Hotel porters $1 to $3 per bag

Hotel maids $2 to $5 a day (left out in room)

Taxi drivers 18% to 20%

LGBTIQ+ Travelers

Seattle is a progressive, liberally minded city with thriving communities across the spectrum of sexual and gender identities; estimates are that approximately 12.9% of the city's population identifies as a member of the broader LGBTIQ+ community. While LGBTIQ+ people may face discriminatory attitudes as they might elsewhere in the US, the city's population as a whole is known for generally welcoming attitudes toward sexual orientations and gender identities other than their own.

Resources and events to look out for include the following:

Seattle Gay News (www. sgn.org) A weekly newspaper focusing on gay issues.

TWIST: Seattle Queer Film Festival (www.threedollar billcinema.org; ☉Oct) Usually held in the third week of October.

Seattle Pride (☑206-322-9561; www.seattlepride.org; ☉Jun) Seattle's pioneering lesbian and gay-pride event (held every year since 1974) usually falls on the last Sunday in June and includes a huge downtown parade followed by PrideFest, during which numerous vendors and entertainers set up in the Seattle Center.

Marijuana

Adults of 21 and up may now buy marijuana products from a licensed retailer on production of photo ID. Individuals are limited to 1oz of pure marijuana flower, 7g of extract (for inhalation), 16oz of solid edibles, or 72oz of liquid product. It is illegal to drive with more than 5 nanograms of marijuana in your blood (basically don't use and drive) and even if you buy weed legally in Washington, it will still be illegal if you bring it to a state or country where marijuana is still criminalized. Use of any marijuana products in public carries a fine of up to $50 in Seattle.

Medical Services

As a visitor, know that all hospital emergency rooms are obliged to receive sick or injured patients whether they can pay or not.

If you're sick or injured, but not bad enough for a trip to the emergency room, try one of the following options:

Harborview Medical Center (☑206-744-3000; www.uw medicine.org/harborview; 325 9th Ave, First Hill; ☐Broadway & Terrace) Full medical care, with emergency room.

US HealthWorks Medical Group (☑206-682-7418; 140 4th Ave N, Seattle Center; ☉7am-4pm Mon-Fri; ⑤Seattle Center) Walk-in clinic for nonemergencies.

Money

The US dollar is divided into 100 cents. US coins come in denominations of 1¢ (penny), 5¢ (nickel), 10¢ (dime), 25¢ (quarter), the practically extinct 50¢ (half-dollar) and the not-often-seen golden dollar coin.

Notes come in $1, $2 (very rare), $5, $10, $20, $50 and $100 denominations.

Exchange Rates

Australia	A$1	$0.68
Canada	C$1	$0.75
China	CN¥1	$0.14
Eurozone	€1	$1.11
Japan	JP¥100	$0.93
NZ	NZ$1	$0.64
UK	UK£1	$1.21

For current exchange rates, see www.xe.com.

ATMs

ATMs are easy to find: there's practically one per block in the busier commercial areas, as well as one outside every bank. Many bars, restaurants and grocery stores also have machines, although the service fees for these can be steep ($2 to $4, plus your own bank's fees).

Credit & Debit Cards

Major credit cards are accepted at most hotels, restaurants and shops throughout Seattle. Places that accept Visa and MasterCard generally also accept (and will often prefer) debit cards, which deduct payments directly from your check or savings account. Be sure to confirm with your bank before you leave that your debit card will be accepted in other states or countries. Debit cards from large commercial banks can often be used worldwide.

Opening Hours

Banks 9am or 10am to 5pm or 6pm weekdays; some also 10am to 2pm Saturday

Businesses 9am to 5pm or 6pm weekdays; some also 10am to 5pm Saturday

Restaurants breakfast 7am to 11am, brunch 9am to 3pm, lunch 11:30am to 2:30pm, dinner 5:30pm to 10pm

Shops 9am or 10am to 5pm or 6pm (or 9pm in shopping malls) weekdays, noon to 5pm (later in malls) weekends; some places open till 8pm or 9pm

Post

At the time of research, rates for 1st-class mail within the US were 55¢ for letters up to 1oz and 35¢ for postcards. For package and international-letter rates, which vary, check with the local post office or with the online postal-rate calculator (http://ircalc.usps.gov). For other postal-service questions, call 800-275-8777 or visit the US Post Office website (www.usps.com).

Seattle's most convenient post office locations:

Main branch (Map p232; ✆206-748-5417; www.usps. com; 301 Union St, Downtown; ◎8:30am-5:30pm Mon-Fri; ▣Westlake)

Queen Anne (Map p240; ✆206-282-0544; www.usps. com; 415 1st Ave N, Queen

Anne; ◎8:30am-6pm Mon-Fri, 9am-3pm Sat; ▣13)

University Station (Map p248; ✆206-675-8114; www.usps. com; 4244 University Way NE; ◎8:30am-5:30pm Mon-Fri, 8:30am-3pm Sat)

Public Holidays

National public holidays are celebrated throughout the USA. On public holidays, banks, schools and government offices (including post offices) are closed and public transportation follows a Sunday schedule. Plan ahead if you're traveling – during

many public holidays flights are full and highways are jammed; on Christmas and Thanksgiving, many grocery stores and restaurants close for the day.

New Year's Day January 1

Martin Luther King Jr Day Third Monday in January

Presidents' Day Third Monday in February

Memorial Day Last Monday in May

Independence Day July 4

Labor Day First Monday in September

Indigenous People's Day Second Monday in October

Veterans' Day November 11

Thanksgiving Day Fourth Thursday in November

Christmas Day December 25

Safe Travel

Judged against other US cities, Seattle is pretty safe, with a lower crime rate (in 2017) than Denver, San Francisco and Phoenix. That being said, normal precautions (stay alert at night, don't flaunt valuables) are still advised.

Smoking

Washington State law prohibits smoking in, or within 25ft (7.6m) of, all public buildings. Most state and private smoking policies also prohibit vaping.

Taxes & Refunds

➡ Seattle's sales tax is 10.1% (a combination of Washington State taxes, King County taxes and city taxes).

➡ The hotel tax is 15.6%.

➡ There are no refunds available on sales taxes paid by travelers visiting the US.

MEDIA

Newspapers & Magazines

Seattle Times (www.seattletimes.com) The state's largest daily paper

The Stranger (www.thestranger.com) Free biweekly alternative newspaper containing the popular sex advice column Savage Love

Seattle Magazine (www.seattlemag.com) A slick monthly lifestyle magazine

Seattle Post-Intelligencer (www.seattlepi.com) The former morning daily, now online only

Northwest Asian Weekly (www.nwasianweekly.com) Serving Washington State's Asian community

Radio

KEXP 90.3FM (stream at http://kexp.org) Legendary independent music and community station

KJR 95.7FM (www.957kjrfm.com) Classic rock

KJR 950AM (www.kjram.com) Sports

KNKX 88.5FM (www.knkx.org) Public radio (NPR) and jazz

KUOW 94.9FM (www.kuow.org) NPR news from the University of Washington

TV

KCPQ Channel 13 (Fox) Airs both new sitcoms and reruns

KCTS Channel 9 (public broadcasting station) Plays local news, weather, and arts and cultural segments

KING Channel 5 (NBC) The nightly news and scripted TV

KIRO Channel 7 (CBS) A news broadcast and reality TV

KOMO Channel 4 (ABC) Lots of sitcoms and hour-long dramas

KSTW Channel 11 (CW Network) Dramas and comedy programming aimed at teens

Telephone

The US uses CDMA-800 and GSM-1900 bands. SIM cards are relatively easy to obtain.

Phone numbers within the USA consist of a three-digit area code followed by a seven-digit local number. If you're calling long distance, dial 1 plus the three-digit area code plus the seven-digit number. To call internationally, first dial 011 then the country code and phone number.

Phone numbers in Seattle have a 206 area code. Even local calls made to the same area code require you to dial the full 10-digit number (there's no need to dial 1 first, though).

Toll-free numbers are prefixed with an 800, 877, 866 or 888 area code. Some toll-free numbers for local businesses or government offices only work within the state or the Seattle region, but most can be dialed from abroad. Just be aware that you'll be connected at regular long-distance rates, which could become a costly option if the line you're dialing tends to park customers on hold.

Time

Seattle is in the Pacific Standard Time zone:

➡ three hours behind New York (Atlantic Standard Time)

➡ eight hours behind London (Greenwich Mean Time)

➡ 17 hours behind Sydney (Australian Eastern Time)

In spring and summer, as in most of the time zones in the US, Pacific Standard Time becomes Pacific Daylight Time. Clocks are reset an hour forward in mid-March, and reset an hour back in early November.

Toilets

Public toilets abound in Seattle. You'll find them most readily in shopping malls and public parks. They are nearly always free of charge. If you're in a pinch, buy something in one of the city's many coffee shops and use theirs.

Tourist Information

Visit Seattle (Map p232; ☑206-461-5800; www. visitseattle.org; 705 Pike St, Downtown; ☺9am-5pm daily Jun-Sep, Mon-Fri Oct-May; ☐Westlake) The main tourist information center is in the Washington State Convention Center in downtown.

Visas

Visa requirements vary widely for entry to the US and are liable to change. For up-to-date information, check www.travel.state.gov.

Foreigners needing visas to travel to the US should plan ahead. There is a reciprocal visa-waiver program (better known as ESTA) in which citizens of 38 countries may enter the USA for stays of 90 days or less with a passport but without first obtaining a visa. Currently these countries include Australia, Austria, Denmark, France, Germany, Italy, Japan, the Netherlands, New Zealand, Spain, Sweden, Switzerland and the UK. Under this program you must have a round-trip ticket that is nonrefundable in the USA, and you will not be allowed to extend your stay beyond 90 days.

Citizens of countries in the US Visa Waiver Program have to register with the government online (https:// esta.cbp.dhs.gov) up to three days before their visit. The registration is valid for two years and costs $14.

Note: Canadian citizens do not need a visa or a visa waiver to travel to the US.

Volunteering

Casual volunteer opportunities abound in Seattle. For a good overview check the 'Volunteering and Participating' page on the official city government website: www. seattle.gov.

The Seattle chapter of the **Sierra Club** (☑206-378-0034; www.sierraclub.org/washington; 180 Nickerson St, Suite 202, Lake Union; ☐62) offers outdoor opportunities such as working on trail maintenance. This is an excellent way to meet and mix with locals and see a bit of the city's surrounding wilderness while you're at it.

Behind the Scenes

SEND US YOUR FEEDBACK

We love to hear from travelers – your comments keep us on our toes and help make our books better. Our well-traveled team reads every word on what you loved or loathed about this book. Although we cannot reply individually to your submissions, we always guarantee that your feedback goes straight to the appropriate authors, in time for the next edition. Each person who sends us information is thanked in the next edition – the most useful submissions are rewarded with a selection of digital PDF chapters.

Visit **lonelyplanet.com/contact** to submit your updates and suggestions or to ask for help. Our award-winning website also features inspirational travel stories, news and discussions.

Note: We may edit, reproduce and incorporate your comments in Lonely Planet products such as guidebooks, websites and digital products, so let us know if you don't want your comments reproduced or your name acknowledged. For a copy of our privacy policy visit lonelyplanet.com/privacy.

WRITER THANKS

Robert Balkovich

Thank you, as always, to my friends and family for your continued support while I run hither and thither and yon. Special thanks to Karin, for sharing your love of Seattle with me and setting me off on the right foot, and to Lynae for the wonderful home away from home where I made many great memories.

ACKNOWLEDGEMENTS

Cover photograph: Seattle Center Monorail exiting through the Museum of Pop Culture, Raimund Koch/Getty Images ©

THIS BOOK

This 8th edition of Lonely Planet's *Seattle* guidebook was researched and written by Robert Balkovich, with Mt Rainier contributions by Becky Ohlsen. The previous edition was written by Brendan Sainsbury, with Celeste Brash writing the Day Trips from Seattle chapter.

Destination Editor
Ben Buckner

Senior Product Editors
Martine Power, Sandie Kestell

Regional Senior Cartographer Alison Lyall

Product Editor
Hannah Cartmel

Book Designer
Lauren Egan

Cartographer Valentina Kremenchutskaya

Assisting Editors Peter Cruttenden, Carly Hall, Lou McGregor, Monique Perrin

Cover Researcher
Meri Blazevski

Thanks to Sarah Bailey, Jessica Boland, Paul Harding, Marcia Riefer Johnston, Andi Jones, Lauren O'Connell, Gabrielle Stefanos

See also separate subindexes for:

✗ **EATING P225**

🍷 **DRINKING & NIGHTLIFE P226**

☆ **ENTERTAINMENT P227**

🛒 **SHOPPING P227**

🏃 **SPORTS & ACTIVITIES P228**

🛌 **SLEEPING P228**

Index

DRINKING & NIGHTLIFE

SPORTS & ACTIVITIES

SLEEPING

Seattle Maps

Sights
- Beach
- Bird Sanctuary
- Buddhist
- Castle/Palace
- Christian
- Confucian
- Hindu
- Islamic
- Jain
- Jewish
- Monument
- Museum/Gallery/Historic Building
- Ruin
- Shinto
- Sikh
- Taoist
- Winery/Vineyard
- Zoo/Wildlife Sanctuary
- Other Sight

Activities, Courses & Tours
- Bodysurfing
- Diving
- Canoeing/Kayaking
- Course/Tour
- Sento Hot Baths/Onsen
- Skiing
- Snorkeling
- Surfing
- Swimming/Pool
- Walking
- Windsurfing
- Other Activity

Sleeping
- Sleeping
- Camping
- Hut/Shelter

Eating
- Eating

Drinking & Nightlife
- Drinking & Nightlife
- Cafe

Entertainment
- Entertainment

Shopping
- Shopping

Information
- Bank
- Embassy/Consulate
- Hospital/Medical
- Internet
- Police
- Post Office
- Telephone
- Toilet
- Tourist Information
- Other Information

Geographic
- Beach
- Gate
- Hut/Shelter
- Lighthouse
- Lookout
- Mountain/Volcano
- Oasis
- Park
- Pass
- Picnic Area
- Waterfall

Population
- Capital (National)
- Capital (State/Province)
- City/Large Town
- Town/Village

Transport
- Airport
- BART station
- Border crossing
- Boston T station
- Bus
- Cable car/Funicular
- Cycling
- Ferry
- Metro/Muni station
- Monorail
- Parking
- Petrol station
- Subway/SkyTrain station
- Taxi
- Train station/Railway
- Tram
- Underground station
- Other Transport

Routes
- Tollway
- Freeway
- Primary
- Secondary
- Tertiary
- Lane
- Unsealed road
- Road under construction
- Plaza/Mall
- Steps
- Tunnel
- Pedestrian overpass
- Walking Tour
- Walking Tour detour
- Path/Walking Trail

Boundaries
- International
- State/Province
- Disputed
- Regional/Suburb
- Marine Park
- Cliff
- Wall

Hydrography
- River, Creek
- Intermittent River
- Canal
- Water
- Dry/Salt/Intermittent Lake
- Reef

Areas
- Airport/Runway
- Beach/Desert
- Cemetery (Christian)
- Cemetery (Other)
- Glacier
- Mudflat
- Park/Forest
- Sight (Building)
- Sportsground
- Swamp/Mangrove

Note: Not all symbols displayed above appear on the maps in this book

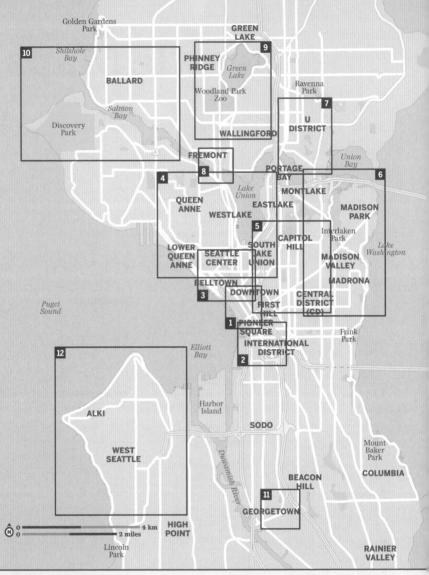

MAP INDEX

DOWNTOWN, PIKE PLACE & WATERFRONT Map on p232

DOWNTOWN, PIKE PLACE & WATERFRONT

Key on p231

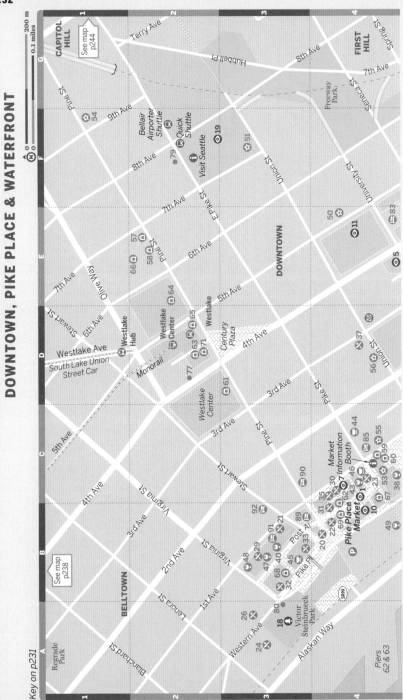

0.1 miles
200 m

See map p244

CAPITOL HILL

FIRST HILL

DOWNTOWN

BELLTOWN

See map p238

Regrade Park

Terry Ave

Pine St

9th Ave

8th Ave

7th Ave

6th Ave

5th Ave

4th Ave

3rd Ave

2nd Ave

1st Ave

Western Ave

Alaskan Way

Hubbell Pl

Union St

Pike St

Pine St

Stewart St

Virginia St

Lenora St

Blanchard St

Olive Way

Westlake Ave

Oliver Way

5th Ave

6th Ave

7th Ave

8th Ave

7th Ave

University St

Seneca St

Spring St

Bellair Airporter Shuttle

Quick Shuttle

Visit Seattle

Freeway Park

Westlake Hub

South Lake Union Street Car

Monorail

Westlake Center

Westlake

Century Plaza

Westlake Center

Market Information Booth

Pike Place Market

Victor Steinbrueck Park

Piers 62 & 63

Post Al

Pike Pl

SR99

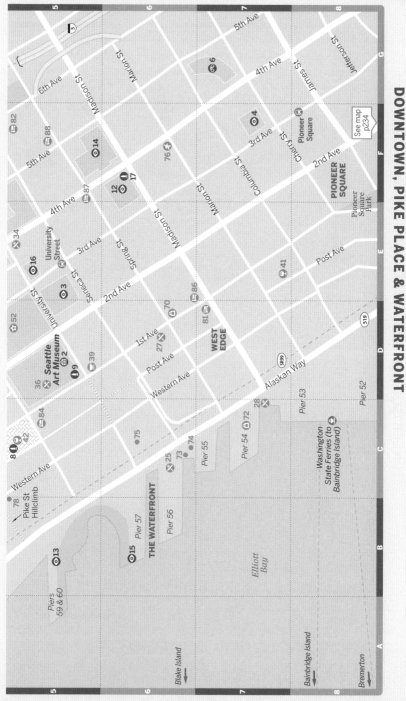

DOWNTOWN, PIKE PLACE & WATERFRONT

See map p234

Elliott Bay

THE WATERFRONT

WEST EDGE

PIONEER SQUARE

Pioneer Square Park

Seattle Art Museum

Washington State Ferries (to Bainbridge Island)

Pike St Hillclimb

Piers 59 & 60

Pier 57
Pier 56
Pier 55
Pier 54
Pier 53
Pier 52

University Street

Blake Island →
Bainbridge Island →
Bremerton →

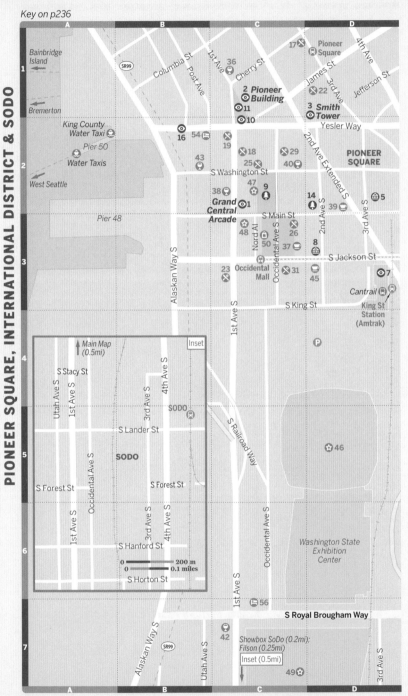

Key on p236

PIONEER SQUARE, INTERNATIONAL DISTRICT & SODO

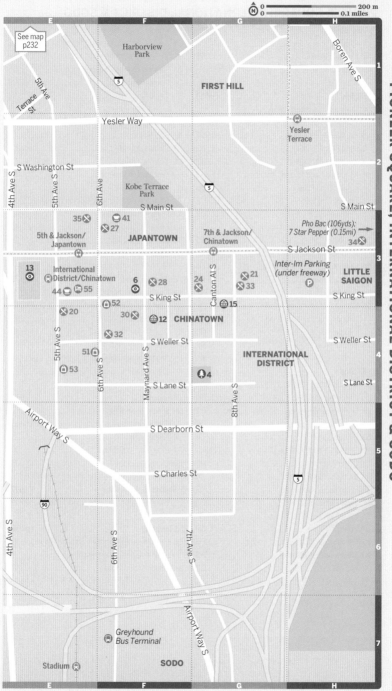

See map p232

N 0 — 200 m
0 — 0.1 miles

Harborview Park

FIRST HILL

5th Ave
Terrace St

I-5

Yesler Way

Yesler Terrace

S Washington St

4th Ave S
5th Ave S
6th Ave

Kobe Terrace Park

S Main St

I-5

S Main St

35
41
27
5th & Jackson/ Japantown
JAPANTOWN

7th & Jackson/ Chinatown

S Jackson St

Pho Bac (106yds);
7 Star Pepper (0.15mi) →

34

13
International District/Chinatown
44
55
6
28
24
21
33
Inter-Im Parking (under freeway)
LITTLE SAIGON

S King St
S King St

20
52
30
12 CHINATOWN
15

32

51
S Weller St
S Weller St

53
INTERNATIONAL DISTRICT

4

S Lane St
S Lane St

Airport Way S

5th Ave S
6th Ave S
Maynard Ave S
8th Ave S

S Dearborn St

I-90

S Charles St

I-5

4th Ave S
6th Ave S
7th Ave S

Airport Way S

Greyhound Bus Terminal

Stadium

SODO

PIONEER SQUARE, INTERNATIONAL DISTRICT & SODO

Boren Ave S

Canton Al S

PIONEER SQUARE, INTERNATIONAL DISTRICT & SODO Map on p234

PIONEER SQUARE, INTERNATIONAL DISTRICT & SODO

BELLTOWN & SEATTLE CENTER *Map on p238*

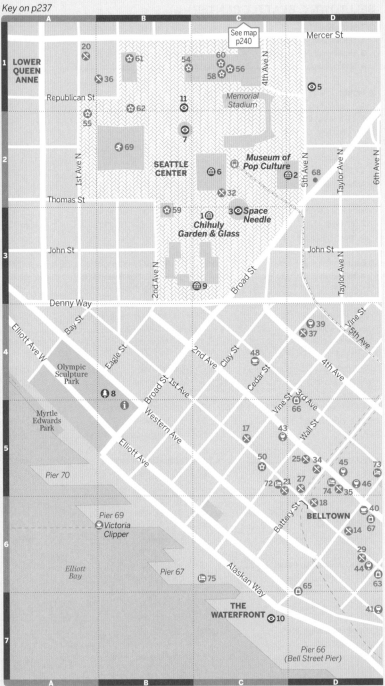

See map p240

Mercer St

LOWER QUEEN ANNE

20

61

54 60 56
58

5

Republican St

36

11

Memorial Stadium

62
55

7

69

SEATTLE CENTER

Museum of Pop Culture

6

2 68

Thomas St

32

59

1 Chihuly Garden & Glass

3 Space Needle

9

John St

John St

Denny Way

Bay St

Elliott Ave W

Eagle St

2nd Ave

Clay St

39
37

Olympic Sculpture Park

8

Cedar St

48

Myrtle Edwards Park

Broad St

1st Ave

Western Ave

Vine St

3rd Ave

66

Wall St

Elliott Ave

17

43

Pier 70

50

25 34

45

73

72 21 27

74 35

46

18

BELLTOWN

40
67

Battery St

14

29
44

63

Elliott Bay

Pier 69
Victoria Clipper

Pier 67

75

Alaskan Way

65

41

Pier 66 (Bell Street Pier)

THE WATERFRONT

10

4th Ave

Vine St

5th Ave N

Taylor Ave N

6th Ave N

1st Ave N

2nd Ave N

Broad St

4th Ave N

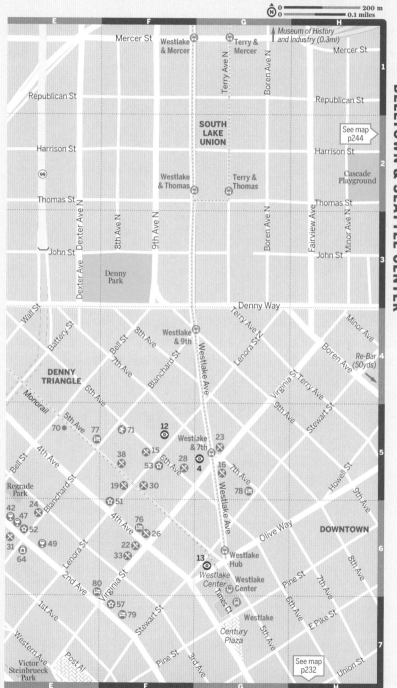

0 200 m
0 0.1 miles

↑ Museum of History
and Industry (0.3mi)

Mercer St

Westlake
& Mercer

Terry &
Mercer

Mercer St

Terry Ave N

Boren Ave N

Republican St

Republican St

See map
p244

SOUTH
LAKE
UNION

Harrison St

Harrison St

99

Cascade
Playground

Westlake
& Thomas

Terry &
Thomas

Thomas St

Thomas St N

Dexter Ave N

8th Ave N

9th Ave N

Boren Ave N

Fairview Ave

Minor Ave N

John St

John St

Denny
Park

Denny Way

Wall St

Battery St

8th Ave

Westlake
& 9th

Terry Ave N

Minor Ave

Re-Bar
(50yds)

Bell St

7th Ave

Blanchard St

Westlake Ave

Lenora St

Boren Ave

DENNY
TRIANGLE

6th Ave

Virginia St

Terry Ave

9th Ave

Stewart St

Monorail

5th Ave

70

77

71

12

Westlake
& 7th

23

4th Ave

Bell St

38

15

28

16

7th Ave

Howell St

9th Ave

53

6th Ave

4

Regrade
Park

19

30

78

42

24

Blanchard St

51

DOWNTOWN

47

76

Olive Way

31

52

26

49

64

22

Westlake
Hub

8th Ave

33

13

2nd Ave

80

Lenora St

Virginia St

57

79

Stewart St

Westlake
Center

Westlake
Center

Pine St

7th Ave

6th Ave

E Pike St

1st Ave

Times Ct

Westlake

5th Ave

Western Ave

Post Al

Pine St

3rd Ave

Century
Plaza

Union St

Victor
Steinbrueck
Park

See map
p232

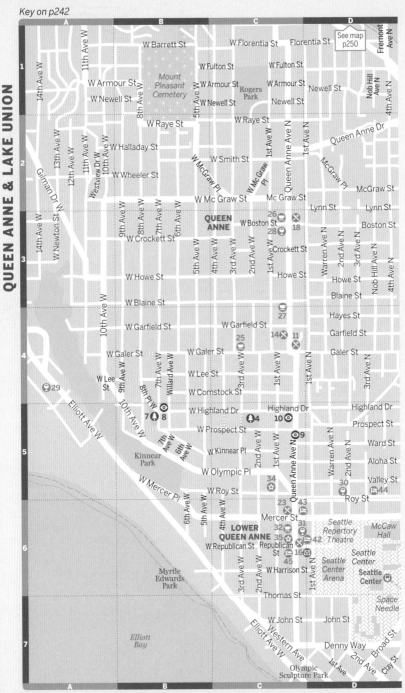

QUEEN ANNE & LAKE UNION

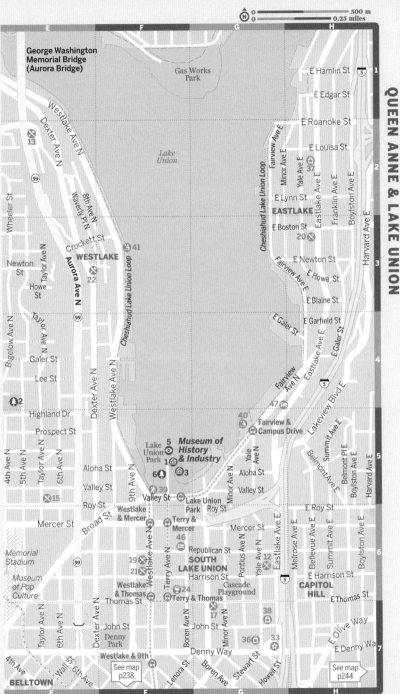

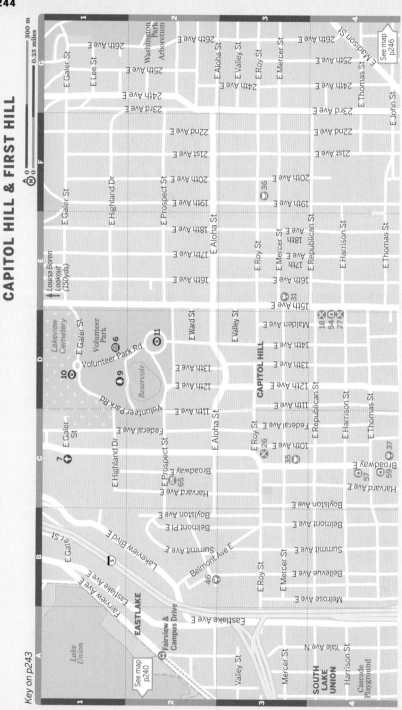

CAPITOL HILL & FIRST HILL

Key on p243

500 m
0.25 miles

See map p246

See map p240

Lake
Union

Lakeview
Cemetery

Volunteer
Park

Reservoir

Washington
Park
Arboretum

Louisa Boren
Lookout (150yds)

CAPITOL HILL

EASTLAKE

SOUTH
LAKE
UNION

Cascade
Playground

Fairview &
Campus Drive

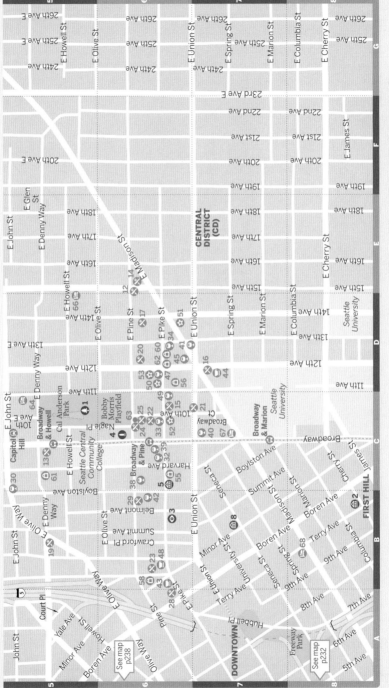

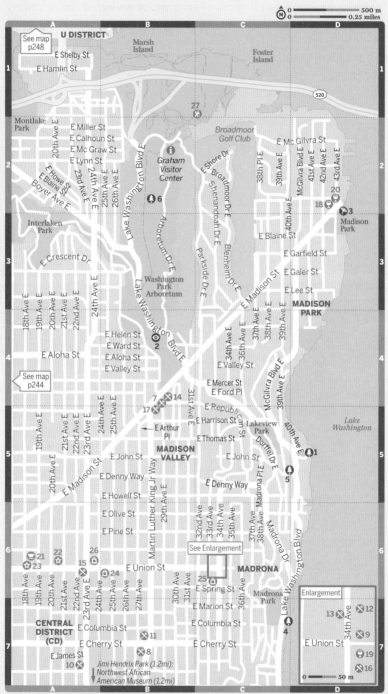

THE CD, MADRONA & MADISON PARK

See map p248

See map p244

U DISTRICT

Marsh Island

Foster Island

E Shelby St

E Hamlin St

Montlake Park

E Miller St

E Calhoun St

E Mc Graw St

E Lynn St

20th Ave E

23rd Ave E

24th Ave E

25th Ave E

26th Ave E

E Howe St

E Blaine St

Boyer Ave E

Interlaken Park

E Crescent Dr

18th Ave E

19th Ave E

20th Ave E

21st Ave E

22nd Ave E

24th Ave E

Lake Washington Blvd E

Lake Washington Blvd E

Arboretum Dr E

Graham Visitor Center

Washington Park Arboretum

Broadmoor Golf Club

E Shore Dr

Broadmoor Dr E

Shenandoah Dr E

Parkside Dr E

Blenheim Dr E

E Madison St

38th Pl E

39th Ave E

40th Ave E

E Mc Gilvra St

McGilvra Blvd E

41st Ave E

42nd Ave E

43rd Ave E

E Blaine St

E Garfield St

E Galer St

E Lee St

MADISON PARK

Madison Park

E Helen St

E Ward St

E Aloha St

E Aloha St

E Valley St

E Valley St

34th Ave E

36th Ave E

37th Ave E

38th Ave E

39th Ave E

E Mercer St

E Ford Pl

E Republican St

E Harrison St

E Thomas St

McGilvra Blvd E

39th Ave E

40th Ave E

Dorffel Dr E

Lakeview Park

Lake Washington

18th Ave E

19th Ave E

20th Ave E

21st Ave E

22nd Ave E

23rd Ave E

24th Ave E

25th Ave E

31st Ave E

E Arthur Pl

E Madison St

MADISON VALLEY

E John St

E John St

E Denny Way

E Denny Way

E Howell St

E Olive St

E Pine St

Martin Luther King Jr Way

29th Ave E

32nd Ave

33rd Ave

34th Ave

35th Ave

37th Ave

38th Ave

Madrona Pl E

Madrona Dr

Lake Washington Blvd

Madrona Park

19th Ave E

20th Ave

18th Ave

21st Ave

22nd Ave E

23rd Ave E

24th Ave

25th Ave

26th Ave

27th Ave

30th Ave

31st Ave

36th Ave

E Union St

E Spring St

E Marion St

E Columbia St

E Cherry St

MADRONA

CENTRAL DISTRICT (CD)

E Columbia St

E Cherry St

E James St

Jimi Hendrix Park (1.2mi); Northwest African American Museum (1.2mi)

Enlargement

13

12

9

19

16

34th Ave

E Union St

0   50 m

0   500 m

0   0.25 miles

THE CD, MADRONA & MADISON PARK

U DISTRICT

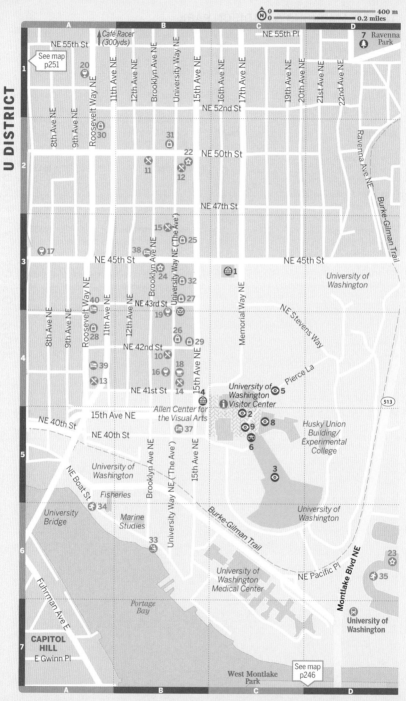

See map p251

NE 55th St

↑Café Racer (300yds)

NE 55th St

NE 55th Pl

7 Ravenna Park

Ravenna Ave NE

Burke-Gilman Trail

8th Ave NE
9th Ave NE
Roosevelt Way NE
11th Ave NE
12th Ave NE
Brooklyn Ave NE
University Way NE
15th Ave NE
16th Ave NE
17th Ave NE
19th Ave NE
20th Ave NE
21st Ave NE
22nd Ave NE

NE 52nd St

30
20

31

NE 50th St
11
22
12

NE 47th St

NE 45th St

15
38
25
24
32
27
19

NE 45th St

University of Washington

1

Memorial Way NE

NE Stevens Way

8th Ave NE
9th Ave NE
Roosevelt Way NE
11th Ave NE
12th Ave NE
Brooklyn Ave NE
University Way NE ('The Ave')

NE 43rd St
40
28
26
29
10
16
18
13
14
4
39

NE 42nd St

NE 41st St

University of Washington Visitor Center
2
5

Pierce La

Allen Center for the Visual Arts

9
6
8

Husky Union Building/ Experimental College

15th Ave NE
NE 40th St
37

15th Ave NE

NE 40th St

University of Washington
Fisheries

Brooklyn Ave NE
University Way NE ('The Ave')
15th Ave NE

3

513

University of Washington

NE Boat St
34

University Bridge

Marine Studies

33

Burke-Gilman Trail

NE Pacific Pl

Montlake Blvd NE

23
35

Fuhrman Ave E

University of Washington Medical Center

University of Washington

Portage Bay

CAPITOL HILL
E Gwinn Pl

West Montlake Park

See map p246

0   400 m
0   0.2 miles
N

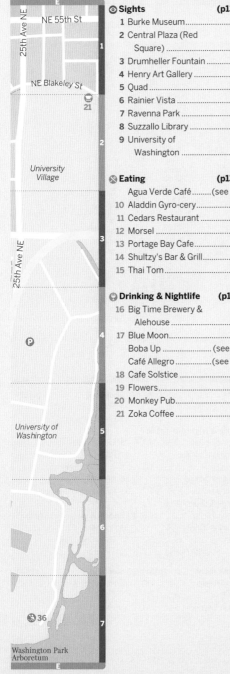

U DISTRICT

FREMONT

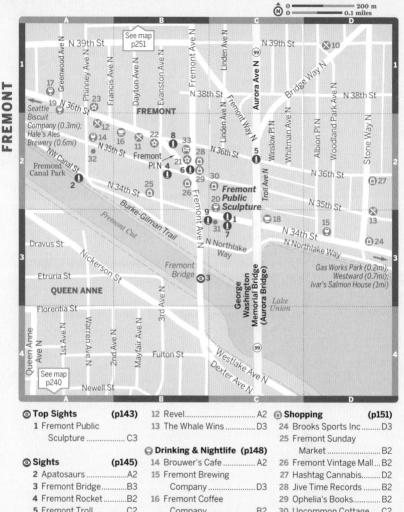

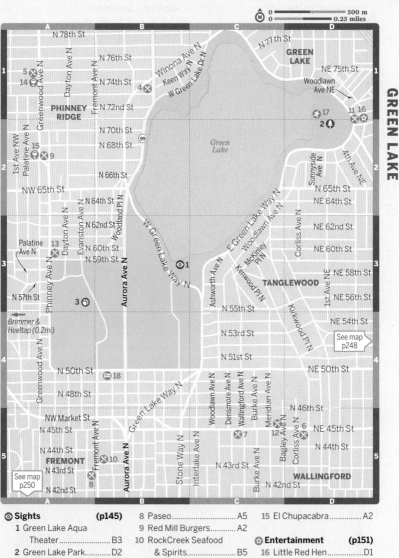

BALLARD & DISCOVERY PARK

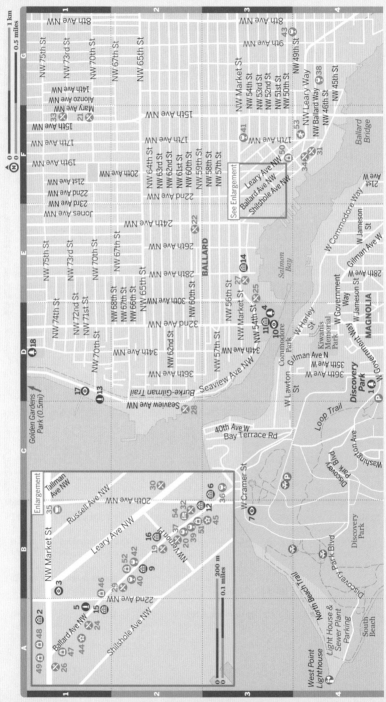

BALLARD & DISCOVERY PARK

GEORGETOWN

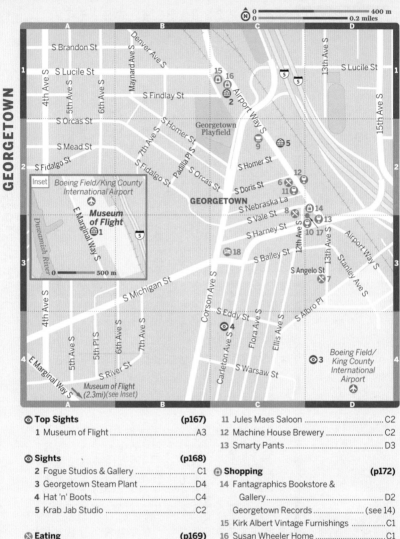

WEST SEATTLE

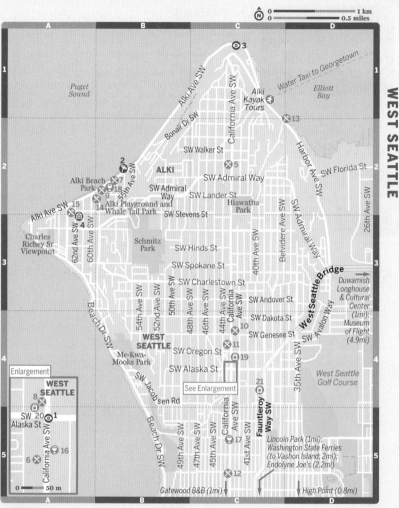

Our Story

A beat-up old car, a few dollars in the pocket and a sense of adventure. In 1972 that's all Tony and Maureen Wheeler needed for the trip of a lifetime – across Europe and Asia overland to Australia. It took several months, and at the end – broke but inspired – they sat at their kitchen table writing and stapling together their first travel guide, *Across Asia on the Cheap*. Within a week they'd sold 1500 copies. Lonely Planet was born.

Today, Lonely Planet has offices in Franklin, London, Melbourne, Oakland, Dublin, Beijing and Delhi, with more than 600 staff and writers. We share Tony's belief that 'a great guidebook should do three things: inform, educate and amuse'.

Our Writer

Robert Balkovich

Robert was born and raised in Oregon, but has called New York City home for almost a decade. When he was a child and other families were going to theme parks and grandma's house he went to Mexico City and toured Eastern Europe by train. He's now a writer and travel enthusiast seeking experiences that are ever so slightly out of the ordinary to report back on. Follow him on Instagram @oh_balky.

Contributing writer: Becky Ohlsen contributed to the Day Trips from Seattle chapter (Mt Rainier).

Published by Lonely Planet Global Limited
CRN 554153
8th edition – Jan 2020
ISBN 978 1 78701 360 5
© Lonely Planet 2020   Photographs © as indicated 2020
10 9 8 7 6 5 4 3 2 1
Printed in China